Fourth Edition

CULTURE SKETCHES
Case Studies in Anthropology

Holly Peters-Golden
The University of Michigan

Boston   Burr Ridge, IL   Dubuque, IA   Madison, WI   New York
San Francisco   St. Louis   Bangkok   Bogotá   Caracas   Kuala Lumpur
Lisbon   London   Madrid   Mexico City   Milan   Montreal   New Delhi
Santiago   Seoul   Singapore   Sydney   Taipei   Toronto

Higher Education

CULTURE SKETCHES: CASE STUDIES IN ANTHROPOLOGY
Published by McGraw-Hill, a business unit of The McGraw-Hill Companies, Inc., 1221 Avenue of the Americas, New York, NY 10020. Copyright © 2006, 2002, 1997, 1994 by The McGraw-Hill Companies, Inc. All rights reserved. No part of this publication may be reproduced or distributed in any form or by any means, or stored in a database or retrieval system, without the prior written consent of The McGraw-Hill Companies, Inc., including, but not limited to, in any network or other electronic storage or transmission, or broadcast for distance learning.

Some ancillaries, including electronic and print components, may not be available to customers outside the United States.

This book is printed on acid-free paper.

1 2 3 4 5 6 7 8 9 0 QPF/QPF 0 9 8 7 6 5

ISBN 0-07-287608-5

Editor in Chief: *Emily Barrosse*
Publisher: *Phillip A. Butcher*
Sponsoring Editor: *Kevin Witt*
Senior Marketing Manager: *Daniel M. Loch*
Developmental Editor: *Larry Goldberg*
Managing Editor: *Jean Dal Porto*
Project Manager: *Richard Hecker*
Manuscript Editor: *Gretlyn Cline*
Associate Designer: *Srdjan Savanovic*
Cover Designer: *Asylum Studios*
Art Manager: *Robin Mouat*
Photo Research Coordinator: *Natalia C. Peschiera*
Cover Credit: © *Philip Game*
Media Project Manager: *Michele Borrelli*
Associate Production Supervisor: *Jason I. Huls*
Composition: *10/12 Sabon by GTS —New Delhi, India Campus*
Printing: *PMS Black, 45# New Era Matte, Quebecor World Fairfield Inc.*

Photo Credits
Page 4: © Betty Press / Panos Pictures; 23: © John Neubauer / PhotoEdit; 42: © GlobalPhoto; 66: © Rob Huibers / Panos Pictures; 82: © A. Ramey / PhotoEdit; 102: © Art Wolfe / Photo Researchers, Inc.; 122: © World Images News Service; 140: © World Images News Service; 163: © Lisa Klopfer; 174: © Hulton-Deutsch Collection / Corbis; 192: © Charles E. Brill; 205: © Paul Beinssen / Lonely Planet Images; 225: © Ludo Kuipers; 241: © Chris Rainer / Corbis; 262: © Jerry Callow / Panos Pictures

Library of Congress Cataloging-in-Publication Data
Peters-Golden, Holly
  Culture sketches: case studies in anthropology / Holly Peters-Golden.—4th ed.
    p. cm.
  Includes bibliographical references and index.
  ISBN 0-07-287608-5 (softcover : alk. paper)
  1. Ethnology—Case studies. I. Title.
GN378.P47 2006
305.8—dc22   2004063170

The Internet addresses listed in the text were accurate at the time of publication. The inclusion of a website does not indicate an endorsement by the authors of McGraw-Hill, and McGraw-Hill does note guarantee the accuracy of the information presented at these sites.
www.mhhe.com

for Rebecca and Jenna,
my first students, my best teachers,
and, I hope, the ones who know

Contents

PREFACE

Anthropology offers a unique perspective. Through its lens we can see, at once, both our kinship with all the rest of humanity as well as our uniqueness. Students peering through this lens for the first time often ask, "How are they the same as we are?" "How are they different?" It is usually with delight that they discover both striking similarities and surprising differences.

This volume is an introduction to 15 societies, and each glimpse is brief and necessarily incomplete. It is my hope that any student who is intrigued will look further into the past and present lives of these people. The following chapters are aimed more at sparking interest than appeasing it.

The groups selected are all peoples whose traditional cultures are uniquely their own. Each has distinctive patterns and practices; each has faced the challenge of an encroaching world, with differing results. Moreover, they often provide the prime illustrations of important concepts in introductory anthropology courses: Azande witchcraft, Aztec human sacrifice, Trobriand *kula* exchange, Minangkabau matriliny. As such, this volume can stand alone as an introduction to those central concepts through these 15 societies, or serve as a valuable companion to anthropology texts, most notably Kottak's introductory texts, which use all of these societies as examples.

Many of the peoples presented herein are involved in the diaspora; some struggle to preserve old ways in new places. While Ojibwa culture flourishes, tribal members contemplate how gaming on the reservation may challenge tradition. Kaluli music has been the vehicle for an aggressive campaign to prevent rainforest destruction. The isolation of the Tiwi was a salient feature in the development of much of their indigenous culture. Today, they are no longer isolated. They encourage tourism, while making sure younger generations are still taught to gather preferred "bush foods." Haitian immigrants and Hmong refugees have envisioned their place in American society quite differently. Nomadic pastoralists like the Basseri face challenges from both governments who think sedentary peoples are more "civilized" and environmental analysts who are concerned about the impact of pastoralism and expanding deserts on agricultural lands. Resettlement and development, such as that undertaken among the Azande, cannot succeed if motivated solely by goals of industrial development but uninformed by indigenous culture.

Our world is more than ever a world of change. The exploration and promotion of cultural diversity has been embraced as a mission on some campuses, feared as a strategy of separatism by others, used as a weapon in other venues. As we are increasingly faced with a global culture, anthropology takes on an even greater responsibility to foster respect for differences in the face of change.

✦ THE FOURTH EDITION

This edition updates most chapters from the third edition to include recent ethnographic information. Each of those contains an expanded discussion of the contemporary situation of each group. The volume includes all new maps in each chapter, showing the location of the group in its region, as well as a world map with each group indicated. Expanded references have been moved to the end of the volume to serve as a bibliography. Also new to this edition are additional sources for further learning about each group, including museums, Web sites, and videos; these can be found on the Web site that accompanies *Culture Sketches* at www.mhhe.com/peters4. This Web site also provides links to maps and other pedagogical aids, including a test bank of multiple-choice questions.

The following is a brief overview of the chapters with the most significant additions:

The Azande

Included is a new section entitled "Azande Today: Resettled, Unsettled," which retains the discussion of the "Zande scheme" and adds a discussion of Azande involvement in Sudan's civil war, their internal displacement, and the struggle to control resources.

The Aztecs

This chapter includes five new ethnographic references, several of which suggest a rereading of the conquest from an indigenous perspective.

The Basseri

Reasons for sedentarization unique to the Basseri are expanded upon in this chapter. Included is a new last section entitled "Customary Strangers: Nomadic Pastoralists in the Modern World" which discusses educational programs for pastoralists ("Iranian tent schools"). This new section contains contemporary scholarship regarding nomadic peoples, examining the changing nature of their social systems, which are challenged by political and environmental transformations in numerous nation-states throughout the world. Also discussed is the demarcation and enforcement of new international borders, which in these tense political times have transformed some pastoralist travel along traditional migration routes.

Haiti

This edition updates the political situation in Haiti, noting the replacement of Aristide's government.

The Ju/'hoansi

An updated section, "The Ju/'hoansi Today," discusses the San court case contesting their displacement, as well as the modern challenges of alcohol abuse and HIV/AIDS in the region. Botswana is the nation with the highest rate of HIV/AIDS in the world; Namibia is fifth. This places the San, 90 percent of whom reside in these two nations, at the epicenter of the epidemic.

The Kaluli

This chapter includes a new section, "'Before' and 'Now': Modernity and the Language of Missionization," that examines cultural change as evidenced by language change.

The Nuer

This chapter has a new section, "Modern Challenges: Civil War and Resettlement." It includes a consideration of the Nuer involvement in Sudan's civil war, its inclusion of the tribal rivalry between Nuer and Dinka, and also expands the examination of Nuer in the United States with a section on the "Lost Boys of Sudan," tens of thousands of children who fled their villages and walked hundreds of miles to refugee camps, 4000 of whom were eventually resettled in the United States.

The Ojibwa

This chapter includes a new section, "Environmental Degradation: Triumph over *Pijibowin*" (poison), that focuses on environmental degradation and land endangerment by industrial development.

The Samoans

This chapter introduces a discussion of the renewed visibility of chiefs in a number of modern nation-states, who mediate local realities and larger spheres of national and transnational interaction.

The Tiwi

This chapter considers the way dance in the *pukamani* ceremony demonstrates kin ties.

The Trobriand Islanders

This chapter includes a new section on tourism that discusses the ways in which Trobrianders create for their "customers" the performance tourists expect to see.

The Yanomamo

This chapter now includes information on the controversy surrounding Patrick Tierney's book *Darkness in El Dorado*.

✦ ACKNOWLEDGMENTS

Errors in fact and judgment in the text that follows are mine alone. I extend thanks, however, to those who share in whatever is most successful therein. To Conrad Kottak for his continued confidence; to Kevin Witt and Larry Goldberg for their editorial skills. My appreciation to those who reviewed the third edition and whose comments helped shape the content of this volume: Michael Murphy, University of Alabama; Mark Tromans, Broward Community College; Greta Uehling, Eastern Michigan University; and Marilyn Walker, Mount Allison University. Their suggestions played a large role in its final form. I am indebted to Professor James Taggart, Franklin and Marshall College, who was the first to open anthropology's door to me and ably guide me over the threshold.

As always, it is my family to whom I offer thanks and admiration of a kind that is reserved for them alone: Rebecca and Jenna, women of grace, passion, and intellect; Marc, who provides all that no one else could.

Holly Peters-Golden

1 The Azande
2 The Aztec
3 The Basseri
4 Haiti
5 The Hmong

6 The Ju/'hoãnsi
7 The Kaluli
8 The Kapauku
9 The Minangkabau
10 The Nuer

11 The Ojibwa
12 Samoa
13 The Tiwi
14 Trobriand Islanders
15 The Yanomamö

Location of Cultures Numbered by Chapter

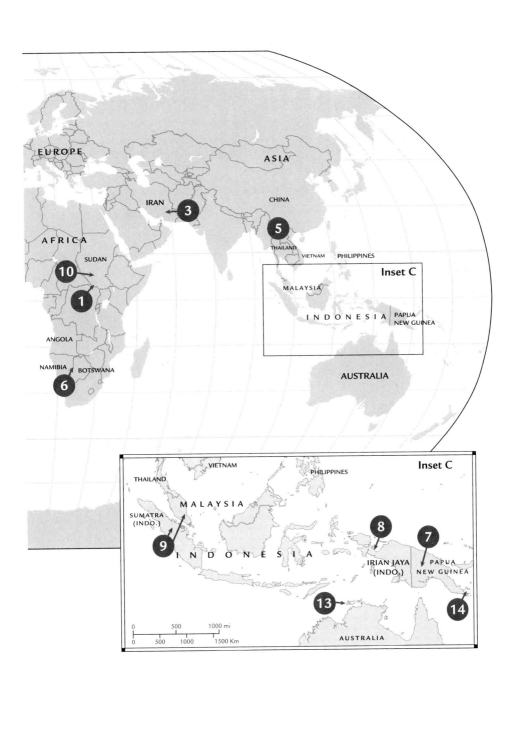

CHAPTER 1

THE AZANDE

Witchcraft and Oracles in Africa

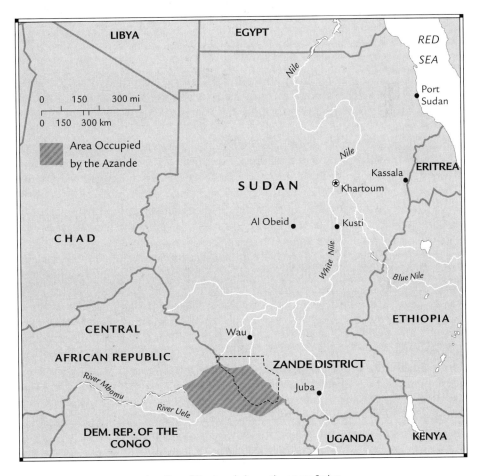

Location of the Azande in southwestern Sudan.

→ THE BEGINNING

There are those who can set broken bones. Only they, and people healed by them, can do this. The first of them long ago fathered a child, and the child had no arms and no legs. He was round, like a cooking pot. People saw him and knew he was a child of Mbori, the supreme being. The ancestor had a dream. In the dream he was told to burn the child, and this he did. He was told to take the child's ashes and mix them with oil; this he could use to heal broken limbs. The ancestor did all he was told to do. He used the ashes of the child born with no limbs and created the clan of those who can heal the broken limbs of others.

→ INTRODUCTION AND HISTORY

The Azande people live in a large area in the center of Africa, in the southwestern Sudan, north of Zaire and to the east of the Central African Republic. Sudan is Africa's largest country, measuring roughly a quarter the size of the United States. This is an area of rolling hills with abundant rivers and streams. On the banks of the waters grow tall trees, which provide shade in which to build homesteads. However, Azande fell victim to sleeping sickness spread by the tse-tse fly, which breeds in thick bush. Sudanese authorities, concerned about this exposure, forced them to relocate to concentrated settlements near roads. (The closeness of the houses in these new settlements was especially problematic. Formerly, structures along the river banks could be spread far apart; this was preferable to the Azande, who feared neighbors' potential witchcraft, which was only effective at close range.)

The peoples known collectively as the Azande are a melding together of what were separate clans in the past. In earliest times, the clans who lived along the banks of the waters were autonomous local groups. Clan disputes were settled within the families of which they were comprised. Disputes between clans were settled by elders from each. Zande history tells of a single individual who, through his wisdom and kindness, gained power within his own clan, the Avongara. Soon, under his able leadership, it became the dominant group. Moving eastward along the riverbanks, the Avongara conquered more than fifty other clans, and eventually amalgamated into one Zande group. The history of the area is characterized by such invasions and warfare (Reining 1966).

In the late nineteenth century, French and Belgian expeditions had set up military outposts in the Sudan; by the early twentieth century the Zande district was under British rule, which lasted until 1953. In that year, growing Sudanese nationalism led to Britain's granting of self-government. Sudan claimed independence in 1956, setting into motion a succession of unstable parliamentary governments and military regimes. Fundamentalist Islamic law was instituted in 1983, and was followed by a series of civil wars among Sudanese of varying religious, ethnic, and political allegiances.

→ SETTLEMENTS

Traditionally, the individual homestead of each couple and their children is the focus of the economic system. The construction and maintenance of homes are constant occupations, especially owing to the toll taken on them by weather, insects, animals, and fast-growing vegetation.

Homes are built of mud and grass framed on wooden poles, and thatched with grass. (One addition to traditional Zande homes is the European introduction of doors fitted with hinges and locks.) In addition to this living space, each household unit has a granary for storing millet. Houses are built around courtyards, which provide ideal places for gathering and conversation. These enclosed courtyards are seen as a window into the household life. Their upkeep is critical since they are seen as evidence of the responsibility or industriousness of their owners. Reining (1966:69) reports that his Zande informants would comment on the state of disrepair of their neighbor's homestead, and "analyzed courtyards as reflections of the inhabitants." They did not exempt themselves from such scrutiny; he continues: "I received a number of apologies from the heads of households about the state of their courtyards, with full explanations for the deficiencies of which they were ashamed" (Reining 1966:69).

The traditional courtyard arrangement appeared to have changed very little with European contact (Reining 1966), with the arrangement of each courtyard reflecting the composition of the household to which it is attached. Because each woman must have her own house and granary, polygynous households will have numerous homes and granaries around its courtyard. In a monogamous household, the average courtyard space is about sixty-five feet in its largest dimension. Households with more adult women may have yards that are one hundred feet square. Courtyards belonging to the households of chiefs are double this size.

"Kitchen gardens" are planted adjacent to the courtyards. These are used for plants that don't require large-scale harvesting or great attention. Pineapple, mango, papaya, and miscellaneous perennial plants used for meals immediately upon picking are found in these plots.

→ SUBSISTENCE AND MANUFACTURE

The Azande practice shifting cultivation (that is, no crop rotation, and incorporating a fallowing period), relying mostly on maize and millet, gourds and pumpkins, manioc and bananas, groundnuts, and beans. The tse-tse fly, problematic to animals as well as humans, makes cattle herding impossible. Whatever meat is consumed is secured through hunting. There is also a tradition of using forested areas to gather plants they do not cultivate. Dogs and chickens are the only domesticated animals.

The region has ample rainfall and many springs. These were a focus of Zande life, because they provided usable water nearly year-round. Water for daily use was carried from stream to homestead and the washing, among other activities, was done at the river banks. In fact, the stream was central to Zande life in conceptual as well as practical terms. For example, distance is expressed by the number of streams between the points in question; the length of a journey is the number of streams crossed during travel. When asked about an exact location (such as an individual's birthplace) the answer will be the stream nearest that location. Given the centrality of the stream to the Azande, their relocation by the European administration caused major disruption in their cultural beliefs and practices.

The year consists of two seasons, one rainy and one dry. During the rainy summer, Azande cultivate their land. Although they have a long growing season and no frosts, the soil is not rich and insects are troublesome. As the hot, dry weather begins, crops mature and are harvested.

Hunting was most feasible in the dry season, when tall grasses had died or were burned, and when the harvest was over. During the rains, vegetation was too dense to allow necessary visibility.

Because rivers were low during this dry season, fish were more accessible. Men employed basket traps, which they set in the rapids of rivers; women dammed the streams into small shallow pools, drained them by bailing, and collected the fish, snakes, and crustaceans that remained. Termites were a favorite food, and their high fat and protein content made them a nutritious part of the diet.

In pre-European days, each family was an independent unit of production. Iron tools and spears were used as bridewealth items, but in general there was no

Zande girl.

tradition of exchange between households, which consisted of a wife or wives, husband, their children, and other dependents (such as widowed elderly). There was a sexual division of labor, and both women's and men's work were necessary to maintain an efficiently functioning household. Construction and repair of the house and granary were the responsibility of men. The arduous task of maintaining the courtyard and its gardens fell solely to women. Wealth, possessed mainly by chiefs, was primarily in the form of foodstuffs; the tradition of destroying a person's worldly goods upon death left little chance of inheritance of property.

Azande have no tradition of occupational specialization. All manufacturing and craftswork were considered largely avocations, done by most. Woodworking and pottery, making nets and baskets, and crafting clothing out of bark were the most important of these skills.

✦ SOCIAL AND POLITICAL ORGANIZATION

Kinship

Among the Azande, clan affiliation was not stressed at the local level. E. E. Evans-Pritchard (1971), the ethnographer most responsible for knowledge about the Azande, found, as he endeavored to gather genealogies, that "except in the royal clan, genealogical relationships between clansmen were very seldom known and usually quite untraceable" (p. 14). Local groups, according to Evans-Pritchard, are, in essence, political units. He reports that his discovering members of the same clan living near one another is due as much to chance as anything else.

Chiefdoms

In pre-European times, the Azande were organized into a number of chiefdoms (sometimes called kingdoms), each of which was independent from the others. The Avongara were nobility; in the days of Zande chiefdoms, it was to Avongara lineages that chiefs belonged. Despite the fact that chiefs of differing groups all belonged to the same clan, there was ongoing hostility and warfare between them.

Chiefs ruled their lands and peoples by appointing emissaries (usually sons, but always Avongara) who were sent out to manage various sections of their territories. Within these communities, commoners were deputized to aid in administration.

Chiefs functioned as military leaders, economic leaders, and political leaders. Unmarried men were recruited into groups that functioned both as warriors and laborers on the king's lands. The governors of the territories had gardens which were also worked by these troops. Both governors and chiefs collected food from the peoples in their domain (provincial governors sending to the chief a portion of their tribute as well) to be redistributed. In addition to food, spears and other items (often payment for fines or bridewealth) were redistributed by the chiefs.

Warfare

Several miles of unsettled forest and bush were maintained between chiefdoms. Watch was kept on these borders by trusted sentinels who were designated to build their houses along these boundaries.

During the rainy season when grass grew tall and provided good cover, surprise attacks were made on these border sentries, usually ordered by the provincial leader. He undertook this action on his own, without permission granted from the chief. Counsel, however, was sought from a poison oracle, a process wherein poison is administered to an animal while questions are posed to the inhabiting spirit. The poisoned animal's behavior, as well as the point at which it succumbed to the poison, were interpreted by those with such skills.

Information was obtained concerning the most propitious days and place for the raid, the expected level of casualties, and which companies of warriors should be entrusted with the most dangerous duties. If the oracle indicated that the time was not right for victory, the plans were abandoned.

The oracle also designated a suitable time and place for the attack, and the proper individual to act as a spy. This individual was sent to report on as many aspects of the homestead to be raided as he could determine. Often the spy went under the pretense of visiting a relative or wishing to trade. The best time for a raid was on a feast day when men would be involved in the festivities, not likely to be armed, and quite likely to be drunk. To determine the exact day of the feast, the spy would plan his visit during the preparations for the festivities. Because beer was always brewed for the celebration, the spy could determine the feast day based on the stage of the brewing process.

A successful raid yielded tools, arms, food, and chickens, some of which were sent to the chief for redistribution. Whatever could not be carried off was destroyed. Huts and granaries were burned.

In addition to raids, there were larger mobilizations of war campaigns on a grand scale. These were ordered by the chief, after having consulted his own poison oracle, and might continue over a period of weeks. While knives and spears were used exclusively in raids, the introduction of rifles into these larger confrontations resulted in a shift from hand-to-hand combat to shots being fired from a distance. Only when ammunition was exhausted would those warriors wielding spears converge on the enemy.

Marriage

The traditional Zande system of marriage was greatly disrupted by European involvement. Administrators legislated broad changes, especially regarding bride payment, divorce, and age at marriage. Although many of these were ostensibly designed to improve the status of women, ethnographer Reining (1966:61–2) regards them rather as "an experiment in altering some aspects of a culture without providing for changes in values. . . . [illustrating] the unpredictability of arbitrary cultural changes." Azande did not share the European view that marriage was especially disadvantageous to women, whom they never regarded as servile, despite administrative interpretation of their customs.

Traditionally, the instigation for marriage among the Azande came from the potential groom. When a man wanted to marry a woman, he asked an intermediary to approach her father with his offer. Unless the suitor was deemed undesirable immediately, her father would discuss the matter first with his brothers and sisters, and next with the woman in question. If she was agreeable, the money sent with the intermediary was accepted.

Several days later, the suitor would visit his promised bride's parents, bringing gifts, and demonstrating his respect. In turn, their daughter visited her suitor's home for a "trial period" of several weeks, after which she returned to her parents home to make her final decision regarding the marriage.

During the time spent in reflection by the woman, the groom-to-be consulted oracles to determine whether the marriage, should it occur, would be a happy one. If both oracle and woman regarded the match favorably, the bride's family traveled to the home of the groom, where the ceremony took place. The marriage was sealed with the installation of the new bride's own cooking hearth.

Reining (1966) describes traditional Zande marriage as a process which continues indefinitely over time, with a protracted payment of brideprice. A small part of the price was paid at the time of the marriage ceremony, but in reality a husband was always indebted to his wife's family. It was always his responsibility to help in his in-laws' fields, and he had mortuary obligations in the event of a death in his wife's family.

The material payment of the agreed-upon brideprice was not, in fact, as important as the attitude and behavior of a husband to his wife and her parents. (Reining 1966) If he was a gentle, loving husband and labored adequately for her parents, remuneration could be forestalled for years. This was often, in reality, the situation preferred by in-laws: it afforded them considerable influence over their daughter's husband. If the husband was not performing his duties adequately, the wife's parents might insist that their daughter move back to their home, forcing the husband to negotiate with her parents for her return. Thus, the relationship of primary emphasis in marriage was that of a son-in-law and his wife's parents. In polygynous situations, a man who had a good relationship with his in-laws often expressed the desire to marry his wife's sister because of the advantages of a good relationship with in-laws.

The topic of homosexuality in Azande culture has been regularly addressed, especially in the context of the unmarried warriors, who, during the several years spent living apart from women, had homosexual relations with the boys who were apprentice warriors. These practices, however, were not necessarily maintained as a lifelong pattern of sexual orientation. Generally, after their experiences with so-called "boy-wives," the warriors entered into heterosexual marriages.

Less attention has been paid to Azande lesbianism, relationships that were often formed between co-wives. Although there is not a wealth of information concerning these practices, according to Evans-Pritchard (1970:1429), "All Azande I have known well enough to discuss this matter have asserted . . . that female homosexuality . . . was practiced in polygamous homes."

Zande husbands felt threatened by such activities, yet could not stop them; thus, women usually kept the sexual nature of their friendships secret. (Blackwood in Suggs and Miracle 1993) Two Zande women who wished to formalize their relationship could do so in a ritual that created a permanent bond. (Evans-Pritchard 1970) In addition to assuring both the emotional and economic support of the partner, it has been suggested that this formalization (a ritual akin to Zande "blood brotherhood") may have both widened a woman's trade network and enhanced her position in the community. Blackwood (in Suggs and Miracle 1993) interprets these relationships as indicating that Azande men's control over women did not extend into the realm of activities between women.

✦ RELIGION, BELIEFS, AND EXPRESSIVE CULTURE

Missionaries settled in the Sudan beginning in the early part of the twentieth century, and attempted to draw on indigenous beliefs as a way to promote Christianity.

Mbori is defined by Evans-Pritchard (1937:11) as "a ghostly being to whom the creation of the world is attributed." Missionaries and government officials writing about the Azande attempted to create out of Mbori a deity that would fit their own tradition. Evans-Pritchard, however, warns against looking for religion, as organized elsewhere, in Azande culture. Mbori is not convincingly portrayed by the Azande as a god analogous to the supreme being as found elsewhere. They have no shrines to Mbori, and no materials used in worship. There is only one ceremony in which his name is invoked, and that is performed infrequently at best. When he attempted to pursue the topic of theology, and Mbori in particular, Evans-Pritchard found the Azande "bored by the subject . . . and unable to express more than the vaguest ideas about him."

The Trickster Tales

One universal motif in folk literature appears to be that of the "trickster," and these tales are told among the Azande as well. To a large extent the tales serve to assert and affirm social rules. They provide examples of the consequences one can expect if moral dictates are not observed. They are always told for the benefit of children, to supplement didactic social training. They are designed to appeal to a young audience (although they often contain very adult themes, and are very much enjoyed by adults) by featuring a main character who possesses a child's curiosity and temptation to break the rules. Demonstrated in the behavior of the trickster are a child's propensity for imitation, the ramifications of overlooking part of a ritual, and the dangers inherent in exhibiting behaviors or assuming a role in society which are inappropriate.

Although there are many groups of trickster tales told among the Azande, the best known concern the adventures of a character named Ture. The stories focus on Ture's elaborate machinations as he attempts to secure what he is after, and end in describing his great success or dismal failure. His wants are generally basics; he is often in pursuit of food, such as meat, termites, porridge, mushrooms, and honey, the items most desirable in a Zande diet.

Ture's rashness often leads him to situations in which he must find a way to prevent his own death, often while in the form of a bird or animal. In many tales he is intrigued by either fire or water, sometimes regarded as necessities, sometimes as playthings. Despite his need for everyday goods, he often pursues items of pure luxury: "salt to improve the taste of his food, a barkcloth which hums harmoniously as the wearer moves, and a means of opening termite mounds to provide him with a home instead of building huts." (Street 1972:83)

Ture often shows poor judgment and questionable values, striving for something only because it is novel, or belongs to someone else, rather than because it is of any use to him. Thus, when he learns that someone possesses the ability to remove his own intestines and clean them, he wants only to be able to learn to do the same; when he obtains a secret formula for putting out fires, he sets his own house ablaze just so he can extinguish it. As the latter example suggests, oftentimes Ture will create ends just for the ability to use the means. (Street 1972)

Once Ture has chosen a goal, he begins to set his strategy for its achievement. However, his strategies tend to ignore all social convention. He usually uses trickery or deception to get what he wants. However, his attempts to use others to satisfy his own needs usually end in failure.

Often Ture tries to use magical spells or rituals that are not his to use. Because he is not the rightful owner of the magic or ceremony, he is unable to obtain the results he seeks. (One is reminded of the troubles encountered by the "sorcerer's apprentice," who borrows his master's hat and attempts to perform his chores with magical assistance, only to be overwhelmed by the power he has unwittingly unleashed.)

For example, Ture overhears a discussion about how two sons found success in hunting after cutting off their dying father's toe. In his eagerness to try this formula for hunting success, Ture murders his father, buries the toe he has severed, and goes out to hunt. To his surprise, he catches very few animals, and most of his companions are killed during the effort. The formula, it turns out, is only effective when the toe is offered willingly.

In other instances, the formula backfires because it is in the wrong hands: Ture has obtained it under false pretenses, and he was not meant to have it. While Ture may overhear a strategy for success, or may be given the tool to implement a strategy, he often has to resort to trickery to get the desired secret or magic.

Although tales end with particular lessons—Don't attempt another's behavior without that person's skill; If you are greedy, your acquisitions will be too much to handle—the Zande tales are more than merely moral examples. They employ themes common to many peoples. Evans-Pritchard suggests that the tales "represent deeper psychological forces present in us all, those elements which we would like to give rein to but cannot because of the rules of society" (Street 1972:86).

The tales also endeavor to teach flexibility, since rules are not always functional in every situation. To instill the message that sometimes rules must be broken, Ture the trickster elaborates the middle ground between order and chaos, and moderation in the application of convention. Classically, trickster tales describe a society's boundaries and rules and assert its unique identity. If viewed from this perspective, the Zande tales help us to understand their society as well as some broader tenets of human nature.

Witchcraft

The Azande are perhaps better known for their pervasive belief in witchcraft than for any other aspect of their culture. However, in his classic description of witchcraft among the Azande, Evans-Pritchard asks the reader to be aware "that the Zande cannot analyze his doctrines as I have done for him. . . . It is no use saying to a Zande 'Now tell me what you Azande think about witchcraft' because the subject is too general and indeterminate . . . to be described concisely. But it is possible to extract the principles of their thought from dozens of situations in which witchcraft is called upon to explain happenings. . . . Their philosophy is explicit, but it is not formally stated as a doctrine." (1937:70) (In such situations, an anthropologist endeavors to construct such a "doctrine" through fieldwork. The resulting product may look quite dissimilar from the indigenous view [Barrett 1991]).

Witchcraft is thought to be an actual physical property residing inside some individuals, who may themselves be unaware of their power. It is inherited, passed from father to son and mother to daughter. Azande believe that if the soul of the father is more powerful, the child conceived will be a boy; if the mother's soul substance is greater, their child will be a girl. Thus, although every child is a product of both parents, each also has more of one particular parent's soul. And if that parent is a witch, inheriting this inherent power to do harm is inevitable.

Because this property is organic, it grows as a person grows. Therefore an older witch is a more dangerous witch. Children, whose witchcraft substance is small, are never accused of major acts of harm (such as murder). They can, however, cause minor misfortunes for other children.

Unlike sorcery, which employs charms and spells, witchcraft is deployed by sheer willpower. Witches send the spirit of their own witchcraft entity to eat the flesh and organs of their intended victims. Thus, a witch may be at home asleep at the time illness or injury occurs. It is the "soul of the witchcraft" that travels through the night. This substance cannot travel great distances, however, and it is for this reason that the Azande feel more secure if they are able to live at a distance from their neighbors. The "short-range" nature of witchcraft allows the perpetrator to be more accurately identified; all those beyond the limits of a witch's capabilities, even with evil intent, may be eliminated. If a person is taken ill while traveling, it is that location where illness struck in which the witch must be found.

The Azande believe that witchcraft is at the base of all misfortune, great or small. If a potter opens his kiln only to discover his pottery cracked, he intimates witchcraft; if a child stubs her toe at play, she suspects witchcraft; if a hunter is gored by an elephant, he lays blame for the injury squarely on a witch.

Azande entertain no concept of "accidental" death. People die only as victims of murder, whether committed by witches or by the magic of revenge reserved for retaliation against suspected witches.

Despite these convictions, the Azande do not live in constant terror of witches. (Nanda 1991) In fact, Douglas (1980) reminds us that Evans-Pritchard's assessment of the Azande was that they were the happiest and most carefree peoples of the Sudan. "The feelings of an Azande man, on finding that he has been bewitched, are not terror, but hearty indignation as one of us might feel on finding himself the victim of embezzlement" (Douglas 1980:1).

Since a witch's motivation is not random, but rather envy or hatred directed at a specific person, a victim searches for a suspect among those with whom he has argued, or in a person who may have cause to be jealous of him. How then can he identify his aggressor? For this, and other purposes, the Azande consult a variety of oracles.

Oracles

The Azande consult oracles regarding a wide range of things about which they need information. They ask for guidance in planning a marriage, taking a journey, building a house, organizing a raid. In addition to whatever their current misfortune may be, they inquire about whether their health will be endangered in the future.

In pre-European times, Zande chiefs consulted oracles to confirm their military decisions, but chiefs were also charged with judicial duties. Every accusation was brought before the chief to adjudicate. To this end, he employed several people whose responsibility it was to assist in the consultation of oracles. It has been said that the Azande belief in witchcraft is the supporting framework of their entire judicial system (Mair 1974:221).

An oracle is a device for revelation. Among the Azande there are many from which to choose, with varying reputations for reliability. By far the most powerful is *benge,* the poison oracle, used by men alone. Its decisions are relied upon without question, and no undertaking of great import is attempted without its authorization. In attempting to convey its centrality, a Zande informant of Evans-Pritchard drew the analogy between the books of Europeans and the poison oracle of his own people. All the knowledge, guidance, memory and truth that are derived from trusted Western writings reside for the Azande within the poison oracle. Evans-Pritchard came to view it as less a ritual than a necessity:

> For how can a Zande do without his poison oracle? His life would be of little worth. Witches would make his wife and children sick and would destroy his crops and render his hunting useless. Every endeavour would be frustrated, every labour and pain would be to no purpose. At any moment a witch might kill him and he could do nothing to protect himself and his family. Men would violate his wife and steal his goods, and how would he be able to identify and avenge himself on adulterer and thief? Without the aid of his poison oracle he knows that he is helpless and at the mercy of every evil person. It is his guide and counsellor (1937:262–3).

Despite this seeming indispensability, later ethnographers have pointed out that *benge* poison, expensive and difficult to obtain, was most likely an oracle available regularly only to men of wealth. This limitation may have acted both to engender social obligations and to grant power and prestige. A man who cannot afford the costly poison, or who does not possess the proper chicken to which the poison must be administered, asks a wealthier kinsman, or deputy of the chief, to consult the oracle on his behalf. It is his duty to oblige. It is older men who are likely to have the means to seek counsel from the oracle: this access to information gives them power over younger men. They not only can ask the oracles about the intentions and behaviors of their juniors, but also are always supported in their decisions by the considerable weight of oracular authority, to which younger or poorer men have no direct access, and so cannot challenge (Evans-Pritchard 1937).

The *benge* poison ordeal is an elaborate procedure, requiring great skill and finesse in both the administration of the poison and the posing of the questions. Poison is administered, by an expert in the task, to a small chicken. The expert must know how much poison is necessary, how much time should elapse between doses, whether it should be shaken to distribute the poison, how long and firmly the chicken should be held, and in what position. Each barely perceptible movement made by the bird is significant to the trained eye.

Once the poison has been administered, the order in which questions are asked, whether they are phrased in a positive or negative frame, must all be determined by the questioner. The oracle is addressed as if it were a person. Every detail of the situation in question is explained, and each individual question may be embedded in five or ten minutes of speech. The *benge* poison shows its answer by responding through the chicken to the directive, "If this is true, *benge* kill the fowl" or "If this is not the truth, *benge* spare the fowl." Each answer is then tested by repeating the interpretation of its reply, prefaced with the question, "Did the oracle speak the truth in saying. . ." (Mair 1974).

An oracle more readily available to all is the termite oracle. This is used as often by women as men, and even children may participate. Two branches are cut, each from a different tree. They are inserted together into a termite mound and left overnight. The answer is indicated by which branch has been eaten. Though certainly less elaborate and costly than the *benge* oracle, consulting termites is a time-consuming affair, since only one question may be posed at a time and one must wait all night long for the answer.

Least reliable but most convenient is the rubbing-board oracle, a device resembling a Ouija board, made of two small pieces of wood, easily carried to be consulted anywhere, at any time. One small piece of wood is carved with a handle, and is rubbed across the top of a second piece, fashioned with legs to stand on. Questions are asked as the wood is moved; as it sticks or catches, so the answer is revealed.

Accusing a Witch

There are two distinct sorts of accusations of witchcraft: one in which illness or misfortune has occurred, the other after someone has died. These differ in both the function of accusing an individual, and the ramifications of being found guilty.

The aim of accusing a person of witchcraft in the former situation is to bring about some resolution to the conflict that induced the attack, and to return the relationship to equilibrium. Speaking ill of a person, or even wishing someone injury, is ineffectual without a social tie: the curse of a stranger cannot do harm. Thus, a relationship with the accused is a prerequisite for bewitchment. (An individual must be suspected, or else his or her name could not have been presented to the oracle for confirmation or denial of guilt.)

When the chicken dies during the *benge* poison ordeal, a wing is cut off, placed on a stick, and brought to the local deputy of the chief, telling him the name of the individual confirmed by the *benge*. A messenger, sent with the wing to the alleged witch, places it on the ground, and announces that *benge* has been consulted regarding the illness of the accuser. Usually this charge is met with denial of any ill intent. At the very least the accused pleads ignorance of harm derived from his or her own *mangu*, or witchcraft substance. As a demonstration of good faith, the alleged witch takes a mouthful of water, and sprays it over the wing. So doing, she or he beseeches the *mangu* to become inactive, allowing the victim to recover. The messenger reports these events to the chief's deputy.

In the event of a "murder," the aim is not pacification but revenge. Restoring amicable relations is clearly not possible; a postmortem accusation is an indictment leading to heavy compensation, sometimes paid with the witch's own life. Exacting such a toll permanently alters the relationship between the kin group of the victim and that of the accused (McLeod 1972).

Witchcraft in Its Social Setting

The Azande chiefdom is formally structured in a clear-cut hierarchy, from the chiefs at the top through their deputies, armies, local governors, and ending with individual householders. Built into this structure is the elimination of most opportunities for unequal competition: that is, chiefly lineages did not compete with those lesser, nor did the rich with the poor, or parents with their children. As Douglas (1980) has observed, accusations of witchcraft arise only in those social situations that fall outside of the political structure. Thus, cowives might accuse each other, as might rivals in other arenas. Because witches could be unintentionally dangerous, their *mangu* could be set into motion by understandable resentments and jealousies. The accusation and eventual demonstration of remorse will set these ill-feelings to rights. Events that can be explained by an individual's lack of technical skill (such as the shoddy work of an inexperienced carpenter) or by personally motivated actions are not likely to be involved in the realm of witchcraft. As Parsons (1969:195) observes, one can imagine many motivations for people to claim that witchcraft was at the root of their adultery, but this would result in ridicule, "because everybody knows witches don't do that."

Witchcraft beliefs can function effectively as a way of managing the anxiety resulting from random misfortune. This is evidenced by the prominence given to illness and death as occasions for witchcraft accusations.

Witchcraft as Social Control and Leveling Mechanism

Witchcraft may serve as an effective agent of social control. The lengthy process involved in making an accusation acts to forestall hasty and emotional confrontations. Charges must have group support behind them and are not leveled carelessly.

An individual's behavior can be guided by the knowledge that wrongdoing might likely result in retaliatory witchcraft. Additionally, cognizance that jealous or hostile behavior might place one in a position of being suspect should misfortune occur might lead one to be quite circumspect. Wishing to be neither suspect nor victim, the Azande possess, in witchcraft, both an effective sanction against socially disruptive behavior and a vehicle for handling hostility.

Because an individual with great wealth is likely to engender the jealousy of others and the attendant bewitchment, Azande are not likely to attempt to outproduce one another. It is in this way that witchcraft acts as a leveling mechanism, indirectly keeping wealth balanced.

The "Logic" of Azande Witchcraft

The attribution of the cause of all misfortune to witchcraft may seem extreme. In fact, Evans-Pritchard himself engaged in lively debate with informants who described as witchcraft events that seemed to him the result of entirely "natural" phenomena. He eventually recognized that they did, in fact, have a very clear understanding about the contribution of the natural world to their misfortune. When Evans-Pritchard suggested to a boy, whose foot had been injured when he tripped over a tree stump, that a witch could not possibly have placed the tree stump in his way, the boy agreed. He recognized that nature had contributed the tree stump and, further, that the tree stump had cut his foot. His evidence of witchcraft was simply that despite his vigilance in watching out for tree stumps, as well as his safe passage on that same path hundreds of other times, *this time* he had been injured. This time, there was witchcraft.

Along these same lines, when a granary collapsed, injuring several people who had been sitting in its shade, Azande saw no contradiction in their dual assertions that termites had eaten at the legs of the building, resulting in its collapse, and that witchcraft was responsible. They further admitted that no witch had "sent" the people underneath the granary in order to trap them: it was afternoon, and they were merely seeking shade. While we would call this series of events coincidence, or perhaps "being in the wrong place at the wrong time," Azande are able to form an explanatory link between these events. That link is provided by witchcraft.

During his stay in the Sudan, Evans-Pritchard witnessed the suicide of a man who was angry with his brothers. Although his despair over his conflict was well known, and when his body was found hanging from a tree, all readily acknowledged that he had, in fact, hanged himself, the cause of death was considered witchcraft. At Evans-Pritchard's behest, a Zande friend explained:

> . . . only crazy people commit suicide; if everyone who was angry with his brothers committed suicide there would soon be no people left in the world; if this man had not been bewitched he would not have done what he did do (1937:71).

Once the supernatural premise that people have witchcraft substance in them and can harm others with it is granted, the Zande argument becomes logical.

These beliefs concerning witchcraft endure today, with some modifications. Resettlement has forced them to accept living in closer quarters, depending upon screens to keep them out of their neighbors' view, if not their reach. When asked about fears concerning the proximity of witches, the Azande report that they feel able to relocate should misfortune occur. This would remove them from any nearby threat.

✧ Azande Today: Resettled, Unsettled

The "Zande Scheme"

The decision by colonial authorities in the 1920s to move Azande out of the valleys to control sleeping sickness was only the first in a series of resettlement and development plans. Before midcentury, the Azande were subsistence cultivators. In the late 1940s and early 1950s, the British introduced the so-called "Zande scheme," a program of cash cropping (chiefly of cotton) and industry (producing cotton cloth). Planners believed they could improve the lot of the Azande, who, it was thought, would be grateful for the introduction of more "modern" comforts and luxuries. The introduction of money and wage labor acted to weaken kinship ties by obviating the need for kin to work together outside the household. Young men and women could more easily leave their parents' homes and set up their own households with income from wages paid by Europeans. As part of the scheme, the Azande were once again resettled—more than 60,000 families by 1950—away from the roads, into farmland. The most detrimental feature of the resettlement plan was the arbitrary assignment of individuals to plots of land. This action was flawed in several ways: it disregarded family groupings, failed to take into account the Azande's desire for mobility and flexible living arrangements, and resulted in some farmers receiving land with good soil, and others that of poor quality. Tensions were engendered among resettled people that were counterproductive to the developers' wishes to create, through resettlement, a stable workforce. Anthropologist Conrad Reining (1966), in a study of the Zande scheme, concluded that while the project demonstrated the feasibility of establishing an industrial center among the Azande (providing cost was no object), and of convincing the Azande to produce copious amounts of cotton, it more convincingly showed how much could not be accomplished. Its primary weaknesses were in the realms of ecology, social organization, and communication, failures it shared with other such attempts. By the mid-1950s, cotton production slowed to a near halt. There was a move to restart the program in the 1970s, but civil war in Sudan, which would continue throughout the twentieth century and into the twenty-first, cut short the attempted revival.

Civil War in Sudan

Strife in Sudan is as old as the independent country itself. From the time Sudan gained independence in 1956, there was inequality between the Arab north and "black African" south. The British government concentrated power in the hands of the north, and the Arab-led government in Khartoum held sway over peoples in the south, Africans who were either Christian or retained their indigenous beliefs. Shortly thereafter, the military seized power and attempted to impose Islam on the southern Sudanese, many of whom fled in response to increasing threats. In the early 1960s, southern refugees formed the Anya-Nya ("snake poison"), a liberation movement advocating an independent southern state. Throughout the 1960s unrest continued as governmental and military rule changed hands. In the early 1970s, the Southern Sudan Liberation Movement (SSLM) was created, finally resulting in a cease-fire. This relative calm was short-lived. In 1983, the Sudanese government instituted Islamic law throughout the country. Numerous opposition groups were formed in the south, chief among them the Sudan Peoples' Liberation Movement (SPLM), that have been accused of showing disregard for the rights of the civilians they champion. (Kebbede 1999) There has been infighting among southern Sudanese peoples—Azande among them—as well as struggles with the powerful north.

By now, the civil war in Sudan is among the longest-running in the world, devastating both the people and the land. Estimates of dead are as high as two million since 1983. In addition, southern Sudan also has one of the world's largest populations of internally displaced people—nearly five million. In recent years, development of exportable oil resources in the south have enriched the government, enabling it to purchase arms for the war against the south. Some scholars contend that while the ethnic and religious conflict in Sudan has long been central, the struggle to control resources is now emerging as a powerful compelling force in the civil war (Kebbede 1999).

✦ FOR FURTHER DISCUSSION

Witchcraft among the Azande traditionally served as an effective means of social control. What are the major institutions and beliefs in your own culture that function similarly? Think about the ways in which members of your society are compelled to behave in socially acceptable ways. How do these differ from one another? There is a "logic" to the Azande belief in witchcraft and the causality of misfortune. Do you employ logic that is similar or different, when explaining negative events? Are there several different "systems of logic" which may be invoked, depending upon the circumstances?

CHAPTER 2

THE AZTECS

Ancient Legacy, Modern Pride

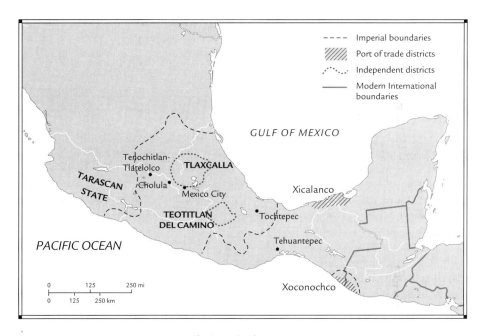

The Aztec Empire, 1519.

✦ THE BEGINNING

The world before had existed not once, but four times, and these were the Ages of the Suns. Water, earth, wind, and fire each had their reign. Each ended in disaster.

The first people were formed of ashes, and when the water came they were carried away and changed into fishes. In the next sun there were giants, and tigers waited for dark to devour them. The giants were weak despite their size, and warned one another: do not fall. But they fell, and when they fell, they fell forever. During the third sun, the rain was made of fire, and all burned. The fourth sun was the wind, and swept everything away. The people became monkeys and fled to the mountains.

Now it is the fifth sun. New people are created from the remains of the old. Quetzalcoatl will restore them, and feed them maize (León-Portilla 1992).

✦ AZTEC HISTORY

Journey to the Valley of Mexico

The people referred to as Aztecs called themselves Mexica. Arriving in central Mexico as nomads in the thirteenth century, they had risen to a position of political and military power by the time the Spanish arrived in 1519. With Tenochtitlan as the capital of their empire, they had forged alliances with neighbors to the east and west.

Mexica migration into the Valley of Mexico began from Aztlan in the northwest some two hundred years before their eventual arrival. As they marched south, they were met with great hardship, expelled from each place they attempted to settle. Throughout the Valley of Mexico, elaborate states were already flourishing. The peoples settled here had complex and specialized technologies, including a sophisticated system of irrigation, which afforded them a variety of crops in abundance. In addition, they possessed intricately organized social and economic systems. The nomadic Mexicas were not welcomed in their attempt to seek out unsettled land.

Their arduous trek was plagued with dissension from within (Berdan 1982) and treachery from without. Evidence for internal rebellion is found in numerous accounts of their journey. Along their route, whenever they stopped they constructed a temple for Huitzilopotchtli, the most revered of the deities, who provided guidance on their exodus. Among the ceremonies conducted at these sites were human sacrifices, for which the Aztecs have come to be known. Many explanations have been offered for the various sacrificial occasions in Aztec culture. Berdan (1982) suggests that those performed en route to their permanent home may have served the purpose of eliminating the dissension in the group, who were agitating to remain where they were and not continue on their journey as Huitzilopotchtli decreed.

The response of the ruler of Calhuacan to the Mexica request for asylum exemplified the rejection they experienced from others. Their petition to settle in his kingdom was met with the granting of territory he knew to be infested with poisonous snakes. He was sure this would put an end to these "undesirable Mexicas" (León-Portilla 1992:31). Instead, they roasted the snakes, ate them, and triumphed. Apparently surprised at the Mexica tenacity and impressed by their military skills, those living in the area engaged the Mexica as their mercenaries. Coupled with some of their more aggressive customs, these martial skills elicited both fear and hatred from surrounding peoples. When a ceremony to dedicate the king's daughter as a goddess resulted in her death and flaying, the Mexica were forced to flee once more.

Tenochtitlan

Camping by the marshy shores of Lake Texcoco, they were instructed by Huitzilopotchtli to look for the sign that would at long last indicate to them the site of their final destination. They saw this sign—an eagle resting atop a prickly pear cactus—and knew they had reached the end of their difficult journey. They named the place Tenochtitlan, "the place of the fruit of the prickly pear cactus" (Berdan 1982). The modern Mexican flag has at its center the eagle perched on the cactus, a snake in its talon.

The founding of Tenochtitlan in 1325 ended their wandering, but certainly not the struggle of the Mexica people. Both the physical and the sociopolitical environment presented enormous challenges. Tenochtitlan was built on an island on the western side of Lake Texcoco. Although the lake provided fish and aquatic birds, ease of canoe transportation, and *chinampas* cultivation (so-called "floating gardens"), the site was not without disadvantages. Chief among these were the lack of wood and stone for use in construction and the threat of floods.

Sociopolitically, the Mexica had established themselves on the boundaries of existing powerful states. Their history of overcoming adversity stood them in good stead. They attached themselves to the ruling Tepanec empire and began to strengthen themselves by forging alliances through marriage.

Within the Tepanec empire, it was the ancient Toltec line of nobility who were viewed as legitimate rulers. The first Mexica ruler in Tenochtitlan married a woman from a royal line, assuring the offspring of this union (and their descendants) legitimate claim to Toltec heritage. The ruler's son further cemented this bond by making a similarly politically astute marriage. Relations between the Mexica and the Tepanec ruler were cemented by these ties (especially after the birth of a son to the Mexica ruler and the Tepanec lord's granddaughter), and the Mexica became allies rather than subordinates.

As a result of these shifts in power relations, the Mexica population became increasingly socially stratified. Rulers headed a class of nobles who claimed private ownership of land and the prerogative to hold important public offices. The largest portion of the Mexica population remained commoners who worked the land and fought the battles. Between these classes of commoners and nobility were occupational specialists: merchants and crafts-people (Berdan 1982).

While attending to war strategy and political power occupied the nobility, the average Mexica devoted themselves to the construction of temples and houses, and *chinampas* cultivation. The latter was of crucial importance, not only because filling their own subsistence needs afforded the Mexica some degree of autonomy, but also because it was a key to necessary expansion.

The Mexica population grew rapidly, in part because immigration supplemented natural growth. As conditions became crowded, people left Tenochtitlan to settle adjacent islands. Successful *chinampas* cultivation provided a consistent resource base, allowing the Mexicas to conquer other groups and exact tribute (Berdan 1982).

During this time, a powerful Mexica military force was being assembled. Joining with two neighboring allies, the Triple Alliance was formed, successfully dethroning the Tepanec empire and beginning the most dramatic expansion in the history of Mesoamerica.

✦ ECONOMIC ORGANIZATION

Tenochtitlan was connected to the mainland by three raised, paved roadways. In the center of the city were eight or nine walled-off ceremonial sites, surrounded by the palaces and homes of the nobility.

Palaces were elaborate edifices with several buildings and courtyards. Housed in the palaces were artists, craftsworkers, servants, nobles, and government officials. Structures included a courthouse, warrior's council chamber, storage space for acquired tribute (and housing for those who looked after it), chambers for singers, dancers, and instruction of various kinds. Occupants and daily visitors to the palace numbered over a thousand.

Cities of this scope rely on material support. Central and southern Mexico was a place of environmental diversity, with intensive production and economic specialization resulting in a surplus of goods. The Valley of Mexico, heart of the Aztec empire, was ideally suited to provide its inhabitants with resources for food, clothing, housing, and tools.

Subsistence

The Aztec empire was built on agriculture, and at the core of this agriculture was maize. It formed the mainstay of the diet in various forms, and could be successfully grown in both the high plateaus and the tropical lowlands. This success was largely climate dependent: maize thrives best where rains are concentrated in the summer, as they are throughout Mesoamerica. Summer rains allow early planting and harvest before early November frosts. The Valley of Mexico yielded one crop of maize per season; in the lower elevations, two crops were possible. It has been suggested (Berdan 1982) that Aztec conquest of the more temperate zones outside the valley may have been spurred by the desire for a reliable source of maize.

In the middle of the fifteenth century central Mexico experienced severe famine. Within fifty years the Triple Alliance had secured control of maize production in widespread ecological zones where maize could be harvested at different times. This acted to assure that the effects of famine were less disastrous to the Mexica. Also helping to offset hunger were ritual feasts given by Aztec rulers in honor of the goddess of maize: prestations of food to people in need helped them through difficult seasons.

Its centrality in subsistence earned maize a glorified position in Aztec culture. Hardly a mere foodstuff, it was intimately involved in Mexica daily life. People personified maize, and addressed it with reverence as it was planted. Poetry, hymns, sayings, and stories all deified the crop and linked people metaphorically to it. An individual speaking out of turn or imprudently was "like an ear of maize split open"; one who had gained great prestige was said to have "reached the season of maize."

Also widely cultivated throughout the Aztec empire were beans, chiles, squash, maguey, and a host of other fruits and vegetables. From cactus were produced alcoholic beverages, fibers for clothing, medicinal remedies, and sewing needles. In the tropical lowlands, cotton and cacao (chocolate) were additionally cultivated.

In those areas of the highlands not conducive to irrigation, most employed systems of fallowing, supplemented by terracing and crop rotations. In shallow lakebeds or flatter stretches, floodwater irrigation was used. *Chinampas* agriculture was by far the most intensive irrigation agriculture strategy. Mud and vegetation were piled in shallow portions of a lake. Posts were attached to secure the plot until the roots of willows planted at the sides and corners could act as anchors. In the areas outside the densely populated urban centers, families cultivated *chinampas* plots that not only supported their own needs, but also yielded enough surplus to be exchanged in the city for specialized goods and services. This funneling of surplus food into the urban area of Tenochtitlan most likely provided the subsistence to those specialists in service to the nobility who could not be provided for by the smaller, more crowded *chinampas* in urban areas.

Cultivation was usually combined with gathering wild foods, hunting, and fishing. Medicinal herbs were of great value, as were peyote and mushrooms. These, along with fruits available predominantly in the lowlands, were in great demand at the marketplaces.

Hunting held an esteemed place among the Mexicas, dating back to their nomadic past. In addition to providing food, fur, and skin, animals were hunted to supply the empire's zoos. Meat from land animals such as armadillo, deer, rabbits, boars, and opossum was all part of the regular diet, and the animals were hunted with snares or bow and arrow. The lakes provided plentiful fish, reptiles, and crustaceans. Duck, quail, pheasant, and partridge were hunted by the lakeshores, and were valued as much for their feathers as for their flesh.

The Mesoamerican food-producing environment allowed both intensive and varied agriculture. This yielded two important consequences. First, it led to specialization in production. Those residing by the lakeshore could devote themselves entirely to fish and waterfowl; farmers in drier areas could specialize in products derived from cactus. Second, these specialized systems of food production resulted in enough of a surplus to allow many people to instead direct their talents to professional occupations other than agriculture.

Occupational Specialization

In the urban centers of Mexico, craft manufacture was highly elaborated, with entire residential sections of town home to painters, goldsmiths, silversmiths, featherworkers and sculptors. While their creations were held in high regard by the entire Aztec population, these products were available only to the nobility. Consequently the artisans themselves enjoyed great prestige, and organized into exclusive guilds that had privileged relationships to the state. They resided separately, and had access to both temples and schools reserved especially for them. Featherworkers appear to have been especially esteemed, creating headdresses, fans, and costumes for nobility and the highest-ranking military personnel. Stoneworkers and metallurgists had similar exclusive residences and were granted political clout.

The craft practiced most widely was weaving, an endeavor reserved only for women, and pursued by women of all classes. Although every girl and woman learned to spin and weave cloth, the materials with which they worked and the garments they produced varied greatly by the status of the weaver. Women of the lowest ranks produced simple goods for household use; noble women engaged in producing the elaborate ceremonial capes, using the finest cotton, rabbit fur, and feathers.

Clothing served the dual purpose of being both utilitarian and identifying the class of the wearer. Commoners were bound to wear garments made from only the coarsest fabrics. Nobility had no apparel forbidden to them, but usually chose to exercise their privilege and wear the most elegant of vestments. Within the highest class, more decorative clothing signaled greater wealth.

Political, military, and religious specialists also emerged, as did "a host of miscellaneous occupations" (Berdan 1982:34), a situation to be expected in such a complex society. Astrologers, midwives, scribes, and prostitutes are counted among these.

Trade and Exchange

Markets were the economic link between different regions of production, the political focus for gossip and information, and the social setting for most neighborhood interaction.

The outdoor marketplace was the hub of every community, providing a meeting place for people of every age and social status to talk and share news, as well as conduct business. Wares reflected the local environment in terms of items abundantly available; larger markets trafficked additionally in luxury items. Barter was typically the medium of exchange, but money in the form of cacao beans and cotton cloaks was common. Less usual were bells, beads, and quills filled with gold dust.

Textiles, which were bartered and sold in the marketplace, functioned as items of trade, religious offerings, marriage payments, decoration, and cremation cloths, among other uses. Trade was carried on by all members of the society, whether they were professional artisans or individual agriculturalists. Families routinely sold their surplus in public marketplaces. These small-scale producers were vendors in the marketplaces and traded their wares to all passersby. Professional merchants were important on an entirely different scale. Their status afforded them political importance, but also economic sway: the luxury items they produced were of paramount importance for the nobility to display as symbols of their status.

Specialization required a fairly sophisticated system of exchange that began in the marketplace. Distribution of goods was also accomplished through tribute and trade routes, numerous enough for individuals to secure a wide range of goods. Trade, both foreign and domestic, forged political ties along with the economic.

The tribute collected from conquered regions provided revenue in exchange for the promise of protection. A wide variety of goods were given in tribute, with the majority typically being the most locally accessible items. Those provinces nearest the Triple Alliance capital cities most often provided surplus agricultural goods, textiles, and wood and paper products. Distant provinces, located in different ecological zones, provided more exotic goods, which might include rubber balls, chocolate, jade, quetzal feathers, and liquid amber.

Nahua ceremonial dress.

It was the commoners on whom the burden of tribute fell most heavily. Cultivators struggled to amass the tremendous amount of food demanded, and artisans turned over the most valuable items they wrought. For those living in provinces on the outskirts of the empire, little more than offers of future protection were given in return. Those closer to the capitals could hope to reap some of the subsistence goods and, as they more often paid tribute in labor than in goods, they were likely to be working on city-improvement tasks that ultimately were of benefit to them.

The enormous stores of tribute were used to sustain the large and complex bureaucracy of the empire, to finance the military, to support the royal palaces, to bestow gifts, and to promote foreign trade.

→ Social Organization

Class Structure

The Aztec empire was a complex, stratified society with social organization guided by the principles of hierarchy and heterogeneity (Berdan 1982). Although one's position at birth (ascribed status) most circumscribed the positions to which one could aspire, there was room for upward social mobility through accomplishments (achieved status).

The most basic social distinction existed between the commoners and the nobility, and these were conferred at birth. Initially, membership in the nobility demanded the ability to trace one's ancestry back to the first Mexica ruler. However, as Berdan (1982) points out, the practice of polygyny and the fact that noble status was passed through both males and females led to an exceedingly high number of people who could lay claim to noble birth. By the early sixteenth century, more stringent rules for reckoning legitimate noble descent were put into place.

Rigid dress codes made status differences readily apparent. Commoners wore simple clothes and their cloaks had to end above the knee. The nobility alone could wear headbands, feathers, gold armbands, and jewels in their lips, ears, and noses. Only the ruler and his second-in-command could wear sandals.

Housing was also a status marker. Only those of noble rank could build two-story houses. When visiting the palace, commoners knew which rooms were open to them, and which were reserved for nobility. Separate courthouses were maintained for passing judgment on individuals of different classes. In these courthouses, nobility were judged more severely than commoners. For example, a commoner charged with public drunkenness was punished by having his head shaved, while a nobleman would be put to death for this same offense. There are reports of rulers sentencing their own children to die for committing adultery.

Of course, the more far-reaching differences between classes were economic and political. Ownership of land, access to public and religious office, and control over important resources were tied to social class.

Along with the rights and privileges accruing (or denied) to each status, there were accompanying expectations of behavior and lifestyle.

The provincial rulers formed the top rank of the nobility. Their power was determined by the size of their territory. Those whose dominion was smaller or less central paid tribute to those who ruled the Triple Alliance capitals, Tenochtitlan, Texcoco, and Tlacopan. The responsibilities of all rulers included collecting tribute from commoners, organizing military expeditions, sponsoring religious feasts, and the ultimate adjudication of legal disputes that could not be settled by the courts. Despite the fact that this status was bestowed by birth, the personal qualities of an individual ruler often greatly influenced his ability to govern successfully. The ideal ruler was one who acted as a protector and unifier, assuming the burdens of leadership as well as its rewards. Although succession usually passed to brother or son, this was often contingent upon personal achievements.

Chiefs formed the rank below rulers, and this status was usually granted to those who had demonstrated superior military valor. Most chiefly duties involved military leadership, either advisory or on the battlefield, or that of judge.

Sons of nobility were a recognized class, to whom rights and privileges afforded nobility accrued, and who could expect to ascend to prestigious posts, even if they did not themselves become rulers or chiefs.

The provincial nobility were largely concerned with agricultural and not urban issues, as might be expected. The administration of land and water rights was of greater import than the military, manufacturing, or trade.

The commoners made up the largest portion of the population. They worked the land, filled the lowest ranks of the military, and paid tribute. They were not, however, a homogeneous group. For example, commoners had varying access to land; some of the more well-off had tenant farmers.

Commoners were organized into *calpulli,* a territorial unit based on kinship, literally meaning "big household." Nuclear families, independent of one another, were strongly favored, but extended households were very common (León-Portilla 1992). Earlier, before the rise of large urban areas, assemblages of households who reckoned descent bilaterally from an apical ancestor constituted a *calpulli.* As these groups settled, *calpulli* came to be the designation for a ward, or barrio. Sometimes these were groups of occupational specialists. In every case, each *calpulli* had its own temple, in which the group recognized a particular *calpulli* deity, and through which they maintained a shared identity. In addition, *calpulli* had their own school, dedicated largely to martial training. *Calpulli* themselves were socially stratified, with a headman, council of elders, and members who worked the land.

There were also "serfs" (rural tenant farmers) and "slaves" in Mexica social structure. Each of these classes of individuals was drawn from the stratum of commoners. People who were homeless, through economic need or through warfare, made up the majority of these ranks. Individuals also sold themselves or family members into slavery for subsistence needs. Those unable to pay debts, tribute, or fines also ran the risk of succumbing to this fate. This was, in almost all cases, an acquired status: children of serfs or slaves were born into freedom.

Kinship, Marriage, and Family

Early reports emphasize kinship as the single most important principle in Mexica society: the lineage was referred to as "the set of cords that unite humans" (León-Portilla 1992:127). The Mexica reckoned descent bilaterally, as did most indigenous central Mexican peoples. Both mother's and father's brothers were called "uncles," and both mother's and father's parents were called "grandparents." Relative age, more than lineality, was a factor in determining social relationships. Distinctions were made between one's older and younger siblings. Beyond one's own generation, however, distinctions continued to be made on the basis of sex in ascending generations (parents, grandparents) and the generation below (son, daughter) but not beyond (all grandchildren were referred to by the same term, regardless of sex). Kinship rules functioned as the guiding factors in marriage, residence, and patterns of inheritance.

Among the nobility, the primary aim of marriage was to strengthen or forge powerful political ties. Ruling houses of neighboring capitals often maintained their relationships through such marriages for hundreds of years. Typically, this pattern allowed for the manipulation of inheritance to the satisfaction of both ruling families. The nobility were polygynous, but the commoners were not. This practice produced many individuals who aspired to relatively few positions. Inheritance was not based solely on the dictates of kinship; achievement often tipped the scale in the awarding of titles to one of many "rightful" pretenders. Unlike titles or official positions, land and houses could be divided among several heirs.

Cross-cousin marriage was common, and class endogamy appears to have been the rule. The *calpulli*, too, tended to be endogamous, which acted to keep resources within a guild, in the case of *calpulli* organized by occupational specialty.

Marriages were arranged for youths by their parents. When they decided a child was of marriageable age, parents prepared a feast of tamales and chocolate to which all the youth's teachers were invited, and at which they ritually discharged the student from their care. There is little evidence that the youth's own wishes were taken into consideration in the search for a suitable mate. Older women of the community served as brokers for the match. Once married, it was the primary responsibility of the new couple to join or establish a household, and have children.

One feature of kinship systems in which descent is reckoned bilaterally is the usual absence of strict postmarital residence rules, and this was the case in Mexica society. Actual residence patterns vary by location. In some areas, nuclear families predominated; in others, joint households were more common. Often the incentive to form either a nuclear or joint household would be provided by the demands of land tenancy and agricultural and subsistence needs. Flexibility in residence patterns assured that family structure could be altered to adapt to available resources.

Aztec Life and Customs

The ideal attributes of a Mexica citizen was to be moderate and discrete in all pursuits. Men were expected to serve as providers and teachers, tending most assiduously to the world outside the household. Women operated in the domain of the household, weaving, educating small children, and overseeing the efficient conduct of the family. Children were expected to show parents respect and obedience.

Young children were expected to be dependent, and little was asked of them. By the age of five or six, greater expectations were placed on all children. These were aimed at instilling the virtues of honesty, obedience, and respect. Boys and girls were expected to be similar in their acquisition of these general characteristics. The practical skills to be developed and the chores assigned to each were different, however. Boys carried water and firewood, brought goods to market, learned to fish or produce feather crafts. Girls learned to spin and weave, to cook, and were expected to be proficient at housework.

Formal education was compulsory for boys and girls, although girls generally attended for a shorter time. Beginning in early adolescence, formal teaching centered around songs, dances, and instrumental music. These were not only essential to ritual and religious participation, their content also transmitted important historical lessons and cultural values. By age fifteen, boys attended schools whose curricula included history, calendrics, dream interpretation, and the skills necessary for various occupations, such as hunter or priest. Military instruction formed the largest substance of commoner boys' formal education.

Law

The Aztec legal system incorporated both secular and supernatural sanctions in order to maintain social control. Behavior was expected to conform to established teachings. When it did not, threats of punishment were the items of first resort. Many religious traditions invoke banishment to "hell" or entry into "heaven" resulting as a consequence of an individual's conduct during life. Aztec belief, however, was that it was a person's death, and not his or her conduct in life, that determined events in the afterlife (Berdan 1982). Thus, no threat directed at an unpleasant afterlife could be issued. Secular law was exacting and punishment was swift. Drunkenness was invoked as the cause of the vast majority of unacceptable public behavior and criminal activity. Adultery resulted in stoning or hanging; homicide was usually punishable by death, although in some cases the murderer was turned over to the victim's family to serve them in slavery. Stealing was less severely punished than any of the foregoing.

Pretending toward a higher social status than one's rightful one, either in the form of dress and personal adornment or acquisition of property, was punishable by death.

Supernatural sanctions were inflicted by the god responsible for punishing that offense, and the consequences would be ones which reflected the affront. Thus, the god Macuilxochitl would punish those who did not practice sexual abstinence during ritual fasts by inflicting venereal diseases. Other gods would retaliate if their shrines were not properly maintained, sending a variety of physical ailments that would identify the sufferer as one who had shirked some ritual responsibility.

✦ POLITICAL ORGANIZATION

The Aztec empire boasted an intricately structured military and government. The type of political organization that predominated from the fourteenth through early sixteenth centuries was the city-state. Central Mexico was divided into some fifty or sixty of these units at this time, varying in size and political prowess.

Leadership and Government

The degree of autonomy enjoyed by rulers (*tlatoani*) of the city-states was variable. Some were not beholden to any other authority, while others were dominated by leadership of a higher order, most typically rulers of Triple Alliance cities (Berdan 1982).

The *tlatoani* functioned as a monarch. He was responsible for ritual, adjudication, waging war, and advocating for the rights of his citizens. In Tenochtitlan, the Mexica *tlatoani* was believed to be a descendent of the god Quetzalcoatl. Berdan (1982:100) reports: "The rulers were earthly counterparts of celestial deities; their rule was by divine right." While the position of *tlatoani* was an inherited one (often from brother to brother, and then to the firstborn son of the oldest brother), rulers had to have been proven valorous in battle before ascending to leadership. In addition to his god-like status, he must possess great personal skills, especially in oratory. (*Tlatoani* means "one who is gifted with the facility of speech.") Possessing both exceptional understanding of the sacred and superior military prowess, the *tlatoani* embodied both "great priest and great military captain" (Carrasco and Matos Moctezuma 2003:22).

The Council of Four, close relatives of the ruling *tlatoani,* chose his successor. Once selected, a series of rituals were set into motion, culminating in the coronation. First, the new *tlatoani* appeared before the priests, who escorted him (along with the council) to a public ceremony, where citizens witnessed an offering of incense. The ruler and his council maintained a four-day fast, after which they returned to the temple and cut themselves, offering blood to Huitzilopotchtli.

The custom after this initial offering was for the newly chosen *tlatoani* to leave for the battlefield and return with prisoners. At the coronation, to which rulers from both allied and enemy lands were invited, a spectacular feast was given, expensive gifts exchanged, and war prisoners captured by the new ruler were sacrificed. This display served to strengthen alliances and warn enemies. It also served as fair warning to any who would contemplate rebellion.

The *tlatoani* was assisted by special counselors, relatives with whom he consulted on all important governmental matters. Advice was given by specialists in each realm of the political structure. For military matters, he had a war council drawn from those professional warriors who had proven themselves in battle. Judicial advice was rendered by high court judges in the complex system of courts.

Warfare

Warfare has been called "a cultural preoccupation" (Berdan 1982) of the Mexica, woven into the fabric of social, political, economic, and religious life. Militaristic themes abound. A boy was declared a soldier at birth, and if his mother died in childbirth she was glorified as a warrior, and assured a blissful afterlife. Men were judged overwhelmingly by their militaristic skills, and rewarded commensurate with their valor. Victory in battle brought privileges in dress and ornamentation, as well as gifts. These returns were thought to inspire continued military success. Death in battle brought rewards in the afterlife.

If warfare was not quite itself a religion, it was at least bound up with religion. Patron gods not only sent soldiers into battle, but also could only be appeased by human sacrifice gathered from enemy troops. There were even particular enemies whom the gods were thought to find especially pleasing (Berdan 1982). War, far from being only a means to expand territory, functioned as an end in itself. The conquest of new lands was a pursuit separate from the warfare engendered by the need to capture people to be offered as sacrifice, and to provide militaristic experience for young soldiers. In fact, Aztecs staged ritual wars—known as "flower wars," for the way in which men fell to the ground like so many colorful blossoms shaken from a bough—expressly for the purpose of gathering prisoners to be sacrificed (Townsend 1992).

Human Sacrifice and Cannibalism

While the topic of human sacrifice and cannibalism among the Aztec has generated much debate, there is no disagreement regarding the centrality of human sacrifice in their culture. The practice arose out of a debt owed to the gods: the consequence of not paying was no less than the end of the world.

Aztec myth describes the creation of the sun and the moon, and the inception of their movement. When the current sun—the fifth—was to be created, all the gods gathered at Teotihuacan to decide who would be willing to throw himself into a great fire and emerge as the sun. Two stepped forward, one wealthy and arrogant; the other poor and humble. As much as he wanted to be the sun, the arrogant god lacked the courage to throw himself into the flames. Instead, the humble god cremated himself, and rose in the sky as the sun. Furious at being outdone, the first god followed, only to emerge as the moon, a pale reflection of the sun's great light. There they sat, together in the sky. The gods knew that they must be separated. One must shine brightly in the day, and the other glow at night. One god threw a rabbit at the moon, some say to dim its light, others say to keep it distant from the sun. Even when this was done, the sun and moon still hung, unmoving, in the sky. It was then that the other gods sacrificed themselves, for only their blood could put the sun in motion. Life for humankind was only possible with a moving sun, and this the gods provided. It then became the responsibility of humanity to feed the sun thereafter, lest it stop and the universe cease with it. Although mythology states that sacrifice is to the sun, the wider notion is that there can be no human life without sacrificial human death (Berdan 1982).

The most common form of sacrifice was to open a man's chest with a sacred blade, tear out the still-beating heart, and offer it to the gods. Women occasionally had their heads severed before their hearts were removed. Children were most often drowned, securing good rainfall (Berdan 1982).

Special occasions and ceremonies dictated variations in the form of sacrifice, although the removal of the heart and display of the head were consistent. Priests upon occasion ceremonially wore the skin of a flayed victim. All forms of sacrifice were sacred, performed without vengeance and endured without regret. A captor honored and respected the person to be sacrificed. Those who died in this fashion were privileged to be the food of the gods. In dying to keep the world alive, they were assured a sublime afterlife.

Often, once the sacrifice was completed, the body was stewed and ritually consumed. Ritual cannibalism has been explained by some anthropologists as a religious phenomenon, while others propose an ecological explanation.

Those who see cannibalism as an extension of the religious motivation behind human sacrifice, suggest that sacrifice made the victims divine. Eating the divine then made the consumer sacred. Thus, the belief that sacrifice is demanded by the gods and necessary for survival makes eating the flesh of the sacrificial victim an extension of the ritual process of maintaining the universe.

Those who argue against such a supernatural stance suggest that there were nutritional reasons for the practice of cannibalism, chief among them the deficiency of protein and fat in the Aztec diet. Formulated by anthropologist Michael Harner (1977), this theory proposes that cannibalism may have been couched in religious explanations, but in fact this practice alleviated a severe need for protein. If there was indeed a shortage of protein, feeding captives would only exacerbate the problem: sacrifice obviated the need to provision a prisoner, and cannibalism provided protein.

This assertion has been severely challenged on many grounds, including the fact that those who might be in greatest need of protein (commoners, children, and adolescents) were least likely to receive human flesh, accessible most typically to nobles. Moreover, there is debate as to whether protein deficiency existed in the first place (Berdan 1982).

Population control is another motivation proposed for cannibalism, although this aim could hardly be best served by the sacrifice of adult males (the most usual offerings) rather than women of childbearing age (Berdan 1982).

✦ RELIGION AND EXPRESSIVE CULTURE

The Aztec worldview maintained that life was precarious, and it was the responsibility of humankind to attempt to control this uncertainty and assure their own continued existence.

Every half-century, a dramatic ritual was undertaken. All fires were extinguished, all houses swept clean, all hearthstones and cooking pots discarded. The entire population was awakened at night; babies, if they slept, would be turned into mice. They waited, poised, to hear of success in the ritual about to begin. Priests climbed to the top of a mountain in the dark, sacrificed a victim, and attempted to kindle a fire in his open chest cavity. If the spark caught, life would continue for another half-century. Citizens were notified of the new fire and, as they waited for messengers to bring them flames to start their own fires, they cut their ears and offered blood to the gods upon hearing the news. Should the fire not start, the sun would grow cold, and the universe end. This ritual embodied the most salient tenets of Aztec culture: that the continuation of life is not assured unless the people actively promote its survival through human sacrifice.

Aztec Gods

Aztec deities functioned in many ways like patron saints. Most were envisioned anthropomorphically, with human traits. Each *calpulli* had its own deity, and because, as we have seen, *calpulli* were often groups of occupational specialists, these deities came to be associated with the occupational group.

When the Mexica arrived in the Valley of Mexico, they found numerous cults that had grown up around gods of nature and which the Aztec made their own. Berdan (1982) describes theirs as an assimilative religion, rather than a proselytizing one. They embraced the deities of those they conquered, and soon had myriad gods. Townsend (1992) suggests that the conquest of each enemy town might be viewed as the "capture" of their deity.

These have been roughly divided into three categories: gods believed responsible for creation, those associated with the elements, and those affiliated with war—and thus with sacrifice.

The creation deities are ones which might best be described as supreme— they are the high gods, more abstract and omnipotent. Included among these are gods of fire, which is an important Aztec theme.

Priests devoted most of their rituals to the gods associated with rain, human fertility, and agricultural fecundity. These gods controlled the elements, on which the survival of the people depended. The majority of female gods, responsible for both subsistence and birth, are found in this pantheon of deities of the elements.

Huitzilopotchli, the patron deity of the Mexica who guided their journey into the valley, is a sun god categorized with the sacrificial war gods. The tie between warriors and the sun was direct and critical: it was only through the blood of sacrifice that the sun could be fed, and kept alive. And it was largely through military capture that the staggering number of victims required could be supplied.

Aztec Priests

Because all the numerous gods claimed their own temples, were honored by their own rituals, and made their own particularistic demands, each needed a host of priests to serve its needs.

The structure of the priesthood closely resembled the structure of the rest of Aztec society, in its hierarchical, "pyramidal" nature (Townsend 1992). It was from among the nobility that the most powerful priests were drawn, although even the lowest-ranking commoner had access to the priestly role.

Both women and men served in the priesthood, and infant girls and boys were often dedicated by their parents at birth. (Fewer women than men remained in the priesthood for the duration of their lifetimes, however.)

The majority of a priest's duties revolved around service to their deity. The idol must be cared for, its surroundings clean, temple fires lighted, and prayers and penance offered day and night. Priests were expected to regularly offer up their own blood, and the display of their penance smeared on their temple was an important sign of their dedication. A secondary duty of the priesthood was interpreting sacred texts and educating boys of the nobility. Priests used meditation, fasting, purifying baths, and occasionally hallucinogenic drugs as means to more effectively serve their deity.

Rites and Ceremonies

Aztec rituals and ceremonies were very much tied up with their reckoning of time. They kept an annual ceremonial calendar based on the 365-day solar year, but also reckoned time by a 260-day ritual calendar. (This calendar contains the "moveable feasts," which are any religious festivals unfixed to the solar calendar, such that they may fall on a different date each year [Berdan 1982]). The 260- and 365-day calendars have been conceptualized as two gears fitted side by side: when turning, the first days would align every fifty-two years. It is this alignment that gives rise to the half-century fire-lighting ceremony mentioned above (Townsend 1992).

Ceremonies occurred with great frequency: there were 18 regularly scheduled rituals each month. The vast majority of these had to do with petitioning the gods associated with fertility, rain, and agriculture. Many of these included fasting, and offerings of some sort—from incense to human sacrifice—were always a part of every ceremony.

Magic and Omens

The formal religious system, with its elaborate rituals and supplication to powerful deities, existed alongside a more intimate and personal system of divination and magic. Shamans acted not on behalf of a deity worshipped by the masses, but for an individual petitioner who wished to manipulate the directives of the supernatural world.

Diviners played an important role in a belief system that saw an individual's fate as being predetermined. Although one's destiny was to a large extent fixed, it could be manipulated to some degree by following the recommendations of a diviner hired to "read" an infant's fate and suggest which days might afford the child the best its destiny could offer.

Divination was relied upon most heavily for prediction, but could also be propitious in healing. To this end, shamans ingested hallucinogens to grant them access to divine information. They were able to read signs of illness by throwing grains of maize on a piece of cloth and interpreting their pattern, predict recovery by whether a knotted rope held fast or gave way, determine the severity of soul loss by the clarity of a child's reflection in a mirror.

Those illnesses with supernatural causes required supernatural intercession to effect a cure, and a shaman would be called upon to intervene.

Because they were ruled by fate, and their destiny was already planned, it was only to be expected that Aztecs must look around them for omens informing them of their destinies. Some omens were to be found in the behavior of birds and animals; others might be supernatural materializations. Each individual was believed to have an animal counterpart, a *nagual,* born at the same moment, sharing the same fate. Kept in the underworld in large corrals, these spiritual twins often revealed themselves in dreams. *Nagual* can serve as allies or prove deadly: any harm befalling the *nagual* is suffered by their "other self" as well (Knab 1995).

✦ AztEC ARTS AND SCIENCES

The arts and sciences of the Aztecs were a blend of the scientific and the symbolic. This body of knowledge included calendars that were based on rigorous astronomical calculations, but were used for ritual purposes. The practice of medicine employed a chemically active pharmacopoeia, but these agents were always used along with shamanistic divination. Complex technologies produced crafts that were used in religious ceremonies (Berdan 1982).

Aztec writing was hieroglyphic, which demanded great skill in memorization, since the glyphs could only serve to jog the memory when looking through a text already known to the reader. Such skills were possessed solely by the nobility, who were the only literate members of Aztec society. The most common form of hieroglyphic was the pictograph, a stylized drawing of the object. Glyphs could also be ideographic, using one aspect of an object to represent the entire object itself; for example, a scroll to represent a speech to be given, footprints to represent a journey, or arrows and a shield to represent war. A third form of hieroglyphics was a phonetic system in which a word for which there was an easily drawn picture was used to represent a more abstract word which sounded the same. (This is a device commonly employed in "rebus" puzzles, where a sheep [ewe] might be drawn to stand for the word "you.")

Stone sculpture of human and animal figures was a skill which was formally taught, and that led to a style of stoneworking that is readily recognizable. Craftwork in mosaics, gold, and feathers was also highly standardized; taught within the guilds, consistency of style is found within each medium.

Literature and music were highly valued, as were oratory skills. While speech-making skills were generally only taught in noble schools, songs and dances were part of all mandatory education. Because a large number of people spanning all the social classes participated in the numerous religious rituals, it was imperative that all citizens be trained in these skills.

→ CONQUEST

For ten years prior to Spanish conquest, the Mexica had been visited by portentous omens. These were difficult to interpret specifically, but rulers were certain they foretold Aztec doom.

Finally, messengers reported sighting strangers off the coast. This was the final and most frightening omen. One year later, these strangers were back, led by Hernán Cortés. In 1519, Cortés and several hundred soldiers began to advance on Tenochtitlan. As they neared the Aztec city, they heard stories about the riches contained within, and pressed on, determined. When Cortés reached the city he captured the Mexica ruler, and violent battles ensued. The siege on the Aztec city lasted more than seventy days, with tens of thousands killed. Despite their valiant defense, the Aztecs were overcome.

Although the Spaniards were smaller in number, their technology and strategies afforded them a great advantage. Their militaristic training taught them to fight to kill, not to capture. They had swords and muskets, horses and large dogs.

One of the first consequences of Spanish conquest was the decimation of the native population. By the early seventeenth century a population of fifteen million had been reduced to just one million. Not only warfare, but also introduced diseases, famine, overwork under Spanish rule, and displacement all took their toll.

Within ten years of the fall of Tenochtitlan, most of Mesoamerica was under Spanish rule. As more Spaniards arrived, the surrounding culture was changed. To the agricultural system were added Spanish technologies: the wheeled cart pulled by draft animals, machetes, plows. The introduction of both livestock and new crops contributed to the decline in the indigenous population by usurping much of the land formerly devoted to maize (Berdan 1982).

Aztec society became less stratified under Spanish rule. As is commonly the case under colonial rule, ascribed statuses gave way to achieved ones. Spaniards, not Aztecs, held the high political offices. Friars converted indigenous peoples to Christianity. Worship of Aztec deities was forbidden, along with its rituals of human sacrifice. Some indigenous peoples found ways to blend many of the similarities of the two systems of belief. Both Christianity and the Aztec religion contained rites of baptism and confession, and a belief in virgin birth. The multitude of Aztec deities became linked with the many Catholic saints.

The Mexica had been conquered. However, Aztec and Spanish cultures were mutually influential, combining over the ensuing hundreds of years to produce an amalgam, a new way of life.

❧ Mexican Nationalism: The Modern Aztec Legacy

With the Conquest, five hundred years ago, Reavis (1990) observes, "Mexico became a country in transition, from a Native American culture to the lifeways of the West" (p. 18). Aztec civilization can be found both within contemporary Nahua villages and throughout the broader culture of Mexico (Smith 1996). There is a wealth of recent scholarship exploring the national identity of modern Mexico, and Aztec history figures prominently into the discourse. Historians reexamining the event are searching for evidence of indigenous perspectives, "rereading the invasion" (Wood 2003), and asking how the native population viewed the conquest (Lockhart 1998, Schwartz 2000, Wood 2003). Mexico is a nation with a mestizo majority and nearly sixty indigenous ethnic groups. In the twentieth century, the state initiated policies which were aimed at unification of the multiethnic population, "a state project of cultural transformation" (Gutiérrez 1999). The identification of modern Nahua as "living tribute to Mexico's noble indigenous past" (Friedlander in Smith 1996:294) is not without its conflicts, since this status is lived within the reality of discrimination "for being Indian in a Mestizo-oriented society" (Friedlander in Smith 1996:294).

Alicja Iwanska (1977) examined two indigenous social movements, which she calls "realism" and "utopianism," each of which was a reaction to governmental plans for "integration of the Indian masses into Mexican society" (p. 2). The "realist" perspective proposed that this process be guided by people (like themselves) who were raised in Indian villages and who had maintained their ties with the families still there. (The slogan of the group was "Let's Mexicanize Indians and not Indianize Mexicans" [Gutiérrez 1999]). The "utopian" plan envisioned transforming Mexico into a modern-day Aztec Empire. This would be accomplished by cultural, economic, and political restructuring on every level: the teaching of Nahua culture and language in schools, the return to a *calpulli* system, the taking of Aztec names and the celebration of Aztec holidays.

Guillermo Bonfil Batalla (1996) writes of two Mexicos: the "imaginary Mexico," the modern nation which is an outgrowth of colonialism and aspires to subjugate Indian culture, and the "deep Mexico" (*México profundo*), grounded in a collective Mesoamerican past. It is out of this deep and shared Indian culture that a true new nation must be formed. Bonfil's perspective has been taken up by others, who also believe that there is a "transcendental Indian character that survives . . . beneath the asphalt" (Lomnitz-Adler 1992). In 1994, an Indian uprising in the Chiapas Highlands drew attention to the demands of indigenous peoples in Mexico. President Salinas had enacted policies which would further the usurpation of Indian land and contribute to the continuing spiral of poverty in the Indian communities, while further enriching the powerful local elite.

As Gutiérrez (1999) points out, access to technology, media, and advanced communication has resulted not only in upward mobility of formerly marginalized indigenous peoples. Such changes have also resulted in heightened ethnic awareness, rather than its rejection for more modern constructions of nationalism. When presented with the culturally integrative plans of the nation-state, Gutiérrez (1999:206) observes that "ethnic peoples in modern times have not rejected their historical past; they remain attached to it because this is the claim that secures their survival."

✦ FOR FURTHER DISCUSSION

Most people regard the Aztec as a civilization which was lost long ago. However, in Mexico today there are indigenous social movements which seek to link the present directly with an Aztec past. What might motivate contemporary Nahua peoples and others in Mexico to do so? What is the significance of the ways in which they have chosen to recognize the Aztec heritage? Is this phenomenon something that you recognize as happening among other groups, in other nations?

CHAPTER 3

THE BASSERI

Pastoral Nomads on the il-Rah

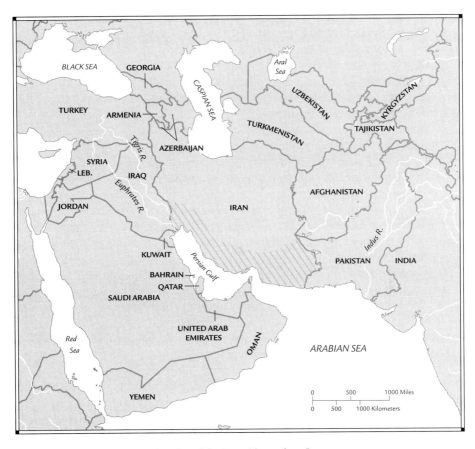

Location of the Basseri in southern Iran.

✦ The Beginning

The Basseri have always been. We have always been on this land; we were created from its dust.

✦ Introduction and Ecology

The Basseri are a pastoral nomadic society in southern Iran, whose migration takes them to the mountains and steppes to the east, north, and south.

The land in which they travel spans about three hundred miles in length, and about fifty miles in width. They are never too greatly dispersed as they journey.

The province in which the Basseri live is quite ethnically heterogeneous, and it has been suggested (Barth 1964) that the tribes in the area are better distinguished from one another on the basis of political organization than by any ethnic or geographic boundaries. Using this criterion, the Basseri do form a discrete unit, operating under the governance of one chief, and they are recognized as such by the Iranian government.

Numbering about sixteen thousand individuals (or three thousand tents), the Basseri are associated with other groups in the area who either claim origins within the Basseri or common heritage with them.

The tribe's nomadic lifestyle was interrupted, for a time, when the reign of Reza Shah dictated enforced settlement. During this period only a small number of Basseri continued their nomadic ways. Many more remained sedentary, to the detriment of their flocks and people. Once Reza Shah's reign was concluded fifty years ago, the Basseri were able to resume their traditional life, and most did so.

Basseri territory is diverse, ranging from desert to mountain. Throughout their range there is little rain; this is concentrated in the winter months. Precipitation in the mountains falls as snow, and thus there is more vegetation and forested land in the mountainous areas. Where the land is flat and low, drought defines the summer and there is very little vegetation, limited to a thin cover of grass during winter rains and into the early spring.

For those sedentary people surrounding the Basseri, agriculture provides the main pattern of subsistence, dependent almost entirely upon irrigation. Rivers and streams in the area provide water for irrigation, and horses and oxen are also employed to pull water up from wells. Access to groundwater is gained by a series of underground aqueducts which link groups of wells, funneling groundwater from higher elevations down to the valley lowlands.

The pastures upon which the Basseri pastoral economy depends are seasonal, necessitating that they have access to an extensive amount of pasture area. The land through which they move affords them this diversity. In the winter, the northern areas are covered with snow, but the south still has usable pasture land. In the spring, areas of low and middle altitude have plentiful grazing areas. As they start to dry out, there are better areas at higher elevations. Although fall is the most tenuous time, once fields are harvested agriculturalists are pleased to have nomads graze their flocks on the land because the manure acts as excellent fertilizer.

The Basseri, like other major nomadic tribes, have a traditional migratory route that they follow annually. In addition to specifying which lands they use, this schedule also elaborates when they will arrive at each location and the duration of their stay. This route and the schedule of utilization along the way is the *il-rah*, the "tribal road," and each *il-rah* is considered the property of that tribe. It grants them rights to particular land at a specific time, and is recognized by the peoples with whom they come in contact. It is important to note that it is not only access to lands, but access at a specific time, that is granted: many tribes use the same land, because the *il-rah* doesn't give exclusive utilization rights. But the lands are validly used only at particular times; thus, tribes who "share" the same land do not overlap in their time there.

The group does not always stay together. As they move north, alternative routes within the *il-rah* allow some dispersal of the tribe, some of whom stay longer in the more abundant spring fields, others choosing to foray east to villages recently made accessible to them.

Breaking camp and moving on is usually a daily activity, but in the summertime the Basseri tend to become more stationary, with movement only local during the day, returning to the same encampment at night. The return journey begins in the late summer and early fall, and usually includes stops to earn cash for labor: otherwise stops are few on this leg of the trek. Fields have the least to offer in this season. Winter too is a more stationary time, when local forays predominate.

✦ ECONOMIC ORGANIZATION

Subsistence and Manufacture

Domesticated animals are of paramount importance to the Basseri. Sheep and goats are the most important because it is they who provide the bulk of subsistence products. Donkeys are used as pack animals and are ridden by women and children. Men ride horses that carry no other load. Camels are burdened with the heaviest items to transport. The Basseri herd no cattle because their trek is long and difficult, and the terrain is too rocky for cattle to navigate (Barth 1964).

Just as different cultigens are suited to particular environments, so too are strains of domesticated animals. There are several varieties of sheep in this area, and the nomadic strain is particularly well-suited for the migratory life of the Basseri. These sheep are ill-suited to the extremes of temperature found in the north and south. While those raised in the north have an increased tolerance for the cold, and those domesticated in the south are better able to withstand drought and dry grazing land, the sheep kept by the Basseri fare best in moderate climate. Thus, the tribe's movement not only ensures access to grazing, it preserves the health of the herds they graze. [Reportedly, nomads who settle in either northern or southern regions and attempt to raise the same strain of sheep with which they are accustomed to migrating lose nearly eighty percent of their animals (Barth 1964).]

Each shepherd is generally responsible for a mixed flock of three or four hundred sheep and goats. Young animals are kept away from older ones, and milk is preserved for human consumption by preventing overnursing of lambs and kids.

Each individual household must own about one hundred sheep and goats in order to provide for itself satisfactorily. Although the average household falls somewhat short of this ideal, the Basseri are known to be possessed of a relatively high standard of living when compared to other populations in their area (Barth 1964).

Milk and milk products are the staples of the Basseri diet. Sheep's and goat's milk, mixed together, is never consumed without being heated. When a bit of sour milk (or the acidic contents of a lamb's stomach) is added, the fresh milk sours. Cheese, which is then made from junket, a sour milk product, is not produced during the times of daily tribal movement. Such production is usually reserved for the more sedentary summer encampment periods.

Sour milk is stored by separating the curds from the whey. The solid curds are shaped into dumpling-like balls, dried in the sun, and are preserved in that fashion through the winter months. The liquid whey can be fed to the watchdogs. When sour milk is churned into buttermilk or butter, it can provide income; while buttermilk is usually immediately consumed, and butter largely eaten fresh, quantities of butter are also stored for sale.

Beyond those numbers of young animals needed to supplement the adult herd, lambs and kids (usually male) are slaughtered for meat and their hides sold. Lambskin is a much-sought product at market, and it is hides that provide all the containers for storage and transport.

In addition to milk products and hides, the animals also provide wool, both for sale and for the tribe's own use. Wool may be spun and woven, or processed into rope. Such spinning and weaving requires great skill and consumes the majority of Basseri women's leisure time. Using threads they have themselves spun, women fashion all the saddlebags and cloth packs in which are carried the entire inventory of the tribe's belongings. Carpets and rugs for sleeping are similarly crafted. Their tents are made of woven goat hair, which renders them impermeable to rain, and insulated such that heat is retained in the cooler months and dissipated in the summertime.

Foraging plays a role of minor importance in the subsistence strategies of the Basseri. Hunting of large game is sport; springtime brings the collection of a few plants and wild mushrooms.

The Basseri milk-based diet is importantly supplemented by cereals and grains, the production of which is a relatively recent phenomenon. During the more settled summer months, wheat and other cereals can be planted upon arrival and will be matured for harvesting before the time camp is broken. Often, they will contract with settled local residents to plant crops before they arrive to do the harvesting. This agricultural work is neither enjoyed nor highly valued: many nomads refuse to participate at all and look down upon those who do (Barth 1964). Some Basseri are landowners and, although they do not settle on the land they own, such possession allows them to avoid all agricultural work by leasing the land to others in return for a portion of the yield.

Given their nomadic lifestyle, many of the tribe's necessities must be secured by trade. The most important of these is flour: unleavened bread is part of every meal. Sugar, tea, fruits, and vegetables are similarly obtained. Basseri bring to market butter, wool, and hides, and occasionally animals. For these they are able to obtain clothing, cooking utensils, saddles, and luxury items—which may include such diverse products as jewelry, narcotics, and portable radios (Barth 1964).

Residence Patterns

Each independent Basseri household is a nuclear family living in a single tent. These constitute the basic unit of production and consumption, and ownership of livestock.

Large tents are pitched for longer stays; for daily travel, smaller versions are employed. Camps are generally made up of thirty or forty tents, each occupied by a married couple and their children, with an occasional widowed or single relative.

Although some goods may be owned by particular family members, it is the household that is regarded as the property-owning unit. Within the household unit, there is a very clear division of labor and vesting of authority. The household is represented in tribal matters and dealings with outsiders by the head, who is invariably male. If the tent consists of a nuclear family, the husband/father is the head. If not, the senior male assumes this role. If there is no adult male residing within the household, a woman may be regarded as the head, but she will actually be represented by a male relative in formal matters.

Within the domestic domain, however, there is much more egalitarianism. Decisions concerning family, children, marriage, kinship, as well as the wider realm of social and group relations are made by adults in consultation with one another. The household's most assertive or wisest member will predominate, regardless of gender (Barth 1964).

Most food preparation, sewing, and washing are by and large girls' and women's chores. Boys and men haul water and wood (although not exclusively so), roast meat, and make tea, and some wash their own clothes.

The Basseri will strike camp and move an average of one day out of every three. This pattern of such frequent movement demands great organization and physical labor. A day when the tribe is planning to move starts long before sunrise. The herds will depart first, under the guidance of a girl, boy, or man. The tent will be down before it is light, and the donkeys are rounded up to be loaded with possessions. The leader of the egress will be a man of the tribe who owns a horse and rides ahead. The average daily trek is about three hours (at a fast pace) before the tents are repitched. The shepherded animals arrive after the people,

Basseri shepherd and herd.

since they cannot travel at the same brisk pace as the caravan of families on donkeys. Once the animals have been milked, a meal can be prepared. At sunset the animals are milked again, and the late meal is eaten before sleep.

Milking is made most efficient by herding the animals into a triangular formation, with the animals at the apex driven past individuals who remain in place filling buckets as the animals are milked and then allowed to wander off. This allows the milkers (a role filled by both men and women) to stay put, and assures that each animal has been milked.

✈ Social Organization

New and Cooperative Households

As is typically found in groups whose households are based on nuclear families, the Basseri are also neolocal; that is, upon marriage a couple starts their own nuclear family in a new tent.

Initially upon marriage, a woman will join her husband in his family's tent, but this is only a temporary arrangement. As soon as they can, a new couple will establish themselves as an independent unit. In order to accomplish this, however, they must be able to support themselves.

Because individual family members may own property, it is common for fathers to give several animals to their sons in times of plenty when the family can afford to do so. This practice, in part, teaches the boy how to care for the animals, which can later be taken to his own household upon his marriage. Boys may also work as shepherds for other households and receive payment in lambs. A diligent worker may be able to build up a small herd of his own.

In addition, the groom's father will pay a cash bride-price to the bride's father; some of this, it is expected, will be used to purchase goods the new couple will need for their own tent—rugs, blankets, cooking utensils. Women of both families weave the cloth to be used by the new couple to construct their tent.

Although all of this helps launch the bride and groom on their way, it does not provide the couple with the size flock necessary for their survival and success. This deficiency is overcome by the practice called "anticipatory inheritance": that is, a son receives upon his marriage that portion of his father's flock to which he would be rightful heir at his father's death (Barth 1964). (When a man actually dies, the additional animals he has amassed, as well as those he originally retained for himself, are also inherited, once his surviving spouse has received her due.)

Once the new couple has been settled in their household and are in possession of their flock, they are faced with the challenge of performing the whole range of tasks associated with the nomadic lifestyle, and this is not possible with a household consisting of only a husband and wife. The ideal configuration has, at minimum, an adult male who performs the labor associated with his role and takes his place in the leadership portion of the migration, an adult female who accomplishes the numerous and difficult domestic tasks, and at least one individual who acts as shepherd. The nuclear family unit can certainly eventually attain this form, but there are long periods of time both before there are children of shepherding age and after the children have grown and are on their own. For these portions of the household's life cycle, the additional labor necessary must be contracted for in some fashion. A shepherd may be hired or a close relative adopted, but more often families band together to form small units which share herding tasks.

Both the strategies of hiring a shepherd or adopting a child allow an individual household to remain an independent unit by relying on labor from outside sources. As Barth (1964:21) points out, "This independence and self-sufficiency of the nomad household, whereby it can survive in economic relation with an external market but in complete isolation from all fellow nomads, is a very striking and fundamental feature of Basseri organization."

However, in tandem with this independence, several households usually combine their flocks under the care of one shepherd. It is not difficult for a single shepherd to control up to four hundred animals; with cooperation among the adults at milking time (who milk their own household's animals), this system is quite efficient.

Those families who have entered into such an arrangement generally pitch their tents together at night and regard each other as equal partners. A family may feel free to cease its participation in this cooperative at any time, and as families shift alliances the clusters of households change over time. Often these shifts in composition are the result either of disagreements or the assessment of the skills of one's current partners relative to the skills of others whom one might join. Because there only has to be one individual in all the joined households who can serve as shepherd, the usual pattern is for smaller or newer households to join more stable or populous ones.

Camps

During the spring when fodder in pastures is plentiful, nomadic tribes can be supported in large numbers. During the winter months, however, it is greatly to their advantage to set up camp in smaller groups. Although each section of land holds little in the way of resources, the total amount of land is extensive. By dispersing over a wide range, they can best use the depleted environment. Thus, while at other times of year Basseri camps may have as many as forty tents, during the winter, local camps generally are made up of just a handful.

Barth (1964) has noted that in many ways these camps resemble the small village of sedentary groups. Whatever sense of community is found among the Basseri is contained in the local encampments they set up along their migratory route, and the members of each camp constitute a "clearly bounded social group" (p. 25). It is only with one another that they have consistent and continuous relationships; all their other contacts are fleeting.

Maintaining this sense of community is a unique challenge among nomadic peoples, as it is unlike that which is found in a sedentary population. For settled peoples, life as a community persists unless some active change is made. Each day the alliances between people are reinforced by the usual progression of the daily routine. Should dissolution of any part of the community be anticipated, it would require that households disband and individuals take dramatic action. For tribes with a nomadic lifestyle, however, the decision to remain a community is not a passive one, dependent upon the inertia of routine. Each day, residents of a local camp must convene and assess their surroundings in order to make the crucial decision of whether or not to move on, and if so, how far. This is not a choice to be made whimsically; the health of their herds and the economic base of their existence are at stake. The wisdom of each individual household head will decide his family's fate, and there must be agreement among tents in order to proceed. Although arguments and differences of opinion between villagers may be resolved after some "cooling off" period—sedentary peoples are unlikely to abandon their homes permanently as a result of a single disputed decision—once nomadic households fail to reach consensus about daily migration, they have effectively changed the composition of their community. As Barth (1964:26) puts it: "by next evening they will be separated by perhaps 20 km of open steppe and by numerous other camps, and it will have become quite complicated to arrange for a reunion. The maintenance of a camp as a social unit thus requires the daily unanimous agreement by all members on economically vital questions."

Reaching consensus about daily movement is greatly facilitated by the recognition of a single leader in each camp. This individual both represents his own local group in dealings with other camps and influences the decision making within his own group.

The Basseri, as will be discussed later, are united as a tribe under the authority of a single chief. The chief appoints local headmen who are recognized as having been so chosen, but are not endowed with any formal means to enforce their own will. There are fewer officially appointed headmen, however, than there are local camps in need of leadership. In those camps where no headman is in residence, informal leaders take the helm. These individual local leaders, however, are not representatives of the chief, and cannot invoke his wishes or support in their own edicts.

The status of headman is typically an inherited one, and usually passes from a man to his next most senior relative. However, camp members claim as their right the ability to bypass such rules and select the person whom they see as most deserving of the position (and, in addition, the right to unseat a headman they deem unfit). The chief is expected to acquiesce in this regard, and generally does so: it is certainly in his best interest to have as his representative the individual most likely to succeed in leading his own group. The chief can then rely on the status and authority already established by a local leader to add weight to his own.

The requirements for acceding to the position of headman is in part dependent upon his economic position within the group, but this is minimal and somewhat tenuous. Wealth is, by and large, livestock. And all Basseri are subject to the loss of animals through circumstances out of their control. Thus, wealth is not a station upon which anyone can depend. It is reported that in some cases of serious animal loss suffered by a headman, group members decide to maintain his position by donating their own animals to reform his herd (Barth 1964). Moreover, even though prestige is gained through ownership of a large herd, it does not appear that wealth is easily converted into political authority.

Because a headman's power is entirely contained within the confines of his own camp, the range of his authority is limited. Barth (1964) reminds us of the structure of Basseri society: each tent is very much an autonomous unit; herding units of two to five tents come together for economic reasons and in so doing form an economic unit which is self-sufficient; the headman receives no specific empowerment by the chief. Therefore, the power base of the headman is very narrow indeed, and often restricted to his own unit. This is, as Barth (1964:29) remarks, "a very small base from which to attempt to tyrannize a whole camp."

Kinship

The Basseri, like other tribal groups in the Middle East, reckon descent patrilineally. Inheritance is usually from father to son, and other patrikin will supplant daughters in obtaining land rights and other goods. A son of a Basseri is a Basseri, regardless of the affiliation of his mother: a woman bestows no membership rights to her own tribe on her offspring. There is a particularly strong solidarity among brothers, and the relationship of a man to his father, father's brothers, and father's father is one of great deference and respect. Local groups are often formed by brothers who have had joint rights to their father's flock before their own marriages and choose to remain associated after their inheritance of animals upon marriage.

While patrilineal kinship is a driving force behind group formation (and access to headman status), there is a strong tie between some matrikin. The relationship between a child and a mother's brother is a particularly affectionate and indulgent one.

Marriage

Alliances between households are most often reinforced by affinal (marital) ties. Marriages are arranged by household heads, which are usually the fathers of the prospective bride and groom. In his absence, a brother or father's brother will serve. Thus, except in the case of an adult man who is arranging his own subsequent marriage, a marital contract is not primarily a bond between a bride and groom, but is rather a transaction between tents. [In fact, the typical term of reference by a man to his daughter-in-law is "my bride" (Barth 1964)].

Bride-price among the Basseri is called "milk-price," which pays for both the woman's hand in marriage as well as the household items she will bring along with her. There is also an "insurance" fee promised, which will be the woman's compensation should the marriage end in divorce. Before the wedding takes place, there are minor tokens given to the bride and her family by the prospective groom, as well as some small acts of bride service (in the form of small favors) to her parents.

Although there are no ongoing debts or obligations between the families once the marriage has taken place, there appears to be great affection engendered between the households of children who marry one another. The woman no longer has a formal affiliation with her parents' household, but since her in-laws and parents will work to actively maintain a friendship, she remains "connected." These warm ties between households are sought in future marriages: sister exchange (in which a groom's sister is given to the bride's family in compensation for the bride) is common, and the Basseri conform to the rules of the levirate and sororate (replacing a deceased spouse with an analogous family member), even in the face of protest by the individuals involved. Families also seek to perpetuate these ties in subsequent generations of marriage arrangements.

Barth (1964) suggests that this extreme affection and active pursuit of the continuation of affinal ties may derive from the political and economic independence of the Basseri nuclear family unit. The only way to ensure the continuation of the community of these autonomous units is to knit households together by marriage. This is especially salient in light of the "anticipatory inheritance" of herds upon marriage. Siblings receive their portion of their father's livestock and establish their own separate households while he is alive. There is no further bond between them save that of affection; no further inheritance of any substantial nature remains to link them economically. (Because women retain no rights in their family of origin, this is equally true for female siblings.) Marital ties, especially if they involve siblings marrying into the same family, can serve to keep tents allied with one another, thus preserving the nomadic community.

A Basseri woman is very important economically; there is a high level of mutual dependence between husband and wife, and women possess tremendous authority within the domestic sphere, which in migratory peoples is the one unchanging portion of their environment. The household cannot survive without a woman's labor. Her family remains important to her both emotionally and also, to some extent, socially, in that they retain influence over her future marriage should she be widowed (or divorced, though this is rare). A husband wishes to maintain friendly relations with his in-laws in part to assure his good relationship with his wife, who is economically crucial to the household.

The desire to maintain ties that will generate goodwill in a local camp, and thus foster consensus in daily migratory decisions and solidarity in general, results in a high number of marriages between close kin. The camp is an endogamous group; when Basseri speak of their camp to outsiders, they refer to it as if it were a single lineage. Barth points out that the truly bilateral camp structure works against the formation of patrilineages. Within each tent, husband and wife are virtual equals; in external dealings, however, the husband is the undisputed head of the household. So it is that while externally giving the impression of revolving around a patrilineal core, the camp is composed, in fact, of "bilateral, nearly self-perpetuating kin groups" (1964:41).

Distance as "Social Idiom"

The actual distance maintained between tents in a Basseri camp can be an indicator of social distance between their occupants. If dissension occurs at the end of a day's journey, participants in the argument will pitch their tents at opposite ends of the campsite. Resolution of differences will be indicated by the tents eventually being pitched in closer proximity in subsequent encampments.

There are practical considerations too in the placement of tents. Households that cooperate in herding must pitch their tents near one another in order to be near their comingled animals. (And, following from this, these units might maintain some distance from other households cooperating together, to avoid mixing corporate herds.) In addition, camp configuration may be determined by the environment: often the shape of the camping site itself will dictate the placement of tents, since with each stop the tribe is presented with a site of potentially different dimensions than the last.

This lack of persistent cohesive groups within the tribe (beyond that of the herding unit) is demonstrated not only when the group is encamped, but also as they migrate. Although the morning ritual of breaking camp usually occurs at the same time for all households, individual families leave whenever their tent is down and their belongings are packed. The group does not wait until everyone is ready before commencing the trek. Smaller families and those with fewer belongings to pack may routinely set out first, with the last family departing half an hour later. This results in the scattering of a group over at least a mile's length, moving at varying paces. The herds move slowest, stopping to graze along the way. The caravan of donkeys and camels who carry the packed belongings stay on the main route and travel at a faster pace. Men on horseback ride on ahead, and are the ones to reach the stopping point first; it is they who choose the campsite.

There are three decisions which face the Basseri daily: whether or not to move on a particular day, which route to follow, and where to make the new camp. The first decision especially demands unanimity, since the routes are limited and the new camp is chosen by the front riders. Each day the leader must attempt to have all heads of households decide to stay on-site another day, or move on. Barth found it quite striking that despite the critical nature of this decision and the necessity for agreement in its resolution, there was a complete lack of any group assemblage to come to a decision. There was such circuitous discussion that often the residents went to sleep at night not knowing whether they would be moving on in the morning.

He explains this phenomenon by invoking the character of the influence possessed by the tribal leaders. The leader's voice is not given much more weight than anyone else's, in an absolute sense. His strategy, then, is to gather together singly or in small groups those people over whom he has sway owing to ties of friendship or kinship. These people can then form a larger group of singular opinion to talk with others, and these become more and more numerous until there is a clear majority opinion. This majority view is so important that often people endeavor to qualify what they say in such a way that it takes a trained listener to know which side the speaker is advocating; he will always present both sides, so as not to end up siding with the minority. This leads to conversation which often seems pointless. (Barth [1964:45] recalls, "Not only does the frustrated anthropologist remain in the dark [as to] whether he will have to pack his stuff and move on next morning; he cannot even learn about herding and nomadic life from these hour-long discussions, when points which are bandied about and emphasized by all, turn out to be without substantive relevance to the problem.")

Association with individuals outside of local camp members is infrequent; even contact with other Basseri is rare. This intense isolation results in part from the great feelings of suspicion borne by the group: no one ventures outside the circle of tents at night. Theirs is a world which is warm and comfortable within the confines of the cluster of tents. Beyond this world lies a world of strangers who are likely robbers and thieves (Barth 1964). Because this is a feeling shared with other local groups, there is rarely any hostility between camps—they are more than willing to keep their distance.

✦ POLITICAL ORGANIZATION

The Basseri encampment's isolation and autonomy is a core feature of life for the members of each local group. Some camps have many tents and some have few; some trace their ancestry such that they claim origins from, or memberships in, larger groupings. They consider themselves—and are considered by others—to be one unified tribe because they are all subsumed under the authority of a single leader, the chief of all Basseri.

Chieftainship

The position of chief among the Basseri is typical of Middle Eastern centralized leadership, in that it is thought that power emanates *from* him, rather than having been vested *in* him by those he leads (Barth 1964).

The chief and his close kin are set apart from all other Basseri in several ways. First, they are seen as descended from a noble lineage, and part of the respect shown them, and the authority granted them, derive from this distinction. Furthermore, they are quite removed from the nomadic life: they own land and houses, villages, and herds numbering in the thousands.

The chief is expected to conduct himself in a manner befitting a man of power and privilege. He is expected to live lavishly and bestow gifts generously. In order to accomplish this, he must depend on more than inheritance to supply his wealth, and he does. Taxes, payable in sheep, are imposed on the tribe members, resulting in the collection of nearly eight thousand sheep a year. (Annual taxes of butter are also paid, and gifts are expected to be brought to the chief by anyone who comes before him.)

In the realm of decision making, the chief's behavior is clearly unique. The typical Basseri style of collective judgments, subtle persuasion, and reaching consensus is not in evidence when chiefly decisions are made. He retains the sole prerogative to command, and to render decisions that affect an individual living in another tent. (Barth [1964] recalls that he was reminded of the chief's monopoly on the right to dictate when he himself made a suggestion regarding the movement of the camp in which he lived, asserting that he would take responsibility for the consequences; he was reprimanded for acting like a chief and attempting to usurp rights that were the chief's alone.)

The headmen appointed by the chief are his representatives but do not act in his stead. They function most often as relayers of information and not as enforcers of his will; thus they are links in the chain of communication, but not in a chain of command (Barth 1964).

The chief's responsibilities revolve around allotting pastures and the organizing of migratory patterns, settling disputes, and acting as the tribe's representative with outside authorities.

The development of patterns of travel and use of grazing land among a large population is a monumental feat. It involves coordinating a regular schedule which eliminates both overuse of land and a logjam of peoples moving along a particular road. This falls to the chief and his administrator, and without this tightly orchestrated direction, a nomadic lifestyle would be unworkable (Salzman 1974). Among other nomadic peoples in Iran, allotment of pastures is often used as a method of sanction, and it has been suggested that this practice exists among the Basseri as well (Salzman 1974). Chiefs among other tribes will limit access to some lands and condemn individuals to the use of lesser pastures as a form of punishment.

The chief's role as adjudicator of disputes is one which is relied upon only after the customary strategies of discussion and compromise at the camp level have been exhausted. Those cases that prove impossible to settle (or involve people with whom it appears "impossible" to reason) are brought before the chief and those involved must abide by his decision.

The Basseri are part of a plural society, and as such the chief's role as their representative to both the Iranian government as well as non-Basseri peoples is crucial. The importance of this function in a plural society rests on the fact that in times of conflict between a Basseri and a sedentary individual, the mere fact of the Basseri's nomadism puts him at a disadvantage. He must move on, or his herds cannot graze; he must move on, or he will be effectively cut off from his entire community, who will move on without him. A farmer can ask neighbors to watch over property, or leave fields unattended; a nomad cannot. A farmer may go to court, and wait for his case to be heard; a nomad cannot.

The fact that the chief does not maintain a nomadic lifestyle becomes of paramount importance. He is not a stranger passing through. He is not a man of lowly means. As the powerful representative of any individual in the tribe, he is invaluable to each and every member. It is he who mediates the nomads' congress with the sedentary society which surrounds them, and can develop the friendly relations and alliances that the mobile tribe cannot.

Relationships with Outsiders

The individual Basseri rarely comes in contact with outsiders. Congress is most likely to occur when an animal has strayed and must be sought out in areas occupied by others. However, chiefs *do* have occasion to come together with chiefs of hostile tribes, and it is of some political importance that they do so. Such visits function to negotiate access to pastures in advance, so as to forestall any fighting of camp members along the migratory route.

Large decorative tents are erected for these occasions, and large communal hunts are arranged to procure game meat. Lavish meals and entertainment are provided, and such occasions are regarded as the most eagerly anticipated events of the year.

Other events which are particularly entertaining are trips to bazaars and markets. The purpose of these forays is to sell livestock and purchase clothes and luxury items. Most of the supplies that Basseri must purchase are not obtained at market, however. Each individual has trading relationships with a number of sedentary people living along the annual route.

✦ ECONOMIC ORGANIZATION

The complete attention of the Basseri people is focused on the most important feature of their economy: the herds. Their daily concerns are to foster the health and well-being of the animals, to ensure that they grow and reproduce, to avoid the risks (predominantly environmental) that place them in jeopardy. Drought, frosts, insects, and veterinary illness all threaten to decimate the herds and, by extension, the herders whose economic survival is invested in the animals.

This constant ongoing focus leaves them little time (or, perhaps, inclination) to attempt to manipulate other features of their environment. For example, in the southern part of their territory are several areas of pasture which, although they hold great potential, are never used. The Basseri admit that this land would be superlative for pasturing were there only a water source for the animals close by. This could be accomplished with relative ease: all these pasture lands could be made usable by the digging of a well. But this is not a project for small, autonomous households to undertake. It requires an organized communal effort. In contemplating this, Barth (1964:102) asks: "who would tend their flocks while they were engaged in the work, and why should one particular camp do it, when the fruits of the labour would be reaped by dozens of other camps as well?"

Thus, it is the animals on which they concentrate. As an individual herd grows, and the wealth of the owner increases, there comes a point at which, ironically, his capital is less secure. This is owing to the inability of an owner, whose herd has grown so large that it is impossible for him to oversee his shepherds effectively, to prevent theft and carelessness. Basseri say they are aware that a shepherd will not watch a flock under contract with the same vigilance he gives to his own; with a large herd, he can appropriate several animals and say they were lost; he can keep or sell dairy products without the owner knowing that he is diminishing the yield. Therefore, it is to the wealthy herd owner's advantage to convert his wealth in livestock to other, less risky forms of wealth. He may purchase jewelry or carpets, or in the best of circumstances, land.

Along their migratory route, nomads can purchase plots which they then lease to sedentary villagers living in the area. The advantages of this are twofold: not only does it allow the Basseri herder a more secure form of wealth, it also affords him great social status in the sedentary society outside the tribe. Basseri purchase land without any intent of settling on it; they are more interested in being able to obtain a portion of the agricultural yield, which they would otherwise have to purchase. Inevitably, however, there are always some landowners whose wealth becomes more and more invested in land, and who grows less interested in his herd and his traditional lifestyle. These individuals compromise by settling on their land for half the year, and spend the other half camping in tents near their former *il-rah*.

Sedentarization

It has been suggested that sedentarization of populations like the Basseri is often in response to the growth experienced by many tribes (Barth 1964). Certainly accumulation of wealth, in the form of land, contributes to this process. Tremendous accumulation is forestalled when men have sons: much of this capital will be drained off via the custom of anticipated inheritance when sons marry. Therefore, such cumulative growth over a life span can really only accrue to fathers of daughters or men with no children at all. It is in this way that lack of male heirs can lead to wealth-induced sedentarization for some households.

On the other end of the scale is sedentarization by impoverishment, which is more often the case. Loss of one's herd may result in the inability to continue the pursuit of a nomadic lifestyle. Thus, too few animals may also result in a family being left behind, their only recourse being to adopt a sedentary lifestyle. Unlike some other Iranian pastoralist nomad tribes, in which wealthier families hire poorer members as shepherds, allowing them to stay within the group, the Basseri have no such mechanism. Impoverished Basseri households were forced to leave the community for a life as agricultural laborers. Bradburd (1989) suggests that one explanation for poor Basseri not being hired within the tribe derives from the nature of their economy. Other Iranian tribes produced trade items such as carpets, horse blankets, and clothing made from wool and cashmere, necessitating large herds of animals to shear. The Basseri economy, in contrast, depends largely on the sale of lambskins, a commodity that depletes herd size, resulting in no need for extra shepherding labor within the community.

✦ RELIGION AND EXPRESSIVE CULTURE

The Basseri are Shiah Moslems, and practice Islam in a less formal manner than some. They are, according to Barth (1964:135), "indifferent" to what he terms "metaphysical problems," and for the most part uninterested in religion.

There are no ritual specialists among the tribe, and upon the occasion of an uninvited visit by people with sacred status, the nomads are as likely to offer ridicule as gifts.

A village mullah (holy man) is likely to be asked to perform marriage ceremonies. Otherwise, Basseri ceremonials are tied to the cycle of seasons, life cycle events, and a few special ritual situations.

Knowledge of the events of the Moslem year are hazy at best, despite the reminders they encounter as they travel through observant villages. Customs are embraced haphazardly, prayer is infrequent and always a solitary act. While Islamic feast days are taken into consideration when migration is being planned, they are not observed by the Basseri. The single deference to the Moslem calendar is in its influence on good luck or misfortune: no sheep shearing is practiced on Moslem holidays, and certain tasks of flock will not be undertaken on Friday, the Moslem sabbath.

By far it is the solar year which is of greater import to the Basseri, because it is on this division of time that the chief plans migration. Celebrations that mark the beginning of a new season or a new year are noted, although there are no elaborate observances that would interfere with packing up the camp and moving on as usual.

Because the migrations are of an annual nature, it is around the yearly cycle that Basseri organize their life and their conceptualization of time. There are shrines set up along the route which mark the graves of important or holy men. They are shown respect when passed by, but have no ceremony, myth, or ritual attached to their acknowledgment. The single exception to this is a shrine which nearly all the camps' migratory routes take them past, and where a stopover is often planned. Animals may be sacrificed and eaten at the site, but the ambiance is one of festivity rather than reverence or solemnity (Barth 1964).

More elaborated are those rituals performed on the occasions of marriages, births, and deaths.

The birth of a child (especially a firstborn) is an occasion for great celebration, with sweets given and the noise of rifles fired in the air. For the first three days of life, and weekly for more than a month, an infant is cut with razor blades on the nose, neck, and chest. (Later in childhood, children are cut on the ears to prevent earache.) This is a measure to prevent a child's blood from becoming polluted later on—a circumstance disclosed by an adolescent's pimples.

Boys are circumcised in infancy by village physicians (or barbers) if travel allows. If not, this is put off until the boy is six or seven, since it is believed that before this age the procedure would be frightening to him. No analogous ritual is performed for girls.

Sexual activity is strictly forbidden before marriage, and when adolescents are found meeting in secret to kiss, girls will generally be beaten. These early romances, which almost never progress past these innocent stages even without discovery, have no bearing on betrothal or marriage, which is arranged without regard for the inclinations of the future bride and groom.

Marriage is perhaps the most elaborate of all ceremonies, with ritual feasting, bathing of the bride and groom, and participation of neighboring camps. The bride and groom are prepared in separate ritual tents, where they are shaved, bathed, and oiled. After the ceremony they retire to the bridal tent, where a guard stands by, rifle in hand, which he will shoot off to alert the community that the marriage has been consummated. The bridal sheets are inspected for the blood believed to signal that the bride was a virgin. If it is not in evidence, the marriage may be immediately dissolved, with the groom under no obligation to give back the dowry (and, often, with the bride-price returned to his family).

Death and burial are attended by minimal ceremony. Household members will spend several hours in their tent, grieving, and the body will be immediately buried in a village cemetery. Before burial, the body is washed and if there is a relative of the deceased who knows the appropriate section of the Koran to chant, this will be done. The atmosphere is not one of expressive mourning, but rather of silence and solemnity. Sorrow and love for the deceased is expressed by gifts of sweets every Friday for what may be an extended period of time. Relatives may become quite emotional on subsequent treks which allow them to visit the gravesite of the deceased, and it is not uncommon for family members to approach the cemetery with weeping and chanting.

Apart from seasonal and life-cycle observances are actions and avoidances designed to promote good luck and avoid misfortune and the evil eye.

Most of the beliefs surrounding good and bad luck pertain to actions with their animals: which ones should not be together during shearing, what practices should be avoided during milking. Beliefs about the evil eye, which derives from envy, are more pervasive but less specific in their proscriptions. This may be because its consequences are thought to be less avoidable. There is no cure for the ills it brings, and it acts out of the awareness of the person in whom it resides.

Envious thoughts on the part of any individual may result in the illness or death of the individual envied. All people have the potential to harbor this power, although those with blue eyes are particularly suspect.

Because spontaneous thoughts of envy may come unbidden into anyone's mind, precautions are taken to distract the onlooker from the potential object of envy, usually a child or animal. This may be accomplished by decorations tied around the animal's leg, or baby's neck, in the hopes that they will signal caution to the person who may unintentionally think covetous thoughts.

Barth (1964) remarks on what seems to be a striking dearth of ritual and expressive culture among the Basseri, but concludes that this assessment may be in error. Although there is surely less ceremonial practice and elaborate display than is found among many other peoples, for the Basseri their movement is their ceremony. That the activities of their days are practical should not eliminate them out of hand for consideration as deeply meaningful. As their *il-rah* unfolds before them and they journey through the seasons and through their year, they are, in effect, celebrating their very existence.

✦ "Customary Strangers": Nomadic Pastoralists in the Modern World

There are roughly twenty million pastoral nomadic households spanning 25 percent of the world's land area (FAO 2001; Krätli 2001). Since early in the twentieth century, efforts have been made to draw them into the *modern world*, propelled by the assessment of pastoral nomadism as both a culturally backward and economically irrational way of life (Dyer 2001; Krätli 2001). The earliest attempts thus focused on sedentarization, presumed to be a prerequisite for a modern, developed, "more civilized" society and the first step out of the "evolutionary *cul de sac*" (Krätli 2001:15) of nomadism. By the mid-1980s, such a view was thoroughly discredited among scholars. It persists, however, among policymakers and those involved in pastoral development programs (Dyer

2001; Krätli 2001). State officials have been described as "[considering] nomads in general as belligerent, difficult to control . . . their continuous movement a sort of offence to the requirements of any modern state" (Dyer 2001:316).

Beginning in the 1920s, international efforts were made to provide formal education for nomadic children, and the promotion of sedentarism was bound up in the program. If parents wanted their children to go to school, they had to stay nearby; children were sometimes sent to boarding schools to expose them to sedentary life; teachers explicitly denigrated nomadic culture in an attempt to instill sedentary values. By the early 1990s, educational programs were deemed unsuccessful for precisely these reasons. A UNICEF report in 1993 explicitly stated "educational programs for nomads have failed primarily because decision makers have sought to use education as a tool for transforming nomadic populations into sedentary ones" (Krätli 2001:17). In response, some countries shifted their educational focus (or at least their formally stated policy), asserting that nomadic pastoralists should be formally educated not to promote sedentarism, but to help them better manage their herds and increase their productivity through more advanced methods of farming and livestock management. Krätli (2001) points out that the critical assumption in all the programs designed to use formal education for this aim is that pastoralism as a way of life could be separated from pastoralism as a means of production, and that abandoning the first would modernize the second. Even when planners succeeded in convincing pastoralists that their resources were dwindling, it was not the economic repercussions that were paramount; rather, such awareness led instead to distress about their cultural identity and existence as a people.

In Iran, a system of tent schools was introduced as part of the Tribal Education Programme instituted in 1955, with the United States providing financial support. The Iranian (then Persian) goal was to transform tribal members into "loyal citizens" (Krätli 2001). By the 1970s there were six hundred tents, each with a blackboard and minimal supplies, set up to teach children along their migratory routes. Glowing reports were published, detailing the ease with which children learned Persian and their enthusiasm in the classroom. In recent years, however, the program has been criticized as having been propelled by a manipulative political agenda, the Persian government aiming to exercise power over restive tribes by chipping away at tribal identity, and the United States interested in both preventing the potential spread of communism and ensuring access to oil (Shahshahani 1995, in Krätli 2001). Although successful in many ways, the Iranian tent school program has been cited as "focused on nation building according to the dominant culture and politics" (Krätli 2001:14).

In 1990, UNESCO (United Nations Educational, Scientific and Cultural Organization) set forth the World Declaration on Education for All, presenting basic formal education as a fundamental human right. This stance is not without complications in the provision of education to nomadic peoples. One central issue in this regard is the program's focus on the individual. The basic unit of pastoral life is the household, or group of households, not the individual. As such, parents often choose to keep their children out of schools in the best interest of the household unit (which includes the best interest of their children). Programs separating children's best interests from those of their households result in an assessment of parents' decisions, out of cultural context, as depriving children of their fundamental right to education, sometimes leading to interventions by state authorities (Krätli 2001:14).

Contemporary scholarship regarding nomadic peoples examines the changing nature of their social systems, challenged by political and environmental transformations in numerous nation-states throughout the world. Although nomadic communities differ in many ways, their long-standing resiliency in the face of sociopolitical challenges has been tied to such shared features as flexibility, resourcefulness, and skill at using different patterns of mobility to successfully exploit the shifting nature of the space around them (Berland and Rao 2004). Not all communities are equally successful in this regard. Deforestation and increasing governmental control of formerly open land limits access to raw materials for manufacturing of trade items; both environmental degradation and attempts to protect endangered wildlife can result in economic loss to those who trap and sell animals. The demarcation and enforcement of new international borders in tense political times has transformed some pastoralist travel along traditional migration routes into criminal activity, reconfiguring trade into "smuggling" goods across borders (Berland and Rao 2004). However, in many cases nomadic peoples' "willingness and capability . . . to perceive, create, adapt old and adopt new strategies in rapidly changing circumstances" (Berland and Rao 2004:22) is the key to their survival. Far from being isolated strangers, their understanding of the political, economic, social, and ecological constraints placed on both their own lives and on those of the communities with whom they have economic dealings allows them to maintain their traditional practices by making astute choices from an array of potential goods or services they have to offer their settled trade partners (Berland and Rao 2004).

✦ FOR FURTHER DISCUSSION

The geographic distance between tents in a Basseri camp can indicate social distance between the people dwelling within them. What are some other examples of physical distance or proximity being used as a "social idiom" to indicate personal, social, or psychological "distance" or "closeness"?

CHAPTER 4

HAITI

A Nation in Turmoil

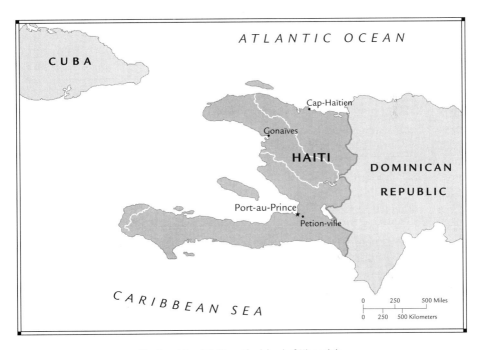

The Republic of Haiti on the island of Hispaniola.

✦ THE BEGINNING

Kric? Krac!

In the beginning, there was only Damballah Wedo, the Great Serpent, whom the Creator asked to hold up the world, lest it topple into the sea. The creature lay underneath the earth, its seven hundred coils unmoving. One day, it began to stir, and the earth trembled. It reached up above the world and unleashed the stars and planets; it slithered along the earth, carving the valleys and rivers, rifting the mountains. It reared into the sky and brought forth thunder and lightning. From its body, Damballah Wedo filled the rivers, and the mist rose, and created Ayida Wedo, the Rainbow, who became the Great Serpent's wife. Together they gave birth to all the spirits in the world, all the blood, all the life, all the people.

✦ INTRODUCTION

The Republic of Haiti occupies the western third of the island of Hispaniola, which is the second largest island in the Caribbean. The remaining two-thirds, to the east, is the Dominican Republic. Situated about six hundred miles southeast of Florida, Haiti spans about eleven thousand square miles, approximately the size of Maryland. Its shape—two jutting peninsulas—is often described as resembling the head of a crocodile, jaws open and aimed menacingly toward Cuba, to the west (Brand 1965, Rotberg 1971).

Haiti was once an environment of tropical rainforest and lush Caribbean pine, but much of it has been cleared for timber and firewood. In fact, one source comments that there are few places in the world where "the destruction of the natural woodland cover [has] been so nearly complete" (Weil 1985:14). Adding to this, severe erosion has left very little commercial forest (Weil 1985). Rainfall is more plentiful on the northern peninsula (which juts into the Atlantic Ocean) than the southern (which is in the Caribbean Sea), and the extensive felling of trees has led to disastrous flooding during the heaviest rains (Rodman 1954).

The word *haiti* means "high land" in the Arawak language of the Taino, the island's original inhabitants. Although Haiti's elevations are lower than the Dominican Republic, nearly half is above one thousand five hundred feet. Two chains of mountains run the lengths of both peninsulas. It has been said that an early European visitor to the island, when asked to describe the terrain, crumpled up a large piece of paper and placed the tortuous shape on the table, as an accurate rendering of the precipitous slopes (Farmer 1994, Rodman 1954). In addition to growing pine and mahogany forests and fruit trees, farming is practiced wherever possible. The hillsides are so steep that farmers often resemble mountain climbers, secured to the slopes by heavy ropes. One author reports hearing "jocular but vivid tales . . . of farmers falling to their deaths off their cornfields" (Weil 1985:7). Lowland regions have richer alluvial soil.

→ HISTORY

Conquest and Slavery

The island which would later be named Hispaniola was originally populated in three separate migrations of nearby peoples, the first from the eastern part of Venezuela about 2600 B.C. Dugout canoes allowed travelers to move from island to island, fishing the coastal waters, gathering wild foods, and seeking shelter in caves or beneath large rock outcroppings by the riverbanks. Some two thousand years later, the Taino, Arawak peoples, reached Hispaniola, displacing or absorbing the local population. Unlike their predecessors, the Taino were horticulturalists with a rich artistic tradition, mostly of ceramics (Anthony 1989, Doggett and Gordon 1999). Villages grew up around an economy of cassava and sweet potato cultivation, and individuals were skilled at fishing with nets and traps. A third wave of travelers, perhaps from the Peruvian Andes or Venezuela's Orinoco region, arrived just shortly before Christopher Columbus, who sailed to the island in 1492, naming it Hispaniola, or "little Spain."

In letters home, Columbus describes the warm greeting he received from the Taino. Writing of the nearly 400,000 inhabitants as "lovable, tractable, peaceable, gentle decorous Indians" (Farmer 1994:60), he assured his sovereigns that the people he encountered could be convinced to trade their gold, and would not resist conquering.

Columbus set out from the island only to meet with disaster: off-shore, the *Santa Maria* ran aground on a coral reef, and was wrecked. Tainos saw the Spaniards' emergency, and hastened to help the stranded sailors, whom they offered shelter. Columbus pressed onward in the *Nina* and *Pinta,* leaving the *Santa Maria* crew behind with orders to seek gold (Weil 1985). Later, other Spanish settlers joined them, enslaving the Taino population and forcing them to mine gold and turn it over to the settlers. For nearly a quarter of a century, the native population was subjected to cruelty and deprivation so harsh that many were driven to suicide (Doggett and Gordon 1999). Hunger and disease ravaged the population, and by early in the sixteenth century, the Taino population stood at less than five hundred.

Sugarcane had by this time been introduced into the island economy. Having decimated the Taino population, Spanish settlers were in need of replacement labor to continue mining gold and raising sugarcane, and turned to the growing slave trade from Africa. By 1540 more than thirty thousand Africans had been brought to Hispaniola (Farmer 1994).

As Spanish interests were piqued elsewhere, chiefly by the discovery of gold and silver in Mexico and Peru, they began to withdraw from Hispaniola. English and French pirates invaded from Tortuga, a small island to the north, and the French eventually gained a stronghold on the island. These "buccaneers," so named for their adoption of the Arawak practice of roasting meat over wooden spits, called boucans, settled in the western part of the island, with the French eventually driving out the English. Although they did not own the land, the French prospered there, and resisted Spanish efforts to displace them. In 1697, the Spanish relented and signed a treaty ceding the western third of Hispaniola to the French colonists, who called it Saint-Domingue. The eastern land (Santo Domingo) remained under Spanish rule, with a border established between them.

Once the territory was officially theirs, French colonists flocked to the island, seeking their fortunes. Using slave labor, French colonists raised coffee, cacao, indigo, and sugarcane. By the end of the eighteenth century, large sugar plantations made Saint-Domingue the richest French colony in the new world, accounting for two-thirds of all of France's overseas investments (Anthony 1989). The need for workers was great, and Saint-Domingue became the main port for West African slave traders, bringing nearly thirty thousand individuals annually. Farmer (1994) reports that by 1791, the island housed nearly half the slave population in all of the Caribbean. The brutality of Saint-Domingue plantation slavery was extreme, the death toll staggering (Anthony 1989). Disease, beatings, exhaustion, and starvation is estimated to have led planters to replace the entire slave population every twenty years (Anthony 1989), with one of every three slaves dying during his first three years of "intense exploitation" (Farmer 1994:63).

Small acts of revolt and resistance began to trouble plantation owners, who redoubled their efforts to keep the nearly half million slaves under control. Farmer writes:

> As the eighteenth century drew to a close, it became clear ... that not even torture would permit such a tiny number of slave holders to control so many slaves. The cycle of repression, hysteria, and atrocities was spinning towards an inescapable finale: "This colony of slaves," observed the Marquis du Rouvray in 1783, "is like a city under the imminence of attack; we are treading on loaded barrels of gunpowder" (1994:66).

And so they were. The French Revolution was soon to spark a counterpart in Saint-Domingue.

Revolution and Independence

In the years leading up to the French Revolution of 1797, Saint-Domingue's population was made up of several distinct segments. These are most often described in terms of skin color: white (French slave owners, who numbered about 35,000); black (500,000 West African slaves); and "mulatto," biracial individuals, originally the offspring of landowners and slaves, who numbered 28,000.

However, social distinctions, also of importance, did not map directly onto skin color. Not all the whites were wealthy plantation owners, and those who were poor artisans hated the planters (Farmer 1994). A group of individuals known as *affranchi* were free by law, but denied the social equality it promised. While the majority of affranchi were "mulatto" (also known as *gens de couleur*, people of color) there were some black *affranchi*. In addition, while the vast majority of slaves were black, there were a proportion who were mulatto (Nicholls 1985).

The French Revolution inspired strong sentiments in all quarters of the Saint-Domingue population. Wealthy plantation owners were alarmed at the burgeoning power of France's lower classes, and did not want to see that situation replicated on the island (Anthony 1989). In addition, they saw an opportunity to declare independence from France. The brutalized slaves had more than ample reason to revolt. But it was the *affranchi,* who owned more than a third of Saint-Domingue property but were denied political or social equality with whites, who seized the opportunity to challenge this status quo (Farmer 1994).

In 1790, France issued a declaration guaranteeing equal rights to the *affranchi,* but the colonial administration of Saint-Domingue made it clear they had no intention of abiding by the law. *Affranchi* owned slaves, sent their children abroad to schools in France, and were determined that they should have rights equal to white landowners. (As Farmer points out, theirs was not the cause of emancipation. He writes "mulatto spokesmen made it abundantly clear that they wanted full civil rights in order to stand on equal terms with whites—as upholders of slavery" [1994:67]). The following year, an *affranchi,* Vincent Ogé, backed by an organization in France called *Les Amis des Noirs* (Friends of the Blacks) led a revolt against the colonial governor, and was captured and executed. This action sparked a slave uprising of huge proportion. Tens of thousands of individuals set fire to 1500 plantations; well over 10,000 lost their lives.

One of the leaders of the uprising was a freed slave, Toussaint Louverture, a man with uncommon military knowledge and charismatic leadership abilities. Over the next several years, war between France and Spain came to the island of Hispaniola. Toussaint led his armies for the Spanish. In 1793 France (some suggest, to gain black support against Spain [Anthony 1989]) abolished slavery in all its colonial holdings, and Toussaint, now a Spanish general, switched his allegiance and joined the French. Followed by his loyal troops, he helped defeat the Spanish armies, and in 1795 Spain ceded their two-thirds of Hispaniola to the French. The following year, Toussaint was installed as lieutenant governor of the island, determined to unite former slaves, whites, and *gens de coleur* in reestablishing the land's former prosperity, without the atrocities of slave labor.

Over the next several years, Toussaint's power increased, much to the dismay of Emperor Napoleon Bonaparte. In 1801, Toussaint wrote a constitution proclaiming Saint-Domingue self-governing, with himself at the helm. Napoleon sent in troops and captured Toussaint, who died in a French prison. Napoleon then announced his intention to reinstate slavery on the island. Two of Toussaint's former officers, Jean-Jacques Dessalines and Henri Christophe, regrouped the armies and drove back the French. In 1804 Dessalines proclaimed independence, renaming Saint-Domingue "Haiti," and began to rule the first black republic, the first independent nation in Latin

America, (and the second in the Western Hemisphere, after the United States) as Emperor Jacques I, a dictator of the first order.

A Nation in Turmoil

One of Dessalines' first acts was to refashion the tricolor French flag into the banner of Haiti. He removed the white stripe, declaring that with it went the white presence in Haiti. What would remain was the red and the blue, symbolizing the blacks and mulattos, though the latter were the object of his scorn. True to his word, he ordered that the whites who remained be killed, and seized all the cultivated land in the country. His plan "was to have the state act as supreme landlord" (Trouillot 1990:45) and within months he had laid claim to all mulatto property. He imposed a military dictatorship, forcing the now-free slaves either back onto plantations or into the army. He refused to establish a system of education, and ruled through fear. By 1806, however, his autocracy could no longer be tolerated, and he was ambushed and assassinated outside the capital, Port-au-Prince.

After his death, the country was riven in two, ruled in the north by Henri Cristophe, a former slave who had served in Toussaint's army, and in the south by Alexandre Pétion, a mulatto educated in France and taken with the tenets of democracy.

It was Christophe's intention to model his reign after the British monarchy. He crowned himself King Henri I, established a court filled with titled nobles, and built several magnificent royal palaces, the most elaborate called *Sans Souci*. In the early years of his rule, he established a sound system of currency, instituted mandatory education patterned after the English system, printed books, created a judicial system, and kept a close eye on his tenant-farmers. Before long, however, his leanings toward tyranny grew. Increasingly fearful that the French would return, Christophe poured much of the country's resources into building an enormous fortress, called the *Citadelle*, which took nearly fifteen years to complete, and which is seen, by some, to embody the last years of his rule: "Threatening, useless, inaccessible, conceived in needless fear and militarily absurd, it was constructed at untold cost of toil, tears and blood" (Rodman 1954:17). As his armies began to plot an overthrow, Christophe was struck down by a massive stroke. Able to move very little, and aware of the growing unrest, he committed suicide, shooting himself through the heart with a silver bullet, in *Sans Souci*. He was buried beneath the *Citadelle*. Meanwhile, Pétion's government in the south of Haiti was dramatically different. Embracing a democratic ideal, he parceled out the large plantations into smaller plots, which he gave to individuals for their own use. The forced labor system of Toussaint, Dessalines, and Christophe had been harsh and unpopular, and Pétion's disinclination to replicate it changed the agricultural base of the southern economy. Christophe's citizenry were serfs, Pétion's were free (Weil 1985), but this freedom resulted in the south becoming a subsistence-farming peasantry, with no export crops and a declining tax base. Foreign loans were obtained, but they carried exorbitant interest rates. Pétion died in 1818, "Haiti's best-loved ruler and the architect of her economic ruin" (Rodman 1954:18).

Jean Pierre Boyer, who had served in the Pétion government, succeeded Pétion in the south in 1818, and upon Christophe's 1820 suicide, reunited the two halves of Haiti. He continued Pétion's practice of dividing up the land into small parcels, with disastrous results. Most of these aliquots were too small for sugar or indigo cultivation. Moreover, societal stratification had taken hold. Although democratic in his distribution of small plots of land to the populace, Pétion and Boyer both fostered a mulatto elite who held both social and political dominance over the black majority (Weil 1985). Boyer attempted to shore up the economy by reinstituting forced labor, hearkening back to the strategies of Dessalines and Christophe. He also looked beyond Haiti's borders. Taking advantage of a revolt against the Spanish, in 1821 he annexed Santo Domingo, the eastern two-thirds of Hispaniola, which Haiti held until 1849, when it claimed independence and became the Dominican Republic. His attempts to forge relations with France were costly, incurring long-lasting debt. In the face of accusations of corruption and treason, Boyer was ousted in 1843.

The years from Boyer's fall to 1915 saw twenty-two dictators come and go, each exacting a toll on the nation. Relations between the majority and the elites continued to be fraught with contention and violence. Of the twenty-two heads of state, most of them black military leaders, only one served a complete term in office. Fourteen were overthrown by civil revolution, the remainder assassinated or forced into exile.

The majority of the rural peasantry was apolitical (Doggett and Gordon 1999), but a substantial number figured quite significantly into Haitian politics, in their function as mercenary guerrillas, employed by the seemingly endless string of men who aspired to ruling the country. Known in the south as *piquets*, but more often as *cacos* in the north, they struck a bargain with those who hired them, overthrowing the current regime in exchange for cash and the opportunity to loot towns en route to the capital with impunity (Anthony 1989, Weil 1985). With seven such presidential coups in as many years, the early years of the twentieth century were filled with bloodshed and civil unrest. They were also marked by increasing interest in Haiti by foreign powers, for economic reasons, but especially for its strategic position in the Caribbean. The United States was especially interested in Haiti.

U.S. Military Occupation

The political situation in Haiti down-spiraled quickly between 1910 and 1915, culminating in the five-month rule of Vilbrun Guillame Sam. Sam, his own position secured by bribing the *caco* rebels, learned of a planned coup, and summarily executed nearly 170 political prisoners, aligned with those who sought to unseat him. A riotous mob (many the family of the murdered prisoners) stormed the embassy, seized Sam, tore his body to pieces, and "paraded through the streets with his remains" (Anthony 1989:66). The United States used this murderous incident as justification for their invasion and occupation of Haiti in July 1915.

The waters between Haiti and Cuba are known as the Windward Passage, and were a crucial shipping route between the United States and the Panama Canal. Germany, amassing World War I victories, sought a naval base in Haiti, and the U.S. feared this would be granted, because of the increasing number of Germans who were currying favor by financing *caco* rebellions (Weil 1985). While purportedly motivated solely by their intentions to stabilize Haitian unrest, the military occupation solidified U.S. economic aims. Taking full control of financial and military affairs, the U.S. rewrote the Haitian constitution to suit its own interests, disbanded the army and replaced it with an American police force. While the United States instituted many positive reforms—building hospitals and schools, repairing roads, engineering reservoirs and sewage systems—they did much of it by seizing peasant land and forming chain gangs of forced prison labor (Anthony 1989, Farmer 1994). Local resistance to the U.S. occupation grew, culminating in 1920 with the *Cacos* Rebellion, led by a "latter-day Toussaint Louverture" (Farmer 1994:96), Charlemagne Péralte. The U.S. Marines reacted quickly and brutally, quashing the rebellion at the cost of 3250 Haitian lives (Farmer 1994).

The United States presence remained in Haiti until 1934, after having shepherded the country through the election of a new president, Stenio Vincent, a mulatto, whose successor, Élie Lescot, was also a mulatto. The army successfully installed the next two presidents, representative of the black majority, Dumarsais Estimé (in 1946) and Paul Magloire (1950), but both were accused of corruption and unseated. For the nine months after Magloire's government was overthrown in 1956, seven unstable governments came and went. In 1957 a new and frightening era would begin in Haiti: the rule of the Duvaliers.

The Duvalier Years

In September 1957, Francois Duvalier, a seemingly unassuming country doctor (Farmer 1994), was elected president. Duvalier had been prominent in the *Noirisme* movement, a popular campaign which urged Haitians to embrace their African roots and reject European influence. Growing in popularity throughout American occupation, it galvanized blacks who were chafing under the favoritism shown mulattos. "Papa Doc" Duvalier wasted no time in assuring his absolute hold over all aspects of Haitian life. Acutely aware of the military's part in the scores of previous government overthrows, he greatly reduced both the size and power of the army. Instead, he relied on his own creation, a private force of terrorists dubbed the *Tontons Mocoutes* (Uncle Knapsack), named for an evil character in Haitian folklore, who captures children and carries them away in his bag. The *Tontons Mocoutes* (officially the National Security Volunteers, or VSN) reportedly killed tens of thousands of Haitians, under Duvalier's orders (Farmer 1994). In response to this brutality, the Vatican excommunicated the Duvaliers from the Catholic Church. In 1964 Duvalier rewrote the constitution, naming himself president for life, and providing for his eventual successor: when Francois Duvalier died in 1971, his nineteen-year-old son, Jean-Claude, stepped into his constitutional place. At first, "Baby Doc" seemed somewhat less dictatorial than his father, but this respite didn't last long. His economic policies alienated both the mulatto minority elite and the black middle class in turn, and with enemies on all sides, he reactivated the *Tontons Mocoutes*. By the early 1980s Haiti's economic system was in utter chaos. Inflation, recession, and rapidly declining tourism all took their toll. Disease wiped out nearly two million pigs, leaving peasant farmers destitute. Antigovernment demonstrations were met with violence, and Duvalier had no choice but to flee to safety. In 1986, taking his family (and millions of dollars from the Haitian treasury), "Baby Doc" escaped to France. There was rejoicing in the streets of Haiti.

Aristide and Beyond

After being purged of the Duvalier regime, Haiti once again went through a string of leaders, four in three years. Jean-Claude Duvalier's successor was General Henri Namphy, who disappointed those hoping for radical change. He was replaced by General Prosper Avril, who was no less repressive. He fled the country, replaced by an interim president, Ertha Pascal-Trouillot, while elections were scheduled. The winner was a young priest, Jean-Bertrand Aristide, who had spent the few years since the end of the Duvalier regime preaching reform from his church at the edge of the Port-au-Prince slums. His campaign slogan, *Lavalas* (flood), resulted in just that: a flood of support from the oppressed Haitian populace, who elected him in a landslide victory. He took office in 1991 and began to implement change, retiring the majority of the army's high command, separating the military and the police force, lobbying to increase the minimum wage, instituting public-works projects to create jobs, and undertaking a battle against crime and corruption. Although his plans were ambitious, he had barely eight months in the attempt: an alliance of wealthy families and displaced army brass, led by General Raoul Cédras, staged a bloody coup. Aristide escaped, but more than two thousand were killed in the first week alone.

Condemning the coup, the Organization of American States (OAS), issued a trade embargo, unsuccessfully attempting to unseat the military dictatorship. By the spring of 1992, however, tens of thousands of Haitians had taken to hastily constructed boats, sailing towards Miami. Of the 40,000 who set forth, the vast majority were intercepted by the U.S. Coast Guard, taken to a naval base, and eventually returned to Haiti on the grounds that they were fleeing poverty, not politics, and thus were not eligible for political asylum. It was a further embargo—on oil—the following year, which resulted in negotiations and an accord, one provision of which was the safe return and reinstatement of President Aristide. Further violence demonstrated that this promise was not to be kept, and in 1994 U.S. troops arrived in Port-au-Prince, exiling Cédras to Panama, and returning Aristide to a welcoming Haitian population.

Haitian children waiting in line for food.

The 1987 constitution provided for no reelections to a second consecutive five-year term. Thus, in 1995, elections were held to choose Aristide's successor. The candidate who prevailed was René Préval, the Lavalas candidate, and Aristide's original prime minister. Other elections, however—for prime minister, legislators, and thousands of local officials to fill empty slots—had been stalled for years, over political infighting and logistical stalemates. Elections were finally held in May 2000, with the presidential election following in November. Aristide, representing the Lavalas party, emerged victorious, winning another five-year term. Aristide's presidency did not bring hoped-for reforms, and by early 2004 violent protests erupted. On the heels of an armed revolt, Aristide fled Haiti in February of 2004, replaced by a United States–backed interim government.

✦ LIFE IN HAITI

Social and Economic Organization

Statistical data on the Haitian population describe unparalleled poverty. Annual income in 1999 was $250 per person (Catanese 1999), with a life expectancy of barely 57 years. More than half the adult population is illiterate.

Haiti is not only the poorest country in the Western Hemisphere, it is also the least urban; of a total population of a little over seven million, nearly 80 percent live in rural areas (Catanese 1999). The vast majority of Haitian citizens are peasants who practice subsistence agriculture. Small plots of land, tilled with hoes and other simple gardening tools, typically yield, beans, maize, bananas, coffee or sweet potatoes. Along the coastline, there is some rice production and fishing. The land is not very productive, owing to the steepness of its mountains, and the poor quality of the eroded soil. Half of the land slopes at a forty-degree angle; most of the population must rely on products grown on 30 percent of the arable land (Miller 1984).

Houses are generally wooden structures, containing two rooms; some have thatched roofs, in the style of ancestral West African dwellings. There is no electricity; cooking is done over charcoal fires outside of the house. Work is hard, and all family members are expected to contribute. Children are often called upon to help with any animals there may be, and women bring whatever surplus the gardens may yield to market. Under ordinary circumstances, men work their land individually. However, when there is a large task to be accomplished—clearing a field, or building a house—they rely on informal local work associations, called *combites*. Friends and neighbors come together to work for the day, and are compensated with a festive meal at the end of the job, accompanied by singing, dancing, and games of riddles and storytelling.

Given the dependence of the majority of Haiti's population on subsistence agriculture, Haiti's crushing poverty is at least partly a result of the extreme deforestation. There is barely a hillside that has not been stripped for firewood or housing: only 2 percent of the country's original forest remains (Catanese 1999). As a consequence, much of the soil has been eroded away, the topsoil running off into the ocean (where it takes its toll on marine life and fishing).

In his discussion of the environmental degradation of the Haitian landscape, Anthony Catanese (1999) points to several historical linkages between rural poverty and deforestation. The first is Haiti's long history of political instability. The succession of violent and chaotic regimes, sometimes lasting only months, made long-range planning for ongoing problems impossible, and concerns about the environment and economy of the rural peasants, singularly unimportant. Second, he points to a shift of power from rural areas to the capital, Port-au-Prince, resulting in "continuing avoidance of investment in rural human and physical capital in ways that would effectively improve agricultural productivity and rural income" (p. 22). Environmental degradation is only a problem in urban areas decades after it begins to take its toll on farmers. A third factor is the long-standing focus on individual needs, to the detriment of the greater societal good. According to Catanese, serious attention to "public welfare . . . has been alien to most regimes" (p. 23).

In the 1980s Haiti's already devastated economy received two more blows. Creole pigs, a staple in the rural peasant economy, were struck by an outbreak of African swine fever. In an attempt to curb the spread of disease, the government (encouraged by the U.S. Agency for International Development, USAID) ordered every pig killed, without offering their owners any form of compensation. Recognizing the catastrophic results of this policy, a small number of an American breed of pigs were brought in, but they were unsuited to the Haitian environment and could not survive.

The second strike was at the tourism industry. Once thriving, the association of AIDS with Haiti, promulgated both by the media and by health experts, brought foreign travel nearly to a halt. In fact, it was American vacation travel which likely brought AIDS to Haiti in the first place, and not the other way around. (Farmer 1994) However, both political unrest and health concerns led to official warnings that American citizens not travel to Haiti. The Haitian tourist market has yet to rebound.

Rising population and diminishing agricultural yield have led to an influx of rural peasants seeking jobs in the capital, Port-au-Prince. While this work was sometimes available in earlier times, over the past twenty years it has become nearly impossible to find, resulting in urban centers of impoverished unemployed. In one such slum, nearly a quarter of a million people are packed into five square kilometers with neither running water nor a sewage system (Doggett and Gordon 1999).

While the law mandates compulsory, free education for all children between the ages of 7 and 13, less than 40 percent of Haitian children attend school, both in the rural areas and in the poor cities, resulting in a literacy rate which hovers somewhere under 50 percent.

There is, however, a different life in Haiti, though it is the privilege of the very few. In the hills above Port-au-Prince reside the Haitian elite, 1 percent of the population who control nearly half the country's wealth. By and large, these are the mulatto descendants of colonial times. The town of Pétionville consists of enclaves of mansions, owned by those who run the import/export businesses, manufacturing, and other lucrative businesses. Their children attend Port-au-Prince private schools. This is not a land-holding aristocracy, as is found in other nations. The countryside belongs to the peasants. The elite of Haiti are an urban elite. While a middle-class is emerging, it is very small. Just as the wealth and power are concentrated in Port-au-Prince and surroundings, so are nearly all the services. More than half of all the medical personnel in the nation are located in the capital city, and it boasts the only complete sewer system. (Weil 1985) There are French restaurants, theaters, and elegant boutiques.

The distraction between Haiti's poor—90 percent of the population—and wealthy—the remaining 10 percent—is often drawn along the lines of religion, language, and skin color. The poor majority are of African descent, speak Creole, and practice *voudon*. The wealthy are most often the descendants of African slaves and French landowners, lighter skinned, French-speaking, and Roman Catholic. Michel-Rolph Trouillot, a Haitian anthropologist, describes the feeling most well-off urban Haitians have for "the common people of Haiti" as "contempt" (1990:229).

Language and Arts
French and Creole
There are two languages spoken in Haiti, but they are far from equal. The official language of Haiti is French, but it is spoken by only 10 percent of the

population. Creole is the language of 90 percent of the Haitian people. This lop-sided distribution is indicative of the chasm in Haitian society, which disadvantages the masses by privileging the few. In colonial times, French was regarded as the "higher" language, spoken by the wealthy slave owners. Creole was "the language of the subordinate and exploited masses constituted of African slaves." (Zéphir 1996) While very few slaves spoke French, most *affranchis* understood Creole. Anthony (1989) points out that the result was that "communication between a black and a mulatto was controlled by the mulatto" (p. 85). Today, most schools are taught in French, the government conducts official business in French, and the judicial system is entirely run in French.

Trouillot (1990) notes that most linguists no longer refer to Haiti as bilingual. Instead, they refer to a bilingual minority elevating one language as "the language of power" (p. 115) over another. He asserts, however, that this linguistic divide does not truly appear at the level of *communication*. All Haitians, even the 8 percent who speak French, speak Creole. (He notes, in fact, that "even the most francophile urbanites often prefer to use [Creole] in situations where everyone is competent in French." [p. 115]) Rather, the cleavage is in the *power* attached to French. Its knowledge provides access to power and prestige that Creole does not.

Culturally, it is Creole that expresses the richness of Haitian culture and through which oral traditions are preserved and passed along (Nicholls 1996). In tone, it has the lilt of French, from which it borrows vocabulary. Additionally, it incorporates some Spanish and English. Many words are derived from several West African languages, and it employs both African pronunciation and sentence structure, which differs from French syntax. The use—or pointed avoidance—of speaking Creole figures prominently in the experience of Haitian immigrants in North America.

The Arts

Art, music, and literature in nineteenth-century Haiti were, for the most part, an extension of those art forms in France (Weil 1985). The intricate architecture and wide boulevards in Port-au-Prince and Cap-Haitien (Haiti's second-largest city) are distinctly French. The time of the American occupation, however, saw a rich blossoming of the arts, and some trace this to a renewed search for national identity while under foreign control (Weil 1985). Others point out that both the visual arts and music and dance have longstanding roots in *voudon*, and before being "discovered" and classified as artistic cultural products, were in the service of religious performance and ritual. In the 1940s, American art collectors visiting Haiti were greatly impressed by the vivid colors, bold lines, and lively movement in Haitian paintings they saw on doors and walls all over the countryside. Classified as "primitive" or "naive" art, paintings depicting religious scenes or everyday market life were brought back to the United States by collectors, who generated tremendous enthusiasm for them in the art world.

Haitian music reflects all aspects of Haitian history, from slavery to revolution. The rhythms and sounds of West Africa and modern struggle and resistance are combined in traditional drumming and politicized lyrics. Both music and dance are central to *voudon* ritual, and are also incorporated into rural daily life. Nearly everyone plays some sort of instrument, and music fills leisure time in the countryside where there is no electricity for radio or television. Bands of musicians often travel from village to village, performing for food and a night's shelter (Anthony 1989). The hard work of a *combite* is modulated by song. A modern jazz form, a fusion of *voudon* music and American jazz (itself of African origin) called *racines* (roots) music, emerged in the 1970s. It, too, combined musical tradition with political call to action in songs which encouraged peasant revolt and called for change. During the years of the military dictatorships in the 1980s and the coups of the 1990s, musicians endured harassment and threats from the army (Doggett and Gordon 1999). During *Carnivál*, before Lent, bands fill the city streets. After *Carnivál* is *Rara Carnivál*, highlighted by *Rara* bands, traveling the countryside until Easter. Bamboo trumpets (*vaskins*) and horns made of hammered tin (*kornets*) combine with maracas, drums, and pieces of metal struck together for percussion.

Storytelling holds a special place in Haitian culture, most likely influenced by the rich oral tradition of West Africa. Traditional fables were collected and published in Creole early in the twentieth century. Stories tell of the creation of the world teach moral lessons, and feature tricksters and *voudon* spirits. Traditional storytelling sessions all begin the same way. The storyteller leans toward the audience and asks *kric?* The audience responds in unison, *krac!* and the tale begins.

Since the initial days of independence, Haitian literature, like music, has been a powerful vehicle for countering colonialism, racism, and imperialist constructions of Haitians as "primitive savages" (Doggett and Gordon 1999). American occupation further stirred Haitian writers to publish their own representations of their cultural identity. The Duvalier regime was a death knoll to Haitian intellectual literary life: *Tontons Mocoutes* murdered at least one renowned writer. Others were exiled or fled in fear but continued to write abroad. During the Duvalier years, there were more Haitian authors working outside the country than within, writing—some in Creole—critiques of the terrorist regime at home (Anthony 1989, Doggett and Gordon 1999).

Catholicism and Voudon

The theme of dualism—French and Creole, African and European, black and mulatto, slave and *affranchi*—extends into Haiti's religious life. It is a well-worn phrase that Haiti is 90 percent Catholic and 100 percent *voudon* (Heinl and Heinl 1978, Stepick 1998, Weil 1985). Roman Catholicism is the official religion in Haiti, and the Catholic Church serves as a powerful institution in urban areas. Between 10 and 20 percent of the population is Protestant.

Weil (1985) points out that French colonial Haiti was not nearly as influenced by Catholicism as were Spanish colonies, and sees this as a result of the priorities of the colonials themselves. Plantation owners and buccaneers alike were not at all interested in converting slaves to their religion; their singular focus was on amassing riches. After independence, the Vatican was unhappy at the official separation of church and state set up in the new constitution, and no longer sent priests to attempt conversion.

However, as the population of mulatto elite embraced French culture wholeheartedly, reinstituting Catholicism as the national religion became an important part of that alignment. They welcomed French and Belgian priests, who were of a similar social class, and used the Church as a symbol of their linkage to Europe and upward mobility, and as a distancing mechanism between themselves and the *voudon* masses.

Voudon has been referred to as "perhaps the world's most misunderstood and maligned religion" (Stepick 1998:86). In fact, "voodoo" is commonly used as an adjective to denigrate whatever follows as unscientific, craven, or primitive. The word is derived from a Dahomean word meaning "god," and the rituals and pantheon draw heavily on West African animist tradition. Haitian *voudon* is heavily interlarded with Catholicism, with influences of the aboriginal Taino religion. One early important function of *voudon* was to provide a sense of unity and common ground among slaves brought from disparate tribal communities. In addition, its dances and songs could be used in the fields as a surreptitious means of revolutionary communication, even when slavemasters were present. It has been suggested that many of the similarities between *voudon* and Catholicism derive in part from a need to placate missionaries and plantation owners while still remaining true to the religion: icons of Catholic saints could be substituted for sacred *voudon* objects, generating a dual pantheon much like the differently named (but comparable) Greek and Roman gods. *Voudon* is, however, more than a syncretism of African and Catholic beliefs. Over time, elements for which there are no African or Catholic counterparts emerged (Bourgignon 1976), resulting in "a distinctly Haitian complex of philosophical tenets, religious beliefs, and ritual practices" (Trouillot 1990:115). While acknowledging African contributions, anthropologist Alfred Métraux (in Farmer 1994:65) describes *voudon* as "fundamentally the products of the plantation economy." *Voudon* centers around a single creator, the *Gran Mâit* (Great Master), served by a pantheon of deities, the *lwa*. *Voudon* rituals center around these spirits, who materialize through possession of the priest's body, during trance. *Lwa* carefully select the people whom they will possess. Although possession is sometimes resisted, it is believed to be an honor to have been called to act as the "horse" which a *lwa* will "mount" during the ceremony (Bourgignon 1976). Each *lwa* is called by its own drum rhythm, which begins the ceremony. Priests—male (*houngon*) or female (*mambo*)—wield their sacred rattle (*asson*) to greet the Spirit of the Crossroads, the *lwa* who has the power to open the gate into the spirit world. Ritual attendants carry brightly colored flags to represent local *voudon* associations. Intricately patterned sacred symbols (*vevés*) are drawn on the ground in cornmeal (likely influenced by Taino tradition), which is then returned to the earth by the pounding feet of the dancers.

Damballah Wedo, the serpent *lwa*, often materializes next, causing the possessed individual to writhe on the ground, snake-like. The intensity and activity of the ceremony increases as more and more individuals are "mounted" by their *lwa*, each heralded by their drum rhythm and special song, playing together in a frenzy of excitement (Courlander 1960).

Perhaps *voudon*'s most sensational feature is what is seen as its darker side, exemplified by animal sacrifice and embodied in the *bocors* (sorcerers who visit illness and death upon their victims) and the legendary zombies, the "living dead" of Hollywood horror movies. In the 1980s attention was focused on the "science" of zombies, when Wade Davis (1985), a graduate student in ethnobotany, ventured to Haiti (financed by a Hollywood film director) in search of the substance which yields zombies. Davis felt he had found the secret: a poison, containing a nerve toxin like that found in the deadly Japanese puffer fish, which lowers the metabolic rate enough to replicate the appearance of death. (Students of Shakespeare will notice the resemblance to Juliet's feigned death, resulting from a potion which left her cold and still long enough to be presumed dead and placed in the Capulet monument.) A Haitian to whom the poison is administered seems to have died and is buried. Under cover of night, the perpetrator digs up the victim, allowing him to emerge from the ground when the effects of the toxin have begun to wear off. The zombie is groggy (and, owing to the power of the poison, perhaps brain damaged; surely traumatized [Stepick 1998]), and walks haltingly, back to the village, with the gait we have come to associate with this character. There is great controversy surrounding Davis' assertions (and the book and film resulting from his journey, both called *The Serpent and the Rainbow*), and Stepick (1998) reminds us that regardless of any pharmacologic "proof" of the existence of zombies, these elements are far from the essence of *voudon*. Like all religions, it seeks answers for the universal questions of life and death, describes a spiritual universe beyond our own, offers order and meaning to its adherents, adds structure and legitimacy to life. He says, of the emphasis placed on gore and fright:

> Black magic's relationship to Voodoo is similar to that of Satanism to Christianity. Concentrating on the darker side of Voodoo is akin to writing a book on the satanic cults of southern California and saying that you have described Christianity (p. 91).

As for the presumed conflict between Haiti's Catholicism and *voudon*, Haitian anthropologist Trouillot (1990) says that the cherished beliefs and practices of *voudon*, embraced by nearly all the population, have never seemed discordant with Christianity to the people who "live" *voudon*. While urban elites may be reticent to admit that they are comfortable holding both sets of beliefs, it is his contention that "they [share] religious beliefs rooted in the same African-dominated cosmology and [take] part in similar rituals" (p. 115). Despite a long history of attempted suppression, "anti-superstition" laws, and official government bans on its practice, *voudon* remains the living religion of Haiti, and, as

Métraux asserted, "belongs to the modern world and is part of our civilization" (in Farmer 1994:65).

→ Haitian Migration and Diaspora: The Tenth Department

Leaving Home

Haiti is divided into nine regions, called *departements*. President Aristide was the first to refer to the estimated 1.5 million Haitians emigrants worldwide as the "Tenth Department" (Jean-Pierre 1995). Nearly one in four Haitians is part of the diaspora (Jean-Pierre 1995), with an estimated 500,000 in North America (Catanese 1999).

Haitians have a history of temporary migration, with rural peasants having long worked as sugarcane harvesters in their neighboring Dominican Republic, and wealthier urbanites sending children to attend school in France. Within the country, rural peasants have moved to the urban centers of Port-au-Prince and Cap-Haitien. In the late 1950s and early 1960s, Haitian intellectuals and professionals who voiced opposition to the Duvalier regime fled to the United States (Zéphir 1996). It was not until the late 1970s and early 1980s, however, that the United States became the destination of poorer Haitians in flight. Dubbed "boat people," tens of thousands of Haitians set sail for south Florida, only 800 miles from home. Their requests for political asylum were rejected by the Immigration and Naturalization Service (INS), which claimed they were economic, and not political, refugees, a distinction which is the difference between welcome and deportation. However, as Miller (1984) points out, the difference between these two categories is hardly more than academic and impossible to disarticulate. Economic conditions *are,* in fact, political situations. The fact that refugee status has been granted to Cubans while denied to Haitians has been a source of much debate, in this regard (Miller 1984, Woldemikael 1989). Critics suggest that this discrimination results from two factors: that Cubans are fleeing a specifically communist regime, and that Haitian refugees are overwhelmingly black (Catanese 1999, Miller 1984).

Coming to America

Because many Haitians enter the United States without documentation, an accurate tally of their total numbers is difficult. One-half million is a reasonable estimate. Miller (1984) cites geographic, economic, historical, sociological, and political factors as all weighing heavily in the choice of the United States as a destination: a reputation for championing liberty, the promise of economic opportunity, a pluralistic society, and its nearest shores only 800 miles away, accessible by boat. The great majority of Haitians who come to the United States settle in New York City and south Florida. These two locations alone account for nearly 75 percent of the population. When expanded to include two more areas of the urban northeast, Boston and New Jersey, fully 85 percent of the Haitian population is accounted for.

Several authors have provided rich ethnographic accounts of Haitians settled in the United States, in New York (Laguerre 1984), South Florida (Stepick 1998), and Chicago (Woldemikael 1989). Others provide insightful analyses of Haitian ethnic identity and struggle (Miller 1984, Zéphir 1996). Many general patterns inhere across enclaves of Haitians in the United States.

The family is the focus of the Haitian American community, beginning with gathering funds to emigrate, continuing with local associations of old and new friends and family members, and throughout the production of a new generation of Haitians born in the United States. In general, it is not the entire nuclear family which leaves Haiti. Laguerre (1984) posits that this is owing to the arduous process and expense of obtaining a visa and paying for transit. Most often, one family member emigrates, and sets to work to reimburse those who have paid for the transit: this is the primary obligation, once resettled. After having done so, other members of the family are brought over, and that household will serve as what Laguerre (1984:86) terms "a stepping stone for newly arrived members of the family."

Stepick (1998) refers to this organized pattern as a migration chain, with each new individual another link. Newcomers, called *just-comes,* are introduced to the neighborhood, to new cultural norms, and are helped to find employment. Individual households are connected through neighborhood organizations and church groups, creating a web of support, both financial and social. Immigrants arrive without money, but not without "social capital" (Stepick 1998), networks of welcome and resource. Extra people are often included in households for days or weeks at a time if they have lost their job or need a place to stay. This "expansive hospitality" is passed along, as just-comes get on their feet, move on, and become hosts to others, creating "a multiple-stranded, dense chain of transnational links between the United States and Haiti, all held together by extended family ties" (Stepick 1998:19).

Obligations to family are not limited to those who are brought over. It is of paramount importance that resettled Haitians send money to the family which remains in Haiti. This responsibility is not taken lightly, and this remittance of funds is substantial enough to have been the impetus for Aristide's designation of the "Tenth Department." Haitians in diaspora send more than $300 million annually to family members at home, an amount equal to the budget of many governmental and non-governmental aid agencies. (Doggett and Gordon 1999) Sent directly to individuals, it is sometimes literally the difference between life and death from starvation. The World Bank contends that, at least in the case of Haitians sending money from New York City in the 1980s, most of the funds go to women in urban areas, with very little reaching men, or the poorest rural residents. Catanese (1999) postulates that when a man is planning to immigrate, he sends his wife and children to the city (usually Port-au-Prince), where he sends money for their support. Stepick (1998) has found that while over time, Haitians living in Miami feel less of an obligation to send funds as time goes by, the practice continues as long as individuals are able because there is a compelling moral component to the economic imperative.

Haitians in Canada

In addition to the northeastern United States and the southeastern Atlantic seaboard, more than 20,000 Haitians have settled in Canada, and the challenges faced by this population provide an interesting contrast. It is Quebec that is home to Canada's Haitians, and their experience is intertwined with the Quebecois struggle. The United States' reputation is of a "melting pot," but according to Dejean (1980), this is most decidedly not the case in Canada. He points out that Canada's history is that of an uneasy federation of two cultures, English and French, resulting in "a two-pronged Canadian nationalism" (p. i) that has demanded that immigrants who are neither French nor English choose between, upon their arrival. Haitians in Quebec find themselves in a peculiar position: arriving in Quebec during a time of intense French nationalism, they are the first immigrant group to be drawn to Canada specifically owing to this fervor. However, the overwhelming majority of the black population in Canada had been English speaking, and Dejean notes that in public situation, black Canadians are automatically assumed to be anglophone, and persistently addressed in English, even if they respond in French. Thus, he concludes, "the Haitians in Quebec find themselves caught between the classic Canadian pattern of cultural-linguistic polarization, one where language operates as a dominant value," and which often sets the English speaking black community at odds with Haitian Canadians. By contrast, it is not language but race which has been the focus of discourse about the complex Haitian experience in the United States.

"Becoming Black" in America

While the first wave of those seeking asylum were more financially secure, the overwhelming majority of Haitians arriving in the United States over the past thirty years have been poor. Although average Haitians working in the United States earn twenty times that of their counterparts at home (Catanese 1999), they are still struggling against numerous odds, not the least of which is racial discrimination. In his examination of Chicago's Haitian community, Woldemikael (1989) outlines the conflicts between racial and cultural identity faced by individuals unprepared for their status in American society. Laguerre (1984) describes similar findings among Haitians in New York. The fundamental conflict centers around the fact that Haitian immigrants define themselves based on their culture and language. However, not surprisingly, given the overwhelming focus on race in America, they are defined from without on the basis of their skin color. Haitians identify themselves as having a culture and history quite distinct from that of African-Americans, but find that being black leads social institutions to gloss them with African-Americans in a misguided (and racist) presumption of homogeneity. Their dilemma, according to Woldemikael (1989) was whether to "accept a new American identity based on race or try to maintain their distinct cultural and national identity" (p. 165). They chose the latter, but there appears to be a discontinuity between generations in this regard.

Both Woldemikael (writing about Chicago) and Laguerre (whose work is in New York City) have found generational differences in Haitian identity. First generation Haitians in Chicago find little motivation to become part of the African-American community. They use other Haitians as their reference point (Woldemikael 1989), socialize with fellow immigrants, maintain strong ties with family back home, and resist ascription to the category of black American. Second generation Haitians, however, often identify more as Americans, having been born in the United States. Children in school especially face pressure by peers to conform to African-American norms, as both white students and school staff "fail to fully acknowledge a differentiated black [sic] student population" persisting in privileging phenotype over culture.

In Miami, Stepick (1998) finds that younger Haitians often attempt to "pass" as African-American. Referred to as "coverups" by the Haitian community, they pretend not to understand the Creole spoken by the just-comes at school, pattern their dress and speech after their African-American classmates, and will even lie about their Haitian heritage. They do this with some ambivalence, he notes; he has also observed some changes afoot.

Pride over Prejudice

In recent years, Stepick (1998) has noted a resurgence of pride in Haitian culture by younger Haitians. In high schools, numbers of students began to speak Creole and volunteered to bring traditional foods into class to demonstrate Haitian cuisine. Others began to dress in Haitian style and advocate for the recognition of Haitian culture in various school events. This was replicated in the wider culture of Little Haiti, as the enclave in Miami is known. Various local societies formally promote Haitian culture by organizing dance and music troupes and mounting Haitian drama in theaters. Storytellers travel to schools with folktales, and Haitian broadcasts can be heard on the radio 24 hours a day.

The vast majority of Haitians in the United States fled a dire political and economic situation in their homeland. Many found a racist and unwelcoming America, and continue to live in poverty. However, in the wake of Aristide's reinstatement, myriad grassroots organizations sprung up, with connections to the popular movement in Haiti (Peters 1995). Their aim is to work for democratic reform. The situation in rural Haiti, however, is still a desperate one. To date, international support has focused on political issues; the call now is for economic support to receive equal attention (Catanese 1999). Perhaps the results of future elections will pave the way for action, for the beginning of a chipping away at the poverty faced by the citizens of the poorest nation in the Western Hemisphere.

→ FOR FURTHER DISCUSSION

It is estimated that there are more than one-half million Haitians now living in North America. In Canada, French-speaking Haitians find themselves at odds with English-speaking black Canadians. In the United States, Haitians find that they are classified on the basis of their skin color, assumed to identify with African-American culture, while they define themselves on the basis of their Haitian history and culture. What do these conflicts and assumptions say about issues of race and ethnicity? Further differences are found between generations: while Haitian immigrants resist identification with mainstream African-American culture, their children, born in the United States, feel differently. Why might this be so?

CHAPTER 5

THE HMONG

Struggle and Perseverance

Hmong Villages are located throughout China, Laos, Thailand, and Vietnam.

✦ THE BEGINNING

Four gods hold up the corners of the world and are responsible for creation. Long ago they sent a flood, and waters covered all the earth. Into a wooden barrel were placed a boy and a girl, who were sent by the Lord of the Sky to populate the earth. When the waters receded, they stepped out of their barrel and saw they were alone in the world. When their baby was born, it looked like an egg, smooth and oval. The boy and girl cut the egg into pieces, and scattered it over the land. Each piece grew into new people, until all the clans of the Hmong were born, and the earth was full of people.

✦ INTRODUCTION AND HISTORY

The Hmong are a tribal people who have traditionally lived in isolated mountain villages throughout China, Laos, Thailand, and Vietnam. Originating in Southern China, the Hmong were historically referred to as Meo or Miao ("primitive" or "barbarian") by outsiders, a pejorative label which they reject (Ovesen 1995). "Hmong" is their own word, meaning "free people." Hmong tales tell of an ancestral past in a land of ice and snow, and perpetual darkness, leading some to posit European ancestry, assuming the stories are of Siberia (Fadiman 1997).

The story of the Hmong is a history of struggle, rebellion, and perseverance. Fadiman (1997:13) describes Hmong history as "a marathon series of bloody scrimmages, punctuated by occasional periods of peace, though hardly any of plenty." Chinese literature mentions the Hmong as early as the twenty-seventh century B.C., when they lived along the basins of the Yellow and Yangtse Rivers for several centuries (Geddes 1976). Relations between the Hmong and the Chinese were never friendly. Hmong chose to retain their own way of life, preferring their own food, dress, language, and music over that of the Chinese, who attempted to incorporate (or at least influence) them. Emperors set up singularly punitive rules for the recalcitrant Hmong, who wanted nothing more than to be left alone (Fadiman 1997). Over hundreds of years, the Hmong skirmished with the Chinese, settling and resettling to avoid extermination. In the sixteenth century, the Ming dynasty constructed a wall one hundred miles long and ten feet high in an attempt to contain the Hmong in one area. In the eighteenth century, bloody battles were a regular occurrence. By the mid-nineteenth century, Chinese practices drove many Hmong out of the north from fertile lands to the rugged mountains southward, and from there to mountainous regions across Southeast Asia. Facing massacre and unwilling to give up their way of life, they chose poorer mountainous terrain because its inaccessibility afforded them greater safety (Yang 1993).

In the 1890s the French took control of Indochina, levying oppressive taxes on the population. The Hmong in Laos, no strangers to conflict with oppressive authorities, rebelled. In 1896, they refused to pay what they considered extortion. Armies were sent into the mountains to intimidate the Hmong, who organized a resistance force, leading to an eventual ceasefire, ordered by French authorities (Yang 1993). A second uprising, far more serious than the first, took place from 1919–1921. It was dubbed "The Madman's War," largely because the rebel leader, Pa Chay, was said to climb trees in order to "receive his military orders directly from heaven" (Fadiman 1997:17). Others bristle at this designation, claiming it makes light of a valiant attempt to resist colonial oppression (Yang 1993). The Hmong insurrection was successful enough to lead the French government to grant them special administrative status, which was essentially an official policy granting the Hmong their centuries-old wish: to be left undisturbed in the mountains with no forced participation in any world but their own. Peace prevailed only until the 1940s, when both World War II and the war in Southeast Asia would prove disastrous for the Hmong.

✦ TRADITIONAL HMONG LIFE

Traditional Economy

The majority of Hmong (roughly six million) still live in Southern China (Koltyk 1998). There are an estimated 350,000 in northern Vietnam, one quarter million in Laos, and 100,000 in northern Thailand (Ovesen 1995).

The Hmong practice slash and burn (swidden) agriculture, as part of their mobile way of life and migratory history. Fields are used until they are infertile, allowed to lie fallow, and then replanted when they have recovered. Land within two hours walk of the village is planted. When this area is no longer usable, villagers move to another mountain and begin again, leaving a landscape dotted with patches of deforestation. The average time one settled area will yield crops is six or seven years, although some fields can be urged into production for as long as fourteen.

A field (*rai*) is selected based on its proximity to the village and its slope, since steep land which has been cleared loses much of its arable soil during monsoon season. Trees are cleared and the remaining brush is burned, with the ashes spread for fertilizer. Unless the plot is very close to the village, farmers construct several small shelters at the edge of each *rai* so they need not travel to and from the village during the peak of the season. In one, the farmer can sleep; in the others, animals can be housed and crops can be stored after harvesting (Yang 1993).

Rice and corn are the most important staple food crops, supplemented by a huge array of vegetables and fruits. Cucumbers, squash, soybeans, and cabbage are the most plentiful. Tropical fruits are cultivated, and the peach, carried to Laos from China over all the years of migration, is especially prized. Nonfood crops are also important, and none more so than the opium poppy.

Opium poppy growing has a long history among the Hmong, playing a central role in their traditional economy for well over one hundred years (Yang 1993). The flower originated in the Middle East, and during the eighteenth century use of the drug derived from its flower spread throughout India, where the trade was controlled by the East India Company, through which it reached China. Profits there were tremendous, but Chinese authorities were alarmed at the consequences of the drug and mounted a campaign to discourage its use, leading to the Opium War between Britain and China in the mid-nineteenth century. It was at this time that the Hmong, driven out of their homes in southern China by the invaders who seized their land, began to cultivate opium in the limestone-rich mountain soil where it thrived. They soon became experts in the care of this difficult crop, and Hmong in China, Laos, and North Vietnam depended on the income (the majority of which they had no choice but to share with government and military officials) (Yang 1993). Opium was, in fact, their only cash crop, and one which was extraordinarily valuable. As Fadiman (1997:123) notes:

> One could hardly invent a more perfect commodity for mountain transport: easily portable, immune to spoilage, and possessing a stratospherically high value-to-weight ratio. One kilogram of opium was worth as much as half a ton of rice.

Lowland merchants (and Europeans) paid for opium with silver bars (or coins, called piasters), which constituted the Hmong definition of wealth. It was melted down for necklaces and used for bride-price. May Ying—Opium Poppy—is considered a name of unparalleled beauty and good fortune to bestow upon a daughter (Fadiman 1997). The Hmong use opium therapeutically, to relieve pain, as well as recreationally, but several studies point to its not being either a social or medical danger when used in traditional, local context (Ovesen 1995, Westermeyer 1968).

Livestock also figure importantly into Hmong traditional economy. Roosters and hens are kept by every family, and their utility goes beyond their value as food. (In fact, eggs are rarely eaten: they are far more valuable for their part in shamanic curing rituals and other ceremonies [Yang 1993]). Poultry is used ritually to retrieve the lost soul of a sick child, to seal a marriage ceremony, and at funerals, to ease the transit of a soul from this world to the next.

Pigs are also owned by every family and are valued for both their flesh and their fat, which is used in cooking. Cattle are used not for agriculture but as objects of sacrifice when asking ancestors for help. Horses are of more help in the fields, carrying baskets of rice and corn to the village from the *rais*.

The Village

Hmong houses (*tsevs*) vary based on location and climate. In Thailand and Vietnam, where villages are at lower elevations (and are thus warmer), houses are often built on stilts above the damp ground to keep them dryer and breezier (Willcox 1986). Reached by wooden steps or bamboo ladders, raised houses also provide distance from snakes and insects, while adding covered storage space. The *tsev* is framed in bamboo, lashed together and covered with grasses, straw, or woven cut bamboo. Roofs are thatched shingles. Houses in Laos, by contrast, are built directly on the ground, often of wooden planks or split bamboo. The floor is packed earth, and the roof thatched with large leaves. Laotian *tsevs* are

Hmong girl in traditional dress.

constructed with heavy support beams, the most important of which is in the center (Ovesen 1995). It is home to a domestic spirit, which guards the house: it is honored by burying the placenta of a baby boy under the floor near its base (Fadiman 1997).

In the main room of the house is the cooking hearth with altars lining one wall. There is storage space under the eaves, and some *tsevs* house a granary inside. (Others have rice and corn storage in an adjacent building.) Married couples have rooms off the center room; visitors are accommodated by sleeping platforms which jut out from the walls. Mats of rice straw are coiled into seats, and large woven baskets serve as storage. Garden plots outside the houses are fenced off with bamboo sticks to prevent hungry pigs from eating the family's produce.

The arrangement of houses in a village is never random, and often entails divination as well as practical considerations. When planning the construction of a new *tsev*, the first requirements is that it be near the *rais*, a source of water, and the houses of family members. After those features are in place, a ceremony is performed to ascertain the spiritual suitability of the location. One method is to place a small pile of uncooked rice in the proposed location of the central pillar. The rice is covered and left overnight. If it is there in the morning, unmoved, then the spirits have approved the site. Alternatively, a measured stick of wood can be positioned in the central pillar's hole. If it is longer by morning, the house may be built (Ovesen 1995). Construction is done communally, and generally takes three or four men the better part of two weeks.

✦ SOCIAL ORGANIZATION

Patrilineal Clans

The meaning of individual households and village differs for Hmong, as compared with their countries' other ethnic groups. For most of these, villages provide the most important organizing principle. The holding of ancestral land is what connects individual households and their members. For the Hmong, their migratory lifestyle and clan organization has resulted in a different set of priorities.

Ovesen (1995) describes Hmong villages as having a relative lack of cohesion as compared with those of other groups in Laos, with the focus directed more toward individual households. This is a result of two factors: the mobility demanded by a slash-and-burn economy, and patrilineal clan organization.

Different sources cite different numbers of Hmong clan divisions: some say there are twelve (Willcox 1986), most list either eighteen (Ovesen 1995) or nineteen (Yang 1993). Children are members of their father's clan (*xeem*), and despite the fact that mobility means that clans are very widely dispersed over great distances, exogamy is very strictly practiced. Clan membership takes precedence over regional or village loyalties, and this solidarity is of great importance given Hmong migratory patterns. When the head of a household decides it is time to move on, he will contact clan members in the new village, and obtain advice and sponsorship for the move. When Hmong are traveling through a village, even one in which they know no one, they may locate members of their own *xeem* and be assured of hospitality. (Ovesen [1995] points out that this practice is demonstrated in Hmong who resettle in the United States by the great importance of owning a telephone: listing ones clan name—used as a surname—in the phone book allows visitors to find their *xeem*.)

Patrilineal clans are further divided into lineages (*kwv tij*), and it is these ties which are depended upon for economic help and daily assistance. In some ways, Ovesen (1995) points out, the lineage functions as a large extended family. While in other groups, lineages may be traced back over many generations, Hmong lineages rarely are reckoned beyond three generations, meaning that the common "ancestor" may, in fact, be living in the household. Lineage members are those who help move a household, provide rice or even money during difficult times, or share land. But material assistance is often secondary to the social, emotional, and spiritual value of lineage connections. Hmong say that they are only happy when they are near their family. Ovesen (1995) notes that the spiritual importance of being close to lineage members is literal, and has practical implications: the oldest lineage member possesses crucial knowledge and authority, as well as being in charge of the family's spiritual life. Thus, when he dies, the residence of his successor dictates the new home of the rest of the family who will move to his village in order to be guided by him in their veneration of the spirits.

Each Hmong household is something of a self-contained unit. The oldest married man is generally considered the head and is the owner of all material goods, from livestock and land to the items in the house itself. As the individual responsible for the family's welfare, it is he who decides when the land is exhausted and it is time to move on. Household size varies from a married couple and their young children to units which include married children and widowed elderly family members. All members must be of the same clan, however: *xeem* spirits do not allow members of different clans to reside together.

The fact that individual households are the focus of Hmong social and economic life, and that villages engender no particular attachments, is demonstrated in the fact that the Hmong do not care to name their villages. Their identity centers on clan and lineage membership, and their villages are named by local Lao authorities. Village organization is also subject to rules set up by district rules, which mandate a village headman be elected by household heads and report in with district authorities. It is his responsibility to settle disputes over land and cattle, and minor domestic squabbles. He has no fixed term of office, remaining in his position as long as everyone is satisfied with his performance and he wishes to do so. Successful headmen rely on elders to advise him on matters ranging from maintaining peaceful interpersonal relations to judging the proper length of time the *rais* must lie fallow before replanting.

Marriage

Traditional Hmong marriages are arranged by the fathers of the bride and groom, with cross-cousin marriage the preferential form. Girls are generally married in their middle teens, boys from ages eighteen to twenty. Polygyny is permitted, though uncommon. Elopement is a permitted traditional alternative to an arranged match, regarded as performative declaration of the desire to marry. The boy and his friends would hide and "capture" the girl (with her happy participation), whose parents would come to her rescue and receive a silver piaster from the boy. Having thus announced their intentions, the fathers would initiate marital negotiations. There is no stigma attached to premarital sex among teenagers, and often pregnancy was a third route to marriage. Today, boys often send a friend with a silver coin to the girl's father, as a request for negotiations to begin. Three days after the presentation of the coin, the couple spends a three-day period at the future groom's house. This begins the girl's entry into his clan, something to which the ancestral spirits must agree. During this time, ceremonies are performed to ensure the young couple's souls do not wander off; the girl in particular is at risk for this consequence, since her incorporation into her betrothed's group is "a spiritually delicate business" (Ovesen 1995).

Once this sojourn at the boy's house is complete, the families begin to negotiate in earnest, setting a bride price and payment for the celebration. The amount spent on the wedding reflects the wealth of the families and the size of the affair. The bride price is generally fixed, by consultation between village elders and district authorities. Because bride-price reflects a woman's potential for reproduction and labor, compensation varies. A girl who has never been married demands the highest price. Women who have been widowed after less than six years of marriage demand a higher bride price than those who have been widowed following a marriage of six to ten years. Women who had been married for more than ten years bring no bride price at all. Various fines are levied around issues of pregnancy and refusal to marry (Ovesen 1995).

✦ RELIGION

While between 10 and 20 percent of the Hmong have been converted to Christianity by missionaries, the vast majority are animists, with a complex system of beliefs and practice revolving around the spirit world. Spirits (*dabs*) of various kinds are involved in every aspect of Hmong life (Nusit 1976, Vang 1984). The shaman (*txiv neeb*) is a crucial mediator between worlds.

The Spirits

The Hmong strive for equilibrium in all they do. Balance is the key to a fulfilling and valuable life. Harmony within oneself, between friends and family, between clans and lineages, and between humanity and nature is what one must strive for. It is with the spirits, whose presence is interwoven in all activities, that Hmong balance and well-being rests. As such, attention must be paid to their demands and requirements.

All spirits are caught up together in an intricate dance of life and afterlife. Ancestral spirits guide living clan members. Animal spirits are often thought of as kindred spirits, who can exchange and share souls with human beings (Conquergood 1989). Every natural feature has an animated spirit, surrounding the Hmong with trees and rivers alive in multiple ways. Conquergood (1989) describes Hmong cosmology by saying:

> The Hmong celebrate their humanity, not as a discrete and impenetrable part
> of the natural order, but as part of the circle of life of all creation—caught
> up in the rotation of the seasons, and deeply connected with the configuration
> of the mountains, and the reincarnation of life from generation to generation,
> even from species to species. Life, in its myriad forms, is intimately articulated
> through souls and spirits (pp. 45–46).

The most important categories of *dabs* are the household spirits, medicine spirits, nature spirits, and shamanic spirits (Ovesen 1995). The household spirits exert their influence before construction begins. Once their approval is obtained, they occupy several sites within the dwelling: there is a spirit of the house, a spirit of the door, a spirit of the center post, and spirits of the large and small hearth (Geddes 1976). It is the spirit of the house whose approval is sought for construction. Once the house is built, an altar to that spirit is constructed opposite the front door. At the beginning of each new year, a chicken or pig is sacrificed and its blood is applied to the altar constructed out of painted paper (Ovesen 1995). It is this spirit who is responsible for the general health and welfare of all who reside in the home. The ceremony for the spirit of the door is also one which must be performed annually, and always at night. Pork and chicken is cooked and arranged near the door. The head of the household closes the door, saying that it is his intent to feed the door spirit and keep good fortune in and ill fortune out. For the next three days, only residents of the house may enter through the door.

The ceremony for the center post of the house is performed every three years and is essential to secure the souls of the household that might wander, resulting in serious illness. As in the other ceremonies, a pig or chicken is sacrificed. These offerings to the spirits are the main impetus for raising chickens, pigs, and cattle, which are far more important as sacrificial animals than as food or draught animals (Geddes 1976).

Certain magical practitioners (*khawvkoobs*) have the ability to call forth the spirits of medicine to assist in warding off sickness. There is an altar to these spirits in most households, and herbs are required to appease them.

Outside of the household reside the spirits of nature, who prefer to live in out of the way places, sometimes preparing to ambush an unsuspecting soul. While they are not evil spirits, they do not like to be disturbed and may take revenge if they are happened upon. The Hmong's main site of vulnerability is the soul (*plig*), several of which inhabit each body, and all of which have the tendency to wander, causing illness or death. There are certain times of life when one is more vulnerable to soul loss, and special ceremonies are performed to prevent such an event or to call back the wandering soul once it has gone off. Calling back the soul (*tu plig*) is always performed for a newborn three days after birth, which is the time it takes for the body and soul to be bound up together, creating a full person (Ovesen 1995). It is performed for a bride on the third day of her married life to assure that her souls will reside in her new home, that of her husband's clan. Calling back a soul is imperative when a person falls ill, and when both household members and *khawvkoobs* are unsuccessful in this, a shaman must be summoned.

Shamans

It is in the person of the shaman through which the most deeply held beliefs of the Hmong are manifest. Through his or her healing trances, core tenets of the culture are performed and reinforced. The shamanic spirits, *dab neeb,* select their own representatives among the Hmong; it is not a matter of human choice. Most often, a person will fall ill, beset by fever and hallucinations. An experienced shaman called in to help is able to recognize that it is not merely soul loss which is causing the illness. Rather, the *dab neeb* of a deceased shaman have selected this individual to receive their gifts. After recovery, the chosen person must study with an established healer for several years, learning the identity and habits of the *dabs,* the chants and rituals to capture wandering souls, and perfecting their ability to go into trance and tremble. The shaking of the shaman, in trance, is an essential component of the healing process, and it is a dangerous and exhausting art, which puts the shaman's own soul at risk.

Language and Arts

For most of their history, Hmong tradition has been an oral tradition. It was not until the 1950s that the language was written, an activity undertaken by Western missionaries in order to promote literacy. There are several Hmong dialects, most of which are mutually intelligible. In Laos, speakers of the two main dialects are referred to as White Hmong and Blue (or sometimes Green) Hmong, a reference to the color of the women's traditional skirts. Most words in the tonal language are monosyllabic.

The fact that Hmong is a tonal language has been linked with the importance of music in everyday traditional life. (Willcox 1986) Improvisational singing and sung poetry set the pace for working in the *rais,* begin ceremonies to honor ancestral spirits, and fill leisure time. Courtship is initiated with music, and at the end of life, the soul is sent to the spirit world with a song.

The most popular musical instruments are flutes made of bamboo reeds. The *qeej,* a mouth organ, is owned by most families, and is often cited as the most beloved emblem of Hmong culture (Willcox 1986, Yang 1993). Its importance may be inferred from the fact that when faced with choosing only a few items to bring to the United States, the majority of refugee families were sure to include a *qeej* to accompany them on the "soul path from Laos, through Thailand, and finally to the United States" (Willcox 1986:31). Two-string violins and various percussive instruments are also important for celebrations and ceremonies. Several drums and rattles are the exclusive purview of shamans, played only during healing rituals or funerals.

Traditional Hmong dress is elaborate and colorful, and Hmong women are renowned textile artists. The traditional process of making clothing begins with cultivation of the plants (hemp and other woody plants). Fibers must then be spun and prepared and dyed, before they can be transformed into the cloth embroidered into breathtaking garments. The most exquisite of these cloth pieces is the *paj ntaub* ("flower cloth"), on which geometric or organic designs are embroidered, appliquéed, or batiked. The stitching is painstaking, with the most prized sewing performed in stitches so tiny they resemble minuscule beads (Fadiman 1997). Dressing for special occasions involves several layers of skirts, vests, fabric belts over twenty feet long, wound around the waist, and triangular cloth leggings. Over these are worn elaborate silver breastplates and a pagoda-shaped hat adorned in bright colors and tinkling coins. The central item is the skirt, which can take even the most skilled woman more than two years to make, but also demands up to three hours of labor simply to put it away after it is worn. The skirts may contain upwards of five hundred tiny pleats. Because it is important that they hold their shape, after wearing, each pleat is stitched in place along its length, with a single thread from waist to hem. In order not to damage the embroidery, the stitching must be very tiny. When the skirt is to be worn, the storage threads are gently eased out of the pleats; they are laboriously stitched back in place to preserve the pleating for the next wearing.

In addition to designs and scenes of nature, Hmong women have often used the skirts to tell stories, preserve traditions, and even communicate with one another. There are folktales about grandmothers finding long-lost grandsons by stitching clan signs onto the skirts and walking through the mountains, and clever women who avoided harm by elaborately embroidering snakes which looked so realistic it protected them from real snakes, who will not attack one another. During the time when Chinese authorities attempted to prevent the Hmong from speaking their own language, women were said to have devised a pictorial code which they appliquéed to the skirts, sending messages to one another and "poking fun at their oppressors" (Willcox 1986:42).

✦ WAR IN INDOCHINA

In the 1940s, the Japanese army attempted to occupy French Indochina. Because the French had paid little attention to the people of Laos except to extract punitive taxes, the Hmong began to organize themselves, and several clans emerged as the most political, competing for local administrative posts which the colonials were willing to let them fill. When the Japanese invaded, some clans aligned themselves with the French colonialists, others with the Japanese troops. The French were loath to lose the revenue they reaped from opium, and officials were sent into the mountains to encourage Hmong loyalty (and to urge the Hmong to increase their opium poppy production) (Chan 1994).

In 1945, just before the Japanese defeat, Laos declared its independence. In 1946, the French retook Laos, and several anti-French movements arose, including the radical Pathet Lao, which became aligned with communist forces in Vietnam. The French were ousted in 1956, and a series of coalition governments ran Laos until the early 1960s, when the war in Vietnam began to take its toll on Laos.

The Hmong figured prominently in this conflict because they were recruited by the CIA to be part of a secret mercenary army, trained by the Green Berets. In 1960 a CIA agent was sent into the Laotian jungle to find Vang Pao, a Hmong military leader who had previously fought against North Vietnamese forces in northern Laos. Vang Pao agreed to help the American forces repel the Communist troops, and set up a meeting with Hmong clan leaders to enlist their support. American officials promised to support the Hmong in defeat or victory, and shipments of guns, ammunition, food, and medical supplies soon began. The Hmong helped to build air bases near their villages, trusting that the American army would keep its end of the bargain.

As the Pathet Lao advanced in Laos, Vang Pao evacuated some hundred thousand Hmong from their villages, resettling them in refugee camps where, unable to rely on their usual mode of subsistence, they became dependent upon CIA supplies in order to survive (Chan 1994). Meanwhile, the Hmong secret army continued to fight for the United States, by 1969 numbering more than forty thousand troops.

Although Laos had been guaranteed neutrality in the 1962 Geneva Protocol, neither the Americans nor the Communists abided by this agreement. Americans secretly began bombing in Laos, eventually dropping over two million tons of bombs on the country in an attempt to stop the Pathet Lao. In the United States, this was referred to as the "Quiet War" (the war in Vietnam being the loud one), but it was hardly so for the Hmong, who endured one bombing raid every eight minutes for nine years (Fadiman 1997). Countless civilians were killed during these sorties, with entire Hmong villages wiped out. Estimates of the price paid by Hmong set the civilian death toll at 50,000 and the CIA-trained Hmong loss of life at 17,000 (Chan 1994). Surviving Hmong suffered as well. Parents, wives, and children of Hmong troops moved through the mountains, attempting to evade Communist forces while planting crops. It was often impossible to stay in one site long enough to harvest what they had grown, and so they were reduced to eating whatever they might find while fleeing through the jungle—leaves, bark, and when lucky, wild fruit.

In 1973 American military involvement in Southeast Asia ended with the Paris Peace Accords. Top-ranking Hmong officers were offered asylum in the United States, but the vast majority of the Hmong people were abandoned. Laos fell to the Pathet Lao, and Vang Pao asked the CIA to evacuate the rest of the Hmong, as promised, because they were seen by the new Laotian government as traitors and would surely be victims of reprisals. He was told that this was impossible; of the ten thousand Hmong who arrived at the Long Chen airbase hoping for help, only several hundred were evacuated. Confused and "stunned by the failure of the Americans to keep their promise" (Chan 1994:45) to provide aid and protection in return for their fighting, those left behind felt they had only two options: to flee into the jungles and attempt to hide from government threatened "torment and death" (Trueba 1990: xxiii) or to attempt to leave the country, on foot.

✦ Refugees and Resettlement

The Pathet Lao took over, and Hmong life was again altered beyond recognition. Those Hmong who were identified as having fought for the United States were captured and sent to "reeducation camps" where the majority died of malnutrition or cruelly hard labor (Chan 1994). Villagers found their world turned upside down by the new government regulations. Communism mandated that all farms be collective; thus, family land was consolidated and the yield was distributed by the state. Traditional slash-and-burn agriculture was outlawed, and anyone found practicing it was arrested (Fadiman 1997). Village leaders were displaced by government appointees. Clan membership, family structure, traditional social and economic relationships were all disrupted. Many Hmong were resettled in lowland areas to work on communist collectivities, and exposed to tropical diseases to which they had no immunities. Previously unencountered malaria—carried by mosquitoes which cannot live in the high altitudes of Hmong mountain villages—took a great toll.

The Pathet Lao troops that patrolled the villages brooked no disobedience. Hmong who seemed rebellious or slow to follow rules were told they needed to attend a "seminar" to learn the new ways. Those dissenters removed from the village by Pathet Lao patrols were sent to seminar camps, and rarely returned. Hones (1999:70) reports being told "if you made a big mistake you'd go to a seminar and never come back." In response, some fled to higher, more inaccessible mountains in an attempt to hide from the troops.

Hundreds of thousands of Hmong chose a different path. Beginning in the spring of 1975, Hmong who expected reprisal, were starving, and filled with terror, set out for Thailand, most on foot. Some traveled in large groups, others as small families. The trip took most travelers a month or two, but there were many whose journey to the border took them years. They inched along, traveling only at night, attempting to avoid both capture and the land mines underfoot. Babies, the elderly, and those who fell ill were carried on the backs of those who were still able to manage. Silence was imperative for survival. Fadiman (1997) was told by one refugee that her son, one month old when the family left their village, knew not a single word when they finally reached Thailand two years later, because no one had dared to talk beyond an occasional whispered direction. To prevent a baby's cry, which could alert the Pathet Lao patrols, mothers would often mix opium in water to assure a child would sleep. If the mixture was too strong, it was fatal. Such babies had to be left, without burial. Frail elders, the sick, and wounded also had to be abandoned, sometimes left with a little food or opium to ease their passing. These were excruciating sacrifices to a people who hold elders in reverence, and who believe that without a proper funeral and burial, a person's soul will wander in eternal distress. Roots and insects were often the best food available. Fadiman (1997:162) was told that when "desperate to fill their stomachs, some people chopped up their sweat-soaked clothes, mixed them with water and salt, and ate them."

The destination of this arduous trek was the Mekong River, which marks the border between Laos and Thailand. It was heavily guarded by government troops, and once there, many who had managed to survive their journey were captured. Those who arrived during monsoon season were swept away in the rushing waters as they attempted to cross, in the dark, with their few possessions— and family members—on their backs. Most mountain-dwelling Hmong could not swim. Some were able to cross in boats; others fashioned make-shift rafts out of what little bamboo was left by the riverside. Some brought empty plastic jugs to use as flotation devices; still others attempted to float by blowing up plastic grocery bags. Stories of crossing the Mekong are told and retold by those who survived the passage. Women embroidered scenes of the exodus in the panels of story cloths (*pandau*). (Hones 1999) Nightmares of the crossing haunted refugees for decades (Fadiman 1997).

Some estimates place at half the number of Hmong who survived their attempt to escape Laos; others set the number lower than that. En route they encountered Pathet Lao and Vietnamese snipers, cluster bombs and land mines, "disease, starvation, exposure, snakebite, tiger maulings, poisoning by toxic plants, and drowning" (Fadiman 1997:165).

By the late 1970s there were more than twenty refugee camps on the Thai border, housing refugees from Vietnam, Cambodia, and Laos. The largest of these was Ban Vinai, which at its fullest, held nearly 43,000, 90 percent of whom were Hmong. It became the largest Hmong settlement in the world, and its area was less than one square mile. Conditions at the camp were squalid; there was no electricity, no running water, no sewage system—and nothing to do. One former occupant explained:

> In Ban Vinai, you don't have the right to do anything except get a ration of
> rice and beans, and go to your tent, and you do that for five or ten years.
> People were born and grew up there. . . . The elderly person just sleep day

and night, they just wait and see and wait and eat and wait and die and wait and die (Fadiman 1997:166).

The Thai government was unwilling to absorb refugees into the local population. They wanted to repatriate the Hmong or have them resettled in another country. Hmong were terrified to return to Laos, but they also became terrified of the prospect of resettlement in the United States. The majority of Hmong who left Ban Vinai for other countries emigrated to America, both because of their previous association with the U.S. military, and because General Vang Pao had settled in Montana (Fadiman 1997). Those still in Ban Vinai received horrifying letters from relatives in the United Statesdescribing urban violence, crumbling tenements, unemployment, and racial prejudice. Daily life in the inner cities—the most common resettlement sites—seemed a nightmare. Despite the egregious conditions at Ban Vinai, many Hmong began to see permanent residence there as preferable to the dangers that would await them back in Laos or in the United States. This was especially true because however crowded and filthy the camp was, unlike the alternatives, it was a place in which Hmong culture was alive and celebrated. Women produced traditional embroidery, families were able to raise vegetables and small livestock, and the sounds of the *qeej* and the chanting of shamans were everywhere (Conquergood 1989, Fadiman 1997). Older Hmong were especially unwilling to leave. Fadiman (1997) cites a Hmong refugee who left Ban Vinai for California as explaining:

> At the camp, the cultural tradition was still there. There was patrilineage. Children still listened to Grandpa. What is the good to come to America if all that change? And a lot of elderly people, though they never, never say it openly to strangers, what really haunt them is they are afraid in America they will not have a good funeral ceremony and a good grave, and that is more important than any other thing in the world (p. 168).

Thailand declared Ban Vinai closed in 1992, and told the 11,500 Hmong who remained that they must choose between returning to Laos and resettling in another country. In preparation, many were periodically moved to other locations. According to Hones (1999:76), "these periodic shifts from camp to camp effectively terrorized the refugees because they could never be certain when they would be uprooted again or, worse yet, sent across the border" and back to Laos. About seven thousand did choose to return, although they were restricted to the lowlands, not permitted access to their home villages, and still prohibited from practicing slash-and-burn agriculture. They were promised that at the very least they would be safe, and there would be no more collective farms and no more "seminars." However, Fadiman (1997:169) reports that although it has been denied by the Thai and Laotian governments (as well as U.S. sources), "some Hmong have been forced to return to Laos against their will, and, once there, have been persecuted or killed." As it turned out, more than 10,000 Hmong, most from Ban Vinai, fled the camps and neither returned to Laos nor chose to leave Thailand. Rather, they fled to an area north of Bangkok, on the land of a Buddhist monastery (Fadiman 1997).

✦ Hmong in the United States

The experience of Hmong resettlement in the United States is unlike that of so many other groups who make up the fabric of the American population. Fadiman (1997) recounts one example of the "Americanization" of European immigrants, who worked at a Ford automotive plant in Dearborn, Michigan, in the early 1920s, and who were given compulsory classes in becoming American, which consisted of instruction in table manners, hygiene, and work habits. (She reports that the first English sentence they were expected to memorize was "I am a good American."):

> During their graduation ceremony they gathered next to a gigantic wooden pot, which their teachers stirred with ten-foot ladles. The students walked through a door into the pot, wearing traditional costumes from their countries of origin and singing songs in their native languages. A few minutes later, a door in the pot opened, and the students walked out again, wearing suits and ties, waving American flags, and singing "The Star-Spangled Banner" (p. 182–183).

The Hmong who fled Laos and Thailand were not searching for a new nationality. Their intent was not to climb into a giant melting pot and emerge transformed. Quite the reverse: their resolve was the same resolve they maintained in the face of Chinese attempts to force assimilation in the nineteenth century. They wanted nothing more than to resist attempts to change them; they wanted to remain Hmong. If they could have done so in Laos, they would surely have stayed in their own land. Fadiman (1997:183) quotes anthropologist Jacques Lemoine as observing that the Hmong "did not come to our countries only to save their lives, they rather came to save their selves, that is, their Hmong ethnicity." Because that is true, the Hmong faced great difficulties in their interactions with officials charged with their resettlement, as well as citizens of many of the places in which they were placed.

To avoid "burdening" communities with too many refugees, the Immigration and Naturalization Service (INS) peppered Hmong throughout the United States, rather than clustering families and clans together. This was extremely difficult for people who were unfamiliar with their new surroundings and who depended greatly on the support of their friends and especially their relatives. When clan members were kept together, they were placed as a group with no other clans in the area, rendering it nearly impossible to find marriage partners within the rubric of exogamy. Nearly all of the locations chosen for the resettlement of these people whose roots were in the mountains and who had never experienced cold weather were in flat lands with bitterly frigid winters. Chicago, Minneapolis, Detroit, and Milwaukee were chief among them, since INS refugee services were more available in these large cities. In addition to urban areas, some individual nuclear families were sent to isolated rural enclaves, which often proved disastrous. With no other Hmong to help them navigate the complex and strange new culture they encountered, there was an alarming incidence of depression, anxiety, and suicide (Fadiman 1997).

General Vang Pao had advised the American government that all they need do to ensure successful resettlement, was to allow the Hmong to be together in traditionally sized groups, on a small amount of land—even inferior land—on which they could raise vegetables and chicken. Most Hmong brought only the few precious things they could carry, and many included a hoe. This suggestion ran counter to the goal of assimilation, and was never considered. In retrospect, officials in charge of coordinating the "catastrophically mishandled" (Fadiman 1997:186) resettlement effort conceded that it had been a disaster, handled "shoddily." One said frankly "It was a kind of hell they landed into. Really, it couldn't have been done much worse" (Fadiman 1997:186).

The overwhelming task of deciphering life in America led one Hmong man to a poignant observation: "In America, we are blind because even though we have eyes, we cannot see. We are deaf because even though we have ears, we cannot hear" (Fadiman 1997:187). In Philadelphia, Chicago, and other cities, Hmong were routinely victims of theft, assault, and racial violence. For some, the solution was what had often been so in the past: moving on. In keeping with the proverb "there is always another mountain," large numbers of Hmong who were without traditional group supports in colder climes migrated to California. Of the 100,000 Hmong reported to be in the United States by the 1990 census, more than 40,000 have settled in California; Minnesota and Wisconsin each have 16,000 Hmong residents (Chan 1994).

In their so-called "secondary migrations" to warmer areas, Hmong families were financed by clan members in the United States. The original resettlement, however, had been contracted out by the federal government to private nonprofit groups, which then found local sponsors. Most of these voluntary resettlement agencies had religious affiliations, and the majority of Hmong found themselves being actively proselytized by church groups and pastors, who visited them at home and attempted to explain that an integral part of their new lives should be the embrace of Christianity. This has had serious consequences for both the Hmong, who have been converted and those who have not. The mere fact that within families there is this divide has led to a breakdown of support. Christianity cannot support many of the most central tenets of Hmong culture, chief among them animism, animal sacrifice, and shamanism. Those who have become Christians refuse to participate in important family ceremonies (the soul calling of a newborn, for example) because of the traditional elements involved. Older Hmong whose children or grandchildren have converted fear that they will not have a traditional funeral, which will result in their souls never finding rest (Ovesen 1995). Within the converted community, clan and lineage solidarity is undermined by the message that the ideal is to consider all people to be your "brothers" and treated as such (Ovesen 1995).

Chan (1994) reports that Hmong elderly in particular have suffered, especially from the social marginalization of old people in American culture. Their status as revered providers of sage advice, respected and consulted on all matters, centrally involved in settling disputes and making decisions seems lost to them. He observes:

> Unable to speak English, dependent on others to drive them places, fearful of taking public transportation in case they get lost, victimized by crime in the low-income neighborhoods where many of them live, many older Hmong may sit at home with nothing to do except watch television (p. 57).

Marginalized and despondent, they say "We have become children in this country" and ask "Where is my dignity if I cannot do anything for myself?" (Chan 1994:57.)

Secondary migration has many motivations beyond relocating to warmer climates. Seeking employment, education, job training programs, or a less hostile environment all figure prominently in families' choice to move on. None of these is as important, however, as migrating to find relatives. In Laos, the extended family household lives under one roof, or in homes that are clustered together In the United States, this family grouping (*tsev neeg*) is more scattered, with separate homes maintained, sometimes even miles apart, but functioning as a unit. Moving to facilitate this web of extended family is of crucial importance. Koltyk (1998), writing about the Hmong community in Wisconsin, reports that individual families from Kansas, Iowa, Colorado, Texas, Minnesota, and California all decided to come together in Wisconsin, to establish a series of homes near one another. Although separate houses, they are thought of as a collective *home,* such that children become accustomed to all of them, sleeping, playing, and eating in multiple residences, being cared for by many adults. Daily life centers around the activities of the sublineage. Women shop and cook together, work in one another's gardens, prepare communally for rituals and holidays, and provide childcare. Although men have dealings with Hmong men of other clans living locally, they spend most of their time with their brothers and their father's brothers' children. When asked to name their friends, Hmong cite their relatives, often to the exclusion of other Hmong who lived in neighboring apartments but who were not family. Koltyk (1998) was surprised to find that while unrelated Hmong do socialize for holidays or ritual events which involve the wider community, their overriding preference for depending only upon kin was paramount: when a young mother's baby became desperately ill and needed hospitalization, she and her husband spent several hours attempting to locate a family member to care for their other children, despite the fact that their next door neighbor was a Hmong woman with whom they attended English classes. Mutual aid organizations have been established in nearly every Hmong community, and they do provide a sense of larger community, organizing athletic leagues and providing counseling, housing information, language classes, and youth programs. While these services are used, and the language and culture classes are popular, they rarely result in extra-familial friendships outside of the classroom.

Hmong in most communities organize similarly. For example, households will almost always have freezers, but rarely washers and dryers (Koltyk 1998).

A freezer, the first major appliance saved for, has come to represent a household's ability to provide for the extended kin group. It is stocked with enough food to share at a moment's notice, serving as a resource to other households in the network, and to allow many members to come together in one place and prepare a large meal. Televisions, videocassette recorders, and videocameras are also popular, both as ways to learn about American culture, but also to view videos in the Hmong language and to record and exchange family events and rituals with lineage members at a distance. Laundromats are a popular place to socialize, and allow women to get out of the house and meet others, while still performing their domestic duties. Many laundromats with mostly Hmong clientele in California have installed VCRs, encouraging groups to watch Hmong videos together while doing their laundry (Koltyk 1998).

Health and illness are major concerns in the Hmong community, and shamans are kept busy caring for their clan members. Bowing to work and school schedules, healing ceremonies tend to be held on the weekends. Extended family members pool their resources to purchase the necessary ritual items, and convene at one home for what is usually an all-day ceremony. When a death occurs, however, a wider net is cast. The news spreads rapidly across the country and abroad, with relatives often traveling great distances to attend the funeral. Performing the requisite funeral rituals is of crucial importance, outpacing most other traditional ceremonies. The soul's passage to the afterworld is a dangerous journey, and must be carefully guided. Accomplishing this in the United States is difficult, because at every step of the ritual process, Hmong face conflict with the law. Upon death, Hmong tradition mandates washing and preparing the corpse at home, which by law must instead be performed at a funeral parlor. Drums, *qeej* playing and chants, which are performed for long hours around the body, to guide the soul on its way, must be tailored both to funeral home visitation hours and noise regulations. Just as Laotian houses are built only on a site which has been divined to be auspicious, so too must a burial place be assessed, which is often a problem for cemeteries. Perhaps the most onerous responsibility for family members, however—and the one which has the potential to cause most trouble—is animal sacrifice, which is imperative. Several cows must be sacrificed, with the meat then used as the meal for mourners. The honor bestowed by performing this ritual obligation is sometimes the greatest consolation a dying person can receive; when death is imminent, family members will inform the ill individual of the number of cows they are planning to purchase, representing their great importance to the family (Koltyk 1998).

Hmong children in the United States are often described as caught between two cultures, expected to act as interpreters of customs they are learning in school, and of a language their parents and grandparents may not know (Treuba 1990). The exclusive focus on socializing with family can lead to difficulties making friends in school. Yet they are also seen as the hope for the future, with higher education the key (Koltyk 1998). More and more, Hmong parents encourage their children to aim for college and beyond. It is clear, however, that this goal is framed neither as a way to become more American, nor as a route to individual success, but rather as a way to achieve economic security that will benefit the entire kin network. This leads to a dilemma: parents fear that their childrens' education will result in a loss of ethnic identity, and that rather than its being a vehicle to allow greater Hmong self-sufficiency and independence, it will instead lead them to reject the traditional way of life (Trueba 1990). In fact, while childrens' economic and professional successes are appreciated, "any earmarks of assimilation [are seen] as an insult and a threat" (Fadiman 1997:207). And, inevitably, children do reflect their American surroundings Fadiman (1997:207) recalls a teenager explaining, "I know how to do *paj ntaub*, but I hate sewing. My mom says, why aren't you doing *paj ntaub*? I say, Mom, this is America."

Fadiman (1997:199) reports that the Hmong are often referred to as America's "least successful refugee," owing to the fact that rates of unemployment are high. She points out, however, that it is only by an economic yardstick that they are thus measured. By other indices—rates of child abuse, crime, domestic violence, responsibility for elderly family members—they can only be admired. That the Hmong community has held on so tenaciously to their ethnic identity runs counter to the American ideal of assimilation, and is likely also used as a measure of "failure." Fadiman (1997:208) cites anthropologist George Scott as observing that in the face of the hardships they have found in the United States, Hmong have responded "by becoming *more* Hmong, rather than less so."

Balance and equilibrium are the key to a healthy Hmong life. Parents hope that by encouraging their children to pursue higher education, they will be creating strong new leaders to maintain Hmong collective identity in future generations (Koltyk 1998). Conquergood (1989:76) believes that "the capacity to hold different ways of knowing in productive tension is both possible and desirable." Perhaps the Hmong in the United States will prove him correct.

✦ FOR FURTHER DISCUSSION

History has shown both the empowerment and the violence which can ensue from ethnic pride and discrimination. As you have read, the story of the Hmong is a history of struggle, rebellion, and perseverance. Over hundreds of years, Hmong suffered persecution at the hands of many groups, while fiercely defending their ethnic heritage. Despite the ravages of war and resettlement, they continue to strive to maintain their traditions.

CHAPTER 6

THE JU/'HOANSI

Reciprocity and Sharing

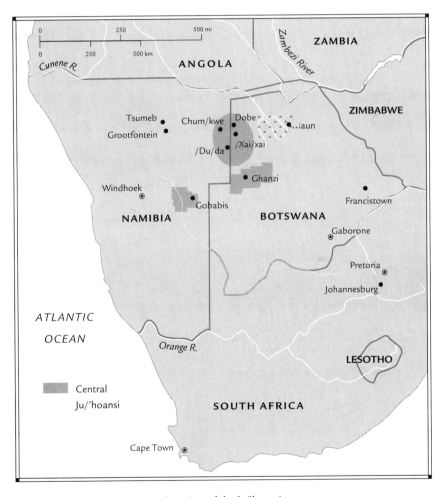

Location of the Ju/'hoansi.

✦ The Beginning

In the world there is life. Why did death come to the world?

"When the moon died, it returned to life again, to pass again across the sky. 'Everyone will do as I do,' said the moon. 'When a person has died, don't think that he will just die and lie there. . . . Take heed, follow what I, the moon, do: I die and then live again, and die again only to live again. Everyone should do as I do.'

But the hare contradicted the moon. 'No!' he said. 'A person is born and he must die also. . . .'

The moon argued with him, and said, 'Watch me. I'm going to die and then I'll come alive again. Watch me and learn, and then we can both do it.' But the hare refused. So the moon split his mouth open. The hare became the split-mouth hare that people chase.

The moon and the hare argued with each other, and harangued each other. The moon said, 'Take my advice . . . a person will die and yet return!' But the hare refused, so the moon took a hatchet and split his mouth. Then the hare scratched the moon's face! That's why you can still see marks on the moon's face, because the hare scratched it and the scratches festered. When the hare had spoiled the moon's face, the two of them separated. They spent the next day separate, and the day after that. That's how their anger rose and they fought, chopping each others' mouths and clawing each other's faces" (Biesele 1976:321–322).

✦ Introduction and History

The San are a hunting and gathering people living in southern Africa. Their nearest neighbors are a herding group, the Khoi, with whom they shared for centuries most of southern Africa west of the Eastern Cape. San are a varied people in terms of looks and language, and include people living in Angola, Botswana, Zambia, and Namibia.

In pre-colonial times, San population was estimated at up to 300,000. However, the arrival of the Dutch in the mid-1650s resulted in the near-decimation of the San people. By the 1850s, Dutch expansion and settlement caused conflict between the groups, escalating into bitter warfare. Systematic genocide of the San by the Dutch led many to fear for their survival as a people.

The group that has been studied most extensively is the Ju/'hoansi of the Dobe area, who are by now most likely the most thoroughly documented foraging society in the world (Lee 1984). The Ju/'hoansi were formerly referred to as the !Kung, but Ju/'hoansi is their preferred referent and is now widely used in accordance with their wishes. The term San is a broader appellation, used to describe a group of foraging peoples living in southern Africa and sharing language features (Lee 1993).

Hunting and gathering peoples around the world find their traditional ways of life threatened, at best, and lost, at worst. Band and tribal societies have been transformed by the "world system" (Lee 1993). However, their current ways of life are informed by all that has gone before.

The Dobe Region

The Dobe area is situated in the northwest portion of the Kalahari Desert and has been home to hunters and gatherers for thousands of years. It is a grouping of ten water holes, arranged in three sections. To the north along a dry riverbed is a peculiar outcropping of granite and limestone with a large foragable area. In the south is one major water hole with several smaller seasonal watering places scattered around it. The center region contains the Aha Hills, made up of several low ranges. This area lacks surface water and thus contains no permanent settlements. These three regions taken together span an area of about three hundred square miles.

Several hundred years ago, San developed trading relationships with peoples to the east. In the late nineteenth century Tswana cattle herders came to the Dobe during the summer rainy season to graze their cattle, hunt, and trade. Tswana relied on San as trackers and butchers, helping to transport the game back to the east when the summer rains ended. It was at about this time that European hunters too came to the Dobe region to secure furs and ivory.

Within the Dobe region currently, the largest group of non-San are the Herero peoples, pastoralists with thousands of head of cattle in their herds.

Access to water is a problem in the northern part of the Kalahari, and permanent water holes are not sufficient for the San's needs. They also depend on seasonal water holes, depressions between the dunes that fill after heavy rains. Some are small and hold water for only a few weeks; others are up to three hundred feet long, holding water for months on end. A small source of water is that which can be found in the hollow interior of some trees; in an emergency, there are roots that can be dug up and their moisture extracted. The San plan their movement around these changing sources of water, spending the rainy summer months near the seasonal water holes, and the wintertime close to the permanent sources.

Plentiful and varied game provide the San with good hunting. They can name over 250 animal species available to them in their environment. Warthog, wildebeest, giraffe, antelope, and other hooved mammals are the most abundant game. Although lions, leopards, and cheetahs are hunting in the same environment, Ju/'hoansi appear not to be fearful of them. They sleep out in the open, even without protective fires, and do not consider themselves in jeopardy.

There are also more than one hundred species of birds in the Dobe area that are hunted for food. Of particular value is the ostrich, whose shells, once the eggs are eaten, can be washed and used for water containers. Reptiles and amphibians are present too, but there are no fish. Insects, although not a part of the diet, provide poison for arrow tips.

The Ju/'hoansi divide the year into five seasons, characterized by differing patterns of rainfall. Although there is a general pattern to the precipitation—rain predominates in the hot summer months and is scarce in the winter—there is considerable yearly variation, resulting in great unpredictability. Consequently, they must be continually adaptive, prepared to accommodate high-rainfall years, low-rainfall years, and extensive variation from region to region.

Settlement

A Ju/'hoan encampment consists of grass huts arranged roughly in a circle, constructed around an area of clearing in the center. Because mobility is the hallmark of Ju/'hoan life, these huts are constructed quickly and rarely used for more than a few months at a time. Camps are located near water holes, and the conventional area that a group exploits is one that can be accomplished in a day's walk, round-trip, in any direction. The Ju/'hoansi houses reflect the season in which they are built. During the dry season, sites are located near dependable sources of water. Huts built for use during the rainy season are constructed with thickly thatched roofs to provide shelter from the punishing rains. During times of the year with less extreme weather, camp is often set up without building shelter of any kind. A fire may be built, the group will sleep, and the next day move on.

In addition to huts, other structures are erected to store belongings to keep them both out of sight and out of reach: arrow poison must not be accessible to children and dried strips of meat must be kept away from the dogs.

Characteristic of traditional camp construction was the circular arrangement of huts or sleeping position: the Ju/'hoansi faced one another. In more recent days, as cattle have become important, some encampments not only are more permanent, but also are oriented with the hut doorway facing the cattle compound, rather than another hut.

✦ SUBSISTENCE

The foraging Ju/'hoansi can provide for themselves a bountiful and varied diet. Plant foods are plentiful and nutritious and make up the majority of their diet. Women have an intricate and complex knowledge of their plant environment, distinguishing more than a hundred varieties of edible plants from those that are poisonous or otherwise undesirable. A single gathering foray can result in fifty pounds of food, easily enough for ten days' sustenance. Most important in their diet is the mongongo, a protein-rich nut found abundantly on trees near every water hole. In addition to their high nutritional value and availability, mongongo nuts are also easily stored and not often affected by seasonal or environmental variation.

A simple digging stick is the only tool required for gathering. It is sufficient for digging up roots and tubers as well as ferreting out burrowing mammals. It can also be used as a carrying pole, slung across the shoulders with the load tied on.

Transporting the food that has been gathered requires more elaboration. A large suede cape, called a kaross, provides the most useful means for carrying both food and firewood by forming a sturdy pouch close to the body. Because it is worn close to the body, it is very efficient for heavy loads. Children too are carried in the kaross, which also doubles as a blanket at night. Leather pouches, net bags, and infant slings are among the other carrying devices so important to the Ju/'hoansi, who rely on containers that can allow them ease of mobility while carrying hundreds of small food items daily.

The Ju/'hoansi follow a very specific pattern in their exploitation of the environment. Richard Lee, an ethnographer who has studied the group extensively, says bluntly, "the !Kung typically occupy a campsite for a period of weeks and eat their way out of it" (1984:44). They do this by venturing out from the campsite in increasing rings, walking further each day to find food. Gathering is done in two ways: some people stay closer to camp and gather all edibles they can; others venture farther afield looking for those things that are particularly appealing. (This leads to longer walking distances each day, as closer supplies are used up.) By pooling their resources at the end of the day, all people have not only enough, they also have a variety.

Even though hunting provides a minor portion of the Ju/'hoansi diet (roughly 30 percent), meat is nonetheless a valuable commodity. Although its scarcity may explain its value, it has been suggested (Lee 1984) that the sociability it occasions may be of even greater importance. Meat provides more than protein; it also provides social opportunity. The killing of a large animal is followed by a commensurately large feast enjoyed by all. Distribution of cooked meat is an arduous affair; it is portioned and reapportioned until everyone has received the amount deemed satisfactory.

Bows and arrows, spears, knives, and ropes are the most reliable tools for hunting. Dogs can be useful, especially in cornering prey and keeping it at bay until it can be speared. Animals need not be out in the open to be fair game. Many are pursued in their burrows by use of a special tool equipped with a hooked end for just this purpose. Older hunters with less agility rely on snares to net unsuspecting hare, guinea fowl, and small antelope.

Essential in successful hunting of this sort are refined tracking skills, possessed amply by the Ju/'hoansi. Not only can hunters tell what sort of animal has made a track, and how many have passed by; they can also determine its sex, age, health, diet, as well as speed and time of travel. For example, the placement of tracks in relation to trees indicate whether the animal was seeking shade from afternoon sun; the amount of sand or twigs in the depression of a hoofprint can indicate how long ago it was made.

✦ EGALITARIANISM

Despite the Ju/'hoansi appreciation for meat, displays of enthusiasm for a successful hunt—and successful hunter—are tempered by the importance of maintaining egalitarianism, which necessitates the avoidance of undue praise for an individual and that person's accomplishments. As Lee (1984:49–50) explains: "Insulting the meat is one of the central practices of the !Kung that serves to

Ju/'hoansi mother and child.

maintain egalitarianism. Even though some men are better hunters than others, their behavior is molded by the group to minimize the tendency toward self-praise and to channel their energies into socially beneficial activities. As a result, the existence of differences in hunting prowess does not lead to a system of Big Men in which a few talented individuals tower over the others in terms of prestige."

In a story that has become perhaps the most widely cited example of this practice, Lee tells of how he learned this lesson, after mistakenly calling attention to his own largesse, despite his best of intentions. His accurate study of the subsistence economy of the Ju/'hoansi mandated that he not interfere with their food procurement in any way. Thus, Lee gave Ju/'hoansi only tobacco and medical supplies in return for their time and talk. His own large supply of canned goods seemed, to him, a glaring inequity in the face of the Ju/'hoansi larder, which was empty by the end of the day.

As he prepared to leave the Kalahari, Lee was determined to provide, as a going-away feast, an ox of such grand proportions that it would provide at least four pounds of meat for every man, woman, and child in attendance. Satisfied that he had found such an animal, Lee was very pleased with himself indeed.

It was not long before word of the purchase began to spread, and people began to approach him for confirmation of the rumor. Lee was only too pleased to confirm that he had, in fact, purchased a large and well-known animal from a neighboring group, and was indeed planning to slaughter and serve it to the Ju/'hoansi. He waited for the delight and gratitude he felt he surely deserved, but was taken aback by the reaction with which he was met instead. One by one, individuals approached him to offer nothing but chastisement for the pitiful specimen he intended to serve. A close friend implored him to explain his stinginess: "What has happened to change your heart? That sack of guts and bones . . . will hardly feed one camp . . . Perhaps you have forgotten that we are not few, but many. Or are you too blind to tell the difference between a proper cow and an old wreck? That ox is thin to the point of death" (1979:156).

Lee was demoralized, and day after day, as the feast drew nearer, was warned that of course he must serve the beast, since it was already paid for, but not to expect much of a festive evening to follow, given the sorry offering that would surely send people home hungry. The feast came and went, and indeed the ox was fat, and served the people for two days and nights of rev-elry. But all the while the Ju/'hoansi were eating they were proclaiming their disdain for the thin, wretched ox. Realizing that he had been fooled, but not sure why, Lee pursued the matter. Finally he was told that the people had been acting in their characteristic manner, the way in which all hunters are treated despite the bounty they might bring home. An informant explained, "Yes, when a young man kills much meat he comes to think of himself as a chief or a big man, and he thinks of the rest of us as his servants or inferiors. We can't accept this. We refuse one who boasts, for someday his pride will make him kill some-body. So we always speak of his meat as worthless. This way we cool his heart and make him gentle" (1979:156).

✦ SOCIAL ORGANIZATION

"Camps" or bands are the traditional form of Ju/'hoan organization. They usu-ally contain between ten and thirty members who live and move together for the majority of the year. Although membership is flexible, it is not random. Individuals are kin to one another, and it is a core of related elders around whom the band is centered.

These older, central group members are generally thought of as the peo-ple to whom the resources "belong." However, the role of the elder is more one of guardian or host of the land and water than one who has formal own-ership since there is no individual ownership of property among the Ju/'hoansi. When an encampment is established around a water hole, the land that sur-rounds it and the bounty contained therein are owned by a kin group. Although permission must be asked of the elders in order to avail oneself of the resources, it is rarely refused. The older members of the camp or band have simply been associated with the resources longest, so it follows that theirs would be the strongest ties. Women and men who function in this capacity also provide the basis for the kinship ties that create the group. The original central members are siblings, who bring their spouses into the group. Their children and their spouses are added as the years go on, with no tradition of unilocality. Both men and women function equally as core elders of the group.

Relations among these groups are maintained in balance by reciprocal vis-iting. Acquiring rights to territories is accomplished through birth (one has rights to parents' territory) and also through marriage (through which there is claim to the spouse's territory). Additionally, visiting between siblings and in-laws acquired through one's children's marriages extend an individual's rightful territory.

Kinship

The flexibility of the Ju/'hoan living arrangement is the key to its success. Mem-bership of the group changes often. Yet flexibility must still have something beneath to give it stability. Among the Ju/'hoansi that is provided by kinship ties.

The band is, at base, a "unit of sharing," which demands peace and cooperation among its members (Lee 1984:61). It must also be balanced in terms of numbers of productive adults who can provide food and labor, and young, dependent members who cannot. Thus, the composition of the group will change as patience wears thin; it will also shift as the number of children becomes too large to support, or too small to ensure a future.

When arguments escalate to the point at which they may jeopardize the cooperation and harmony of the group, the Ju/'hoan penchant for going off and visiting kin in another group functions as a sort of "safety valve." Lee (1984) observes that it is more often the depletion of patience than the depletion of food resources in an area that causes some to move on and regroup.

The Ju/'hoan system of kinship is extremely complex, and presented quite a challenge to ethnographers attempting to understand both how people reckoned their connections to one another, and also the functions served by their associations.

All kinship relations among the Ju/'hoansi are of one of two types, either "joking" or playful relationships, or "avoidance" relationships, based on "fear" or, more accurately, respect. One's actions with a joking relative are characterized by comfort, relaxation, and familiarity. With some (for example, grandparents) there is a great display of affection. With others (such as peers, and especially those of the opposite sex) there may be an element of flirtation, and even outright bawdiness. However, with avoidance relatives, manners are refined and more aloof. The relationship between parents and children falls into this category, demonstrating the authority parents have over their children, and the respect children are expected to show their parents. Parents-in-law and children-in-law are also avoidance relatives, and it is the mother-in-law/son-in-law and father-in-law/daughter-in-law relationships that are the most severely constrained. Although custom forbids conversation between them, in practice they usually do speak to one another (Lee 1984).

One unique feature of the system is the relationships forged by special naming practices. There are very few names found among the Ju/'hoansi because children are supposed to be given names of their ancestors. Since everyone must be named for someone, many people have the same name. Ju/'hoansi have only a single name (not a "first" and "last" name), and thus rely on nicknames to identify individuals. The sharing of a name with someone else engenders a special kinship relation with that person, carrying with it a host of other connections, all based on the coincidental sharing of the same name. Thus, for example, a woman married to a man with a particular name calls any man with that name "husband." If your mother's name is the same as another person's mother, you and that person are siblings because you are children of the "same" mother.

These relationships forged by naming have a direct impact on marriage rules: one may not marry a person with the same name as one's parent or sibling. If you are a woman whose father has a common name and, in addition, have several brothers with common names as well, fully half the population may be eliminated as marriage partners solely on the basis of their names.

Marriage

Traditionally, marriages are arranged for children by their parents, who begin to contemplate their children's marriage partners soon after their babies are born. Parents whose children are betrothed to each other in early childhood may exchange gifts for ten years or more before it is time for the children to wed.

There is a rigid system of rules guiding the universe that defines an appropriate marriage partner. Incest taboos extend beyond parents and siblings to what we would term first and second cousins, as well as aunts, uncles, nieces, and nephews. Beyond these proscriptions based on ties of blood and naming, individuals belonging to the avoidance categories of kin are likewise eliminated. This severely restricts the number of potential spouses.

Once the proper kinship and name relationship has been settled, there are personal characteristics that parents also consider necessary in a marital partner for their child. Parents are especially cautious in choosing sons-in-law who must be good hunters, not given to fighting, and belong to a friendly family who enjoy participating in exchange. To this end, couples may begin their lives together in adolescence, with the chosen boy coming to live with the "bride's" family for as much as a decade, hunting for them and remaining under close scrutiny.

Ju/'hoan marriages sometimes have a stormy beginning, presumably due to the tradition of a "marriage-by-capture" ceremony in which the bride is forcibly removed from her hut and presented to her groom. Because all first marriages are arranged by parents, the couple involved have had no say in choosing a partner. Girls who are very displeased with their parents' selection may protest violently—often kicking and screaming during "capture" and running away at the conclusion of the ceremony—which can sometimes result in the dissolution of the arrangement. Even if the protests are ignored and eventually stop, Lee (1984:79) suggests that this behavior is "eloquent testimony to the independence of !Kung women from both parents and husbands." In fact, more than half of all Ju/'hoansi first marriages end in divorce. Subsequent alliances are forged by the couple's own desire to be married to one another and are generally very stable.

Relations between divorced individuals is usually quite amicable, with former partners living near one another and maintaining a cordial relationship.

Connection and Conflict

The nature of marriage in Ju/'hoan society is uniquely adapted to this highly mobile society in which broad access to resources ensures ample food, and flexible band membership can provide "escape." Marriage is the major form of alliance formation between groups of Ju/'hoansi, and friendly relationships with in-laws are crucial to survival. Given that mobility is a key feature in Ju/'hoan life, in-laws in other groups provide the assurance of another home when resources (and tempers) wear thin. A good marriage and good relations with in-laws are the best assurance of both individual and group survival. An individual will never go hungry, and the group will never be riven by conflict from which one participant cannot literally simply walk away.

Lee (1984) has pointed out that without either material wealth or the aspiration for high status to generate conflict, it is usually marriage and sexual relations that provide the stage on which both conflict and alliance are played out. In fact, there has been some speculation that the very young age at which girls were traditionally betrothed and married (sometimes as early as eight or nine) was in part to forestall conflicts arising in these two domains. Early marriage prevented rivalries among too many suitors. Moreover, if a girl were married before she became interested in courtship, it would be unlikely that she would have extramarital affairs. These conflicts are of no small significance: the most likely cause for a dispute which ends in murder is arguing between men over their affections for the same woman.

Talking and Telling Tales

Marshall (1976:351), referring to the Ju/'hoansi as "the most loquacious people," suggests that one useful strategy in maintaining peace and diffusing tensions is talking. People engage in conversation all day long and well into the night. They talk as they work, as they eat, as they gather around the fires with their children at night, as they visit with other families. Often, people who have hunted or gathered separately during the day will recount in exhaustive detail the tracks of animals, amounts of berries, abundance of certain plants. They then plan the next day's activities. Where might there be game? To whom will they give nuts?

Songs pepper the conversation and can be used as a disciplinary measure or to head off a conflict by warning an individual to correct inappropriate behavior. They compose songs specifically for this purpose, walk to the edge of the camp at night, and sing their disapproval.

In addition to the informal conversation that drives so much of Ju/'hoan daily life, there is a rich tradition of storytelling among all the San. Most of these tales are set in a long-ago past, when people were not yet real humans, but animals, and many strange things that would never happen today were commonplace.

In some places, a few individuals are expert storytellers, known for their skills and set apart from others in this talent. Among the Ju/'hoansi, however, it is old people who are storytellers—and every old person rises to the occasion. Rather than gathering children around the fire to teach them the ways of the Ju/'hoansi, elders are more content to spend time telling stories among themselves. Children listen informally; young adults do so with perhaps a little more intent. But storytelling is largely an activity "of a small group of old people getting together for some real grown-up enjoyment" (Biesele 1976:307). This is not because the older Ju/'hoansi have no other way to fill what are increasingly emptier hours: storytelling is not "something to do when you are old" (because there are few other things to do) so much as "something *that* you do when you are old" (that is, a welcomed privilege bestowed by age). (Biesele 1976:307) As one storyteller succinctly put it, "the old person who does not tell stories just does not exist" (Biesele 1993:20).

Leadership and Combat

It is clear that harmony is the linchpin to an adaptive Ju/'hoan life. The members of each band must cooperate and share within their corporate group. Marriage must establish strong and warm ties between families in different encampments so that a pattern of reciprocal visiting is established, allowing movement between bands for personal or subsistence reasons.

The apparent harmony among the Ju/'hoansi, not enforced by external authority, has been of great interest to outside observers. Richard Lee (1984) has endeavored to explain the ability of the Ju/'hoansi to establish the order and peace that come only "from the hearts and goodwill of the people themselves" (p. 87).

It seems logical to ask the question, Who is responsible for seeing that permission to hunt and gather in a territory is requested, and granted, and the balance of territorial use maintained, and disputes settled if access is denied?

Early accounts of the Ju/'hoansi suggested that there was, in fact, the familiar role of "headman" or "big man" among the Ju/'hoansi (Marshall 1976). This, in fact, is not the case. Although individuals in each group do emerge in leadership positions, these are informal and based not on an inherited right to such status, but rather owing to a modest demeanor, interpersonal skills, and successful handling of past conflicts.

Although harmony is certainly the hallmark of traditional Ju/'hoan life, conflict—sometimes fatal—does occur. Ju/'hoansi themselves describe three spheres of conflict: arguing, fighting, and deadly combat.

It is not surprising that among people who so enjoy talking and verbal jousting, arguments would ensue. Talking about food may lead to arguing about meat distribution. Talking about gifts may engender arguing about exchange. Often a conversation starts out as joking, only to escalate into something more serious as tempers flare. This culminates in a "talk," the rapid-fire hurling of insults, often sexual in nature, which may itself become a "fight."

Fighting involves two individuals, male or female, physically grappling with one another. They last only a few minutes before others pull them apart and hold them back until they calm down. Although wrestling and hitting may have occurred only moments before, after the two are separated they often joke with one another about their behavior. Matters are not always resolved so quickly, but there is ample opportunity for simply going away for a cooling-off period.

The potential for the most serious violence exists among men between the ages of twenty and fifty, who will resort to using poisoned arrows if pressed beyond their limits. The poison employed is very potent and is fatal as often as not.

Hxaro Exchange

The Ju/'hoansi effectively employ talking and joking to avert the escalation of a fight, but perhaps the most important mechanism for maintaining goodwill is the *hxaro* exchange, a system of gift giving, which not only fosters friendly relations, but also serves to circulate goods and even maintain environmental balance.

The essence of *hxaro* is exchange between individuals that is not as immediate as barter: one person gives an item to another, and in the future an item is returned. The exact nature of the item—its equivalency in value—is of lesser importance than the consistency of give and take maintained in the relationship between the people involved. In attempting to learn the rules for *hxaro*, anthropologist Lee presented an informant with a series of questions as to the acceptability of items for exchange: In return for a spear, would five strings of beads be sufficient? Four? One? His Ju/'hoan informant laughed at Lee's desperation to understand the rules, saying, "I see what your problem is! . . . you don't understand our way. One string, five strings, any return would be all right. You see, we don't trade with things, we trade with people!" (1984:98)

All Ju/'hoansi are eligible to enter into *hxaro* together with the primary pathways emanating from a husband and wife who exchange with their children, who exchange with their spouses, who then exchange with their own parents, thus solidifying bonds between families whose children have married. All manner of items are exchanged in *hxaro*, from glass beads and other craftwork to arrows, spears and knives, and even dogs. The only items restricted from *hxaro* exchange are food and people.

As visiting plays a central role in Ju/'hoan mobility and social ties, it is not surprising that *hxaro* exchange is a focal point in any visit. Not only does such gift giving extend established relationships, it can also serve as a safety valve for diffusing conflict; going off to do *hxaro* can function as a valid excuse to leave a group when involved in escalating dissension. Further, *hxaro* ties established with other groups allow Ju/'hoansi to effectively exploit the environment by relocating when food sources become scarce in one area while remaining abundant in another.

✦ RELIGION AND THE SUPERNATURAL

Gods

The Ju/'hoansi have no single explanation for the origin of life on earth. They tell stories about a time at the beginning of the world when people and animals were the same, and all lived in one village under the guidance of an elephant, sometimes thought of as the "higher God." Many of their stories about their "lesser God" portrays him as a trickster, someone who is a practical joker of grand proportion, always leading people astray and causing trouble in the village.

Ghosts

The Ju/'hoansi have successful strategies for coping with their environment and their relationships with one another. However, as in any human group, they have little or no control over natural forces. Ju/'hoansi fall ill and die; adversity of all sorts is no stranger. They have devised ways to explain and understand these circumstances, and as is often the case, their explanations transcend the forces of nature.

It is the ancestral ghosts—the *gangwasi*—who are responsible for most of the illnesses and other misfortunes that befall their living kin. *Gangwasi* wait near the villages and send their destruction. It may seem surprising that a people who, in life, live harmoniously together would attribute such evil intent to their loved ones once dead. The Ju/'hoansi explain this by saying that it is death that turns people bad. All people are good when alive. They believe, in fact, that the great affection that people feel for one another in life is what motivates their spirits to send illness and death to the loved ones they have left behind. For although the *gangwasi* have all they need—food, and clothing, and the company of other *gangwasi*—they do not have those they love the most. It is the intense longing to be reunited with their dearest kin whom they have left behind which compels the *gangwasi* to send illness and death.

Admittedly, not all *gangwasi* harbor the same degree of malevolence toward their living kin. Many Ju/'hoansi live their lives relatively free from misfortune; others seem to meet sorrow and adversity at every turn. Although this is difficult to explain, some Ju/'hoansi postulate that it is misbehavior on the part of the living that engenders the ill will of their own kin's *gangwasi*. One man suggested, ". . . we know [*gangwasi*] expect certain behavior of us. We must eat so, and act so. When you are quarrelsome and unpleasant to other people, and people are angry with you, the *gangwasi* see this and come to kill you. The *gangwasi* can judge who is right and who is wrong." (Lee 1984:107–108) Thus, avoidance of *gangwasi's* censure can also function as an effective measure of social control, acting to reinforce adherence to shared social norms.

The Ju/'hoansi are far from helpless in defending themselves against the malevolent entreaties of the *gangwasi*. They possess a wide array of magical spells and healing herbs with which to counteract the *gangwasi's* attack. The most potent item in their armamentarium, however, is *num*, the healing energy that enables indigenous healers to enter a trance, and while in this state, effect a cure.

Healing

Lee (1984) asserts that the Ju/'hoansi are not overly given to philosophizing about their gods and ghosts except at the prodding of an anthropologist. They are, however, quite concerned with the threat of illness and death and have devoted much time and energy to addressing these challenges.

To become a healer is a grand aspiration of many, and the Ju/'hoansi believe it is a status accessible to all. Nearly half the men and one-third of the woman are acknowledged as having the power to heal. Although this power is not restricted, neither is it gained without great hardship and pain. Those who are too young, or too immature are discouraged from attempting the long apprenticeship required to become a healer. The apprentice receives lessons from older, established healers who go into trance to teach the novices, rubbing their own sweat onto the pupils' healing centers—their bellies, backs, foreheads, and spines. The novices require frequent breaks, because it takes time for those less experienced to be able to manage the intense pain that is engendered by the healing power. They can only go so far; then they must rest, gather their resolve, and go on a little longer.

Healing is most often accomplished in the context of a *!kia* dance beginning at sundown and continuing through the night. These are held several times a week and are attended by all who are in the camp. Although designed to effect healing, these dances accomplish other things. They provide a unifying experience for the whole community as well as an outlet for grief, tension, hostility, and fear. *!Kia* is the "primary expression of a religious existence and a cosmological perspective" (Katz 1976:286).

The *!kia* depends on the activation of *num,* which resides in the bellies of the women and men who are healers. When they dance, in preparation for entering a trance state to effect a cure, the substance heats up and, boiling, travels up the healer's spine to explode with therapeutic power in the brain. One healer described it as "[boiling] in my belly and . . . up to my head like beer. When the women start singing and I start dancing, at first I feel quite all right. Then, in the middle, the medicine begins to rise from my stomach. After that I see all the people like small birds, the whole place will be spinning around, and that is why we run around. The trees will be circling also. You feel your blood become very hot, just like blood boiling on fire, and then you start healing" (Lee 1984:109).

Women healers have a special medicine, *gwah,* in their stomachs and kidneys. In the Drum Dance, their legs tremble and they enter the *!kia* trance state. As they dance the *gwah* travels up the spine as *num* does, lodging in the neck. To gain the *gwah* power, women chop up the root of a short shrub, boil it into a tea, and drink it. They need not do this before every Drum Dance; the power they secure from the tea consumed at the beginning of their healing career is so strong that it lasts a lifetime.

Melvin Konner (1987), a medical anthropologist who investigated the healing practices of the Ju/'hoansi before undertaking his own medical training in the United States, writes, in a compelling account of his time spent in both medical systems, of the great power in the Ju/'hoansi men's healing ritual:

> Women sit in a circle around a small fire, clapping in complex rhythms and singing in a yodeling way. Men with rattles strapped to their legs dance around in a circle behind them, always in one direction, steadily, monotonously.
> Through a combination of dance, concentration, listening to the music, and practice, some of these men enter altered states of consciousness—trances—in which healing by the laying on of hands is believed to be possible.

In these trances the men take great risks and experience great pain—especially when they are learning. Their souls may leave their bodies never to return. Injury, pain, and death are part of the expected risk of learning to heal. Physically, when in trance, they may injure themselves by running at full tilt into the pitch-dark savannah, or by pouring glowing red coals over their heads. Furthermore, the medicine itself is said to boil up in the flanks of each healer, and this effect, essential for healing power, is said to cause a pain like no other. Spiritually, they believe that their souls leave their bodies when they are in this state. As mature healers they can use this phenomenon to advantage, arguing in the spirit-world on behalf of the ill person (p. 374).

Konner (1987:373–374) writes of the *!kia* lessons, "the best insurance against the risks is the support of the community of healers. Trusting in your fellow-healers, especially your teachers, you can let go psychologically and spiritually; they will pull you away from the coals or prevent you from running into a tree; they will teach you how to turn the pain in your flanks into healing power; they will slowly bring your soul back into your body."

This seems as though it could be said of the Ju/'hoansi in more realms than healing. Lee (1984) has characterized them as a people with a sense of their own importance, a people of biting humor and, above all, the deepest regard for one another.

✦ THE JU/'HOANSI TODAY

Lee (1993) describes changes in traditional Ju/'hoansi life beginning as early as the 1970s. By now, those anticipated changes—and many others which were not foreseen—have taken hold. The people who, in 1963, had never heard of Africa, the continent on which they lived, are now thoroughly familiar with the vicissitudes of governmental control. Forty years ago, three-quarters of the Ju/'hoansi were hunter-gatherers, unfamiliar with schools, stores, clinics, and airstrips. Modern Ju/'hoansi life includes all these, and more: sedentarization, resettlement, militarization, apartheid, and a market economy have all been at work over the last several decades.

In 1965, the Ju/'hoansi of Botswana and of Namibia were cut off from one another by the construction of a fence at the border. Climbing the fence was the only way for Dobe Ju/'hoansi to continue foraging in Nyae Nyae, the Namibian land adjacent to the Dobe, as they had previously done. In the mid-1970s, the houses built around the cattle kraals came to be more permanent settlements than they had previously been. Several schools were built, and boreholes for water were established. However, severe drought toward the end of the decade led to the institution of a government-run food program, further undermining Ju/'hoansi independence (Lee 1993). The 1980s brought government restrictions on hunting. As a result, the Ju/'hoansi could not survive solely on their own foraging or herding; they had little choice but to depend on supplemental government rations. By the 1990s, Lee (1993) describes Ju/'hoansi villages as all but unrecognizable. Dwellings are no longer conical grass huts, arranged in a close circle to represent the interdependence of the people, but mud-walled houses distributed in a long line, attending more to the their property, the herds. The change in their traditional foraging diet—most significantly the reliance on refined carbohydrates and domesticated meat and dairy products—has resulted in previously unknown hypertension and heart disease. The addition of alcohol and cigarettes has greatly exacerbated the problem.

When the government shut down the food distribution programs in the 1990s, the Dobe Ju/'hoansi were ill prepared to cope. Attempts to recapture hunting skills were somewhat successful, but when the government reinstituted food distribution, they were abandoned. Lee (1993) comments that the government's changing practices left the Ju/'hoansi unable to predict what future policies might be. It became increasingly apparent that the government of Botswana was "anti-San" (Lee 1993:157). Schools forbade Ju/'hoansi children to speak their language and allowed teachers the use of corporal punishment, unheard of among the Ju/'hoansi. More ominous was a policy of displacement, with Ju/'hoansi land being sold to local ranchers.

The Namibian Ju/'hoansi in Nyae Nyae faced an even more desperate situation. In 1970, the government of Namibia established "Bushmanland," designated to be a "homeland." The result was the loss of from 70 (Marshall and Ritchie 1984) to 90 (Biesele 1990) percent of the Nyae Nyae, and with it all the resources there. One thousand Ju/'hoansi were resettled into an area which previously supported 275. Because it was impossible to survive through traditional means, the government provided rations. The resulting "enforced idleness and unaccustomed crowding" (Lee 1993:161) exacted a great price. Rising alcohol consumption, family violence, and the disruption of egalitarianism left the community in disarray. In the 1980s, further disruption was planned: government conservationists began to lobby for declaring the Nyae Nyae area a game reserve, excluding all herding, farming, and foraging activities. An additional part of the plan was to have several Ju/'hoansi "dress up in traditional clothes, dance, and sell curios to the wealthy tourists who were to flock in droves to the spectacle" (Lee 1993:162). The plan was eventually abandoned, owing not only to local protest, but also to the horror expressed by international media.

Warfare between South Africa and South West Africa drew the Ju/'hoansi in. In response to the South African's attempt to impose apartheid on Namibia, a counterinsurgency movement was mounted, and Ju/'hoansi men were recruited into the military. At its peak, the army had 700 Ju/'hoansi soldiers, resulting in the Ju/'hoansi's being "one of the most heavily militarized peoples in Africa" (Lee 1993:161).

In 1990, Namibia gained its independence from South Africa, but this proved not entirely positive for the Ju/'hoansi. The new country was poor, and the end of the war meant a loss of livelihood for the hundreds of Ju/'hoansi soldiers and their families. Moreover, the dismantling of the apartheid system led to local ethnic groups with hundreds of cattle moving into "Bushmanland"—now the Tsumkwe District—to take over the grazing land and waterholes.

The Ju/'hoansi have responded with the help of the Nyae Nyae Development Foundation of Namibia (NNDFN), a group founded by anthropologists John Marshall and Claire Ritchie in the early 1980s to help preserve Ju/'hoansi land rights. Lee (1993) reports that the initial impetus behind the NNDFN was the Ju/'hoansi themselves, who were determined to take back their traditional lands. The NNDFN helped raise funds for the Ju/'hoansi to purchase cattle and drill waterholes, under the auspices of a cooperative they organized, the Nyae Nyae Farmers' Cooperative (NNFC). Still, it is a struggle for a foraging people who were then subject to decades of colonialism to reemerge as successful pastoralists or farmers. Biesele (1990:25) cites one man as posing this poignant rhetorical question: "Why do we have to live like this? What have we done wrong? Growing up as a child I used to know the taste of meat. These days we do not even get to smell it very often."

In 1993, the Ju/'hoansi prevailed and were able expel the pastoralists who were illegally encroaching on their lands. In 1998, the Nyae Nyae Farmers' Cooperative collaborated with the government of Namibia and several NGOs to establish the Nyae Nyae Conservancy, 9000 square kilometers of communal land, over which the Ju/'hoansi have control. With help from the NNDFN, the Ju/'hoansi established 35 villages, arranged by traditional kin memberships. Tsumkwe, a town of 1000, is the administrative center and informal "capital." Participation in such an endeavor was challenging for the Ju/'hoansi: their tradition of egalitarianism led to meetings in which hundreds of people attempted to make decisions by coming to a consensus. Eventually, each community elected two representatives (with the stipulation that at least one must be a woman) to attend the meetings and speak for their constituencies (Hitchcock and Biesele 2002).

One successful program among Ju/'hoansi in Nyae Nyae is the Village Schools Project, a program which has brought community members together to create educational materials in the local language. An important feature of the project is its modeling of education on the traditional Ju/'hoansi methods of teaching and childrearing, which grow out of their core values of equality and sharing. Five Village Schools serving the thirty five Ju/'hoansi villages are structured to reflect the importance of egalitarianism and the view of children and their work as valuable, with children of all ages involved in storytelling and hands-on experience, involving both local teachers and adults from their communities. Local people, with the help of linguists and anthropologists, are writing storybooks and nonfiction readers in the Ju/'hoansi language, beginning a tradition of literacy (Hitchcock et al. 2003).

The Ju/'hoansi residing in the Nyae Nyae Conservancy are more fortunate than many other San, in that they have regained rights to some of their land and can continue some traditional practices. San in Botswana are embroiled in a land battle with the government, in a dispute that may set a precedent for other hunters and gatherers attempting to resist state control across Southern Africa and elsewhere. In 1961, the Central Kalahari Game Reserve, encompassing more than 16,000 square miles, was established to protect both the habitats and the ancestral lands of the San. In recent years, however, the Botswana government began forcing San off the reserve, and in 2002 they cut off all provisions of food, water, and health care. By 2004, nearly all twenty-five hundred San residing there had been relocated to its periphery. Government officials claim their motivation for relocating the San is to facilitate their participation as modern citizens of the state, but human rights organizations and others assert that the real issue is mineral rights: Botswana is one of the world's largest producers of diamonds, and removal of the San from their land would permit the government to begin diamond mining in the extensive reserve (Hitchcock et al. 2003). In an unprecedented move, the San have taken the matter to the courts, charging that the termination of services to the reserve and their removal from their ancestral lands are illegal.

Problems remain for the Ju/'hoansi. The Tsumkwe District West, just outside of Nyae Nyae, is a site proposed for the resettlement of more than 20,000 Angolan refugees (Hitchcock et al. 2003) and repatriation of more than 5000 Herero from Botswana has contributed to land pressure (Hitchcock and Biesele 2002). In 2002, hunger was a problem in Nyae Nyae. The government's distribution of corn meal to Namibian Ju/'hoansi in 2003 has helped, but additional foods and other goods (such as oil) are needed (Hitchcock et al. 2003).

Among the most serious challenges to the Ju/'hoansi are alcohol use and the introduction of HIV/AIDS, both of which involve the town of Tsumkwe, the administrative center of the Nyae Nyae that contains shops, the police station, a clinic, and a hotel. Traditionally, the San produced alcohol by fermenting fruit and honey. This was done mostly for ceremonial occasions, in part because prior to the drilling of wells and boreholes, lack of fresh water limited the amount of alcohol that could be produced (Gujadhur 2000). With settlement and the coming of stores, the ability to purchase sugar gave rise to a new commodity, a locally brewed beer made from sugar and berries. Ju/'hoansi women buy sugar, brew beer, and sell it by the cup at local bars called shebeens. Shebeens located in Tsumkwe are frequented by outsiders—men working on road crews, state workers, traders—who seek out liaisons with Ju/'hoansi women.

Anthropologists Richard Lee and Ida Susser have been assessing HIV/AIDS among the San for nearly a decade. Botswana is the nation with the highest rate of HIV/AIDS in the world; Namibia is fifth. This places the San, ninety percent of whom reside in these two nations, at the epicenter of the epidemic (Lee and Susser 2003). Lee and Susser point out two opposing factors salient to San exposure: those who live in remote areas with little access to outside populations ought to be protected; however, poverty and low social status add to their vulnerability. Estimates of Ju/'hoansi seropositivity show the emergence of 50 to 100 cases, or a rate of roughly 3 to 6 percent. Given that Botswana has an overall seropositive rate of 38 percent and Namibia 23 percent, the Ju/'hoansi are clearly far less affected than the general population. In seeking an explanation, Lee and Susser feel isolation is not the sole factor, especially with the advent, in recent years, of male traders, civil servants, soldiers, and tourism workers with whom San women come into contact, especially at the shebeens. They point instead to a central feature of Ju/'hoansi life: gender equality. After speaking with women of several local ethnic groups, they recognized that Ju/'hoan women and girls expressed a sense of autonomy, empowerment, and confidence in their abilities to negotiate sexual situations that was absent in other informants. They felt entitled and open about making sexual decisions, and seemed unaffected by the peer pressure to engage in unsafe sex expressed by young women in neighboring communities. Interviews with Ju/'hoansi men yielded support for the women's assertions. They confirmed women's power to rebuff sexual advances, adding that a woman's willingness to engage in sexual activities provided the occasion to propose marriage.

Tsumkwe was seen as a far more dangerous place than the surrounding villages. Teenage girls reported being told that sleeping with men there would put them in danger, acknowledging that some among them were taking risks. Lee and Susser point out that the attitudes held by Ju/'hoansi men were not shared by the outsiders frequenting the shebeens at Tsumkwe, and their most recent work indicates that it is likely those men, with money to spend and less regard for women's autonomy, who were placing Ju/'hoansi women at risk. They caution that without intervention, rising HIV rates among the Ju/'hoansi are inevitable.

In 1994, Richard Lee observed:

> The Ju/'hoansi are enduring but not unchanging; they are adapting to the world system as fast as they can. Their newfound political and technical skills augment a formidable array of knowledge and practices inherited from their foremothers and forefathers: their language, kinship and naming systems, rituals and mythology, subsistence practices, and above all, their ironic sensibility are the firm bases on which they are constructing their future (p. 174).

He went on to note that the modern-day Dobe Ju/'hoansi commitment to a system based on reciprocity and egalitarianism remains unwavering. Underpinning whatever changes may come to pass is the belief that all Ju/'hoansi are entitled to life's necessities, simply because they are Ju/'hoansi. While social leveling mechanisms limit the accumulation of wealth and power, the belief that no one should be denied the basics of food, care, and community ensure that no one falls below an acceptable standard. He was hopeful that what the future holds for the Ju/'hoansi is a life within which the interests of the modern world system and the communal mode of production and management may work in concert. In 2000, Grant McCall found that the introduction of a cash economy created strains between traditional egalitarianism and capitalism, between sharing and capitalist accumulation, between the unencumbered open reciprocity of foragers and the sort of exchange that demands something in return. However, he also reports that despite smaller *hxaro* networks, traditional gift exchange is still a central feature of Ju/'hoansi life, forging ties within and between people of different villages. In fact, half of all possessions had been received as *hxaro* gifts. He reminds us that hunting and gathering serve as more than food-getting strategies; they also facilitate the egalitarianism and collectivism that typify social relations. He found that nearly 70 percent of meals involved shared food.

Once numbering in the millions, there are roughly one-hundred thousand San left in southern Africa. In a 2003 report to the Committee for Human Rights of the American Anthropological Association, Robert Hitchcock, Megan Biesele, and Richard Lee, three anthropologists long associated with the Ju/'hoansi, report that these one-hundred thousand San experience disparate social, economic, and political constraints. Some are able to continue hunting and gathering at least part of the time; most others are poorly paid wage laborers for African farmers. They wrote:

> While many San continue to experience injustice and cultural loss, this is tempered by success stories, examples of political mobilization, and a new spirit of community resistance. It is a tribute to San resilience and cultural strength that they have overcome many obstacles in an effort to retain their languages, cultures, and religious beliefs even if circumstances have forced them to give up their mobility and foraging systems (Hitchcock et al. 2003).

✦ FOR FURTHER DISCUSSION

Hunting and gathering societies find their ways of life threatened. People who two or three decades ago maintained traditional lifestyles, now find themselves fully drawn into the market economy, affected not only by institutions such as schools and hospitals, but also by militarization, civil war, sedentarization, resettlement, and governmental control. The Ju/'hoansi tradition is that of egalitarianism and reciprocity. Richard Lee reports that the Dobe Ju/'hoansi still hold these values above all else. Do you think they will be able to integrate their belief that no one should be denied the basic necessities of life with the demands of their modern situation? Why?/Why not?

CHAPTER 7

THE KALULI

Story, Song, and Ceremony

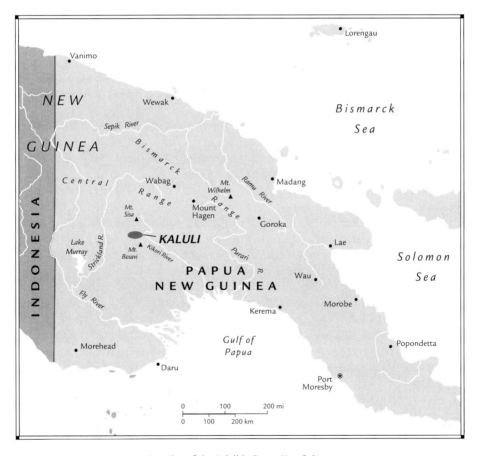

Location of the Kaluli in Papua New Guinea.

✦ THE BEGINNING

"When the land came into form" there were no trees, there were no animals, there were no streams, there was no food. But there were people. People covered the earth. The people had no food, and so they were hungry. They had no homes, so they were cold. One stood up and gathered all the people together. He told one group to be trees, and they became trees. He told one group to be fish, and they became fish. He told one group to be banana, one sago and, finally all the plants and animals, rivers and hills, were there. The few who were left became the human beings (Schieffelin 1976).

✦ INTRODUCTION AND HISTORY

The Kaluli live in the tropical rainforest in the Southern Highlands Province of Papua New Guinea on the Great Papuan Plateau. They are the most numerous of four related horticultural groups who collectively call themselves Bosavi kalu, "people of Bosavi." The addition of the suffix -li (real) makes the meaning of Kaluli "real people."

The Bosavi people, whose number has been approximated from twelve hundred to two thousand, live in about twenty longhouse communities built on ridges throughout the dense forest. Each community is about an hour's walk from the next, and the vegetation is nearly unbroken between them.

Although there are signs suggesting that the Kaluli are perhaps more closely related to lowland groups than to their closer neighbors in the New Guinea highlands, Bosavi tell no stories of their people coming to their present land from somewhere else. Their mythology tells that they have always lived on the plateau. Over the past several generations they have been slowly moving eastward into unsettled, more heavily forested terrain. This movement may be a search for better gardening lands, an attempt to escape enemies, or flight from epidemics with which they have had to contend.

Kaluli traded extensively with friendly neighbors, but it was in the middle 1930s that the first Europeans visited the Great Papuan Plateau, bringing trade goods that had never been encountered. Chief among these were steel axes and knives, mirrors, beads, and pearl shells. World War II intervened, and European contact was broken until the 1950s. Between these two times, however, disaster struck the plateau in the form of measles and influenza epidemics. The populations of several groups were decimated, with the loss of lives ranging from 30 percent to, in some places, 70 percent of the population. The Kaluli lost fully one-quarter of their population. This threat is ongoing; despite public health programs, infant mortality is high and influenza epidemics still sweep the lowlands annually, resulting in a slowly declining population rate.

In the 1960s and 1970s the impact of evangelical Christianity could be seen in Kaluli communities. Schieffelin (1976) reports that earlier attempts by Seventh Day Adventist missionaries were unsuccessful. When it was learned that this religion forbade eating pork, it was concluded that the minister was crazy and he was forced to abandon his mission.

The Life of the Land

It is significant that longhouse identity is associated more with the land on which it sits than the clan affiliation of the people within. The name of a community's land becomes an integral part of their identity, and it is invoked in both friendly and hostile interactions. It is used much like a name in friendly socializing; in war these place names served other purposes. Enemies on the attack were on unfamiliar turf, with no knowledge of which ridges and trails might be well suited for defenders to hide behind in ambush. As they raced into battle, those defending their home territory hurled names of landmarks like weapons; these were met with the frantic cries of the enemies' own territorial names. Those that identified places of past victories were particularly powerful. Such a display was effective because it took advantage of the fright assumed to be felt by parties who were on strange land, who were someplace they didn't belong.

In both uses of place names—to identify themselves in friendly conversation and to verbally attack their enemies in battle—Kaluli are demonstrating how much their land is part of themselves. Edward Schieffelin, an anthropologist who has spent much time with the Kaluli, says it was explained to him this way: "When a man lives somewhere for a long time . . . his name is in the ground just like you put your name in that book" (1976:44). Often as he walked through the forest with informants, a Kaluli would point to a faintly discernible spot where the trees were thinner and remark that he had lived there as a small boy. A patch of weeds or remnant of a wooden post would be identified, with the individual remarking casually on whose garden or house it had been. Schieffelin came to understand that these places held for the Kaluli the content of their past; they call themselves by their places because they see themselves in their land.

The Kaluli traditionally marked time in a predominantly seasonal way. Their terms for seasonal change and the progression of time are not based on changes in weather, however, or phases of the moon, but rather are based on changes in forest vegetation. These changes are further demarcated by changes in the bird population. The appearance of a particular bird during the month of April hearkens the onset of a time that lasts through September, and is often heralded by enthusiastic cries that the season is "really here: we heard *bili*," the bird that appears at this time, a comment sounding much like our "first robin of spring." Days, too, are apportioned by the birds—the morning calls of one awaken the children; the late-afternoon sounds of another alert people to come sit together for their meal. Not only time, but also space may be demarcated by birds. Their eating or nesting places may be used to describe portions of villages or trails, or to indicate direction.

✦ SETTLEMENTS

The patrilocal village is made up of men belonging to the lineages of several patrilineal clans, along with their wives, children, and other female relatives. Relationships between villages are maintained by ties of marriage and matrilineal affiliation.

Each Kaluli community is structured with one longhouse and several smaller houses centered around a clearing. The longhouse is the main residence; smaller houses function more as temporary shelters for families from the longhouse who live nearer the gardens when it is time to harvest. A large longhouse may be sixty by thirty feet, with porches built onto either end. The entire structure is built up off the ground from five to twelve feet, and supported by poles. This elevation provides the best vantage point from which to see enemy raiders. Surrounding forests are cut down to enhance visibility, and the cavernous space left beneath the longhouse is inhabited by domesticated pigs, whose noise at the approach of strangers makes them effective "watchdogs."

The interior of the longhouse is divided in half by a hall running down its length. On either side are the men's sleeping platforms, made of bark and raised a foot or so off the floor. Near each is a firebox used for curing meat, and piles of firewood and smoked game are heaped near them. Other foods and possessions are hung by strings from the rafters, to keep them out of the reach of rats. Women, children, and piglets not yet consigned to the space beneath the longhouse sleep in closer quarters in passageways running down the sides of the house. Elderly men and unmarried youths occupy one corner of these, and older women of prestige, along with unmarried girls, share a section of the women's area.

Individual fireboxes are used for smaller, solitary meals or "snacks," but the longhouse functions as much as a town hall as it does a residence. When there are important matters to discuss, visitors to entertain, or important ceremonial occasions, the community fireboxes in the central hallway are the focal point. In all, about fifteen families, usually totaling about sixty people, reside in each longhouse. It is the longhouse community, more so than any other tie, that engenders feelings of loyalty in the Kaluli. People usually refer to themselves by the location of their longhouse rather than that of their clan. The residents build their house and plant their gardens together. They hunt and fish, sing and cook, in unison. When a youth is to be married, most longhouse residents contribute to the bride-price; when a gift of meat is received, it is shared with co-residents.

Although it may seem as if living in the longhouse would be cramped and might engender squabbling, this is usually not the case because families are often absent from the longhouse for weeks at a time. Small houses near garden sites, although certainly temporary shelters, are used often in two- and three-week blocks. At times when their own gardens are less demanding, families may travel to other longhouse communities to assist clan members with their own planting and gardening. In addition to local travel and gardening chores, hunting and trading expeditions take Kaluli away from the longhouses for extended periods of time. Old longhouses give way to new ones when gardens become exhausted. After two or three years of use, longhouses fall into disrepair, and the residents plant new gardens and construct a new longhouse. Often the old structure is used less and less, as the garden fails, until finally it is abandoned and the new structure becomes permanent.

✦ Economic and Political Organization

In several ways, Kaluli society stands in great contrast to other groups in the New Guinea highlands.

Both politically and economically, Kaluli society is highly egalitarian. There are no formal positions of leadership, and also no role of "big man," the wealthy individual who rises to an informal position of great influence found so widely among other highland groups.

Absent, too, is the highland pattern of elaborate exchange for personal wealth. Whether exchange be formal and ceremonial or in the context of everyday activity, Kaluli do not use it as an occasion for enhancing status. Exchanges generally engaged in elsewhere in the region revolve primarily around life-cycle events and political activity. The most significant occasion of formal exchange in Kaluli society is marriage.

Subsistence Activities

The Kaluli are intimately familiar with the land they garden. Trees, hills, and streams are all referred to by their own names. Not only forest growth, but also inhabitants and travelers are recognizable; Kaluli can identify the footprints not only of one another, but also of individual pigs.

Kaluli practice swidden horticulture in extensive gardens and have a rich and varied diet. Their daily staple food is sago, a starch that they extract from wild sago palms that grow along streams a short walk from each village. Bananas, pandanus, breadfruit, sugarcane, sweet potatoes, and green vegetables from their gardens supplement the sago eaten at every meal. Most of the daily protein is gathered casually, by scooping up a small crayfish from underneath a rock, or dipping a hand into a brook for a small fish. Small rodents or lizards darting across a Kaluli's path will be stabbed with a stick or summarily stamped underfoot.

There are fish in abundance in numerous rivers and streams throughout the area, and small game is easily come by in surrounding forests. The Kaluli may venture on several-day trips to unsettled forests where game is more abundant, but usually these treks are reserved for times when larger amounts of game are needed for an exchange. A small number of domestic pigs are kept. Forest foods are in dependable supply, particularly owing to the low population density.

Trade and Manufacture

Kaluli trade both with other groups and within their own community of Kaluli. While they have the most long-standing trade relationships with people to the north, trade has been more recently established with those living in the east. Each of several important trade routes was characterized by its own specific items. From the people in the west they secured hornbill beaks and strings of dogs' teeth; from the south came tree oil. To these items they added their own net bags, and traded all of these to the highland Huli. In return, the Huli provided salt, tobacco, and aprons woven from net.

Trade between longhouse groups was active, and relationships between the longhouses were forged by chains of marital alliances. These marriage ties and trading relations afforded the opportunity to travel between communities with hospitality assured, as well as provide allies when needed for conflict resolution.

Kaluli manufacture tools for gardening, stone adzes, bows from palm trees, and net bags. The forest provides materials for constructing longhouses and fences. The most elaborate items of manufacture are the extravagant costumes created for important ceremonial occasions.

Division of Labor

Although the everyday activities of men and women are separate, and male and female gender roles are clearly differentiated, there is among the Kaluli none of the hostility between men and women often reported in the New Guinea highlands. Daily activities of labor and socialization are cooperative, and men and women are more complementary than competitive.

Women tend the gardens, look after the pigs, hunt small forest game, and gather other small protein sources. They are responsible for processing the staple starch, sago. It is to women that the important task of socializing the children is primarily entrusted.

Men often organize their labor as group activity, drawing on their networks of reciprocity and obligation to accomplish the strenuous tasks of cutting down and dividing trees, clearing large garden plots, building dams and fences, and planting.

Kaluli men.

Conflict and Control

Given that there is no formal system of control in the absence of a leader with the authority to enforce rules and exact punishment, such control is left to methods of informal sanction. Usually this is accomplished through gossip or ostracism. A person who has strayed outside the boundaries of personal or social parameters may be confronted by the injured parties and asked for compensation. Strong beliefs in the power of the supernatural to redress violations of taboos function as effective deterrents to misbehavior. In the past, the anticipation of enemy raids as retaliation was quite effective too, put in recent years this activity has been disallowed by the government. Schieffelin (1976) reports that rather than feeling resentment toward this official outside interference, most Kaluli are instead relieved that the danger inherent in the old days of retaliatory murder is gone.

The usual causes of conflict among the Kaluli are theft and death. It is the latter that, before government sanction, gave rise to intense violence. Deaths are believed to result from witchcraft; it was the offending witch who was the object of the counterattack. Witches are still held accountable for their actions, but are not routed out of their longhouses and clubbed to death. Compensation of another sort is requested, although without formal sanctions in place such payment cannot be assured.

✦ SOCIAL ORGANIZATION

Kinship and Descent

Kaluli are organized into exogamous, patrilineal clans that are scattered throughout all the longhouse communities. In any single longhouse there reside the localized lineages of two or more clans. Even though clan membership is conferred through the male line, each Kaluli individual claims kinship to both mother's and father's groups. Paternal kin provide those ties within the residential longhouse; maternal ties connect an individual to relatives living in other longhouses. The group of individuals to whom one feels closest—those with whom one has grown up, or sees most often—take food from each other's gardens, and share food in return. More distant kin (with distance in this case being two or more generations away) are lumped together with the same term "grandparent" or "grandchild") used to refer to people who are no relation at all.

The most important tie in establishing relationships, however, is that of sibship. Siblings, among the Kaluli, are those who are one's actual siblings as well as parallel cousins (mother's sister's children and father's brother's children).

Marriage

The preferred Kaluli marriage is one in which the man and woman belong to different clans, and refer to one another with the term reserved for distant kin and unrelated individuals.

Arrangements for marriage are instigated by the elders in the groom's longhouse, often quite without his knowledge. A woman is selected and the bridewealth collected, all unbeknownst to the couple. Schieffelin (1976) remarks that by the time arrangements are nearing completion, the groom is often the last to know, and his closest friends delight in being the ones to shock him with the news.

Marriage sets in motion a life-long relationship of exchange. A formal relationship is begun with the collection and bestowal of bridewealth. Friends and relatives of the groom contribute goods, thereby solidifying their previous relationship with the groom and establishing a new one with the bride. This relationship involves the usual extension of food and hospitality that one might ordinarily expect from kin; but it further binds the contributors to the ongoing state of the couple's marriage. If the wife should die as a result of witchcraft, a bridewealth contributor seeks revenge. Should a woman commit adultery, he supports the husband in his dispute. In the event of the husband's death, contributors "officially" have the right to give their opinion on the fate of the children, but this option is rarely exercised. The relationship comes full circle when the friends and kin who contributed to the original bridewealth receive part of the bridewealth of the couple's daughters, commensurate to that which they contributed long ago.

The compensation inherent in bridewealth is both in recognition of the nurturance provided by her family as she grew, and also for loss: loss of the daughter they love, who will go away with her husband, and loss of her important contributions to the economy of their own longhouse. Especially affected are the girl's unmarried brothers, for whom she has labored domestically, much in the way a wife would. Although the ideal compensation is the groom's donation of a sister to the bride's family, such so-called "sister exchange" doesn't occur with great frequency. Another function of bridewealth payment is to describe the universe of in-laws as those who have received part of the payment.

✦ SOCIALIZATION

The socialization of children in Kaluli society has been elegantly described by Bambi Schieffelin (1990), a linguistic anthropologist who weaves the general socialization of children together with the teaching of language.

Girls and Boys

One of the first social lessons children learn is the appropriate content of their sex roles. Because it is the mother who interacts most intensively with her children, the task of emphasizing the child's sex, taken up in the first days of life, falls to her. Whether she and the child are alone or surrounded by others, she calls attention to the child's sex by the way she structures the content of her conversation and interaction.

Sons are told how strong they will one day be. Mothers structure games and other activities that employ aggression and assertive behavior. Boys are expressly taught that they will get what they want if they are endlessly demanding and never give up their pursuit. They are taught to beg, to wheedle, and even to have vigorous tantrums until their needs are finally met. They are expected to perfect the talents to ensure both their behavior and their wishes will be attended to.

Daughters are taught something very different. Although all young children are recognized to be naturally "helpless," girls are not permitted to maintain this pose for very long. Unlike boys, who are endlessly needy and always on the receiving end, girls are assigned chores to do as soon as they are physically coordinated enough to begin to manage them. Their activities are those that are designed to serve others; daily they fetch firewood, carry water, weed gardens. In addition to this sort of labor, their nurturing skills are an important focus of girls' socialization. As soon as a new baby is born, a little girl becomes an older sister, which is a role of extreme importance in Kaluli life. She already knows that her own wants are secondary to those of others; when her mother presents her with a new sibling, this lesson is intensified. (In fact, so special is the relationship of an older sister to her younger brother, that in order to facilitate his integration into the community, Steven Feld, an anthropologist studying Bosavi music, was introduced to the community by Schieffelin as her younger brother. The Kaluli welcomed him warmly as her sibling.)

As will be elaborated later, sharing plays a critical role in Bosavi social life. For any Kaluli to say, "I have none" is such a basic strategy that it is a named kind of talk (*gesema*, "make one feel sorrow or pity") and usually results in the receipt of whatever goods were lacking. Saying this conveys to the potential donor, "You have something I don't; I want it, and have rightful claim to it; you must give me some, while feeling sorry I have none." This basic mode of expression is elaborated in a boy's relationship with his older sister, as he is taught explicitly the proper whining and begging appeal with which to approach her.

"Hardening" Language and Behavior

It is recognized that all children—not just boys—are naturally dependent when they are small. Children, it seems, are always hungry; they beg and whine for food endlessly. Adults feel pity at such plaintive appeals and children are never denied.

But children cannot continue indefinitely in this vein. They are thought to beg and whine "naturally;" they must learn other important forms of communication socially. This they learn through lessons in language.

Reciprocity and sharing are the anchors of Kaluli life, and it is important that children learn to participate in a variety of important social exchanges. It is through learning appropriate language that children become participants in all varieties of social exchange. Although they may start out as helpless, by the time they are three years old, children are expected to be able to be join in reciprocity—to be able to give as well as receive, and to ask and offer with the proper words.

Babies are thought of as "soft." They are unable to understand what is said around them, they have no control over their bodies' movements or functions; they are loose and "floppy." Children's early physical and mental development parallel one another; both are conceptualized as "firming up." They must not only become more physically sturdy and socially assertive, but must also "firm up" their language and be taught to be articulate members of their speech community. The process of a child's mind and body maturing together is called "hardening." When Schieffelin, raising her own small child among the Kaluli, asked for some indicators that such a process was in fact taking place, she was told that sometimes one can count a child's teeth as a marker of developmental stage; teeth allow for more exact speech.

"Hardening" of children puts them in control of themselves and others. Mothers actively guide their children in language use that will "harden" them. They tell their toddlers what to say and how to say it in "hard" language. Asking for something in the child's "natural" language of whining and cajoling must be supplanted by the hard way of asking for what one needs. This is important preparation for a life based on sharing and exchange. Once a child can use "hard" language to ask, then others may do the same and ask the child to share with them. Thus, a child can be drawn into the important activity of sharing with others in the household. The aim of socialization, therefore, is not only to "harden" them physically and mentally; once they have been "hardened" linguistically, they can be responsible members of the community.

The qualities of "hard" and "soft" are ones that go beyond the realm of childhood development. The world was once a "soft" place, until the mud was stamped on and made hard. A "hard" man is one who is strong and outspoken—who possesses the skill of using "hard" language.

In song and ceremony, key elements of Kaluli culture, a successful performance is one that brings the audience to tears. To have this facility in singing and composition is to "harden" the song, and only a "hardened" performance is a skillful one.

"Soft" things are likened to weakness and decay. Things that are "soft" can in fact be dangerous, in that they can impede the process of hardening. Children (thought to be themselves "soft") must never eat eggs, which are mushy, or any foods that are yellow, a color that symbolizes frailty and spoilage. They must also avoid the meat of birds whose high-pitched calls are "soft."

✦ THE GIVING AND SHARING OF FOOD

The *Muni* Bird

A girl and her younger brother set off to a stream together to catch crayfish; while the girl was soon successful, her brother had made no catch. He whined to his sister, "I have no crayfish," but her reply was that he could not have hers, as it was for their mother. Soon she caught a second but her brother still had none, and again whined for hers (and was again refused: it was for father). Upon her third catch her younger brother begged for the crayfish, only to be told it was for their older brother. Shortly after, the young boy caught a tiny shrimp, whose shell he placed on his nose, turning it bright red. As he looked at his hands, which held the meat of the shrimp, they became red wings. His older sister, frightened at her brother's transformation into a bird, begged him not to fly away. His reply was only the high, mournful cry of the *muni* bird he had become, as he flew off. Weeping, his sister called to him to take the crayfish she had caught, take them all, eat them all, but his song only continued; crying, he sang that he had no sister and he was hungry (Feld 1990).

The giving and sharing of food is perhaps the most fundamental theme in Kaluli interpersonal relations. It promotes friendship and familiarity; it is a vehicle for showing fondness.

Food is an avocation, an interest beyond mere survival. At times when he has no chores that need accomplishing, a man will stroll to his gardens to check the growth of his fruits, or make some other observation about the gathering of grubs or other food preparation.

Food is one of the primary ways of relating to children. They can be calmed, made unafraid of new faces, and shown affection all by the offer of food. Even as little as a day after their birth, Kaluli babies will be taken to the forest for several days' fishing and grub gathering. Newborns will be fed these gathered treats to make them strong, as well as to welcome them into this world and urge them not to return to the place from which they came. Such sharing of food with a baby allows a child's father and other family members to forge the crucial bond made by feeding which would otherwise be exclusive to the baby and breast-feeding mother.

This sets in motion the lifelong Kaluli pattern of sharing food as a form of sharing affection. A small piece of meat or portion of salt is an unequivocal declaration of feeling from one unmarried adolescent to another, and the exclamation, "He gave me pork!" is a heartfelt expression of the depth of loss felt after the death of a friend (Schieffelin 1976:48).

Sharing of food is the expected norm. When one family within the longhouse cooks, it is understood that all who are hungry will have some. Likewise, when one is in need of extra shoots to plant in a garden, or food at mealtime, it is expected that one will be provided for. This is especially true when the food in question is a delicacy, such as game meat.

At times when food is not, or cannot be, shared, Kaluli manners dictate that it should be consumed discretely. Even if there is no greedy intent, excluded individuals are to be sheltered from any offense this might engender. For example, men eating fish of a kind taboo to their wives and children will be considerate enough to do so out of the sight of their families.

Anthropologist Edward Schieffelin, at the beginning of his years among the Kaluli, found that when he could enlist no aid from individuals for even double the expected wages, he could entice them to help for a cup of rice or a tin of meat. He reminds us that this interest in food does not derive from the lack of it. The importance of food is found in its use as a focus of social relations. Schieffelin (1976) explains:

> I became aware of this as soon as I entered a longhouse on the plateau for the first time. I sat down wearily on the edge of the men's sleeping platform and was pulling leeches out of my socks when a man approached with a blackened, loaf-shaped packet in his hand. He broke off a piece and handed me a chalky-looking substance covered with grayish, rubbery skin. There was a pause while the people of the longhouse watched to see what I would do. Reluctantly, I took a bite. The flavor was strongly reminiscent of plaster of paris. *"Nafa?"* ("Good?") asked one of my hosts hopefully, using one of the few Kaluli words I knew at the time. *"Nafa,"* I answered when I could get some saliva back in my mouth. "Ah," said my host, looking around to the others. They relaxed. Having eaten sago, I was established as a fellow creature (p. 47).

Kaluli do not share food because of the obligations of a relationship as much as to solidify and actualize the relationship through the giving of food. As Schieffelin (1976:63) explains, "it is through giving and sharing food that the relationship becomes socially real." In fact, the true definition of a mother, for the Kaluli, is less the woman who gives birth to a child as the one who feeds a child. By extension, if a woman feeds a child over some period of time her children "become" that child's siblings.

In the myth of the boy who became a *muni* bird, told on pages 126–127, we can identify several of what have now become familiar Kaluli themes—the sharing of food, the responsibility of a sister to her brother, the opposing postures of pleading boys and nurturing girls, and birds and their sad sounds.

A young boy, plaintive and whining in an appropriate manner, asks his older sister for what among the Kaluli should be his due; denying a child food is unthinkable. For an older sister to deny food, three times, to her younger brother runs counter to the most basic Kaluli social norms. As the younger brother is denied food by his older sister, he ceases to be her brother; even more—he is, in fact, no longer a person at all.

Birth and death, illness and health, mourning and joy all have mandates and taboos revolving around foodstuffs. The reason given for the Kaluli's appropriation of food as the ultimate vehicle for constructing social relationships and expressing affection is that food is the cornerstone of life. If food shows affection, then what does it mean to go hungry? It means more than an empty belly: it means loneliness.

✢ Religion and Expressive Culture

The Unseen World

All that cannot be seen is a very real part of Kaluli life. The forest is thick and hides many things from the eyes, but is full of sound. The skittering flight and screech of a bird tells you of someone approaching as precisely as catching sight of the visitor does. Morning is not sunrise, but birdsong. Evening is not dusk, but cicadas. Schieffelin (1976) was unable to convey to a Kaluli friend the kind of bird whose name he wanted to know, however detailed his report of its appearance. But when he remembered the rattle of its wings and crumpled a piece of paper in description, the bird was immediately recognized.

These sounds are not merely sounds. When a Kaluli draws attention to the mournful call of a pigeon, saying that it is a little child calling for its mother, it may in fact be just that. It is not only that the bird's call sounds that way; there are spirits that live unseen, and indeed the soul of a child may call for its mother. (It is not unusual that birds and their sounds are prime examples of the importance to the Kaluli of what is heard. They hold a prominent place in Kaluli life, as we will see.)

There are people in the unseen world who are called with a term meaning "shadow" or "reflection." In this unseen world every person has a shadow. Shadows of men are wild pigs; shadows of women are cassowaries. These shadows lead their own lives in the unseen world, roaming the forests. Should the shadow be hurt, the person would suffer too. If the shadow is killed, it means death for its Kaluli counterpart.

Spirits of the dead also live in this unseen world, along with spirits who have never had a human life. These are not fearful sorts of spirits; on the contrary, they might once have been friends or relatives. Unlike other New Guinea peoples, the Kaluli think it impossible that the dead would bear the living any ill will.

There are large invisible longhouses on Mt. Bosavi that are home to another sort of spirit, quite different from the spirits of the dead. As humans have spirit reflections that are wild pigs and cassowaries, so these "people" have the reciprocal spirit; their shadows are the wild pigs and cassowaries that live in Bosavi. These shadows are not evil, but they are responsible for dangerous thunderstorms.

There is, however, a third kind of spirit, which lives in certain well-known areas of the land and whose anger can only be prevented by taking certain precautions. These shadows are dangerous, and may send foul weather, sickness, and even death.

Mediums and Witches

It is through mediums that Kaluli have knowledge of the unseen world. Men who have married spirit women in a dream gain access to this world when they have a child with their spirit wife. As the medium sleeps he leaves his body behind and wanders the unseen world. Once he has gone, spirits can enter his body and use his mouth to speak to the living.

Such seances are exciting occasions for Kaluli who wish to speak to departed loved ones. They are eager to learn what animal form friends and relatives have taken in the unseen world, inquire if they have enough to eat, and ask advice about curing the sick and locating lost property. They also petition their help to identify the *seis,* witches who live among them in the community.

Every Kaluli death, whatever the outward cause may appear to be (old age, illness, an accident), is caused by a *sei,* a term used to describe both an evil spirit and the person whom the spirit inhabits. *Seis* are usually men, but sometimes women, who have evil spirits lodged in their hearts about which they themselves may be unaware. While they sleep, the shadow creatures that dwell within them stalk the night for prey. *Seis* typically attack only strangers, but hunger or anger can cause them to turn on their own kin.

Although the *seis* are generally unseen, some people on their deathbed or with particular abilities have in fact seen them, and describe them as hideous. Their attacks leave sickness and disabilities that are often as invisible as they are: a painful, distended belly contains unseen stones; legs that cannot move have been amputated by the *sei,* but can still be seen. When the victim is fully compromised, the *sei* will pull out the victim's heart, killing him. Once the prey is dead, the *sei* will finish eating the rest of the body. This is evidenced by a corpse's ongoing decomposition and eventual disappearance.

Death and Afterlife

At death, a person's spirit is freed from the still body and retreats to the forest. There it begins a journey along a river, which to the spirit is a wide westward path, only to arrive at an enormous bonfire where it burns until finding deliverance in another spirit. This rescuer carries the burnt soul back to its own spirit longhouse, attending healing ceremonies along the way until the restoration is complete. Finally, the two are married. After this union the newly departed will assume a new form, and will resemble any other wild creature in the forest. Loved ones will not see it again, but may look forward to conversation and advice through a medium.

Traditional mortuary practices have been outlawed by the government, which now requires that Kaluli bury bodies in a cemetery. Prior to this edict, issued in 1968, the body would be placed in a hammock outside the longhouse, with fires lit around it. Mourners would come for several days; afterward the body was removed to a small structure built near the longhouse, where it would decompose. Small possessions treasured by the deceased would be placed there with him or her, as sentimental reminders. These were not meant to travel to the afterlife with their former owner; what use would a wild pig in the forest, or a bird soon to live in a treetop have for a necklace or bow and arrow? As soon as only bones remained, they would be gathered into a net bag and placed under the eaves of the longhouse front porch.

The children and spouse of the deceased were required to follow several taboos established for mourners; often others did so too, simply out of affection. If a woman has gathered food to eat with another before her own death, her intended companion might refuse to eat it, sad that they could not share it together as they had planned. One man gave up breadfruit upon his brother's death, because it had been his brother's favorite food (Schieffelin 1976).

✦ STORY, SONG, AND CEREMONY

Songs of Birds, Sounds of Tears

Steven Feld was an anthropology student making a living as a jazz musician while he pondered the question of returning to school to complete his degree. At the home of his friends, anthropologists Edward and Bambi Schieffelin, he heard Kaluli music and was smitten. Deciding to merge his musical and anthropological interests, he went to Bosavi with the Schieffelins and studied sound—in the performance of poetry reading, song, and weeping—as a symbolic system.

Kaluli myth and music were the vehicles for his understanding of the way Kaluli relate to their world. Many Kaluli stories are about birds and their connection with sadness, often because of the sorrowful nature of their calls. As Feld listened to such stories, he began to reflect upon similar associations in his own musical culture, especially American blues and jazz. He recalled "literary and musical imagery, such as the common use of the mournful sounds of the whippoorwill in poetry and songs about sadness and love . . . associating a bird of the night with minor or descending pitches, sad sounds, blacks, the South, and the beginning of instrumental blues" (1990:23). Feld found a theme present in music and folklore in many diverse places. He began then to regard the themes woven through Kaluli myth and the sounds repeated in Kaluli music as "expressive embodiments of basic Kaluli concepts of sentiment and appeal" (p. 24).

Birds and their music are for the Kaluli, who are avid bird watchers, metaphors for their own society. It is most often birds that become the "spirit reflections" of the dead. Skillful at identifying birds by their sounds, Kaluli analogize the particular pitches and melodies of different birds with different segments of their population. (As when the whining and whimpering complaints of children are likened to that of the dove, whose call is said to be like that of "a hungry child calling for its mother.")

Once Feld discovered the centrality of birds and their songs to Kaluli culture, he proceeded to collect and organize all the information he could about the birds in the Bosavi environment, and the ways in which the Kaluli regarded them. This endeavor inadvertently taught him more than he anticipated; he expected to discover Kaluli notions of bird classification, perception, and symbolism. What he learned instead grew out of the sheer frustration of his Kaluli informant who, after hours of imitating bird calls and nesting behaviors, blurted out, "Listen— to you they are birds, to me they are voices in the forest." Feld realized that he could not continue to impose his own system of classification on the Kaluli experience of these important "voices;" that the Kaluli understanding of birds and their songs is "based on certain fundamental premises about the world, such as the belief that things have a visible and invisible aspect; that sounds and behaviors have an outside, an inside, and an underneath; or that human relationships are reflected in the ecology and natural order of the forest" (1990:45).

Weeping conveys an emotional message from one person to another, which is very much connected to singing. In response to sorrow or loss, Kaluli may begin to cry. But feelings of disappointment, frustration, or self-pity may also lead Kaluli to burst into song.

Weeping and singing are very much bound up together. There are many "wept songs," usually about a lost loved one. Men and women have different socially dictated modes of weeping. Men begin with a high-pitched wail, which turns into an imitation of the short-burst call of the *muni* bird. They cry for a short period of time and stop abruptly. Weeping is a more common expressive form among women. Although both men and women cry similarly in response to a moving song, it is women who are likely to blend weeping and singing into the sung text of a "wept song." As Feld (1990:33) explains, "while sadness moves both men and women to weeping, it is weeping that moves women to song."

Out of the attempt to preserve the musical heritage of the Kaluli, Feld has joined with other musicians to produce a recording of Bosavi music, *Voices of the Rainforest*. Profits from its sale benefit the Bosavi People's Fund, set up to provide financial aid in the struggle to maintain Kaluli cultural survival in the face of threats to their rainforest environment.

The *Gisaro*

The usual occasions for Kaluli formal ceremonies are those they celebrate with neighboring longhouses, most often marriages or large gifts of meat. Pig feasts and similar large events take months to prepare.

Underlying these community events is the theme of reciprocity and exchange. After a particularly complex and moving ceremony, guests may be inspired to host a return event in their own longhouse community in great haste. Schieffelin (1976) reports witnessing a dance performed to ward off sickness. Guest dancers from another village came to the host community, singing throughout the night, and performing so poignantly that it moved many to tears. As soon as the dancers departed, elders called in kin from other longhouses and within two days had staged a ceremony at the dancers' village that (they were proud to note) caused all assembled to weep.

Of all the ceremonies performed in Kaluli life, none is as important as the *gisaro*. It is presented as part of a larger ceremony (such as a wedding or pork prestation), and performed inside a host longhouse by guest dancers who begin at dusk and continue until dawn.

The cast is assembled by sending out requests to those who might like to participate, and it is rare that there are not enough men who respond to the call. For weeks before the event, *gisaro* dancers compose songs and prepare elaborate costumes. The intended effect of the *gisaro* performance is to overwhelm the listeners with powerful emotion. To this end, it is imperative to maintain the element of surprise, as to the identity of the dancers, pattern of makeup and costume, and content of the songs.

While the performers are rehearsing at least a dozen new songs and dances, the hosts are preparing food. On the day of the feast, dancers wait for dark and enter the longhouse which is lit with the torches soon to be a central part of the *gisaro*.

Gisaro dancers are painted and costumed alike, so as to be indistinguishable from one another. A rested dancer can thus replace an exhausted one, allowing the dancing and singing to continue unabated. The songs are heartbreaking, and purposely so. They tell of people and places loved and lost. The audience hangs on every word, their sorrow building until they can no longer contain themselves. Sobbing and wailing fills the longhouse, but the *gisaro* performers continue, seemingly oblivious to the anguish they are causing, never showing any trace of emotion on their faces.

Amid their wailing and stamping, hosts angered by the pain inflicted on them by the wrenching *gisaro* songs, jump up and grab the huge resin torches. These they jam into the backs and necks of the dancers, searing their flesh. Still they continue, singing and dancing, as the enraged and grieving hosts continue to burn the dancers. The wailing and burning continues throughout the night. The visiting dancers inflict emotional pain on their hosts; the hosts, in turn, visit physical pain on the dancers (Houseman 1998).

Before the ceremony, dancers coat their bodies with sweet-smelling vegetable resin whose scent mingles with the burning flesh. It is thought to afford the skin some protection from the burns and diminish the pain somewhat, but most dancers suffer extensive second-degree burns across their backs, upper arms, and shoulders. The skin will sometimes blister and peel off during the dance; otherwise, it sloughs off in a day or two. Dancers generally spend the first ten days after their ordeal convalescing; after three or four weeks they have healed.

Edward Schieffelin (1976) details in his ethnography of the Kaluli the ways in which the *gisaro* can be understood as the dramatic embodiment and crystallization of the major premises on which Kaluli culture is built. *Gisaro* is a way for them to understand and express their view of the world, the loss and sorrow contained within it, their link with those now invisible to them. He concludes, "the Kaluli [feel] that the forces of growth and life are generated in oppositions, and it is with this, as a life condition, with all its beauty, exuberance, tragedy, and violence, that they try to come to terms in *Gisaro*" (p. 223).

⇥ KALULI TODAY

"Before" and "Now": Modernity and the Language of Missionization

Bambi Schieffelin (2002) reports that in 1961, a brochure printed by the Unevangelized Fields Mission (UFM; now the Asia Pacific Christian Mission, APCM) described the Kaluli as "stone age savages . . . primitive people [who] are half man, half animal" (p. S5). A fundamentalist group interpreting the Bible literally, they believed there was no time to waste in introducing Christianity to Mt. Bosavi. In the 1970s, missionaries built an airstrip, church, elementary school, clinic, and trade store. Missionized Papua New Guineans served as teachers, pastors, and nurses. Mission staff conducted daily church services and Bible study groups (Schieffelin 2000). By the 1990s, dramatic change had been wrought, altering the ways in which Kaluli "interpret events, establish facts, convey opinions, and imagine themselves" (Schieffelin 2000:294).

As we have seen earlier in the chapter, a sense of place is central to traditional Kaluli life. Place-names were the mooring for ceremonies, significant events, and interpersonal experiences (Schieffelin 1976). Feld's (1990, 1996) investigation of Kaluli music describes the ways in which events and relationships are located in the places recalled in song. In her study of childhood socialization, Bambi Schieffelin (1990) notes the ways in which place-names link people to places, forging identity. Thus, it was place and not time that was used to invoke remembrance. Missionization demanded the adoption of European-based time. Bells, clocks, calendars, and schedules organized the mission's daily activities. But, as Schieffelin (2002) notes, "[t]he mission effort to control time was not just a practical strategy but a way of asserting hierarchic power and governance. By changing time the mission hoped to transform persons by changing their daily activities and the ways in which they thought and talked about them" (p. S7).

The introduction of European-based time allowed missionaries to construct the crucial opposition of "before" (the past) and "now" (the present). "Before" was the time prior to the arrival of missionaries, and the newly introduced word was used "to construct the past as amoral, chaotic, irrelevant" and a stumbling block to salvation, the fundamentalist goal for the Kaluli (Schieffelin 2002:S15). "Now" began with 1970s mission contact, and continues through the present day. These new categories moved Kaluli from their traditional relationship to time and place to a fundamentalist orientation, "one with no need for a Bosavi past, a present charged with change, and a future that depended on choices made in the present" (Schieffelin 2002:S6). Kaluli Christians who embraced both the vocabulary of missionaries and the new temporal focus reshaped not only their language, but their identities as well. They were set apart from their non-Christian kin in such a way as to mark what Schieffelin (2002) identifies as the beginning of Bosavi social stratification. Traditional ways of constructing and marking relationships were discouraged by missionaries, who considered even *thoughts* about the times "before" to be a threat to conversion and belief. One aim of missionization was to align the Kaluli with the global anticipation of the Second Coming. In order to accomplish this, Bosavi peoples must share the same sense of time with other Christians, a change that would separate them from their unique Kaluli selves. As Schieffelin (2002:S16) explains, "[w]hat mattered was only whether they were saved; that would become their only meaningful identity."

Many indigenous peoples confront modernity in the form of Christianity, and are challenged by its reliance more on speech than on ritual. (Robbins 2001) In his work with a group in the New Guinea Highlands, anthropologist Joel Robbins (2001) reports the local populations frustration over just this aspect. On many occasions, he was told "God is nothing but talk" (p. 904).

As a linguistic anthropologist, Schieffelin pays particular attention to the ways in which the introduction of new vocabularies and particular verbal expressions were used to accomplish missionary goals. She became aware of the pattern of language change while preparing a dictionary of English and two local languages. The project began in the mid-1970s. In the mid-1990s, she and her collaborators were rechecking earlier entries with Kaluli assistants, who consistently claimed that many words were wrong, or not understandable, or no longer used. The team found it puzzling that they would have gotten so many words "wrong," and in an attempt to solve the mystery they presented their original texts—many of which had been provided by the fathers of those very Kaluli assistants. Their memories jogged, the assistants agreed that the translations were, in fact, correct. The most significant discovery, however, was *which* words had been dismissed by the Kaluli. Words that had been used in myths and traditional stories, employed in curing ceremonies, or associated with witchcraft were all reported to be no longer in use in the 1990s. Certain categories of emotions—for example, "anger"—were also diminished. When asked for an explanation, Schieffelin was told that "Christians no longer became angry, and therefore such words were no longer necessary" (2002:S9). The significance of this linguistic change went beyond the compilation of a dictionary. As Schieffelin points out, the loss of particular words in the Kaluli language "indicated the extent to which an alternative view of the Bosavi world . . . was being refashioned in its ways of speaking" (2002:S9).

Thus, these changes were representative of broader changes, especially the ways in which Kaluli had accepted the fundamentalist teachings of the primitive "before" and the enlightened "now" (which would prepare Kaluli for the inevitable Biblical future.) Schieffelin (2002) notes that "in order to catch up, people who were 'behind the times' were required to detach themselves from their particular past. One way to do this was to make it impossible to speak about a past that increasingly had negative connotations; the erasure of words seemed like one way to do it." This, coupled with the introduction of new ideas about time, allowed the missionaries to accomplish their goal of Kaluli conversion, reorganizing both social and cosmological spheres. The Kaluli were told that the whole world awaited the Second Coming, and part of their preparation for salvation must be to join in keeping time on a world clock. As Schieffelin (2000) concludes, "under conditions of rapid social change, every language choice is a social choice that has critical links to the active construction of culture" (p. 323).

✦ For Further Discussion

The sharing of food is at the center of Kaluli social relations. Is this something you have seen as important in other societies as well? How is food used to create and solidify bonds in your own experience? What sorts of cultural messages can be transmitted through the giving and taking of food? Among the Kaluli, food shows affection; thus, to go hungry is to be lonely. What are some of the meanings of hunger in your society?

CHAPTER 8

THE KAPAUKU

New Guinea "Capitalists"?

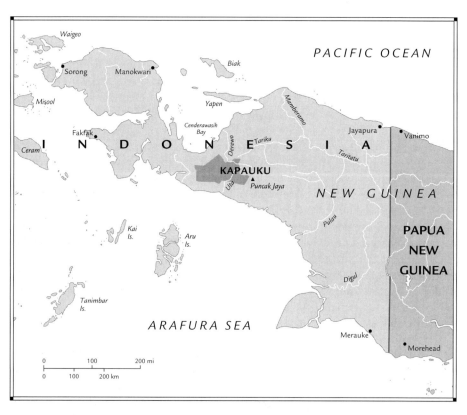

Location of the Kapauku.

✦ THE BEGINNING

Ugatame designed the universe and is of two natures, male and female, like the sun and the moon are two. Sun is light and warm and like a ball of fire. Moon is cool like the light of a firefly. But the sun and the moon are not Ugatame; they are proof that there is Ugatame.

The world is a flat slab of stone, covered with earth, and edged all around with water. There is nothing below it; it goes down as far as there is to go. No dark world beneath the real world exists. Above the world is a bowl turned upside down, and this blue bowl is the sky. The sun begins cupped under the bowl at its eastern lip. It moves through the day to the western edge. As evening comes, the sun slips under the western lip of the blue bowl, and all through the night travels above the curve of the bowl. At last it slides underneath the eastern edge, and it is morning. As the sun moves above the outer convexity of the bowl, tiny breaches in the bowl allow pinpoints of light to seep through; these are the stars. Above the bowl is another world, and it may look like this one. It is Ugatame's home.

✦ INTRODUCTION AND HISTORY

The western half of the main island of New Guinea was originally colonized by the Dutch. In 1969 it came under the jurisdiction of Indonesia, and it is now Irian Jaya. The central highlands of West Irian are rugged, with mountains whose peaks may soar to 4000 meters, and deep valleys below. Three large lakes act as reservoirs and flow south to the Indian Ocean. Of the five vegetational zones, tropical rainforest predominates, with a variety of beeches and oaks. The undergrowth bears ferns and pandanus. Higher altitudes are covered with stunted alpine growth; valley bottoms are swampy and covered with reeds. It is among these mountains that the one-hundred thousand Kapauku make their home.

Their tribe was named Kapauku by the people to the south; their neighbors to the north call them Ekari. They call themselves "Me"—"the people."

The south coast of New Guinea was linked to the interior by an important intertribal trade network. Because this ran directly through the Kapauku's region, they had extensive contact with both people and goods from beyond the borders of their own territory. However, their mountain ranges, swamps, and extensive rainforests ensured their isolation from Western influence until 1938, when the Dutch government stationed officers at an outpost they created near one of the large lakes. This initial contact was brief. The Japanese attack in the southwestern Pacific resulted in the abandonment of this post, and it was not reestablished for nearly ten years. When a new outpost was established, Christian missionaries arrived, their goal being "to see to the spiritual welfare of the people" (Posposil 1963:3).

→ Kapauku Economy: The "Primitive Capitalists"

The Kapauku Papuans are often cited as the prime example of a "simple" society with an egalitarian redistributive system that nevertheless boasts features typical of contemporary capitalist orientation (Harris 1988; Nanda 1991). In fact, Leopold Pospisil, the leading authority on the Kapauku, labels their economy as "primitive capitalism," characterized by the pursuit of wealth in the form of cowrie shell money, status distinctions based on such wealth, and an ethic of individualism (1963:3).

Subsistence

Large game is absent in this environment, relegating hunting and trapping to small importance among the Kapauku. There is a paucity, too, of small game animals; the lakes offer no edible fish. Although hunting provides distraction as sport, it is the gathering of crayfish, insects, frogs, rats, and bats that provides important supplements to the daily diet. (It is also a crucial part of the Kapauku economy in that it supplies the raw materials for construction and manufacturing.)

Kapauku subsistence is dependent on two items: sweet potatoes, the staple of the native diet, and pigs.

The Kamu Valley's two very different types of terrain demand the use of two kinds of cultivation, and each household usually maintains some of each type of garden. Shifting cultivation, with areas cleared by burning, planted with sweet potatoes, and harvested daily, is employed in the mountainous areas. Extensive gardens on the rocky slopes are laboriously fenced off to protect them from wild boars and hungry domesticated pigs, and left fallow when plots are exhausted.

The valley is exploited more intensively, employing two methods of rotating crops of sweet potatoes, sugarcane, taro, bananas, cucumbers, gourds, and beans. In all garden types, it is the sweet potato that assumes primacy, with 90 percent of all land devoted to its production.

The domesticated pig plays a role in Kapauku society that can scarcely be overestimated, and which is intricately tied up with other fundamental aspects of Kapauku life and culture.

Pospisil explains that the sweet potato and the pig can be separated neither from one another nor from the essence of Kapauku economy. Both people and pigs are fed on sweet potatoes. It is the sale of pigs (and pork) that contributes the largest portion of the individual Kapauku's income. And because fat, healthy, fertile pigs depend on the plentiful harvest of sweet potatoes, the two are economically bound together. Each is food and each is wealth—and wealth is the driving force behind Kapauku society. Pospisil reports that "the highest prestige in this society and the highest status of political and legal leadership are achieved not through heritage, bravery in warfare, or knowledge and achievements in religious ceremonialism, but through accumulation and redistribution of capital" (1963:5). Capital is amassed in the form of shell money, and successful pig breeding is the means to acquire it. So, indirectly, sweet potatoes not only feed human and animal alike, but also provide a way to achieve political power. By providing a way to achieve great wealth—and it is only a wealthy man who rises to leadership and authority—the pig and the sweet potato are joined in "a pivotal role in the wealth-oriented Kapauku society."

Manufacture

Kapauku's limited scope in manufacturing provides contrast to their agricultural sophistication. It is, for the most part, not specialized. Manufactured tools include flint chips, stone axes and knives, and grinding stones. Women's aprons are fashioned from woven tree bark, which is also employed in creating decorative necklaces and armbands worn by both women and men. Knives, used both for surgery and the carving of pork, are made of bamboo splinters that have broken off during the construction of water and insect containers. Rat teeth and bird claws provide raw material to create other carving tools. Agricultural tools, needed for digging, planting, and harvesting are generally made of wood.

Bows and arrows are the first line of weaponry, although mostly used for killing small game, and not in combat. Enemies (and any large game available) are more likely to be challenged with projectiles tipped with long, sharp bamboo blades.

Although these manufactured tools and weapons are strictly utilitarian in design, the Kapauku demonstrate great artistic skill in their manufacture of net bags, used for both practical and decorative purposes (Posposil 1963). They are woven in intricate designs made of string spun from soft inner bark, and often decorated with colored orchid stems. Large nets for fishing and roomy carrying bags are woven by women; the smaller decorative bags worn around the neck or on the shoulder for adornment or used to carry money are festooned with bright feathers and shells, and are manufactured by men.

Settlement

A Kapauku village typically houses about 120 people and is a scattered arrangement of about fifteen houses. These vary in size and are constructed of upright planks thatched with reeds or pandanus leaves. This vegetation is also used as insulation between plank layers, with large strips of bark providing the flooring. Each room has a fire, built beneath a chink in the joining of the walls and roof left expressly for smoke to escape.

Large houses are elevated, leaving a space beneath the structure, which houses domesticated pigs. The planking used for walls is also used to build a partition, which runs across the width of the building, dividing it in two. The front section houses the men and adolescent boys in a communal dormitory. The back half is further divided into individual "apartments," one for each married woman and her children.

Some households outgrow this traditional arrangement. If the back section has insufficient room for the number of wives and children, small shelters near the main house are built for each unprovisioned woman and her children.

Money

Reminiscent of the contrast between elaborate techniques of cultivation and simple technology of manufacture, Posposil (1963) also draws attention to the unusual juxtaposition of "one of the world's most primitive technologies" with what he describes as a "sophisticated and complex" economy (p. 18).

Kapauku economy rests on the use of money. Cowrie shells and two types of necklaces are used both as money for purchase and exchange and as a measure of value and worth. Both of these types of money can be used to buy food, crops, animals, land, and to purchase cultivation labor, medical care, and magical skills. If one is without money, one is without both respect and social standing. It is only money that affords access to what is important: marriage, social status, livelihood, and personal relationships.

Shells and glass beads, the units of worth, are arranged into denominations and, because they are not locally produced, must be secured through trade with peoples living in the coastal lowlands.

Although there is generally an established "customary" or "ideal" price for goods and services, there is also considerable fluctuation that follows the

Kapauku men.

rubric of supply and demand. In addition, prices often reflect the relationship between the individuals involved in the transaction. Often prices are lowered between close relatives, or in dealings with someone whose favor is likely to be valuable in the future or has been depended on in the past.

As would be expected, because they are close by, most buying and selling occurs between close relatives, members of local patrilineal kin groups. Barter—that is, exchanging commodities rather than money—has been reduced to a fairly insignificant position among Kapauku, and money payment is mandated for favors and behaviors that in other economic systems would not involve such a transfer. For example, the expression of grief over the death of one's relative must be paid for in money. And there is rarely a crime committed that cannot be erased through adequate shell money payment.

Perhaps the most elaborate rules of sale are constructed for pigs, which is not surprising given their importance in Kapauku culture. In fact, it is the ceremonial pig feast that is the occasion of most active business transactions. Salt is another important item of sale.

In addition to outright buying and selling, the extension of credit has been elaborated (perhaps beyond that of Western economies) as a means of redistributing money. Because there is no mechanism of giving an outright gift, loans assume an important role in establishing oneself as generous and prestigious. "Interest" on a loan is informal and may be promised by the borrower rather than demanded by the lender. Although there is no legal recourse if this promise isn't kept, it carries with it the social sanction of dishonesty and the likelihood that there will be no further extension of credit in the future.

Pospisil (1963) recounts a story explicating the extent to which the Kapauku "profit motive" has extended to their interactions with Christian missionaries on the island. A missionary church was established and enjoyed popularity among villagers, who, after Sunday services, received tobacco and other desired goods. Feeling as if his efforts toward their conversion were close to fruition, the missionary grew puzzled as attendance at services began to drop off dramatically over a period of several weeks during which he was waiting for his supplies of goods to be replenished. Once the supplies were finally gone, so were all the attendees at his church. He went to the village to inquire about this distressing turn of events, and was told in no uncertain terms: "No tobacco, no hallelujah" (p. 94).

✦ SOCIAL ORGANIZATION

Kinship and Descent

Each Kapauku can place other people in one of three groups: close friends and kin; acquaintances and strangers; and enemies.

One can trust only those in the first category. Close friends and relatives are the people who offer financial, economic, political, and emotional support.

The second classification merges individuals who are only casual acquaintances with those who are completely unknown. It is worth remembering that because "every stranger is a potential customer" (Posposil 1963:34) and therefore a potential source of increased wealth, strangers are usually treated with courtesy.

The category of enemy does not necessarily imply personal enmity on an individual's part. Rather, enemies are defined more by group membership than any hostile interaction. An enemy is someone who belongs to a group that has traditionally had warlike relations with one's father's group.

Although Kapauku reckon descent along both maternal and paternal lines, villages are patrilineal and exogamous, and generally patrilocal. The sib, which is the kinship group of most importance, is a totemic, patrilineal (ideally exogamous) group whose members reckon their descent from a common apical ancestor. The diffuseness of the Kapauku patrilineage renders it of little use for political purposes, limiting its focus to the regulation of marriage and the construction of personal and economic obligatory relationships.

Most day-to-day rights and obligations are incurred within the localized patrilineal group; it is members of this group that an individual will depend upon for amassing bride-price or gathering allies in times of conflict with outsiders. Larger political amalgamations (confederations) are established through kinship ties, forged by marriages, with other lineages.

Marriage

The arrangement of a marriage ideally occurs between the families of the prospective groom and brothers and mother of the prospective bride. Collecting a high bride-price takes precedence over the preferences expressed by the woman to be married. However, mothers may set a bride-price they know cannot be met expressly for the purpose of discouraging an undesirable prospect.

Elopements are not infrequent, despite the fact that they are considered improper. When this occurs, it is set right by negotiating a bride-price after the fact, indicating that families of the eloping couple have accepted the union. The pig feast, an occasion for men and women of marriageable age from neighboring villages to come together, is a primary opportunity for courtship. Premarital sex is generally not punished, although it is frowned upon for its potential to diminish a woman's bride-price. Premarital pregnancy, however, is a much more highly disapproved of matter.

When divorce occurs, the bride-price must be returned, which is a serious consequence. (Divorce—usually occurring because a woman has left her husband—is, in fact, cited as a common instigator of warfare.) In such an instance, small children generally remain with their mother, and when they reach the age of about seven, are likely to join their father's village. Unless advanced age or illness prevents it, a widow is expected to remarry within a reasonable amount of time after her husband's death.

One reason polygyny is widely practiced is that it provides an opportunity for men to gain status. The acquisition of multiple wives, granting status because it is an indicator of the husband's ability to pay multiple bride-prices, is a display of wealth among the Kapauku much in the same way that the acquisition of expensive jewelry and other luxury items is in the United States.

However, while polygyny is an ideal for which Kapauku men will strive, it is an expensive venture and not easily attained. (About one-third of all marriages are polygynous.) As we have seen, Kapauku economy depends largely on plant cultivation and pig husbandry. Although it is the agricultural activities that provide most of the food, it is through pigs that men achieve status, power, and authority. If a husband can afford multiple wives, they will ultimately help him earn more money and prestige through their tending of pigs and sweet potatoes.

Family and Household

Household composition varies somewhat. It always consists, minimally, of a nuclear family, but usually also includes other consanguineal or affinal kin. In addition to being the basic Kapauku unit of residence it is also, to a large extent, the basic unit of production and consumption.

Whoever owns the house is considered the "head" within the household; he is responsible for organizing production and harvesting activities, because he is ultimately responsible for assuring that household members are adequately fed. He is also charged with maintaining harmony and cooperation among the other men, which must be accomplished by setting an example and through his own personal skills of persuasion. Despite owning the house he has no formal recourse for enforcing his wishes. He must also be careful not to overstep certain boundaries in exercising control over the members of other nuclear families living within the household.

✦ Political Organization

Authority and leadership in the setting of a family (nuclear or polygynous) or an individual household is well defined among the Kapauku. It may be based on ownership; it may be based on kinship. Authority and leadership on a larger level is not formally defined in this way.

Positions of leadership in Kapauku society are held exclusively by men, who appropriate the products of women's labor in order to play their political games. That men are in formal positions of leadership must be viewed in the context of the entire fabric of Kapauku society, however. Posposil (1963) points out that, despite whatever "ideal" may be espoused formally, one must not overlook the reality that, in many instances, "the father and husband is only a figurehead, while the actual power rests with his wife" (p. 42). He says of one such woman, with whom he was negotiating a purchase of pork, "despite the fact that she is the individual who makes the important decisions in the family, she never forgets the conventions of Kapauku culture" (p. 42).

Found in many societies throughout Melanesia and New Guinea is a person in a position of leadership called the "big man." It is through personal attributes and achievements that such stature is achieved. Big man status is neither inherited nor elected. As a result of public behaviors—generosity chief among them—and the great wealth that facilitates such behavior, a man sets himself apart from others in the community, attracting loyal followers. As he continues to amass wealth, so too he gathers his reputation. He sponsors feasts, helps young men gather bridewealth, and by so doing engenders the obligation of those whom he has helped.

Among the Kapauku there is such a big man role. It is called *tonowi*, which means "rich one."

The *Tonowi*

The Kapauku *tonowi* embodies the typical traits of the characteristic big man. His position is an informal one; he sets himself apart from his fellows with his wealth, his generosity, and his verbal skills. Often he may have proven to be brave in war or well versed in shamanism, but these are traits that only enhance his power; they are not essential to be a *tonowi*.

A *tonowi* does not have the formal authority to enforce his will. He offers his suggestions, makes his wishes known, and encourages people to accept his decisions. Although his position is an informal one, the *tonowi* assumes the mantle of leadership on a great number of occasions. It is he who acts as a representative of his own group in their dealings with outsiders and other villages. Within his group he negotiates settlements and judges blame in disputes. It is generally the case that social control among the Kapauku is effected by persuasion rather than by force. Owing to the desirability of amassing a fortune, economic inducements often act as the most effective incentive. Fines or threats of fines are frequently enough to exact conformity.

Given the extreme value Kapauku culture places on wealth, it is hardly surprising that one who has achieved great wealth would be deemed successful and worthy of admiration. When speaking of big man status, however, mere possession of wealth is never enough; not all who are rich are *tonowi*. The wealth must be generously distributed, and Posposil notes there may be severe consequences if it is not: "[I]n some regions . . . selfish and greedy individuals, who have amassed huge personal properties, but who have failed to comply with the Kapauku requirement of 'generosity' towards their less fortunate tribesmen may be, and actually frequently are, put to death" (p. 49). Posposil was, in fact, among the Kapauku at a time when just such an occurrence took place.

Even in those regions where these measures are not taken, wealthy individuals who hoard rather than share their fortunes are shunned, ridiculed, and eventually brought into line, thus ensuring more equitable distribution of capital.

Of course, given the nature of his position and the lack of formal recourse, even a *tonowi* who is generous and well respected cannot force others to do what he wishes. This is one instance where his personal charm and verbal gifts become of the utmost importance. If met with resistance, he may become agitated and begin to shout taunts; he makes long eloquent speeches outlining the wisdom of his decision, citing rules that support his position, finally offering threats to solidify his position. In extreme cases, he may begin to perform what is known as "the mad dance," or abruptly stop his ranting and cry piteously about the misconduct in question and the obstinence of the transgressor. Some *tonowi* are so adept at this performance that they can summon genuine tears, a sight that usually proves moving enough to at last secure the compliance of any unwilling party (Posposil 1963). This facet of the role is crucial enough to jeopardize a wealthy man's ability to become a *tonowi* in its absence. Wealthy and generous individuals who are shy and soft spoken, or who disdain public confrontation, cannot ascend to the position.

The generosity required of a wealthy individual must be expressed in culturally appropriate forms. Because the native economy does not include gift giving, it is through his willingness to make loans that the *tonowi* acquires his political power. By extending credit to those in need, wealthy men gain both the prestige that accrues from generosity and the indebtedness and loyalty of their creditors. The *tonowi* is then in a good position to have others follow his dictates. Those who are already in his debt comply so as not to have repayment of their loans demanded; those who have not yet asked for extensions of credit comply lest they jeopardize their chance of successful borrowing in the future. Thus the widest possible alliances are forged, and the *tonowi* exacts loyalty from the majority of the villagers.

Besides those to whom he has extended credit, a *tonowi* also finds support by taking "apprentices" into his household. Since every Kapauku man aspires to riches, a young man seizes the opportunity to join the household of an older, wealthy man. He is lent a pig, and is given room and board and the opportunity to benefit from the *tonowi*'s business acumen. If the young man appears to be a promising pupil, his benefactor might allow him to buy a female piglet in order to begin accumulating his wealth in earnest. The final act of generosity is a loan to make up the bride-price he will need to marry. In return, these apprentices work in the garden and household and act as bodyguards. They are loyal in the event of a dispute; in war, they offer their lives. Once they are established in their own right, those the *tonowi* has called "my boys" continue to function as loyal supporters.

A *tonowi,* much like any Kapauku, also depends upon his close kin for political support. Members of his kin group will follow a *tonowi* for all the same economic reasons others do, but will additionally acquiesce out of genuine affection.

Because the *tonowi*'s wealth is dependent upon successful pig breeding, it is far from secure. If a *tonowi* makes a poor management decision or has a run of bad luck, his fortune may be lost. Because the loss of wealth will result in the loss of *tonowi* status, Kapauku political structure is rarely static over long periods of time. Pig breeding offers a vehicle for wealth that is accessible to many Kapauku, contributing to the flux in the status system. As one man loses power, another steps in to take his place. The result is a flexible, frequently shifting power structure, with no individual in a position of authority for an extended period of time.

✦ The Culture of Individualism

Economic Individualism

One of the most striking features of Kapauku culture is the overriding emphasis on the individual. Evidence for this orientation, as well as its consequences, is found throughout their beliefs, behaviors, and institutions.

Posposil asserts: "All Kapauku economic undertakings are executed primarily because . . . 'I need,' or 'I want to do it for my own benefit.' I have never heard an economic argument in which the needs of the social group have been put forward as a justification for a position taken by a discussant" (1963:89).

This attention to one's own needs, and the attempt to acquire that which will satisfy them, has resulted in individual ownership of all goods, with practically nothing viewed as communal property. Houses, pigs, land, canoes are all cited as items owned by a single individual. More surprisingly, even large areas of forest are claimed by individual owners. The exceptions to this are rocky mountainous areas and large streams not claimed by individuals but rather the property of lineages and sublineages. Posposil (1963) suggests that fishless waters and barren, rocky land on which nothing will grow hold no economic interest. Thus, they are not claimed by individuals because no one cares to own something of no economic value. What *is* valuable, however, are any game animals which may roam around these mountaintops and streams. They, when caught, become the property of the individual trapper because of the access granted by the lineage ownership.

Upon occasion, two individuals may jointly own a house. When this is the case, however, each individual can identify which sheets of bark and planks of wood are his contribution to the building—and hence his own. Those items that service the village as a whole—for example, fences, bridges, and main ditches—are in fact owned piecemeal by individuals who claim ownership to particular sections of the structures.

Individualism is the vantage point from which to view all economic cooperation within each household. No single meal served is exempt from individual ownership. Each meal has a host who owns the food. When household residents work in the garden, tend the pigs, or dig a ditch, they are entering into an individual contract with the owner of the house, and they will be paid, either in shell money, pork, or other goods. When the work is completed, even if the task was performed by several household members, it is still not viewed in the aggregate as a single large accomplishment with many contributors. In fact, rather than striving for consistency of the overall project when working together, Kapauku will take pains to make their own contribution unique enough that it can be recognized as distinct from the portion done by any other individual. If a fence is to be built, individual workers build sections they can remember as their own, refer to as their property, and for which they will be solely responsible. Garden work is divided up such that each individual is only responsible for one discrete section.

Multiple Leaders without Consensus

The cultural thread of Kapauku individualism can be found running through the institutions of the society. As we have seen, the *tonowi*—the most important of these political institutions—rises to his position based on individually acquired, and not inherited, wealth. However, great wealth without the assertive and polished personal characteristics is not sufficient for success as a *tonowi*.

There is also no formal cooperation among the men who achieve *tonowi* status at the same time. Generally, one man is charged with settling the legal aspects of conflicts and another with attending to more broadly stated political issues. Conventionally, they do not confer and attempt to reach consensus. Rather, each one considers the facts and renders a judgment independent of the other. If a dispute arises, deciding whose authority takes precedence is simple: the leader who arrives on the scene first is the one who renders judgment. Thus, there is, in Kapauku political and legal organization, no council of elders or any formal group that deliberates for the benefit of the community as a whole. A *tonowi*'s verdict is presented, and then it is up to him to sway opinion to support it.

Socialization into Individualism

Individualism and independence are among the most important lessons in the education of young Kapauku. Often this teaching begins in the all-important setting of the garden. Early on, boys and girls are given gardens or sections of a garden to care for on their own. A girl plants, weeds, and harvests her own plot, which is separated from those of her mother and older sisters. This allows her success or failure to be plainly seen on its own merit.

A boy's garden, too, is an occasion to begin learning the necessary skills that will serve him later on as he aspires to amassing his fortune. The yield of his garden belongs solely to the boy, who enters into financial relationships, as debtor or creditor, with his father and older brothers. To teach him a lesson, a father may purposely cheat his son to see what the child will do.

Pospisil (1963) observed a "lesson" that proved to him the seriousness with which this education is regarded. He recounts that one day "I heard a loud howling and lamentation coming from one of the houses. When I entered the structure I found to my surprise a middle-aged, muscular man squatting in the middle of the room, crying and yelling while a boy, about eleven years old, was screaming at him and hitting him with a stick. The man was being beaten by his own son. The reason for the excitement was that the father owed his son two bomoje shells which he refused to pay back. Thus the boy had a right to punish his debtor. However, by inflicting the beating he abrogated his right to the debt; the father's obligation to repay was annulled After the beating was over and the enraged boy departed, the father wiped away his tears and smiled with great satisfaction: 'My boy will be quite a businessman, but he must learn not to trust anybody.' In addition to the lesson in commerce the whole affair proved to be most satisfactory to the happy father, as he assured me. Not only had he gained 2 cowries, but the beating administered by his son, he insisted, was so painless that he received the wealth for practically nothing" (p. 30).

When children misbehave they are punished, but as a learning tool rather than a tactic to engender enforcement born of fear. Children should ideally view reprimand as a consequence of past behavior. It is not desirable for a child to be "well-behaved" in an unthinking way. Punishment conveys information that the child is expected to use in *choosing* his or her own course in the future. Likewise, children are asked, and not told, to do things. This, too, derives from the belief that an individual must be allowed the freedom to choose. The true essence of life is thought to be an unfettered cooperation of the mind and the body. Without the individual freedom to allow the soul to direct the actions of the body, the soul attempts to leave—resulting in death. Kapauku society has no institutions that limit this individual freedom; there is no slavery, there are no jails, and they never take prisoners of war. Killing, to their way of thinking, is far more humane than incarceration, which would result in a slow death caused by the absence of personal freedom.

Individualism in Warfare

Unlike so many of their lowland neighbors, the Kapauku do not relish the idea of war. They regard it as an occasion for the destruction of gardens and pigs, and the loss of loved ones. The economic consequences of such occurrences are dreaded. If a close relative instigates a conflict, one is obliged to help, but not without regret. (And, in fact, the cause of any war can be traced back to one individual engaged in a dispute with another.) In the rare instances when war erupts, fighting follows an individualistic pattern. There is no strategizing among groups of warriors, no attacks planned en masse. In fact, participants spread out so that when an enemy is shot there is no doubt as to the identity of the killer, who is later recognized in a personal victory dance. If several snipers stalk an enemy in his village, only one man is designated to carry out the attack, with the others waiting under cover.

✦ Religion and Expressive Culture

The Kapauku believe that Ugatame, who dwells beyond the sky, created the universe and has predetermined all the events within it, past, present, and future. Spirits of Ugatame's creation frequently appear to Kapauku as shadows in the trees, which make rustling or scraping sounds as evidence. Less often, these shadows appear in dreams or visions, sometimes in human form. These incarnations can be used by the dreamer as helpers or protectors, for either good or evil purposes. Likewise, the souls of dead kindred can be called upon to provide aid to their living kin.

Science, Secularism, and the Supernatural

The religious philosophy of the group is intriguing in that it is not, as Posposil (1963) puts it, "studded with numerous rationally inexplicable dogmas that are so characteristic of the world's great religions" (p. 92).

The Kapauku hold a rationalistic and logical view of the world that resembles scientific thought. Their outlook on the world is internally consistent, depending upon that which can be perceived through the senses, and follows logically from those perceptions. Once these premises are granted, that which contradicts these expectations is rejected out of hand. Following from this, because the only things that exist are things that can be perceived by the senses, the supernatural does not exist. People believe in it, but it is not real. They are thus none too eager to explain the unknown and speculate on the whys and wherefores of the world's mysteries. When asked to do so, they are most likely to reply, "I don't know," and be satisfied to leave it at that. Ethnographer Posposil (1963) reports never having witnessed any purely philosophical musings, speculations on the enigmas of life, or arguments focusing solely on the supernatural.

This logical universe is relativistic. Determining "bad" and "good" can only be accomplished in context. Hence, when asked, "Is killing a man good or bad?" the reaction is one of both surprise and confusion. After some thought, the answer will be itself a question: "Killing of which man, and good for whom?" (Posposil 1963)

Ceremonies

Kapauku ceremonies stand in contrast to the elaborate rituals found in the lowlands. Unlike ceremonial events, which typically focus on religion and the supernatural and are often communal in nature, Kapauku ceremonies appear both secular and individualistic. All have "owners" who are individually responsible for their outcomes and who will personally gain prestige if they are successful.

The lack of preoccupation with the supernatural is reflected in the fact that Kapauku ceremonial life revolves primarily around the realm of economics. Any elements one might deem "magical" are very minor portions of ceremonial events such as weddings, births, or feasts. Certainly the magical acts are not considered essential: *tonowi* sponsoring feasts assert that the success of an event is due solely to their own labor, and not to any supernatural guidance.

Absent from Kapauku culture are artistic renderings of supernatural beings, fertility rites, elaborate mortuary customs, and group initiation ceremonies. The most elaborate ceremonial production, the pig feast, is not religious in nature, but is designed to gain wealth and display status. Performers in the ceremonies are not attempting to influence the supernatural to send good fortune their way; they expect direct economic benefit as a result of their participation.

Pig Feasts

The most important Kapauku ceremony, and certainly one that is economic in focus, is the pig feast, which is a cycle of events lasting several months.

It is instigated by a *tonowi*'s decision to host the feast. Here, he can sell pork for shell money, give away pork to gain prestige, and establish his primacy over other rich men who may aspire to his position. The construction of a dance house and feasting houses is then begun, and these endeavors have a series of rituals associated with them. Following their construction, there is a three-month period of nightly dances, attended by nearby villagers. Special songs are composed for singing in the dance houses during these months, and are regarded as the valuable personal property of the single individual who composed them.

There are actually several grand feasts before the final one. Dancing, singing, and courtship is ongoing. By the time the culminating feast is held, there have been perhaps two thousand guests and several hundred pigs slaughtered and distributed. Profits in shell money may be enormous. Great feasts are talked about for years after their occurrence.

Illness, Curing, and Death

Illness is sent by spirits or sorcerers, and cured by shamans, who often are helped by spirits of their own. A shaman's curative armamentarium includes spells and prayers, treatments made from medicinal and magical plants, ritual washings of the ailing individual, and the removal of foreign objects from a victim's body. Shamans also have the power of preventive medicine should an individual be aware of a sorcerer's evil attempt and wish to forestall the anticipated illness.

Both shamans—whose magic is used toward positive ends—and sorcerers—whose gifts are essentially evil—can acquire status through spiritual or dreaming visitations. Women and men who are shamans practice preventive magic and curative ceremonies. Those who are sorcerers can send illness, economic ruin, or death.

Certain older women, whose souls have been eaten by flesh-hungry spirits, and replaced by the spirits' evil presence while they sleep, appear ordinary by day. But during the night they pursue all the corpses who have been former victims of the evil spirits now residing within their souls, and consume what is left of the corpses' flesh. Punishment of these ghouls does not include death, which action would only release the spirits possessing them, sending them in search of new homes. Instead, because ghouls are believed to be so possessed due to the black magic of a sorcerer, the individual sorcerer deemed responsible is sought out and killed, thus effectively ending a ghoul's ordeal.

Death is invariably attributed to spirits or sorcerers, no matter what its outward cause. The soul, once it has departed the body, will spend the day among the forests, but comes home to the village at nightfall, in case kin-group members need help or seek vengeance. Days spent by departed souls in the forest are the totality of the Kapauku "afterworld" beliefs; there is no sense that there is another dwelling place for the dead after life in the village. Given the expectations of the Kapauku that the souls of the dead may act in their behalf, it is not surprising that great care is taken with burial practices to achieve this end. Whereas the torso of the dead is buried, the head is left above-ground, sheltered from the elements by a web of branches with enough open space between them to provide a window.

A World of Quantity

As an outgrowth of their emphasis on objectivity, profit, and exactness, Kapauku are oriented to a world where the quantitative holds sway over the qualitative. They have outstanding mathematical abilities and a highly elaborate counting system, both valuable skills in their money economy. They value high numbers and large volume. When shown pictures in an American magazine, they directed most of their attention to counting the number of teeth in a smile, windows in office buildings, cars on the street, and, with most enthusiasm, the huge number of spectators in the crowd at a football game.

Posposil (1963) found that informants gained great pleasure in being able to count the thousands of glass beads he used as money. After many hours spent counting, he would be told: "You have 6722 beads in your boxes. That means you have spent 623 beads since Gubeeni counted your money three days ago" (p. 94). He reflects on this with the admission that his finances were never so much in order as during his times in the field among the Kapauku.

He also benefited from their understanding of his work back home. After giving the villagers a "lecture" on agriculture, he in turn was handed several chickens, with the explanation that they remembered that he was always paid to lecture to his anthropology students in the United States (Muller 1990).

✦ For Further Discussion

An important role in Kapauku society is the *tonowi*, a "big man." How is the importance of the tonowi connected to the other important features of Kapauku society, such as individualism and economics?

CHAPTER 9

THE MINANGKABAU

Matriliny and Merantau

The Minangkabau live in West Sumatra and Malaysia.

✦ THE BEGINNING

In the beginning, there was only the Light of Mohammad, through which God created the universe. From the Light came angels and Adam, and from Adam descended Alexander the Great, whose wife was a nymph from Paradise. Upon his death, the three sons of Alexander the Great, Diraja, Alif, and Depang, set sail around the world, taking with them their late father's crown. Some say the princes argued rightful ownership; some say their ship ran aground. But the crown was lost in the sea. A follower of Diraja, a trickster and master goldsmith, fashioned a replica of the crown and urged Diraja to tell his brothers he had found the original. Diraja did so, claiming the crown as his own. At this, the brothers parted. Prince Depang sailed off to the Land of Sunrise, becoming Emperor of Japan; Prince Alif traveled to the Land of Sunset, where he proclaimed himself Sultan of Turkey. Prince Diraja found the Land between Sunrise and Sunset, finding himself at the top of a mountain. It was there that the Minangkabau world began, with Maharaja Diraja as its first king.

✦ INTRODUCTION

Indonesia comprises more than 13,600 islands peppered over 3400 miles, roughly the distance from the Atlantic coast to the Pacific (Peacock 1973). Of these, roughly 6000 are named, and less than 1000 permanently populated by Indonesia's 180,000,000 citizens. Geographers divide Indonesia's islands into three groups: the Greater Sunda Islands, the Lesser Sunda Islands, and the Moluccas. It is the Greater Sunda Islands (Borneo, Sulawesi, Java, and Sumatra) that are home to the majority of Indonesia's population, and in which the nation's principle economic activities are centered.

Sumatra is the largest of the Great Sundas and the world's sixth largest island. Towering along the length of its western coast is a massive wall of nearly one hundred volcanic peaks, several of which are active. Made of two chains folded together, the tallest of the summits reach twelve thousand feet. At the base of the mountain's eastern slope is a lush plain, blanketed by dense tropical rainforest. In a valley between the two mountain folds rests a series of lakes. The Equator slices the island, and the climate is hot and humid. There is no dry season here, and 145 inches of rain falls annually. Sumatran wildlife includes elephants, tapirs, leopards, tigers, rhinoceros, proboscis monkeys and orangutans. The east coast is swampy; the south sparsely populated, but wealthy with oilfields. The north boasts waterfalls and tropical jungle. West Sumatra is home to the Minangkabau.

In the center of the island, along the western coast facing the Indian Ocean, live the four million Minangkabau. Legend has it that the name derives from triumph in an unusual battle with Javanese invaders in the fourteenth century. A Javanese king, Adityawarman, sent word to West Sumatra that he intended to annex their land. Unwilling to cede their autonomy, they proposed a buffalo battle. The Javanese provided a huge bull; the Sumatrans a young calf that had not been fed for days on end. Attaching sharp knives to the calf's small horns, the Sumatrans released their representative, who mistook the larger buffalo for its mother. Hungrily, the calf ran to the Javanese bull and began to suckle at its belly, driving the knives deep into the larger buffalo, killing it. The victors took their name from this triumph: *minang* (victorious) *kerbau* (buffalo) (Koentjaraningrat 1975, Vreeland et al. 1977). While this story is told more for its charm than out of a sure sense of truth, the buffalo's horns can be seen in the unique sweeping roof points of traditional architecture and the hornlike projections of women's ceremonial headdress. A more prosaic explanation is that Minangkabau is derived from *pinang kabu*, meaning "original home" (Loeb 1989 [1935]).

→ HISTORY

Early Influences

Although much has been written about the history of the Minangkabau, there is some dispute about its earliest beginnings (Unny 1994). Indian influences were in evidence in Indonesia as early as the fifth century, with small kingdoms developing in Sumatra. Srivijaya, a powerful Buddhist kingdom, arose in south Sumatra, in the seventh century. The Srivijaya Empire dominated Indonesian waters, situated in the center of international trade routes. By the early part of the fourteenth century, the Srivijayan preeminence waned, and it is widely assumed that the Minangkabau kingdom arose as an extension of this large trading empire to the south, although there is debate about the timing of its emergence (Josselin de Jong 1980 [1952], Kahn 1980, Loeb 1989 [1935], Unny 1994). By the middle of the fourteenth century, all of central Sumatra was the kingdom of Minangkabau. The Minangkabau kingdom flourished until the early nineteenth century, when the royal family was challenged by a bloody rebellion, and, in mid-century, finally overthrown.

European Trade and Colonial Dominance

Sumatra's contact with Europe began as early as the thirteenth century with Marco Polo's expeditions to the northern part of the island. The riches to be had far outweighed the extreme hardships of travel to the Indies, and there was fierce competition for spices, gold, and textiles. (Peacock [1973] reports that a quarter of the Dutch crews died on each voyage, often because the water they had to drink was so polluted that they chose instead to drink their own urine.) The Portuguese were the earliest Europeans to dominate trade in Indonesia. By the early sixteenth century, they controlled the ports. After the Portuguese, both the British and Dutch arrived in Indonesia in search of spice trade, early in the seventeenth century. The British established trade relations on the west coast of Sumatra, engaging in near constant conflict with the Dutch, to whom they eventually traded West Sumatran possessions for the port of Malacca, on the Malay peninsula to the north. While British, Portuguese, and Spanish traders all were a presence in the Indonesian waters, it was the Dutch who eventually held sway.

At the beginning of the seventeenth century, a group of Dutch traders formed the Netherlands East India Company in an attempt to monopolize Indonesian trade and force their Portuguese and British rivals from the area. They encountered formidable competitors in the Chinese, Indian, Arab, and Asian merchants, but persevered, and by the end of the century they had gained control through a combination of industry and arms. The Netherlands East India Company negotiated directly with the Minangkabau, contracting with the royal family for exclusive rights to the pepper and gold trade on the western coast (Kahn 1980).

At the turn of the century, the Company declined into bankruptcy, and by 1800 the Dutch government took over their land, exerting control mainly on Java. There, the Dutch instituted a system wherein export crops were to be delivered to the Dutch. West Sumatra was one of the areas outside of Java where this tribute was also demanded, and the Minangkabau highlands provided coffee to profit the Dutch government, with the proviso that they could not sell coffee on the open market.

The Rise of Nationalism

By the late nineteenth century, there was growing Indonesian resistance to Dutch rule. Among the Minangkabau, as coffee production began to decrease, the Dutch imposed instead a monetary tax. While this freed the Minangkabau to sell their coffee at higher prices, it ran counter to an earlier promise by the Dutch never to levy direct taxation on the Minangkabau.

Throughout the region, nationalist organizations arose in protest to the colonial regime. The Minangkabau, among the most educated Indonesians, were seen as intellectual leaders in the early twentieth century nationalist movements, acting as advisors to several charismatic leaders. It was Sukarno who emerged as the most influential of these, establishing the Indonesian Nationalist Party (PNI) in 1926. Demanding independence, the PNI was quashed by Dutch colonial authorities, and Sukarno was imprisoned. Indonesia fell to the Japanese in 1942, and they released Sukarno and other political prisoners in exchange for their work in propagandizing the Japanese cause (Peacock 1973). In 1945 when the Japanese surrendered to the Allies, Indonesia declared its independence, with Sukarno as the first president of the Republic of Indonesia. The Dutch, however, attempted to regain control. For the next several years, there was bitter fighting, despite the new nation's attempts to negotiate peacefully. In 1949 independence was finally won, and the United States of Indonesia joined the United Nations in 1950.

Over the next several decades, the new country experienced devastating social and economic troubles. There was dissension between military, religious, and governmental factions, and Sukarno reestablished the constitution, seizing far more power for himself. In the mid-sixties, members of Indonesia's Communist Party attempted a coup. After murdering army officers, the rebels were defeated by troops mobilized by a general, Suharto. In the wake of the uprising, Sukarno's power waned, and in 1968, Suharto replaced him as president. He held office until May 1998, when violent riots erupted, and Suharto was replaced by his vice president, B.J. Habibie. Habibie remained in power for seventeen months, until October 1999, when he became the first Indonesian president ever voted out of office. Abdurrahman Wahid won the nation's first democratic election, with Megawati Sukarnoputri, Sukarno's daughter, as vice president. In 2001, Megawati replaced Wahid as Indonesian president. In 2004, Susilo Bambang Yudhoyono became Indonesia's first directly elected president.

→ MINANGKABAU TRADITION

West Sumatra's population of roughly 3.4 million is nearly all Minangkabau, Indonesia's fourth largest ethnic group. The Minangkabau refer to their home as *Alam Minangkabau*, the Minangkabau World. *Alam Minangkabau* is divided into two regions, *darat* and *rantau*. These are geographic designations, but also cultural phenomena (Kahn 1980). While *darat* refers specifically to the highland home of the Minangkabau, it also refers to the "culture core" of home (Kahn 1980:8). *Rantau* is the term applied to outlying districts, and figures prominently into Minangkabau social and economic life. The *darat* is further divided into three districts or *luaks*, Tanah Datar, Agam, and Lima Puluh Koto.

Within these three core districts are the village communities, or *nagari*. *Nagari* are larger than many traditional villages, and thus are sometimes referred to as "village-republics." The largest may be home to several thousand (Young 1982). Each *nagari* has at least one mosque, and one council hall, the *balai*, in which the governing council sits.

The first Minangkabau *nagari*, according to the *tambo* (Minangkabau historical legend), was Pariangan Padang Panjang. It was in this first *nagari* that the four matriclans (*suku*) originated. Out of these ancestral clans—Koto, Piliang, Bodi, and Caniago—grew all the Minangkabau people, who left the original *nagari* to settle others as their numbers grew. It was in this way that the entire *Alam Minangkabau* came into being. Although there are now many clans, it has been established that every *nagari* contain at least four, in keeping with the original number of *suku* (van Reenan 1996). Each *suku* is further divided into six lineages, or *kaums*, each with a clan leader, or *penghulu*. The *kaum* is a social unit of individuals descended from a common ancestor, and it both possesses communal property and bears communal social responsibility for the actions of its members. *Kaum* members live together in a neighborhood (*kampuang*), which shares rights to the land, and they bear social obligations to one another, both ceremonial and mundane. Individuals have rights and obligations at each level of social organization. They are loyal to their *kaum* in dealings with other *kaums*; defend their *suku* to other *sukus*; stand by their *nagari* in relations with other *nagari* (Abdullah 1972).

At the heart of Minangkabau social structure is *adat*. In fact, any discussion of traditional Minangkabau life must begin with *adat*.

✦ CUSTOM AND BELIEF

Adat

The concept of *adat* is of crucial importance in Minangkabau life, past and present. It is a term that is most often translated as "customary law," the traditional rules of conduct, belief, and social organization. It is what is right and proper; it is what is essentially Minangkabau. Peletz (1981:15) describes *adat* as "a unitary, all-embracing concept encompassing an expansive set of institutions governing the conduct of all personal, kin, and local affairs." In addition, it includes "the reciprocally based relationships between humans and the natural and supernatural realms." The pervasive and solid reality of the power of *adat* is captured in the well-known saying that claims that the living are anchored and guided in their lives by *adat* in the same way that the dead are surrounded and held firm by the packed earth of their graves (Peletz 1981).

It was at the inception of the *Alam Minangkabau* that *adat* was established. The *tambo* recounts the beginnings of Minangkabau history, the time before memory, in which the rules of *adat* were given and the royal family was established. Taufik Abdullah, a scholar of Minangkabau history, explains that the *tambo* provides both "mystical sanction to the existing order" and "categories for the perception of reality" (1972:184). It is not only a recounting of the history of the Minangkabau world, but also a template with which events in modern times may be interpreted.

Tambo legend has it that two men, Datuk Katumangguangan and Datuk Perpetiah nan Sabatang, codified *adat*. They divided the *darat* into the *nagari*, *suku*, and their *penghulu*, and established the rules for governance. Half-brothers and descendants of the king Maharaja Diraja, Katumangguangan was of pure royal blood; Perpetiah nan Sabatang's father was a commoner. Thus, each developed a political tradition derived out of their own birth; the followers of Katumangguangan created a system of aristocracy, and those of Perpetiah nan Sabatang the commons system (Frey 1986). The brothers divided the three *luaks* into these two systems, or *laras*. Those settlements (called Koto-Piliang), which follow the Adat Katumangguangan, are in keeping with his aristocratic heritage. Its adherents have a hierarchical lineage system, with some *penghulu* of higher status. They built their village council halls (*balai adat*) to represent this authority structure; the ends of the building were raised above the middle section, with the *penghulu* of higher rank sitting above the others. Those adherents of Adat Perpetiah nan Sabatang (Bodi-Caniago) follow a system that is more democratic in form. The *penghulu* lineage chiefs who make up the village council are all regarded as having equal stature. Unlike the seating in the Koto-Piliang *balai adat*, in the council houses here it is said of the *penghulu* "when they sit they are equally low, and when they stand they are equally high" (van Reenan 1996:71). In addition to these two systems, some *nagari* chose a mixture of the two, with the villages home to some clans that follow the *adat* of the Koto-Piliang, and others the *adat* of Bodi-Caniago.

Traditional Minangkabau *adat* encompasses four distinct categories, which speak to different levels of society and institutions, and which differentially guide belief, behavior, and choices. They are *adat nan sabana adat, adat nan teradat, adat nan diadatkan,* and *adat istiadat.*

The first *adat* category, *adat nan sabana adat* (*adat* which is truly *adat*), refers to the immutable laws of nature. These are represented by general natural laws: the nature of water is to be wet, the nature of fire is to burn, the nature of that which is sharp is to wound (Tan-Wong 1992). The physical world is that within which the social world must operate. It is therefore of primary importance that these be understood. They are the most "fundamental *adat,* the real self-evident *adat* where no human intervention can change its course" (Kling 1997:47).

The second category, *adat nan teradat,* is the essence of Minangkabau social organization. These are all of the principles set out at the beginning of the world. The rules constituting the *nagari, luak, suku,* and *penghulu* are all in this category, as is the principle of matrilineality, which we will see is fundamental to the *Alam Minangkabau.* The survival of Minangkabau life and the continuity of its traditions are ensured by adherence to this *adat.*

Adat yang diadatkan, the third category, is best rendered as local *adat.* While *adat nan teradat* is focused on the maintenance of tradition, it is this *adat* that allows for change over time. Its tenets are based on decisions made by deliberation by the village council, which has the wisdom to recognize that rigidity in the face of new situations is dysfunctional. Consensus is the guiding principle in considering change in local rules, which is proposed to all, and adopted if there is unanimous approval (*muafakat*).

Last are the *adat istiadat,* daily customs and practices, "social behaviours that are considered appropriate, but not obligatory" (van Reenen 1996).

The rules of *adat,* then, are the customs and guiding principles that govern all the realms of human experience, physical, social, and spiritual. Above and beyond the specific rules are two overarching principles: consensual agreement and cooperative group effort (Tan-Wong 1992). All members of *Alam Minangkabau* have an obligation to all others and to achieve the aims of a unified world. Challenges must be approached with an eye to compromise and unity.

The Rise of Islam

Most sources cite reasons of expanding trade for the initial introduction and eventual spread of Islam through Malaysia and Indonesia (Abdullah 1972, Frey 1986, Hall 1964, Peacock 1973). As early as the seventh century, Muslim traders had brought Islam to the islands. By the time of the Crusades, late in the eleventh century, Southeast Asia was well-linked by trade and shipping to the Far East, Asia, and the Mediterranean. While there is evidence for small Islamic settlements by the end of the thirteenth century (Peacock 1973), it was not until the fourteenth and fifteenth centuries that Islam predominated.

In the early fifteenth century, Melaka, a port on the southwestern coast of the Malay peninsula, controlled the Strait of Melaka, a crucial trade route between Malaya and Sumatra. As Islamic rulers settled there, Melaka soon became a Muslim state, and northern Sumatra followed. It was the local rulers who converted to Islam first, with their subjects following. Both politics and economics were at work. Peacock (1973) suggests that Muslim merchants were more likely to choose one port over another for their trade if the ruler were Islamic and not Hindu. Moreover, as Europeans competed both for trade and for religious converts (to Christianity), local rulers embracing Islam could find wider Muslim support against European (especially Portuguese) encroachment.

The Aceh, who live on the northernmost tip of Sumatra, were most likely the earliest Sumatran converts to Islam. (Frey [1986:69] recounts the Minangkabau saying, "*adat* descended from the hills, while religion ascended from the shores.") However, the Minangkabau have long been a source of interest in discussions of Islamic dominance in Indonesia, for both historical and ideological reasons. Historically, because of the bloody *Padri* wars; ideologically, owing to the co-existence of belief systems which would seem unlikely to blend easily together: the matrilineal *adat* and the patrifocused Islam.

Adat and Islam Together

The Minangkabau world, with Islam and traditional *adat* side by side, was a harmonious one. Peacock (1973:106) describes traditional Minangkabau society as embracing two traditions, "the one a masculine *adat* which recognized the power of Muslim law and the jurisdiction of the patrilineal royal family over the entire society; the other a feminine *adat* which recognized only matrilineal custom and local communities." Kahn (1980) suggests that in fact the Minangkabau practiced something of a dual descent system, during the centuries of royal rule. That is, royal power was patrilineal, while the rules for inheriting both land and other forms of wealth followed the matrilineal *adat*. Noting the considerable attention that has been paid to what would seem to be contradictory systems— matrilineal custom and devotion to Islam—Kahn (1993) asserts that demanding the sort of internal cultural consistency that would render these two in conflict is a mistake, born of a misguided search for single unifying principles. He points out that there are, in fact, rules in place for choosing between instances where each tradition is to be applied. Inheritance of property, for example, sometimes follows Muslim law, and other times (most notably when ancestral land is at issue) is inherited through the matriline.

While sometimes prescribing conflictual actions (for example, in matters of marriage patterns, or residence rules) (Peletz 1981), there are many fundamental ways in which *adat* and Islam resemble and reinforce one another. Both traditions place great stock in the ideal of *muafakat*, consensual agreement, both value reciprocity and social obligations, both stress compassion and loyalty (Peletz 1981). An often-cited aphorism is that *adat* is based on religious law, and religious law is based on the Koran (Abdullah 1972, Peletz 1981, Frey 1986).

The harmonious integration of two traditions was represented in the tradition of three kings, who ruled collectively. In matters of religion, the Raja Ibadat was king. In matters of *adat,* the Raja Adat ruled. The King of the World (Raja Alam) was the ultimate authority, demonstrating the unity of *adat* and Islam together forming, in effect, the world. At the level of the *nagari,* there is again a blend of *adat* and Islam, with the presence of both the *balai adat,* the traditional council hall, and the mosque. Abdullah (1971) explains that *adat* is the underpinning of harmony within society, while Islamic religious law shows the way to find harmony between the mortal and the divine. He sees this embodied in the neighboring *nagari* structures of *balai adat* and mosque.

The harmonious co-existence of Islam and *adat* was violently shaken in the early nineteenth century by the *Padri* wars. The Wahabis, fundamentalist Muslims, were committed to Islamic purity. The ways of the Minangkabau royal family and the centrality of *adat* was unacceptable to them. Small Islamic schools in the Minangkabau highlands were run by teachers who came under the influence of the Wahabis, who proclaimed that *adat* was blasphemy (Peacock 1973). In 1820, after making a pilgrimage to Mecca, three of these men set out to invoke war, beginning what has been referred to as a "fundamentalist reign of terror" (Josselin de Jong 1980 [1952], Unny 1994). This civil war raged for twenty years, the *Padri* killing or enslaving resistors (Lee 1999) and murdering nearly all members of the royal family (Unny 1994).

Rejecting the possibility of a peaceful integration of *adat* and Islam, *Padri* leaders attempted to appeal to local Minangkabau farmers. In addition to their violent objections to the practices of the Minangkabau royal family, which included drinking and gambling, they also resented the Dutch colonialists, who controlled trade. The *Padris* gained followers among poorer farmers, whose lands were unsuitable for wet-rice cultivation, by urging them to grow coffee and refuse to cede the crops to the Dutch (Frey 1986). Encouraged by the possibility of greater wealth and inspired by nationalist feelings, local peoples fell into line. The Dutch, realizing that their own colonial power was far better served by traditional *nagari penghulu* leaders than by an upsurge in Islamic fundamentalism, intervened. By the time the *Padris* were defeated, it was apparent that despite their zeal, they had not succeeded in displacing *adat* and substituting a strict fundamentalist Islam. They did, however, greatly enlarge the scope and power of Islamic teachings, resulting in the Minangkabau being recognized as among the most devoted Muslims in Indonesia. Rather than supplanting *adat,* Islam became further intertwined. New formulations of *adat* emerged, ones that saw *adat* as a manifestation of religious law (Abdullah 1971).

→ Matriliny and *Merantau*

The Minangkabau are perhaps best known for two features of their society: the rule of matrilineal descent, and the male practice of *merantau,* or outmigration. These two are interrelated.

Matriliny

Matrilineal descent has long been intriguing to ethnographers. In the nineteenth century, evolutionary views held that matriliny was the initial form of social organization, and as such was destined to evolve into the more "advanced" patriarchal system. Over the past fifty years or so, arguments about theories of descent have waxed and waned, with debates circling around issues such as the instability of matrilineal systems, the conflict between authoritative and reproductive roles, strains between allegiances to different lineages, and imbalances in power and gender relations, all pointing towards its eventual demise (van Reenan 1996). It is often the Minangkabau who are mentioned in such discussions, perhaps because matrineality has survived, despite social and economic change.

In matrilineal systems, individuals belong to the family group of their mother. Women retain membership in their own groups after marriage, and generally continue to live among their matrikin, practicing matrilocality. In Minangkabau society, the most basic genealogical unit is the *semande* (one mother), a mother and her children. The core belief of matrilineality is that this mother-child bond is the most basic to society (van Reenan 1996).

Minangkabau social structure, as we have seen, is guided by *adat* law, which sets forth the rules of matriliny regarding village organization, group membership, residence, and inheritance of property. As is the case in most matrilineal systems, a man is differently responsible to his children, who are not a part of his family, and to his sister's children, who are. The Minangkabau have a *mamak-kemenakan* (uncle-niece/nephew) network (Abdullah 1972). The *mamak,* generally the oldest male member of the *suku,* is the head of the family and is responsible for the welfare of his sisters' children. He represents the family in *suku* affairs (Abdullah 1972). However, despite the fact that they are not members of the same clan, fathers have a close and important relationship with their children. Abdullah (1972) writes that although an uncle:

> is responsible for the material welfare of his [nephew] . . . it is the father who is expected to see to the spiritual growth of his children. An individual, who is father to his children and mamak to his sisters' children, is expected to fulfill both sets of responsibilities. (p. 196)

The distinction between a man's role as father versus that as uncle is perhaps best expressed by the adage that he "holds his children in his lap, but guides his nieces and nephews with his right hand" (Frey 1986:84).

The earliest writings on Minangkabau residence reported that marriage was something of a visiting arrangement. A man visited his wife at night, but in the morning returned to the home of his mother and sisters (Josselin de Jong 1980 [1952]). However, more recently, van Reenen (1996) notes it has been deemed useful to think of residence as being made up of several aspects. Domestic residence—eating, sleeping, childrearing—has always been uxorilocal, in the wife's home. Political residence, defined as the place where an individual enacts rights and duties as a community member, is matrilocal, at the site of the matrilineage. Economic residence is the site of labor and other productive activities. For men, these used to be almost exclusively located at the matrilineal home. Now, men tend to work near their wives and children as well.

Merantau

The *Alam Minangkabau* is divided into *darat*, home, and *rantau*, the lands beyond. Perhaps one of the most distinctive features of Minangkabau social life is the practice of *merantau*, or voluntary outmigration. *Merantau*, taken literally, means to go to the *rantau*, the outlying territories of the *Alam Minangkabau* (Kahn 1980). It has been suggested that the more modern practice of *merantau* has its roots in the earlier, less formal practice of village segmentation (Kato in van Reenan 1996). Minangkabau were originally sedentary agriculturalists, and their land in the *darat* was rich and productive, resulting in bountiful rice harvests. In response to rapid population growth, lineages and sublineages left their original *nagari*, and set off to establish new ones. Their intent was to stay in the newly settled village. In addition to agriculturalists establishing new *nagari*, Minangkabau traders also ventured to the *rantau* with gold and other goods. Van Reenan (1996) points out that this was only practical: outsiders rarely visited the inland, because the *darat* was difficult land to traverse. Thus, it became necessary for merchants to take their goods to the *rantau*.

Perhaps the most concentrated and best-known early migration of Minangkabau was to the Malaysian state of Negeri Sembilan. More than four centuries ago. Minangkabau going *merantau* sailed across the Straits of Melaka, and established new *nagari* settlements. These initial migrants were followed by more, and Negeri Sembilan is now a stronghold of matrilineal *adat* and Islamic law, tracing its origins to the Minangkabau highlands.

By the nineteenth century, several factors—among them the *Padri* wars, Dutch colonialism, and a rapidly increasing money economy, partly related to the valuable coffee crop—contributed to a change in the aims and structure of migration, largely owing to a rapid increase in population and colonial impediments to new *nagari* formation. The Minangkabau system of matrilineality was instrumental in facilitating the changes in migration. Men were not tied to the village in the same way women were. It was women who owned the ancestral land, women who stayed in their natal homes. The position of men in a matrilineal system—more free, but less secure—made *merantau* an appealing option, both for economic and personal reasons.

A husband (*sumando*) is, in essence, a guest in his wife's ancestral house. During the time he is there—for meals, or to visit with his children—he has restrictions placed on his behavior, and has no domestic power to speak of. In his own home—that is, the ancestral home of his mother and sisters—he is in the position of *mamak,* with rights and obligations pertaining to his sisters' children. However, he does not own the ancestral property he manages there. Burdened with obligations to two households, but only partially belonging in each, Naim (1984 in van Reenan 1996) concludes that rather than continue to "float" between them, his feelings of discomfort and restlessness propel him to go *merantau.* There he can work unburdened by the marginality and daily conflicts engendered by his dual role as *sumando* and *mamik.* By the middle of the nineteenth century, *merantau* was no longer solely the permanent institution of new settlements. It was "an institutionalized flow of merchants, artisans, students, clerks, government officials, political activists, professionals, and religious teachers" (Kato in van Reenan 1996:115).

Minangkabau in the *rantau* were often the most fervent missionaries for Islam. Their tradition of migration made it easy for men to travel to Islamic seats of learning and then travel abroad, spreading the faith. Unny (1994) reports that even those men who were less observant in the *darat* became active proponents of Islam in the *rantau.* He reports that in Jakarta, a city which is second only to West Sumatra in its Minangkabau population, more than 60 percent of the Moslem priests are Minangkabau. He goes on to suggest that whatever conflicts between *adat* and Islam may be experienced at home are absent in the *rantau.*

The modern practice of *merantau* has changed in terms of its location, duration, and practitioners. Originally *merantau* meant specifically those

Minangkabau women in a wet rice field.

migrants who stayed within the *Alam Minangkabau,* leaving the *darat* for the *rantau*. Today, the term also applies more broadly to individuals who, while retaining ties to their home village, travel elsewhere to work and live. Minangkabau increasingly go *merantau* on other islands (Java, Sulawesi, Bali, Borneo) and abroad, settling in Singapore, Malaysia and the Philippines (Unny 1994). It has been estimated (Naim in Kahn 1980) that there are now as many Minangkabau living outside of West Sumatra as there are at home. The majority maintain strong ties with their *nagari,* visiting home frequently and often buying a house and land there, serving for some as a place to retire. While *merantau,* some Minangkabau have formed associations of migrants from the same *nagari,* which, in addition to social functions, collect monies to send home for various village projects, such as building schools or mosques. (Kahn 1980) Furthermore, the past meaning of *merantau* was generally a temporary migration. Men left their *nagari* to earn money, further their education, or gain outside experience, and returned home regularly. Certainly, they returned home permanently in their old age (van Reenan 1996). While this so-called circulatory migration is still practiced, many who go *merantau* do so with the intention of settling permanently in their new homes. Last, *merantau* used to be exclusively the provenance of young men. Peacock (1973:108) describes the practice as "freeing the young bachelor from the local community." However, going *merantau* is no longer limited to either the young or to men. In the past, men who left their wives behind would often divorce them and remarry in their new community (or, invoking the Islamic privilege of polygyny, take another wife). In modern times, single women as well as men migrate; married couples migrate together.

→ LIFE IN THE NAGARI

Economic Organization

A combination of wet-rice cultivation and agriculture in dry fields has been the mainstay of Minangkabau economics for hundreds of years (van Reenan 1996). The plains areas are ideal for the wet-rice fields, where it is used locally for subsistence, and sold in the uplands. Surrounding these are the volcanic highlands, whose land is better suited to crops grown by dry agriculture, as well as coffee, which thrives in many hill villages, and is a much sought-after commodity around the world. Most Minangkabau are still farmers living in ancestral *nagari*. In addition to rice, villagers grow a variety of fruit and vegetable crops in their irrigated fields (*sawah*)—peanuts, peppers, maize, and tomatoes chief among them.

Local markets, which often move around from *nagari* to *nagari,* sell not only produce, but also fish and meat, clothes and jewelry, and other items such as books and textiles. Merchants from various communities follow the market as it travels.

Different *nagari* boast skilled artisans, whose works are sold both locally and in larger cities. Jewelry, woven purses, silver and other metallurgy, weaving, bamboo carving, and pottery number among them. In addition, commodities such as rubber, tea, spices, and especially coffee are sold on the worldwide market. In turn, manufactured goods from abroad find their way into the village markets. According to Kahn (1980), there is no *nagari* in West Sumatra today that does not participate in the global economy.

Residence, Property, and Inheritance

The traditional Minangkabau house is the *rumah gadang*, a large structure housing a matrilineage (*paruik*, meaning womb) of up to four generations. Built above ground (with chickens and other small livestock living below), and with the traditional sloping roof resembling buffalo horns, it has, at its center, a long inner room. This serves as communal living space as well as a ceremonial area for marriages or clan business. The kitchen is at one end, and there is often a long porch running the length of the front of the structure. Each of the adult women who form the residential core of the household has her own room (*bilik*), surrounding this central chamber, where she receives her husband at night when he comes from his own mother's *rumah gadang*. This communal lineage house serves as the symbol of the matriline, and the senior women are sometimes spoken of as the "central pillars of the house" (van Reenan 1996).

Young children eat and sleep in their matrilineal *rumah gadang*, playing outside during the day, accompanying mothers and aunts at their work. By the time they are six or seven, they are ready to begin formal Islamic schooling in the *nagari*'s prayer house, or *surau*. Boys sleep in the *surau*, until they are married (and begin to sleep in their wife's *bilik*) or go *merantau*. Girls sleep at home in the *rumah gadang*. In many *nagari* today, small structures are built next to the once-crowded *rumah gadang*, so women may have more space for themselves and their children and their husbands (when they are not absent) than their single *bilik*. Van Reenan (1996) warns against the assumption that this indicates a trend towards the standard nuclear family. There are still *rumah gadang* that host communal living, matrilocality is still the rule, and the smaller houses are always located nearby, keeping the matrikin as close neighbors.

The ownership and inheritance of Minangkabau property is governed by *adat*. Property consists of *harto pusako*, ancestral property, and *harto pencarian*, that which is acquired by an individual or couple. *Harto pusako* encompasses the rice fields (*sawah*), the ancestral home, and all other property owned by the lineage. These two types of property are governed by different rules. *Harto pencarian*, acquired goods, are inherited by either sons or daughters, and the mandates are more flexible. Sometimes acquired property is passed by mothers to their daughters and by fathers to their sons, a system found not uncommonly in Malaysia and Indonesia. Should the owner wish, *harto pencarian* may be sold (Kahn 1980).

Harto pusako, ancestral property, however, has much more stringent rules attached. It is always the possession of women, passed from mother to daughter, and never sold. Rights to the ancestral land are passed along from senior women to their adult daughters, with each receiving an equal share (van Reenan 1996). Such ownership contributes to women's socio-economic autonomy (Davis 1997). Even when land is parceled out for this inheritance, however, it remains ancestral land, the property of the matrilineage. (van Reenan [1996:100] cites an illustrative saying: "*harto pusako* may be divided but not separated.") This land *adat* is very strong, although there are allowances made for unusual circumstances (no direct female descendants, financial need that may result in the "pawning" of land, though this is frowned upon): (Kahn 1980, van Reenan 1996.)

It is through their wives that most men have access to land, by farming it and eating what they have grown (van Reenan 1996). However, some men will receive gifts of some proportion of the land's yields from their sisters or nieces, in recognition of their special bond. If a man falls on hard times, his sisters may allow him the use of some ancestral land (van Reenan 1996).

Sociopolitical Organization

Each matrilineal segment is headed by the lineage chief, the *penghulu*. Although these groupings are matrilineal, they have male leaders. *Adat* law mandates that the *penghulu*'s powers extend across all important categories—political, economic, social, and ceremonial (Manan in van Reenan 1996). Conflict resolution is always attempted at the lowest level of social organization (household, sub-lineage, lineage, *laras*, etc.), each of which has its own *penghulu* leader, and the ideal of *muafakat*—consensus—is paramount. The *penghulu* have three associates, each of whom is responsible for a different sphere: one assists in resolving disputes, the second watches over security in the *nagari*, and the third advises the *penghulu* in matters of Islamic law. *Penghulu* council meetings are held in the *balai adat* (council hall), with proceedings run according to the *adat* which prevails (*Adat* Koto-Piliang or *Adat* Bodi-Caniago).

✦ Minangkabau Today

West Sumatra is a popular destination for tourism. Padang is the provincial capital of West Sumatra, and the lesser tourist attraction, despite its share of traditional architecture and long history. Bukittinggi, "the administrative and cultural center for the Minangkabau people" (Parkes 1998:301) is the leading attraction. There are remnants of the colonial past, chief among them a clock tower constructed by the Dutch in the early nineteenth century (and referred to as Bukittinggi's Big Ben), as well as an old fort dating from the same time. The Bukittinggi Museum is housed in several traditional *rumah gadang*, which display clothing, musical instruments and arts and crafts. Tourism has also extended into dozens of Minangkabau *nagari* in the surrounding countryside.

The Minangkabau are still regarded as the "world's largest matrilineal society" (Unny 1994:5), despite changes in the traditional ways of life. There is much debate regarding shifting residence patterns and whether there has, in fact, been a "nuclearization" (van Reenan 1996) of the family. It is true that the role played by men has changed in the last fifty years or so.

Marriage, in the past, was entirely dictated and arranged by the matrikin. According to the 1950 census, Minangkabau had the dubious distinction of having the highest divorce rates in the entire Malay-Indonesian archipelago. Both the process of men going *merantau* for extended periods of time, as well as the tenuous place men hold in matriliny have been cited as contributory (van Reenan 1996, Unny 1994). Government intervention (specifically, the National Marriage Act of 1974, which enforced strict penalties for divorce) has played a part in the great reduction of divorce rates, but so have changing relations within the family. The *sumando* is no longer exclusively a peripheral visitor to his wife and children. As more women set up residence near, but not in, the *rumah gadang,* marital bonds strengthen. Matrilineality remains strong, as does the *mamak-kemenakan* bond. Some researchers (van Reenan 1996) find evidence that the relationship between *mamak* and sisters' children no longer carries either the huge economic burdens or the overarching authority it once did, to the detriment of the father-child tie. Minangkabau women still stand as the bridge between their own kin and that of their husbands, with their focus remaining primarily on their matrilineage. In some villages, men have increased their involvement in their wives' kin groups, often at the expense of their own matriclan (van Reenan 1996). In most others, men retain an overarching interest in their matrilineage, where they have a voice in decision making, in contrast to their status in their wife's house (Blackwood 2000).

Traditional Minangkabau culture thrives, in tandem with full participation in modern Indonesia. Despite state-level ideologies of men as heads of households, and the official constraints of Islamic law, women remain at the center of social networks, exercising their power as heads of their households and heirs to land (Blackwood 2000). A large proportion of Indonesian scholars are Minangkabau (Abdullah 1972, Kahn 1980, Unny 1994), and they continue to prize education, revere Islam, and enlarge their economic and scholarly opportunities through *merantau*. Balancing and integrating oppositions—*mamak* and *sumando, adat* and Islam, homeland and *rantau*—are still at the center of *Alam Minangkabau.*

✦ For Further Discussion

Many scholars have noted the seeming oppositions in Minangkabau society: Islam and *adat, merantau* and matriliny. How have the Minangkabau managed to weave together these apparently contradictory categories? What are some examples from your own society of traditions, values, and institutions that seem to be oppositional or contradictory, but are integrated into the workings of cultural life?

CHAPTER 10

THE NUER
Cattle and Kinship in Sudan

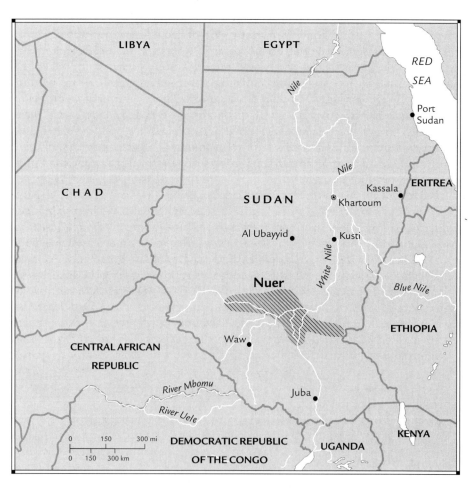

Location of the Nuer in southern Sudan.

✦ THE BEGINNING

Kwoth is everywhere. He is like wind; he is like air. He falls in the rain and roars in the thunder. The rainbow is his necklace. We are like little ants in his sight. *Ne walka*—in the beginning—there was a tamarind tree in the western land. Her name was Lic, and she was the mother. *Kwoth* created us to drop from her branches like ripened fruit. *Ne walka*—in the beginning—we were as the fruit of a tamarind tree.

✦ INTRODUCTION AND GEOGRAPHY

Sudan is the largest country in Africa, its area encompassing nearly one million square miles. It lies in the northeastern part of the continent and is a land of widely differing geography. In the north, it is covered with vast deserts; grassy palms fill the central region; and steamy jungles and swamps lie to the south. The Nile River is by far Sudan's most important geographic feature. Most of southern Sudan consists of a flood plain formed by its branches, with dense, jungle-like vegetation covering much of the region. Mountain ranges rise along the borders shared with Uganda, Kenya, and Ethiopia. Rainfall averages from thirty-two to fifty-five inches annually. Wild animals, including gazelles, giraffes, lions, leopards, and elephants roam the south. Along the Nile's branches live hippopotamuses and crocodiles.

The Nuer, now the second largest ethnic group in southern Sudan (Holtzman 2000), number more than a million (Hutchinson 1996) and live in the open savannah and swamps that line both sides of the Nile. E. E. Evans-Pritchard, best-known ethnographer of the Nuer, observed that "from a European's point of view Nuerland has no favourable qualities" (1940:51), cycling seasonally as it does through a state of parched grass or soggy swamp. The Nuer themselves, however, held a very different view. "Nuer," Evans-Pritchard reports, "think that they live in the finest country on earth" (1940:51). As herders, they indeed assess their land correctly. Their soil is made of thick clay, which cracks in the sun during droughts. These deep grooves are soaked and filled in the rainy season, cradling enough water to allow certain species of grasses to thrive even during the driest of seasons, providing pasture for the cattle. During times of intense flooding, sandy areas in somewhat higher elevations offer refuge.

Rainfall and flooding from the rivers that cross their lands provide the Nuer with surface water and abundant grasses, which, at their peak, reach shoulder high. However, the change of seasons, from wet to dry and back again, are sudden and often cataclysmic. Soggy swampland is rendered sere in a short time, as the blazing sun quickly evaporates the surface water from the clay soil. This, coupled with insufficient rainfall, may result in a shortage of pastureland.

This cycle of flooding and drought results in an environmental system that steers the direction of Nuer social and economic life, as we shall see.

⇢ ECOLOGY

Subsistence

Nuer economy is a mixture of pastoralism and horticulture. Such a mixed economy is dictated by their environment, as neither strategy alone would be sufficient to provide for their needs or those of their cattle. Of the two strategies,
pastoralism is the one favored both by the environment and by the Nuer themselves. As Evans-Pritchard remarks, "the environmental bias coincides with the
bias of their interest" (1940:57).

Although the Nuer might be able to rely solely on pastoralism, were it not
for the threat of certain cattle diseases, the balance in their economic strategy
could never shift such that horticulture would predominate. Climate, flooding,
and the flatness of the land result in an inability to cultivate most Central
African food plants. Their staple crop is millet, consumed in the form of porridge and beer, and they supplement this with a small amount of maize, and
an even lesser quantity of beans. Some tobacco is encouraged to grow under
the eaves of their huts, and gourds can send their vines up along the fences of
cattle corrals.

Millet's hardiness is such that the Nuer can reap two harvests per year,
but even so it will not survive too much standing water, and thus gardens have
to be established on higher ground. If the elevation is such that water from the
gardens may be lost, running down the slope, small dams are often constructed
as a solution.

Although millet is able to weather the harsh climate once it has been
established, the process of it taking hold initially can be undependable. Even
a short drought can cause new shoots to wither; unexpected rains can beat
small plants into the ground or wash them away. Weather is not the only environmental threat to crops. Evans-Pritchard (1940:78) reports having witnessed
the toll taken by such events as swarms of locusts, unfettered grazing by
ostriches and antelopes, and a parade of elephants stomping across the
seedling beds.

The Nuer practice neither crop rotation nor fallowing, and neither fertilize
nor irrigate. Instead, they move on to another site when the land is depleted.

Moving with the Seasons

The alternating floods and drought make it impossible for the Nuer to live in
one location year-round. Floods send Nuer and their herds to higher ground;
drought forces them out again. Those foodstuffs provided by their cattle—meat
and milk products—must be supplemented by fish and grain. Millet is best sown
inland; the rivers where fish are abundant are far away from these inland sites.
During the rainy season, cattle must be moved to protected ground, because
standing in sodden land quickly results in hoof disease. It is for this reason that
villages are constructed on the highest ground available. However, once the rains

cease, these elevated sites, selected precisely because they were the highest (and thus, driest) locations, soon must be abandoned for sites closer to pools and lakes in order to secure adequate water supplies. The vicissitudes of finding water are echoed in the search for vegetation. As they move seasonally, Nuer seek out both pastureland and drinking water, and drive their cattle to locations where they know both will be available. Their movement across the vast plains is never haphazard in nature, but rather aimed directly toward the most succulent grasslands. It is in this way that changing water supplies and vegetational growth determine both the time and direction of Nuer movement. When the rains begin again, they can return to their villages.

✦ SETTLEMENTS

Nuer are forced to build villages for protection against the flooding rains (and mosquitoes) and to practice horticulture. They are driven out of these villages into migratory camps to escape drought and to fish.

The aim, in choosing a village site, is to secure enough room for building homesteads, planting gardens, and grazing cattle. Most villages are built on elevated mounds, above the floodline and the mosquitoes breeding in the standing water, which stretch for a mile or two in length. In front of these sandy ridges there is land for grazing; gardens are cultivated in the back. Open ground is preferable to wooded areas, as it provides better protection to the cattle (from insect pests and predators in the woodlands) and because millet fares better in an open environment. Construction is of wood, and termites are generally better avoided in these open stretches of ground.

A typical Nuer homestead consists of a hut and a cattle barn. Families move from one section of the village to another, especially if there have been quarrels or pastures are exhausted. Huts and barns last about five years before they need to be rebuilt. After a decade or so, the gardens and pastures are no longer usable, and the entire village community may seek out a new site.

Camps, the Nuer settlements in the dry season, consist of flimsier structures, built close to the water source, and oriented so that their backs are to the wind and their front faces the cattle. These shelters can be erected in a few hours, using grassy material plastered with dung.

Throughout the dry season and in years when crops fail or herds fall victim to disease, it is fishing that sustains the Nuer. Opportunities to exploit the rivers, teeming with a variety of fish species, are as significant a factor as pasture and water when Nuer choose their campsites.

Nuer have no need of complex fishing techniques because the rise of the rivers during floods carries huge numbers of fish downstream, depositing them into streams and lagoons where they are easily speared. At nightfall, dams are constructed and fishers wait downstream by firelight. In a single night, as many as a hundred fish may be speared. As the dry season advances, fish are trapped in pools, the outlets of which have dried up and receded. It is a simple matter for the Nuer to stand along the pool's edge and spear all the fish within. Nuer can rarely see the fish they spear, but the sheer numbers of the prey yield adequate results even when spears are flung into the water at random.

Although Nuer territory is rich in game, hunting is not a strategy much relied upon. They rarely set out to hunt, pursuing only those gazelle and giraffe who present themselves at the camps. Their herds provide them with meat enough to suit them. Lions may be killed to protect cattle; leopards are valued for their skins, which figure prominently in Nuer social life.

✦ CATTLE

"Their Social Idiom Is a Bovine Idiom"

Cattle are the focus of Nuer life. They depend on the herds for their very existence; they delight in caring for them; and their love for cattle and zeal for acquiring them are at the core of Nuer culture. Cattle are the thread that runs through Nuer institutions, language, rites of passage, politics, economy, and allegiances.

Nuer relations with their neighbors are directed in large part by their preoccupation with the herds. They have nothing but disdain for neighboring tribes who own few or no cattle; they have entered into warfare with others solely for the purpose of stealing cattle and pastures. Internecine disputes are most often about cattle, and political divisions follow tribal distribution of pastures and water. Disputes that *result* from cattle are often *settled* with cattle—such conflict often ends in grave injury or death, and cattle are the only acceptable compensation.

Cattle are cared for by groups of families because an individual household cannot protect or herd their cattle alone. In the dry season, when huts are hastily constructed around the cattle *kraal* (corral), one can identify which groups own and care for cattle together. Male household heads are identified as owning the herds, but wives and sons have some rights to their use. Sons marry in order of seniority, given head of cattle when they do. It is not until the stock has been replaced that the next son may marry and take his share. The bond between brothers, forged by co-ownership of cattle, persists even after they have married and started families of their own. The bridewealth paid for a daughter of one's brother is shared among the brothers, and kinship becomes defined in large part by reference to cattle payments. It is as if the transfer of cattle from one individual to another is equivalent to the lines drawn on a genealogy chart (Evans-Pritchard 1940). When cattle are sacrificed, the meat is divided along kinship lines.

Personal names are frequently derived from features of the herd animals. Men are often called by names that refer to the color of a favorite ox; women take names from the cows they milk. When children play in the pastures, they call one another by cattle names; sometimes these names are proper names given at birth and handed down through the generations. Evans-Pritchard remarked that the genealogies he collected during his fieldwork often resembled the cattle inventory of a *kraal* more than a family tree (Evans-Pritchard 1940).

It is not surprising that the centrality of cattle would be reflected in Nuer ritual life. If one endeavors to contact the spirit world, this may be accomplished only through the cattle. Cows are dedicated to spirits—those spirits that are attached to the lineage of the owner, have possessed a living family member, or are the ghosts of ancestors. Thus, when asking about the history of any cow in the herd, one receives information not only about the ways in which that cow links one person to another—having been secured as bridewealth, for example, or as payment for a dispute—but also of the spirit world connections the animal represents. By rubbing ashes on the back of the cow, its owner may contact a spirit and seek its intervention or assistance.

As Evans-Pritchard soon learned, in order to understand the culture of the Nuer, one must first be thoroughly versed in the language of cattle. The complex negotiations surrounding marriage exchange, ritual, and the settlement of disputes were only intelligible once he could decipher the terminology of cattle colors, ages, size, sex, and other features. He laments, "I used sometimes to despair that I never discussed anything with young men but livestock and girls, and even the subject of girls led inevitably to that of cattle" (1940:19). Try though he might, every subject, approached in any way, soon yielded commentary on cows, heifers, oxen, steers, or kids. As he observed, "their social idiom is a bovine idiom"(1940:19).

Cattle are, of course, essential in a more mundane sense as well. Milk and millet are the mainstays of the Nuer diet, and whereas millet rarely lasts through the year, milk can be depended upon as a daily food. A single cow can sustain an entire family when milk is supplemented with fish. Even when the millet crop is abundant, Nuer depend on milk and cheese to make it palatable. Children especially need milk daily, and the Nuer say that children cannot be happy, much less healthy, without a dependable daily source of milk, of which elders will deprive themselves in order to assure the children's share. When there is milk enough for the children, extra can be made into cheese. If a family cannot secure enough milk for their small children, relatives will unhesitatingly provide a cow, because kinship obligations include caring for the children of one's kin and neighbors. This is never thought to be the sole responsibility of the child's parents.

Because milk is so essential, cows are often judged by the amount of milk they produce, and one cow is never equivalent to another if its milk production is not commensurate. Any Nuer can immediately list, in rank order, the best and worst cows of the herd, paying no attention to those qualities he might cite in his oxen—fatness or color or horn shape—but only those features that promise a good milk cow. Nuer can scrutinize the back and haunches, veins, and bone structure of a cow and predict with great accuracy its lactating capacity.

Their dependence on dairy products directly influences other aspects of Nuer life and social structure. Cattle are not as numerous as they once were, owing largely to disease caused by cattle pests, and this relative shortage prevents the Nuer from leading an exclusively pastoral lifestyle, although this might be their preference. A mixed economy is essential to supplement their diet. As previously mentioned, one family unit often needs to depend on the larger kin group for dairy products, mandating that the basic economic unit for the Nuer must be a larger one than a single household. However, the importance of milk products not only introduces constraints, such as the foregoing, into Nuer daily life, but also provides flexibility. For example, while their need for horticulture prevents them from leading an exclusively nomadic life, their reliance on dairy products does allow them considerable mobility. Milk can be both stored and transported in the form of the dairy cows, and is accessible wherever the herd may be. Moreover, since the production of milk depends on water and pastureland, this diet not only permits, but also *requires,* frequent movement.

Although herds are not raised for the purpose of slaughter, meat is important to the Nuer diet and economy as well. Honoring a ghost or spirit, mortuary rites, and marriage ceremonies are all occasions during which barren cows are sacrificed and consumed. (Such rituals are more commonplace in the rainy season, or early into the draught, because the festivities are never complete without beer, brewed from the millet available during these times of year.) Never do Nuer slaughter animals solely because they desire to eat meat. There is the danger of the ox's spirit visiting a curse on any individual who would slaughter it without ritual intent, aiming only to use it for food. Any animal that dies of natural causes is eaten, although Evans-Pritchard notes that when a favorite animal has died, its owner often has to be persuaded to overcome his sorrow and share the meat. On an occasion such as this, the Nuer explain "The eyes and the heart are sad, but the teeth and the stomach are glad" (Evans-Pritchard 1940:26).

Nuer man.

In addition to their value as foodstuff and ritual objects, oxen are also items of great prestige. Wealth is defined differently in different places; among the Nuer, it is only cattle that are truly valued in this way (Gross 1992:44). Prestige is derived from the shape, color, size, and form of the oxen, and Nuer will actively intervene in shaping the oxen, beginning at birth. They will manipulate the humps on a newborn ox's back, or train its horns to grow in a certain configuration. Cattle also provide raw materials for the manufacture of leather goods, drums, rugs, clothing, pipes, spears and shields, containers, ornaments, and cutlery. Their dung is used as plaster in construction and burned to provide ashes both for ritual use and also as "toothpaste" and mouthwash. Their urine is used not only for churning cheese, but to wash hands and face.

✦ SOCIOPOLITICAL ORGANIZATION

The Nuer have no centralized political leadership. Theirs is a kin-based society, and it is only through an understanding of the kinship organization that one can apprehend the way in which their social system functions.

Evans-Pritchard found the Nuer to be a "deeply democratic" (1956:181) people, with an egalitarian approach to their communal life. It is the obligation of kin to help one another. When one household has a surplus, it is shared with neighbors. Amassing wealth is not an aim. Although a man who owns a large herd of cattle may be envied, his possession of numerous animals does not garner him any special privilege or treatment.

Segmentary Lineage Organization

The Nuer are perhaps best known as the most often cited example of the segmentary lineage organization. Marshall Sahlins (1961), in his classic study of this type of system, describes it as the inevitable result of tribal growth.

Among the Nuer, there are roughly twenty patrilineal clans. Each of these can be divided into maximal lineages, which can in turn be divided into major lineages. These are segmented into minor lineages, which are divided into minimal lineages. A minimal lineage group reckons its descent from one great-grandfather. It is these most minimal groups around which Nuer daily life revolves. There is neither leadership nor formal organization in the higher levels. They are potential connections waiting to be activated should the need arise. In a dispute between different minimal lineages, alliances can be formed by drawing from people related at a higher level. Each side of the conflict can mobilize more and more kin by reaching out to more and more distant kin. Mary Douglas (1966) comments, "[t]he Nuer afford a natural illustration of how people can create and maintain a social structure in the realm of ideas and not primarily, or at all, in the external, physical realm of ceremonial, palaces or courts of justice" (p 143).

Warfare, Raiding, and Blood-Feuds

In the early nineteenth century, Nuer territory spanned about 8700 square miles. Their neighbors, the Dinka, held nearly ten times that amount of land. By the end of that century, however, the Nuer had expanded their territory at the expense of the neighboring Dinka. The Nuer cut a wide swath through Dinka territory, in the end increasing their holdings to 35,000 square miles. Dinka culture resembled that of the Nuer in many respects, save the one that seems to have given the Nuer a significant military advantage—the segmentary lineage organization (Evans-Pritchard 1940:240).

The Dinka, who were the first to settle in the Sudan, had no neighbors to defend against, and thus had none of the mechanisms in place to mobilize distant tribal members. Sahlins (1961) suggests that the unique alliance-forming properties of the segmentary lineage system of organization allow its members to raid nearby territories held by groups without the ability to mobilize forces. Relatives are available for defense, too, but it especially allows groups to decide to make the first strike because lineage segments are assured that they can draw reinforcements from other lineages related to them at a higher level of the clan.

The Nuer are a people with a penchant for fighting (Evans-Pritchard 1956), and these disputes frequently end in death. One is unlikely to find an older tribe member without copious evidence of the visit of clubs and spears. An insult is justification for a fight, and the Nuer have been described as easily taking offense. Since there is no formal mechanism for redress if an insult has been hurled, an individual must take it upon himself to seek justice. He issues a challenge to a duel, and the challenge must be accepted. Children are instructed to settle any grievance by fighting, and skill in this endeavor is uniformly admired.

Whereas boys fight one another with spiked bracelets attached to their wrists, men fight those closest to them with clubs. Spears are reserved for use outside the local community, as there is a greater danger for more serious injury or death, and this has the potential to escalate into a blood-feud. After the battle is joined, no onlooker may intervene, and the combat rages until one of the parties is severely injured, at which point they will generally be pulled apart by those gathered around to watch the spectacle.

When the dispute involves men from different villages, however, it generally takes a different form. Spears are the weapons of choice, and every man in both villages is expected to participate. Because such a fight cannot end until there are several dead, Nuer are loath to enter into such a battle lightly. Instead, they will allow the conflict to be mediated by an informal adjudicator, the leopard-skin chief.

The Leopard-Skin Chief

Despite their reluctance to enter into a blood-feud, the Nuer fight often, and homicide is not uncommon as the battles escalate. When a life is taken, there must be compensation. Because the Nuer have no formal system of adjudication, it falls to the holder of an informal ritual office of mediation, the leopard-skin chief, to intervene and prevent further bloodshed. Although one advantage of the segmentary lineage organization is its effectiveness in mobilizing allied kin, the ease with which full-scale disruption can escalate is something that must be kept in check. Although the leopard-skin chief has no power to enforce his judgments, his intervention is generally successful.

Part of the leopard-skin chief's effectiveness derives from his status as an outsider to the lineage network. Such an individual is generally a man whose own lineage is not one of the local village. This affords him a more neutral stance, so neither his attempts at mediation nor his judgment about payment of compensation are seen as favoring one side or the other.

Sometimes a leopard-skin chief can step in and encourage de-escalation of a dispute before blood is shed. More often, however, he is sought out after there has already been a murder, and his role is to arrange settlement between the aggrieved lineages, allowing both sides to step back from the battle without admitting defeat and preventing any further bloodshed.

When one man has killed another, he retreats at once to the home of the leopard-skin chief, so named for the skin he wears draped about his shoulders as the insignia of his office. This is neutral ground for the murderer. While he is in residence there, no kinsmen of the deceased will seek revenge. The leopard-skin chief has the ability to ritually cleanse the slayer, and this begins immediately. The murderer must neither eat nor drink until the leopard-skin chief has released the blood of the dead man out of his body, which is accomplished by making several incisions down the length of his arm with a fishing spear. Once this is accomplished, the murderer presents the leopard-skin chief with an animal to sacrifice, and the cleansing is complete.

A man may remain in the sanctuary of a leopard-skin chief's home for quite some time, because negotiations cannot begin in earnest until the family of the deceased have completed their mortuary ceremonies and anger has begun to cool. His first attempts at negotiations may be met with some resistance. After ascertaining how many head of cattle the culprit's family are willing to offer as compensation, the chief approaches the victim's kin. It is a point of honor that they refuse this first overture. Negotiations proceed slowly, and generally the injured family begrudgingly accepts the payment—in theory forty to fifty animals, paid out over the course of several years—when they determine that the chief has made his best offer and is becoming increasingly impatient with their refusals. When at least twenty head of cattle have been paid, the family of the murderer may begin to feel safe, no longer fearful of being ambushed by the enemy family as they walk abroad. It is the leopard-skin chief who delivers the payment, with the murderer remaining in the asylum of the chief's home until completion of the initial transfer.

Even years after the debt has been paid, there is enmity between the two families. There is official prohibition against the families' eating or drinking together until the entire payment and all accompanying sacrifice are complete. However, in actuality they may choose not to share food for years, or even generations, out of injured feelings. Of this they say, "a bone lies between us." The healing is never really complete, as the murdered man's family is thought ever after "to have war in their hearts" (Evans-Pritchard 1956:154).

✦ Religion and Expressive Culture

The Nuer speak of *kwoth,* spirit, as the creator, as a father and judge, as a guiding force and recipient of their prayers. Evans-Pritchard (1956) suggested that this overarching concept could be roughly analogized to a Western notion of "God." However, there are also two other categories of supernatural beings that figure prominently in Nuer religious thought. These are the "spirits of the above" and "spirits of the below." One of the ways in which these spirits differ from the rather larger concept of *kwoth* is that different individuals accord various spirits of the above and below varying interest and respect. A certain spirit may be significant for some individuals and families but not for others, whereas *kwoth* is recognized and revered similarly by all Nuer.

Spirits of the Above

Whether a person feels distinctly connected to any of the spirits ordinarily has to do with whether or not the individual or any family member has had direct contact with the spirit, usually in the form of possession. Sudden illness may be seen as possession and, once recovered, the sufferer may come to regard the spirit that has sent the illness as one of his or her own *kuth,* the term applied to all spirits. Descendants of this individual may then continue to attend to this spirit. If they do not, the inherited spirit may send a reminder to alert the family to its need for attention. When the Nuer fall sick without an obvious cause, they may realize they have been neglecting a *kuth* who has visited an illness as a signal that it is not happy to have been forgotten.

Temporary spirit possession can be remedied by sacrifice. An animal is dedicated to the offending spirit, and recovery is expected to follow. There are instances, however, of spirit possession that is permanent. This may occur independent of an episode of illness, or may follow it. Abnormal behavior may be manifest for some time, and it is then realized by others that this individual has been given, by the possessing spirit, powers of healing, prophecy, and divination. That person is then *gwan kwoth,* the owner of that spirit, hollowed out by the possession, and filled up with the gifts bestowed by the spirit. Such an individual's character is forever altered (Evans-Pritchard 1956).

In this new role, the prophet—usually male—is relied upon for certain ritual functions. He may perform sacrifices, or aid in curing. But the most important function of one permanently possessed by a spirit of the above is in the realm of warfare. Orders to fight come through him, the possibility of victory is in his hands, and no large-scale military effort is ever undertaken without these prophets performing sacrifices and singing hymns. The main social function of such prophets is to direct cattle raids on neighboring tribes, most notably the Dinka.

One sort of spirit of the above is the *colwic,* who were once Nuer themselves. Individuals who have been struck by lightning, killed in windstorms, or found dead in the bush, unaccountably, are thought to have undergone a metamorphosis and emerged divine. Most lineages can cite at least one *colwic* patron spirit. Death by lightning is not uncommon, and violent electrical storms are cause for great anxiety. However, such a death is not thought to be retribution for any misconduct on the part of the deceased, as some deaths are regarded. Rather, the electrocuted person is seen as having been chosen by *kwoth* to be changed into a *colwic.* It is said that the individual has actually entered into a kinship relation with *kwoth,* as a result of this special selection (Evans-Pritchard 1956:54).

Spirits of the Below

Spirits of the above are also known as "spirits of the air." They are "great spirits" and much revered. Spirits of the below, however, are regarded quite differently. They are believed to have fallen from above, and as "spirits of the earth" they are "little spirits" and not held in the same reverence.

Spirits of the below can be classified into several categories, the most important of which is that of totemic spirits. These attach to specific clans and lineages, and are usually described in animal form—lion, lizard, crocodile, various birds, and snakes. Plants may be inspirited too, as may rivers and streams. Each of these aspects of nature is a material representation of a "spirit of the below." These spirits can act positively through the plant or animal, if the totem by which they are represented is shown the proper "respect" by the Nuer. This respect can be demonstrated by refraining from hurting or eating it; paying it the courtesy of acknowledgment, should it be met along one's way; or by some act meant to demonstrate regret, should it be encountered dead or hurt.

Spirits as Social Refraction

It is evident that the spiritual conceptualizations of the Nuer are intricately bound up with their social order. Spirits who "belong" to one lineage do not visit individuals of another lineage. Those that are represented by totems can act only for the clans whose totems they rightfully are. However, there are larger spiritual representations that do indeed belong to all Nuer, and in this way their religious structure resembles their social structure. The principle of segmentary lineage organization is that although lineages may be distinct and opposed to one another at one level, those same lineages may be affiliated with one another and opposed to another lineage at a different level of segmentation. It is in this same way that they can conceive of the spiritual realm as being specific to a smaller group at one level, yet "belong" to a larger segment, higher up.

Kwoth and Nuer: Death, Soul, and Sin

Evans-Pritchard (1956) points out that to the Nuer, religion is a "reciprocal relation" between *kwoth* and humanity. Their religious tenets tell them not only about the nature of *kwoth* and various spirits, but also about their own nature.

The Nuer fear death, and it has been suggested that this is because they have no tradition of an afterlife. They profess neither knowledge nor interest in what happens to them after they die. Life comes from *kwoth,* and it returns to *kwoth,* in some sense, after death. They make a distinction between the mere "life" or "breath" of an individual, that which demonstrates being alive, and what might be thought of as the "soul," that property that bestows unique personhood on an individual. Mere animation is not sufficient to demonstrate this latter property. This is demonstrated by the story of Gatbuogh, a man who returned to his village after years of wandering, having been given up for dead. He returned changed—he was distracted, disengaged, not communicative. It was said of him that he was alive but he no longer had his soul. Similarly, mortuary rites and mourning periods are not observed in the event of a small child's death. Although the Nuer describe conception as a result of male sperm entering the uterus, a child is also created by *kwoth,* and is thus a product of both human and divine construction. Only when children are old enough to have begun to participate in the social life of the Nuer will they be deemed "real people." They are certainly alive, but not in possession of souls.

In the relationship of human to divine, sin is of paramount importance. The Nuer say that *kwoth* is both very near and very distant. This is what they want, as he can be of assistance if close, but not dangerous in his powers of retribution if far away. The greatest "sinful" transgression regards a failure to show respect. This demonstration of respect is a broad concept, incorporating elements of avoidance, abstention, modesty, deference, and restraint. Such respectful relationships—*thek*—exist in a wide range of configurations. They are found between a man and his wife's parents, a woman and her bridewealth cattle, an individual and food belonging to strangers, the living and a corpse. Transgressions in these relationships bring dire consequences. Evans-Pritchard (1956) says of *thek* relationships that "[t]hey are intended to keep people apart from other people or from creatures or things, either altogether or in certain circumstances or with regard to certain matters, and this is what they achieve" (pp. 180–181). The result of sinning in these circumstances is the highest form of shame and despicability, in addition to the prospect of more corporeal punishment, such as illness, blindness, and death. Homicide, adultery, and incest are among the most serious infractions a Nuer can commit. These acts, however, pose particular dilemmas for the Nuer.

Evans-Pritchard reports that incest is something much talked about among the Nuer, and it is not difficult to see why. Two factors contribute to the frequency of incest outside close kin: the first is the lack of disapproval accorded to casual sexual relations before marriage, and the second is the nature of kinship relations in Nuer society. An individual may not be able to reckon with complete certainty whether a particular person in fact occupies a relational role that is prohibited or not. Homicide poses a dilemma as well, in that while the Nuer believe that killing a member of one's community is wrong, this disapproved behavior may occur as a result of following another *approved* behavioral code. Douglas (1966) points out that Nuer boys are instructed from an early age to use force in defending their rights. This may at times lead to homicidal behavior, however unintentional. Adultery, according to Evans-Pritchard (1951, in Douglas 1966) may be regarded "as a risky sport in which any man may normally be tempted to indulge." But it is dangerous behavior because it brings sickness to the wronged husband, who is at risk for severe pains in his lower back, caused by the pollution of his subsequent relations with his wife. Payment of an ox to the husband can avert this fate.

Mary Douglas, in her classic volume *Purity and Danger,* reflects on the utility of these threats of pollution, which she asserts can "serve to settle uncertain moral issues." Regarding incest, she writes:

> The Nuer cannot always tell whether they have committed incest or not. But they believe that incest brings misfortune in the form of skin disease, which can be averted by sacrifice. If they know they have incurred the risk they can have the sacrifice performed; if they reckon the degree of relationship was very distant, and the risk therefore slight, they can leave the matter to be settled *post hoc* by the appearance or non-appearance of the skin-disease (1966).

As she goes on to point out, in a system such as the Nuer's, where the social structure is made up entirely of individuals whose relationships to one another are defined by marital categories and incest prohibitions, violations of the rules regarding incest and adultery strike at the heart of the local community's integrity. "To have produced such a society the Nuer have evidently needed to make complicated rules about incest and adultery, and to maintain it they have underpinned the rules by threats of the danger of forbidden contacts. These rules and sanctions express the public conscience." Moreover, because there is often no general outrage over adultery, Douglas suggests that the threat of pollution can act, in an impersonal way, to take up the moral slack when indignation is not engendered.

❖ MODERN CHALLENGES: CIVIL WAR AND RESETTLEMENT

The Nuer figure prominently into the decades-long civil war in Sudan. As discussed in the Azande chapter, Sudanese independence from Britain in 1956 was established with inequities in place. The powerful north, home of the capital city Khartoum, seat of the Arab-led government, sought to impose Islam on the south, populated by Africans who adhered to Christianity or indigenous belief systems. Brutal violence inflicted by the military forced thousands to flee the south, and inspired formation of civilian-led independence movements. The most powerful of these, the Southern Sudan Liberation Movement (SSLM), effected a brief cease-fire in the 1970s, but violence soon erupted once more.

In addition to the enforced Islamization of southern Sudan, with policies in place to undermine the cultural identities of southern peoples, the northern elite set into motion a plan to gain control of land, oil, and water resources in the south (Kebbede 1999). A canal was planned, engineered to span the southern homelands of both the Nuer and the neighboring Dinka, among other groups. This canal, the Jonglei, was designed to channel water north from the Nile, to provide water for northern farmers whose agriculture produced cash crops, such as cotton, for export. This diversion of water would have resulted in the destruction of southern pasturelands crucial to pastoralists, such as the Nuer, who depend on their herds for their lives and livelihood. The expectation of Sudan's government was that nomadic groups would acquiesce to assuming a more "advanced" sedentary lifestyle, and southerners were neither included in the planning nor considered in the consequences (Kebbede 1999). The Nuer economy was deemed lesser, devalued because it provided mere subsistence, and not a marketable product (Kottak 1997). Faced with the loss of both grazing land and the inevitable change in their way of life, southerners in the SSLM succeeded in forcing a halt to the construction, and focusing attention on environmental degradation and the struggle for resources as well as religion and cultural identity.

The civil war in Sudan is among the longest running in the world. Since 1983 there have been an estimated loss of two million lives. The Nuer continue to play a central role. Although at its inception in 1983 the dozen leaders of the Sudan Peoples' Liberation Movement (SPLM) were drawn from all the area's ethnic groups, the majority of the rank and file were drawn from the Nuer and their southern neighbors (and traditional rivals), the Dinka. In 1991, a Nuer commander attempted to overthrow the SPLM founder, a Dinka, inciting warfare that claimed many thousands of lives. The coup resulted in the group's split into two factions, one Dinka-led and one Nuer. Violent battles continued between the two for several years, wreaking havoc on local civilians, their cattle holdings, and their lands. Hoping to find a resolution to the tribal fighting, a conference was held in 1998, resulting in an accord calling for future peace conferences. Such conferences were held in 1999, 2000, and 2001, furthering reconciliation between the Dinka and Nuer.

Nuer in the United States

Southern Sudan has one of the world's largest populations of internally displaced people—nearly five million (Kebbede 1999). An additional half million, many of them Nuer, took refuge in camps in Ethiopia. The subsequent Ethiopian revolution forced many to move to settlements in Kenya, which provided not only a safe haven, but the opportunity for an escape from refugee life. Programs designed to assist in finding permanent new homes allowed Nuer to emigrate, and by 1996 nearly four thousand southern Sudanese were living in the United States (Holtzman 2000). In the Midwest, Nuer are challenged to forge a new community without the kinship ties and village links which are the underpinnings of traditional Nuer solidarity. Jon Holtzman, an anthropologist who has done fieldwork among Nuer both in Sudan and in Minnesota, has found that local church congregations have reached out to Nuer refugees. Since most of the resettled Nuer had been converted to Christianity by missionaries in Sudanese schools or Ethiopian camps, Holtzman observes that the church offers "perhaps the only continuity between Nuer life in Africa and Minnesota" (2000:123).

Church affiliation in Minnesota may derive from prior association in Sudan, but may often be an extension of the resettlement effort. Individual church members, or the congregation at large, offered sponsorship to Nuer families, securing for them the ability to seek refuge in the United States. Thus, families often chose to join the sponsoring congregation. This was not necessarily part of the bargain; often Nuer sought out the denominations most familiar to their home community. Holtzman (2000) points out that Nuer often found joining any congregation a challenge, owing to their understandable desire to conduct services in their own language. One church accommodated their wishes, providing separate space for worship at the same time as regular services. Problems soon arose:

> [T]he Nuer service was a raucous, lively affair, with spirited singing to the
> pounding beat of African drums. This proved incompatible with the English
> service going on upstairs, and the minister was upset at having the
> tranquility of the chapel interrupted by persistent drumming—not to mention
> the effect this had on his sermon (Holtzman 2000:126).

In addition to the sponsorship instrumental in helping Nuer gain resettlement permission, church groups often continued to raise money to provide material goods for resettled families. Thus, Holtzman found that "spiritual relationships have become deeply entangled in the negotiation of material ones" (2000:127), although the aid is provided out of a sincere dedication to humanitarianism and the promotion of Christianity.

The majority of Minnesotan Nuer are young families and single men in their late teens and twenties. Holtzman (2000) explains that parents were eager for their adult children to resettle, adventure being a prerogative of youth, while they remained to care for the family's traditional home. Close ties are maintained with relatives in Sudan or Ethiopia, to whom remittances are sent, and who are often called upon to fulfill ritual requirements in their relatives' absence.

Traditionally, kinship is the paramount social bond in Nuer society, where everyone is related, however distantly, to everyone else. These various sorts of kinship bonds, activated at times when alliances need to be forged, are diffused in resettled Nuer, whose daily lives take on a more individualistic focus. Minnesotan Nuer find ways to reconstitute allegiances, often focusing on the larger shared "Nuer identity" than on Sudanese concepts of kinship. Holtzman found that his questions about the tribal, clan, and subclan affiliations of a Minnesotan community were brushed aside dismissively with the comment, "Those things don't matter here. Here we are just all Nuer" (2000:44).

Some Minnesotan Nuer express the desire to return to their homeland, if peace can be found in Sudan. The high cost of living, long hours at work, and missing those who remained behind are all reasons which tug at those who wait for the opportunity to go home (Holtzman 2000). Not all who have resettled consider their move a temporary one, however. Those who have found educational opportunities and employment are committed to finding even greater success for themselves and their children. They look to the future, content to carve out a new life in a new land.

"The Lost Boys of Sudan"

One group of south Sudanese refugees has received particular attention: the so-called Lost Boys of Sudan, a group of more than thirty thousand children, mostly Nuer and Dinka boys whose villages had been destroyed and families killed.

In 1987, government militia raided southern villages, killing the adults and capturing the girls. Terrified young boys, many outside of the village tending cattle, fled at the sight of the violence, meeting up with other children, mostly boys, as they trudged through desert and wilderness. Small groups found one another, and soon tens became hundreds, and hundreds became thousands. Together they walked hundreds of miles over several months toward Ethiopia. Many died of thirst and starvation; some fell prey to wild animals. When the survivors arrived at Ethiopian refugee camps, they had formed small cadres in which the older children—some only nine or ten—looked after the younger ones. Relief workers named them the Lost Boys, after Peter Pan's band of orphans. In 1991, after three years in the camps, Ethiopian civil war forced them to flee again. Some perished as they attempted to ford the crocodile-infested rivers under gunfire. Survivors set off to seek shelter in Kenya, one thousand miles away, many walking for more than a year. Thousands were lost on the journey: more than twenty thousand children set out from Ethiopia; eleven thousand (three thousand of them girls) eventually arrived at Kenya's Kakuma Refugee Camp.

After surviving for nearly a decade in Kenyan camps on a single daily meal, in 2000 and 2001 nearly four thousand Lost Boys—now teenagers—began to be resettled in the United States under international rules allowing for the resettlement of minor children. Younger children were placed in foster homes; older ones traveled in groups of three or four and were placed in group homes or apartments sponsored by local churches and refugee aid organizations. In 2004, a publisher in Dallas who was moved by the stories of several Lost Boys in his church congregation, turned the tales of their harrowing experiences into a series of graphic novels, entitled *Echoes of the Lost Boys of Sudan*. Modeled after comic books depicting feats of superheroes, the series follows the lives of those four Lost Boys, now in their midtwenties, with part of the proceeds going to a national refugee education fund.

Where Are the "Lost Girls"?

Of the four thousand children resettled in the United States, fewer than ninety were girls. Whereas boys in the refugee camps were kept together in small groups, girls were generally placed with guardians. The boys formed a visible group, the target of outreach by aid workers. It was assumed that the girls were being cared for. Some lived with families, but not all had the girls' best interests at heart. They were valuable as unpaid domestic workers and would eventually bring in a dowry. Now young women, many married and with young children, they no longer meet the requirements for resettlement. Sudanese activists and refugee organizations have been urging humanitarian and government agencies to investigate their plight.

The first national conference and reunion for Lost Boys and Girls was held in Phoenix during 2004. Planned by elected leaders of fifteen communities of Lost Boys across the United States in an attempt to unify those individuals scattered across the country, organizers hope to forge a new solidarity among resettled Sudanese refugees.

✦ For Further Discussion

The Nuer traditionally employed a form of political organization called the segmentary lineage organization (SLO). It provided an effective way to resolve disputes and mobilize support. In the 1990s, however, civil war in Sudan brought a grave challenge to the Nuer and their neighbors. War has cost millions of lives, and resulted in widespread resettlement. Many Nuer took refuge in camps in Ethiopia. The subsequent Ethiopian revolution forced many to move on to settlements in Kenya. The search for permanent new homes brought many thousands of Nuer to the United States. Given the importance of political systems and the traditional Nuer way of life, what might be some of the challenges of forging a new community without the political ties and village links that are the underpinnings of traditional Nuer solidarity?

CHAPTER 11

THE OJIBWA

"The People" Endure

Ojibwa Country in North America.

✦ THE BEGINNING

Long before the world began, there was Gitchimanito, the Great Spirit. He made wind and water, fire and rock; he made the sun and stars and Earth. To the Earth he gave tall trees and green plants. He created animals that ran on four legs, animals that flew, animals that swam and, last, he created the people.

Gitchimanito arranged all he created by the four sacred directions—north, south, west, and east—and then two more: the sky above, and the earth below.

Not long after, the seas flooded the earth, and the animals tried to find it again, to no avail. One after the other, they searched beneath the seas, until finally the muskrat scraped a pawful of soil from the submerged earth, and from that scrap the world was recreated. Gitchimanito envisioned a purpose for the spirit of all he created. Trees would grow large and give shade and protection. Plants would flourish and give food and medicine. Animals would be bountiful and their lives offered up as food and clothing for the people. But all this goodness would be recognized and appreciated by the people whose benefit it would serve. Nothing would be sacrificed without praise and thanks and a token of appreciation.

The people lived first by the great ocean in the east, but a vision carried them westward and, following it, they found the Great Lakes.

This is the beginning of the Ojibwa's tale, the explanation of their creation and of finding their home.

✦ OVERVIEW

The Ojibwa, a Native American group living in the northern midwest in the United States and south-central Canada, refer to themselves as *Anishinabe,* which literally means "human being," a term by which many of the world's people are known to themselves. There is some speculation and disagreement about the origin of the name Ojibwa. It has been said to refer to their style of moccasin (*"ojibwa"* meaning puckered up, and referring to the crimped stitching that edges the moccasins). Others (Tanner 1992) suggest that it is instead derived from *"ojibiweg,"* which means "those who make pictographs," and that their name refers instead to the paintings on birch bark that were traditionally used as a form of writing.

Originally, an area extending north of Lakes Superior and Huron was home to the Ojibwa. Beginning in the seventeenth century, their geographic expansion resulted in a four-part division. These groups are: the Salteaux (Northern Ojibwa); the Plains Ojibwa, or Bungee; the Southeastern Ojibwa, and the Southwestern Chippewa. By the end of the eighteenth century the Salteaux occupied the Canadian Shield north of Lake Superior and south and west of Hudson and James Bays. This is a flat area of poor soil, and numerous lakes and swamps. Plains Ojibwa country, in southern Saskatchewan and Manitoba, is a region forested with oak and ash, with great rolling hills. The Southeastern

Ojibwa in Michigan's lower peninsula, eastern upper peninsula, and adjacent areas of Ontario share an environment similar to that of the Southwestern Chippewa in northern Minnesota, extreme northern Wisconsin, Michigan's western upper peninsula, and Ontario between Lake Superior and the Manitoba border. Both live in countries of rolling hills, deciduous forests of maple, birch, poplar, and oak, and marshes, prairies, rivers, and lakes. They live with long, cold winters and short, hot summers.

The Ojibwa, one of the largest American Indian groups north of Mexico, numbered at least thirty-five thousand in the mid-seventeenth century. Today the Ojibwa have been given one hundred or more small reservations in Michigan, Wisconsin, Minnesota, North Dakota, Montana, and Oklahoma. The majority of the roughly two-hundred thousand individuals live in the Canadian provinces of Ontario, Manitoba, and Saskatchewan.

✦ HISTORY

In the mid-seventeenth century, the Ojibwa first encountered Europeans on their land. These explorers found an impressive natural bounty in rivers and forests. It wasn't long before the Gulf of St. Lawrence was crowded with fishing expeditions. The market for native furs—mink, bear, wolf, otter, and beaver—was tremendous, and by the end of the century Ojibwa were heavily involved in the fur trade, and eager to expand their trade for European goods.

The burgeoning desire for European trade goods led to escalating intertribal conflict centering on the rights to exclusive fur-trading privileges, especially fierce between the Iroquois and the Huron. In the middle 1600s, the combined effect of Dutch-issued firearms and the decimation by newly introduced diseases (smallpox chief among the epidemics) exacted a dramatic toll.

Earlier, the Ojibwa were closely allied to the Huron to their south. However, after the Huron were defeated by the Iroquois in their battle for control of the fur trade, the Ojibwa came under forceful Iroquois attack. In a successful attack that put an end to Iroquois power in their region, Ojibwa expanded both southward and westward.

Eventually, representatives from fifteen Indian nations negotiated peace in the trade wars, but not without great cost. By the beginning of the eighteenth century, Ojibwa culture had changed dramatically. Animals that had been hunted mainly for subsistence were now trapped primarily to be used in trade, and as dependence upon European trade goods increased, traditional patterns and activities diminished.

Also, with the development of the European fur trade, the exploitation of a particular hunting and trapping territory (which had been vaguely defined areas) evolved into discrete territories over which hunting and trapping groups had exclusive rights to fur resources. By the century's end their major geographical expansion resulted in the four-part tribal fracturing.

With migration, too, came some significant modifications in traditional hunting, fishing, and gathering subsistence patterns. These modifications were most evident among the Northern Ojibwa, who adopted a subarctic cultural pattern, borrowing extensively from the Cree, and the Plains Ojibwa, who incorporated numerous aspects of Plains Indian culture.

During the first half of the nineteenth century, Ojibwa began to experience the influence of the American government. They became, once again, increasingly dependent on traders, this time Americans. Although fishing was plentiful in the summertime, winter found the Ojibwa without large game, which had been depleted, and left them in need of provisions owned by traders. Large parcels of land were ceded in return for the promise of continued blacksmith service (upon which they had come to rely for gun and trap repair, as well as fishing spears and ice cutters); and payments of salt and tobacco on an annual basis. Hunting and fishing rights on the land were given up. Demands for farmland forced Southeastern Ojibwa to cede their territory, and the movement toward reservations began in earnest.

Canadian officials attempted what they termed a "civilization" program, aimed at redirecting Ojibwa life to a reservation-based farming economy to replace traditional fishing, hunting, and gathering. Missionaries across North America embraced the "civilization" programs as a way to facilitate conversion to Christianity, which appeared easier to effect with a population that was less dispersed. With harsh winters and a short growing season the copper-rich, forested land in Wisconsin and Minnesota was unsuitable for farming, and thus not in jeopardy of being ceded to agriculturalists by government decree. But Ojibwa resistance was challenged by copper miners and the lumbering industry, eager to exploit the abundant resources on Ojibwa land and loath to allow the Ojibwa to remain living on land they had ceded, a right which had been granted them by the United States government.

In keeping with their plan for Ojibwa to adopt a farming economy, and under pressure from these burgeoning industries, the government attempted to resettle the Ojibwa west of the Mississippi, where they could live in permanent shelters and farm the land. This initial attempt was unsuccessful, and an alternative program—to allot individual parcels of land within reservations to individual families—was introduced. A series of treaty conferences ensued, during which Native American leaders presented their complaints: promised payments had not materialized; settlers on Ojibwa land had gone through the woods and taken the game that had been left hanging on trees to cure; government-financed schools were not educating Ojibwa children, but only those of the traders. Perhaps the point of most contention was presented by Ojibwa from Sault Ste. Marie, whose land was destroyed by the construction of a shipping canal. Unsuspecting villagers were taken by surprise as four hundred workers arrived in their village and began construction, which destroyed not only fishing sites, but the village itself. Families were forced to flee their homes as the canal building proceeded.

Although treaties were signed promising permanent homes, farming acreage, equipment, and carpentry tools, this allotment process never came to fruition. By the time an official Act was passed into law, nearly 90 percent of the land promised to the Ojibwa and others was already owned and settled.

Despite their desire to maintain their way of life, Ojibwa resettled on reservations could neither fish nor gather wild rice on land unsuitable for these economies. Thus, consequences to Ojibwa culture, beginning with the earliest days of the fur trade, were cataclysmic. The technology introduced, the scattering and removal of the indigenous population, and the intertribal conflict engendered had dramatic effects on Ojibwa culture.

Before the middle of the nineteenth century, Ojibwa tools were fashioned of stone and bone. Bowls and spoons, canoe paddles and sleds, drums and snowshoes were all made of wood. Birch bark provided the material for canoes and containers. Spears and bows and arrows were the tools of the hunt, with animal skins providing the material for clothing, blankets, and tailoring. Hooks and nets were used for fishing.

With the advent of the fur trade, iron tools (scissors, needles, axes, knives), cooking utensils (kettles and pots), as well as guns and alcohol, were introduced, with tremendous consequences. Iron tools transformed the approach to hunting. Pottery craft was reduced to obsolescence with the availability of sturdier and more efficient iron kettles. The European demand for fur, coincident with governmental plans to encourage a shift from the traditional economy to one based on farming, created an ironic dilemma, as Hallowell (Hallowell and Brown 1992:18) explains: "the continuing demand for furs, in the long run, entrenched most of these Indians more firmly in their occupation as hunters since so many of them were compelled to remain in a region where any transition to agriculture was impossible."

The European system of buying and selling introduced to the indigenous peoples a system of "debt" which was to them wholly unfamiliar. Goods were sold to hunters on credit, with payment in furs expected subsequently. European traders attempted to offset the risks inherent in giving goods on credit by establishing considerably higher prices for the goods they sold to the hunters. A host of factors, not the least of which was the unstable, seasonally changing availability of game, ensured that native peoples were rarely able to escape perpetual indebtedness. Although they were becoming more dependent upon trade goods, they were not able to incorporate the technology for producing or repairing such goods on their own, and thus were never able to benefit from the new technologies by employing them to become economically independent.

✦ SETTLEMENTS

Ojibwa patterns of movement and settlement were guided largely by the seasons, and varied among groups as their environments varied. In general, bands dispersed in the winter, moving to hunting grounds where deer, moose, bear, and a variety of small game were available. In the spring, maple trees were tapped, and the sap was gathered and boiled to produce maple syrup. Early Ojibwa established semipermanent villages in the summer and maintained temporary camps during the rest of the year, in keeping with their need to move in order to efficiently exploit fish, game, and wild plant resources.

Although the strategy of seasonal settlement and movement was found to some degree in all the Ojibwa groups, it was differently elaborated in each. Southeastern Ojibwa and Southwestern Chippewa returned to permanently established summer village bases to plant gardens. Plains Ojibwa were highly mobile, and moved to the open plains in the summertime to hunt the bison herds upon which they focused their economy and whose skins were used to construct their familiar *tipis*.

The Northern Ojibwa spent the late fall, winter, and spring moving in dispersed winter hunting groups. As the ice melted, these small groups met up with other such bands, spending the summer months congregated in fishing settlements. In contrast to the isolation of winter hunting movement, the assembly of large groups at fishing sites afforded the opportunity to renew social ties and perform important communal ceremonies. In addition, many of these summer sites were near trading posts, where supplies could be secured for the coming year.

During the summer months spent in the villages, the gathering of wild nuts and berries, and planting of small gardens of maize, beans, squash, and pumpkins supplemented fishing. Wild rice, available most easily to the Southeastern Ojibwa and the Southwestern Chippewa, was harvested in the fall.

✦ KINSHIP AND SOCIOPOLITICAL ORGANIZATION

Despite the fact that there was seasonal movement, sometimes of small groups, these smaller units of Ojibwa belonged to a larger whole. In earliest times, the Ojibwa were organized into small autonomous bands of interrelated families. As is characteristic of band organization, these were flexible groups with an egalitarian structure. Band size and characteristics varied somewhat among different groups. Southeastern Ojibwa and Southwestern Chippewa bands were made up of several hundred people; Northern Ojibwa bands were smaller, each numbering from fifty to seventy-five individuals. Plains Ojibwa bands tended to be looser, more shifting units.

Kinship terms, used as both reference and address, functioned not only to identify the relationship of one person to another, but also as a vehicle to guide behavior and express the content of role relations and expectations. (For example, a child came to recognize that those men addressed by his father as "brother" all act toward the child as his own father might.) Beginning with earliest childhood, kinship terms directed social interaction, allowing relations with both extended family and members of other groups as they moved among them.

Generally, Ojibwa society was organized into a number of exogamous totemic clans, with membership reckoned patrilineally. (Northern Ojibwa in the Berens River area of Manitoba were more likely to be endogamous within their bands.) Because these clans were not localized, most individuals could depend on finding some members of their own clan in any settlement to which their summer movement took them. Marriages, which involved little formal ceremony, were generally arranged by parents or guardians. Cross-cousin marriage, although practiced, was not preferred; most marriages were monogamous, even though polygyny was possible.

Ojibwa political organization was, like other aspects of their sociocultural system, dramatically influenced by contact with European fur traders. Traditionally, there were no powerful political "chiefs" among the Ojibwa. However, European traders sought to identify an individual within each band with whom they could negotiate. One individual was designated by a trader, and an official relationship was structured between the two men, a vitally important link for the trader whose livelihood depended on maintaining his access to pelts. As a result of the status granted and attention paid to the "chief," this individual gained status and prestige, which were reinforced by goods he was given to distribute as gifts. This newly defined position, "a convenient means of dealing with Indians whose native culture did not function through persons whose role it was to represent them in transactions with outsiders," was instituted among all the Ojibwan groups (Hallowell and Brown 1992:35).

Among the eighteenth-century Southeastern Ojibwa, bands were headed by less formal chiefs; as farming and more permanent settlement patterns were encouraged by the government, an elected chief, assistant chiefs, and a local council became the characteristic local political organization. Among the Northern Ojibwa, the individual selected for band leadership was usually a skilled trader whose kin group formed the basis of the band's membership. Plains Ojibwa bands had several chiefs, with one recognized as the head chief and secondary chiefs designated based on hunting skills, achievements in battle, generosity, and leadership ability. Elected councilars assisted the chiefs.

Ojibwa across the generations.

As Hallowell points out, the power held by these chiefs and councilars was derived primarily from their function as trade representatives, but this authority did not extend to matters arising within their "bands," which were also groups that were conceived largely by government agencies. Groups that were defined by the people themselves did not correspond to those conceptualized by traders and government officials. To the Ojibwa, the true seat of individual power was to be found in the indigenous healers, whose abilities acquired through dreams were truly matters of life and death.

✦ OJIBWA CULTURE

The belief system of the Ojibwa centers on the important relationship between people and those who are other-than-people. Although skills and knowledge obtained from fellow Ojibwa are certainly important, there are crucial aspects of a successful life that can only be known and achieved through dependence upon those who are not human. Hallowell reports that he found "neither myth, tale, nor tradition [portraying] a human being as making any discovery, bringing about any change, or achieving any status or influence unaided by other than human persons" (1992:80).

To understand this, one must first understand that in the Ojibwa conceptualization there is no sharp division between the natural and the supernatural as defined by the Western scientific cultural model. There are animate and inanimate objects. The latter category is made up largely of manufactured items (although pipes are spoken of as animate); plants, fish, animals, and humans beings are all classified as animate, as are the sun and wind and other elements. Also found among the category of animate beings are those animals that are known to exist but are rarely, if ever, seen. These include Large Snakes, Great Frogs, and Big Turtles. Of even greater importance are the Thunder Birds, whose wings make the sound of the thunder, and whose blinking eyes are the accompanying lightning. Thunder Birds are classified with other birds whose migratory patterns correspond to the stormy seasons during which thunder and lightning occur.

All plants and animals are controlled by their "owners," whose permission is an absolute prerequisite to securing them through hunting or gathering. This belief means that skillful techniques and an exhaustive knowledge of their environment are necessary but not sufficient talents for successful subsistence. To know the owners of each species, and to make certain that each plant and animal is correctly treated is the only insurance against failure. The remains of an animal, which would be killed only for a useful purpose, must be disposed of and honored with proper ceremonial respect. Failure to accord plants and animals this right would inevitably result in retribution by the owner, generally the inability to secure that plant or animal again in the future. A hunter has a relationship with the owner of the species he hunts; the "use" of an animal results in a debt owed the species' owner, and such obligations must be fulfilled. Likewise, when plants are gathered, owners must be properly addressed and an offering (usually of tobacco) is left in the ground.

To the Ojibwa, the category of "persons" includes not only themselves—*Anishinabe*, human beings—but also animate beings who are not human. These beings are more powerful than human beings, and might be classified as "supernatural" beings in another cultural context. These persons are referred to as "our grandfathers" by the Ojibwa who, from childhood, have knowledge and experience with these beings. They have a real place in the lives of Ojibwa, through myth, ceremony, and dreams.

Myths told about "our grandfathers" were thought to be heard not only by the people assembled to listen, but also by the objects of the stories themselves. It is believed that their delight in hearing them was so great that long ago one urged the others: "We'll try to make everything suit the Indians so long as any of them exist, so that they will never forget us and always talk about us" (Hallowell and Brown 1992:66).

Tales told about the "grandfathers" were generally told by elders—human grandparents—who were revered members of society. They educated adults and children alike, teaching through myths and dance and song those parts of wisdom deemed every bit as important as the practical skills of hunting, sewing, cooking, and fishing. Children, raised with little strictness and rarely reprimanded or punished, were in the care of women and elders for the first years of their lives. Boys of seven began to be instructed by adult men in the ways of hunting and fishing; girls continued to be instructed about domestic life by their mothers. When an Ojibwa girl received the "gift . . . denied to men" (Tanner 1992:27)—her first menstruation—she became a woman, leaving the village for a time, and returning with a new status. Special instruction was afforded to those young women and men who displayed the gift of healing powers, the gift to be among the *Midé*.

Religion and View of the World

Ojibwa religion is bound up with several distinctive features: dreaming, fasting, visions, and, above all else, the relationship with "the grandfathers," the other-than-human beings.

According to Hallowell, "faith in the power of the other than human persons, trust in the essential help they can offer human beings, and dependence upon them in order to achieve a good life define the . . . core of Ojibwa religion" (Hallowell and Brown 1992:81). Religious beliefs that emphasize this critical relationship direct behavior, and thus function as a primary way of maintaining the social order.

The primary contact between individuals and these other beings is achieved during dreaming, a state of primary importance in Ojibwa life. It is during dreams that power is given and received, and while contact can be made with "the grandfathers" outside of dreams, it is only in the dreaming state that the most intimate and powerful relationship is forged.

Just as a sharp dichotomy between the natural and the supernatural cannot be effectively drawn for the Ojibwa, neither can experience gained through waking and dreaming teachings be set in opposition. The world experienced while dreaming is not one of fantasy and unreality; it is another occasion for reflective thought. One difference between the experiences of sleep and waking, however, is the ability of the soul during sleep to break free of the body, allowing the most intense contact with other-than-human beings. During such contact, "blessings" of knowledge, and, thus, power, are bestowed; beginning in early childhood, one is encouraged to dream in order to receive these blessings.

To facilitate visionary dreams, boys especially were encouraged in a fast, during which time they would be visited by "the grandfathers." During this state, the fasting boy would be approached by one who would take him under his wing and tutelage, whom he could see and hear. The fasting period might last a week before such "guardian spirits" would appear; the boy's father or grandfather might appeal to their own long-ago recognized teachers to help secure the boy's own blessing.

Once secured, the vision was not discussed. In fact, if a boy began to discuss his experience, or ask for guidance in interpreting what he had dreamt, he was cautioned against it; seeking clarification through discussion of one's vision might be grounds to lose the blessing and the power it bestowed. A dreamer's family was made aware obliquely of the fast's fruition by a boy's change in behavior. He became somewhat withdrawn and introspective, observed new ritual obligations assumed to have been demanded of him in his dream. His proud family let his achievement be known to the rest of the community, but also only inferentially: they had found him in an altered state of consciousness, his manner had changed, they had seen differences in his behavior.

Dreams and visions varied greatly, in both content and intensity, from person to person. Some "dream visitors" impart only knowledge and access to trapping and fishing; others to warfare; still others imparted the skills necessary for curing. One person may be visited by many guardian spirits; others may never fulfill their quest for a vision. Whether blessed by many or none, the dreamer was to remain equally silent, both because boasting is unacceptable and because it jeopardizes one's ability to hold onto the power received.

It has been suggested that one reason that Ojibwa feel a strong link between humans and the other-than-human spirits that are "the grandfathers" is that both classes of persons are bound by the same moral order. Primary among these shared values is the importance of mutual exchange. The guardian spirits give blessings and knowledge to their human grandchildren; they have an excess of power, more than they need, and thus they must share it.

The egalitarian focus that serves to distribute goods and services in a society without a market economy also guides the act of sharing across human and nonhuman boundaries. The accumulation of excess goods, indicative of greed, is as unbefitting to "the grandfathers" as it is to those who dream of them. Self-deprivation can be taken to excess as much as overacquisitiveness. One boy was reported to have been dissatisfied with the blessing he received during his initial fasting vision. His desire was to know everything in the world, to dream of every leaf on every tree so he could see beyond them to know all. He continued to fast. This desire, considered greedy, was granted, but with the proviso that as the leaves fell from the tree, so too would the boy fall ill. And when the trees were at last bare, his life too would end. As Hallowell explains, "Overfasting is considered as greedy as hoarding. It violates a basic moral value of the cosmic society of the Ojibwa" (Hallowell and Brown 1992:92).

In keeping with the rights and duties bound up in sharing and reciprocity, the blessings received during the dreams were not bestowed without obligation. If one was to utilize the knowledge and power obtained through vision to their fullest extent, both prohibitions and "debts" must be attended to. In some cases, food taboos were imposed by guardian spirits who were owners of that animal species. In others, items of clothing or adornment associated through myth with the bestower of one's blessings must be worn. Often contact was forbidden between the dreamer and certain other individuals. None of these observances may be explained; consequently, recipients of blessings often are forced to endure misunderstanding by others, requiring the exercise of great self-control. Infractions result not only in the withdrawal of the blessing; even unintentional violation of such taboos extracted a penalty, usually illness. Any breach of conduct between people or between humans and other-than-humans is punished eventually; there is no comfort to be taken in the passage of time. "Bad conduct . . . 'will keep following you.' Sooner or later you will suffer because of it" (Hallowell and Brown 1992:93). Moreover, it may be those closest to you who will pay the price for your own infraction; it may be your children who fall ill and die.

Thus, the fear of falling ill functions, in traditional Ojibwa society, as a powerful sanction against behavior that fails to conform to that which is expected. Ethnographers have pointed out that this set of beliefs—grounded in individual responsibility for behavior and a commitment to exercise self-control without explanation—acted against the acceptance of the government-introduced system of chiefdoms, which sought to impose sanctions by dictum from without.

In those settings where illness functions as a check on antisocial behavior, becoming ill has ramifications on two levels: not only as personal misfortune, but also as a clear indicator of some moral or behavioral transgression against wider cultural values. This is further reinforced by the public disclosure of the violation that has brought on the illness. A confession of sorts is a necessary element in the curative process; once the misconduct has been identified and made known, it functions as a warning to others.

In their elegant recounting of Ojibwa myths, Overholt and Callicott (1982) alert the reader of these tales to some of the important elements out of which they are spun. It is through the telling of the myths that central values are passed on from Ojibwa to Ojibwa; for people outside their tradition, examining the themes contained within the stories can be a window into the Ojibwa world.

Power is a recurrent theme in Ojibwa life, especially the power possessed and granted by the "grandfathers." One power possessed by humans and other-than-humans alike is that of metamorphosis, the changing of one's shape. Hallowell counts this as "one of the distinctive generic attributes of persons in Ojibwa thought" (Hallowell and Brown 1992:66–67). This thought is never more in evidence than when considering the bestowal of blessings, through dreams and visions. These are parts of life and awareness that are no less real than the more mundane pieces of one's day; and surely no less powerful. The

Ojibwa view of themselves as not solely people who live with other people, but as human beings who live in a more broadly defined society, with other-than-human persons, is exemplified in two other features of Ojibwa culture: the *Midéwiwin*, or Grand Medicine Society, and the shaking tent.

The Shaking Tent

The shaking tent (or shaking lodge) is a performance aimed at divining information not available through other means. Most often the questions asked have to do with the diagnosis and treatment of illness, the welfare of loved ones far away, or the location of game animals. The practice involves persons and powers from all the important realms of the Ojibwa world: the audience of Ojibwa, the "spirits" to be contacted, and the diviner.

In preparation for the event, a structure is erected. Poles are lashed together to form a barrel-shaped tent, or lodge, with skins, canvas, or birch bark draped over the framework. The diviner enters the tent after dark with the assembled audience outside. Songs and drumming are the vehicles by which the diviner calls his spirits to him. These are never a random assemblage of visitors whom he importunes: they are his own *pawaganak*, his own guardians.

The evidence of their arrival is the movement of the tent, which shakes from side to side with their appearance within. At times this movement is rendered even more impressive by the binding, hand and foot, of the diviner. Thus tied with rope, it could not be he creating the rhythmic motion. Hallowell (Hallowell and Brown 1992) tells of a diviner of such potency that he was said to have requested that four tents be constructed. He placed articles of his clothing in three, and himself entered the fourth. Once he had begun his songs, all four tents began to sway.

It is not only the movement of the tent that signals the arrival of the *pawaganak*; they can also be heard to respond to the diviner's song with singing of their own. In addition to guardian spirits, the souls of those living persons being inquired about can visit the tent to offer information and advice. These voices and songs are not believed to be "channeled" through the diviner; they speak for themselves. Although it is true that sometimes their voices could be heard by the audience outside the tent and sometimes not, they are always intelligible to the diviner who, though he may be interpreting them, is surely not creating them (Brown and Brightman 1988:153).

The *Midéwiwin*

One of the best known features of rich Ojibwa culture is the *Midéwiwin* (literally "mystic doings") of the *Midé* (mystic) Society, sometimes referred to as the Grand Medicine Society.

The *Midéwiwin* is an organized society of men and women who possess the knowledge to cure by the use of plants and herbs. Initiates, who have experienced a vision in which curing powers have been imparted, must serve an extended apprenticeship, during which they are tutored, for a price, by an established *Midé* priest.

Much of the accumulated knowledge of the *Midéwiwin*—stories, songs, and dances—are inscribed as pictographs on birch bark scrolls. After sufficient time, the aspiring *Midé* member participates in an initiation ceremony, during which he or she is "shot" with a white shell, ordinarily carried in the medicine bag of a member. Participants, in trance and falling unconscious after the magical shots, regain consciousness to spit the powerful shells from their mouths.

The earliest accounts of the *Midéwiwin* portray it as far more than a vehicle for curing illness. Beliefs about illness and curing in general reflect, as do other aspects of Ojibwa belief and practice, an individualism found at the core of Ojibwa culture. Ojibwa religion has been called "very much an individual affair," focused as it is on the personal experience through visions and dreams of an individual, which resulted in a unique relationship forged between one person and a guardian spirit (or, in some cases, spirits). So, too, illness is believed to be caused by sorcery or as retribution for misconduct toward the "grandfathers" or one's fellow humans. Although certainly important in the realm of solidarity among Ojibwa, it also has a strong flavor of singularity.

There are several categories of shamans, or professional healers, among the Ojibwa, quite apart from the *Midé* priests of the *Midéwiwin*. These other healers receive their gifts as individual blessings, bestowed upon them during dreaming or visions. Once learned, this medical knowledge is "private property, the visionary or dream inspiration of specific medicines and techniques exhibiting a high degree of individualism and variation" (Brown and Brightman 1988:174).

This individualism did not exclude the practitioners in the *Midéwiwin*; there was no standard curriculum taught to all their members either, no remedy known to all, leading to the interchangeability of practitioners so common to Western biomedicine. When asked about a cure, a *Midé* priest might reply, "I can tell you about my own medicines. I do not know about other people's medicines. . ." (Brown and Brightman 1988:174).

Thus, those early writers (for example, Schoolcraft 1851), describing the *Midéwiwin*, characterize it as transcending the limits of its curing responsibilities, having national participation, and engendering national pride. Others who observed the rites emphasized what they regarded as its unifying aspects: "Every person who had been initiated into the secrets of this mysterious society . . . [was] imperatively obliged to be present on every occasion when its grand ceremonies were solemnized. This created yearly a national gathering, and . . . bonds which united one member to another" (Hickerson 1988:56).

In recent years, there has been reexamination of the *Midéwiwin* and its origin and place in Ojibwa history. It had earlier been assumed to represent an aboriginal institution—that is, to have been part of Ojibwa culture arising from within its own tradition, present before contact with outside groups. This assumption has been challenged by more recent anthropological investigation.

Ojibwa culture and society, along with that of other native peoples, was forced to undergo major changes during European contact. One consequence of stressful contact, which challenges traditional patterns of both belief and behavior, is the appearance of "nativistic" or "revitalization" movements. The most well-known of these include Melanesian cargo cults, the Ghost Dance of western Native peoples, and the Handsome Lake religion of the Iroquois.

It is the contention of anthropologist Harold Hickerson (1988) that the *Midéwiwin*, rather than originating in pre-contact times, is in fact another example of such a phenomenon. In a thoughtful and well-supported treatise, he details the evidence for his claim that the *Midéwiwin* among the Ojibwa and other groups emerged out of a reaction to the challenges of Christianity and European contact, and that its ceremonies "represented and reflected new modes of organization, not ancient ones" (p. 63).

✦ Ojibwa Today

Historical descriptions of the Ojibwa detail the traditional life of the past. But in many ways, the current experiences of modern Ojibwa are portrayed in them too. The rich cultural heritage of the people who call themselves *Anishinabe* survives through their continuing celebration of themselves in art, language, and ceremony.

Relocation: "This Hole in Our Heart"

Following the Great Depression in the United States, the economy of the Ojibwa suffered along with that of the rest of the nation, only to rebound during World War II. Ojibwa joined other native peoples in moving to urban areas and laboring variously in shipyards, factories, and aircraft plants for the war effort. As Tanner (1992) points out, however, diversion of funds to the military from domestic programs had an adverse effect on schools, roads, and hospitals on the reservation.

In the 1950s, a government relocation program attempted to reduce reservation living (thus government expenses) by urging Native Americans to migrate to urban areas and assimilate into mainstream American society. Nearly half the native population of Minnesota had been relocated to urban areas by the middle of the 1970s. The desire among some urban Native populations to blend into the non-Native mainstream was very much like that of a number of immigrant populations, eager to "become real Americans" by distancing themselves from other traditions. However, Deborah Davis Jackson, an ethnographer whose fieldwork was conducted among Michigan *Anishinabe* communities, eloquently describes the experiences of individuals who were raised in urban environments with a veiled sense of their *Anishinabe* heritage. The classic three-generation model of European immigrants to the United States describes the first immigrant generation as remaining distinctly "foreign", their American-born children as rejecting any vestiges of that ethnicity, and their own children rediscovering the cultural heritage of their immigrant grandparents. Jackson (2002) points out that this model is not entirely applicable to the situation or urban Native peoples. In the case of those who left reservations and rural communities for the city, two generations in the European immigrant model are compressed into one— these relocated individual are both "leaving the Old Country" and "becoming mainstream Americans." Moreover, unlike "white ethnics," an invisible blending into the Caucasian population is not possible. Last, the collapse of the first two generations into one results in the loss of that "cushion" between an immigrant generation, and a third generation raised by already assimilated parents. Jackson (2002:111) describes "an ambiguity, an ambivalence, a poignant tension" in the identity of those Ojibwa relocated to an urban environment. This results in their grown children's' description of their unresolved position:

> The majority of us [city-raised Indian people] walk around with this hole in our heart. We know we're different, that there's a piece of our life that is missing (Jackson 2002:100).

It was also during the 1970s, however, that government policy began to become more sensitive to the needs and desires of Native Americans, and both laws and funds began to be aimed at preserving traditional culture. Alternative schools offering instruction in Ojibwa language and beginning the day with traditional ceremonial observances came into existence. This was in direct contrast to the tradition of former "Indian boarding schools" run by the government from 1880 to 1930 and often explicitly aimed at assimilation (Northrup 1997, Paquin and Doherty 1992). Ojibwa tribal councils provided scholarship money for students to attend universities, where they increasingly found programs allowing them to continue to learn about their own heritage and culture.

Tribal Casinos

In recent decades, gaming in tribal-owned casinos has garnered popular attention, and is a source of debate both within Native communities and without (Northrup 1997, Vizenor 1990). Proponents believe it provides an opportunity for financial independence and the enhanced welfare of the tribe: Gaming revenues, by law, must be used exclusively for tribal government operations, charitable contributions, and the economic development of the tribe and its members (Anders 1999). Such potential comes at a time when federal support of tribal operations is on the wane.

As we will see in further discussion, it was revenues from native casinos that provided funds to effect a recent sweeping environmental victory.

Some non-Native critics claim that Native gaming privileges are an unfair government sanction. Within Native communities concerns are voiced about the negative social potential of gambling, as well as the erosion of traditional values. Perhaps the argument central to the Native position is one of sovereignty, the ability of individual tribal communities—sovereign nations—to make their own choices about the place of casinos on their reservations.

Environmental Degradation: Triumph over *Pijibowin*

Logging, mining, oil drilling, dam construction, and toxic waste storage and disposal are among the threats to habitats all over the world. The Ojibwa are among those indigenous peoples whose lands and economies are endangered by industrial development. Zoltan Grossman (1995) has remarked that "it is one of history's ironies that the 'wastelands' to which Native peoples were exiled are now coveted for their rich mineral resources."

In Northern Ontario, mercury seeped into the Grassy Narrows Band Ojibwa river systems from a paper mill upstream, contaminating fish consumed by those living on the reserve (Erikson 1994). In addition to toxic health effects, there were economic consequences as well: commercial fishing was halted once the river was declared unsafe, and Ojibwa could no longer earn income as guides for local sports fishing groups. As disastrous as it was to lose the only sources of outside employment and to fear the onset of mercury poisoning, Erikson (1994) observes that there was a third tragedy: the deeply spiritual blow of losing faith in the natural world. A Grassy Narrows elder told him:

> "We call it *pijibowin*. This is the Ojibwa word for poison. You can't see it or smell it, you can't taste it or feel it, but you know it's there. You know it can hurt you, make your limbs go numb, make your spirit sick. But I don't understand it. I don't understand how the land can turn against us" (1994:38).

Stuart Kirsch (1996), writing about eco-politics in Papua New Guinea, notes that "indigenous peoples are becoming global activists in order to survive" (p. 15). In a struggle spanning nearly 30 years and eventually rallying support as far away as Australia, Wisconsin Ojibwa joined forces with local Potawatomi and Menominee to mount a battle against no less an opponent than Exxon, which in 1975 announced plans to build a zinc and copper mine just a mile from the Mole Lake Sokaogon Ojibwa's wild rice lake (Gedicks 1993, Grossman and McNutt 2003). This site is at the center of local Ojibwa culture, economy, and spiritual life. Wild rice is a dietary staple, an important cash crop, and a central aspect of sacred and ritual life (Gedicks and Grossman 2001). In surveying the site, an Exxon biologist referred to the wild rice as "a bunch of weeds" (Gedicks 1993:61).

The proposed site of the mine was at the headwaters of Wolf River, the state's largest whitewater trout stream, and a popular tourist attraction. The estimated 58 million tons of acid waste that would be generated over the life of the mine, contaminating groundwater, was a potential disaster. Native groups protested with little community support throughout the late 1970s. In fact, the 1980s found Ojibwa and non-Native sport fishers embroiled in an acrimonious battle over fishing rights, a conflict which culminated in racist taunting, the assault of tribal elders, and vandalism to Ojibwa property (Grossman and McNutt 2003). However, within a few years these unlikely allies had come together to fight a larger mutual enemy. The environmental threat posed by the proposed mine provided common ground. An alliance of Ojibwa, Potawatomi, Menominee, and Oneida tribal governments, joined by environmental groups, local sport fishers, and grassroots organizations worked tirelessly, mounting speaking tours and rallies, resulting in Exxon's withdrawal from the project in the mid-1980s. In 1993, Exxon returned with a new mining partner, intent on reviving their plan. In the intervening years, however, the four tribes had established casinos on their reservations, providing substantial resources. The Nii Win Intertribal Council (*Nii Win* is Ojibwa for "four") hired lawyers and technical experts, established Web sites, and forged international alliances. Their success was stunning: not only did they defeat both Exxon and BHP Billiton, the world's largest mining company, they achieved a far greater victory. In October 2003, the Mole Lake Sokaogon Ojibwa and Forest County Potawatomi communities pooled $16.5 million in gaming revenues and purchased the zinc and copper mine site along with the surrounding 6000 acres of land. The tribes will share stewardship for the land, protecting wild rice lakes, Spirit Hill, an Ojibwa burial ground, and all the surrounding resources. In announcing their victory, the Mole Lake tribal secretary explained, "Protecting these lands has required a great personal sacrifice for tribal members. But it is a sacrifice that honors our ancestors and our children, Our ancestors lived here. They fought and died to protect these lands for future generations. It is our responsibility to continue that tradition" (Pommer 2003).

Still *Anishinabe*

Although the Ojibwa people are not a homogeneous group, there is still widespread adherence to traditional values and culture. Oral literature, art and craftwork, language and religion are still passed along to new generations. Hunting, gathering, and fishing continue. Tanner reminds us, that "in ceremonies, dancing, and drumming, they are still *Anishinabe*" (1992:111).

✦ For Further Discussion

How do the changes from traditional to modern Ojibwa life compare to those among the other groups about which you have read? What are some of the challenges faced by groups who comprise an ethnic minority within a nation? Are Native North Americans in a unique situation?

CHAPTER 12

THE SAMOANS
Matai *and Migration*

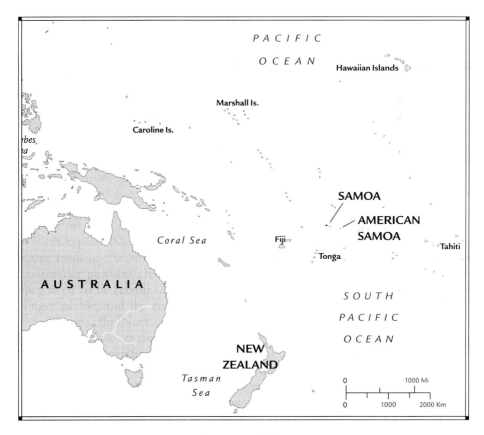

The Samoan Islands.

✦ THE BEGINNING

There were heavens above and water below, and no place to stand. Tagaloa looked down from above and thought he would make such a standing place. This he did, and called the rock he had created Manu'atele. So pleased was he with his creation that he thought to make a second rock. He divided the first into little stepping stones—Tonga, Fiji, and other islands—and he tossed these into the sea. Tagaloa returned to Samoa and fashioned a vine to hug all the rocks in the sea. The vine spread and spread, and soon the leaves fell from the vine. Tagaloa saw that from the leaves emerged worms—worms that had no heads nor arms nor true life. Tagaloa gave them these things— arms and legs, heart and head—and thus made them people. He reached down and took pairs of these new people—one woman, one man—and set each pair upon an island. These islands needed a king, and so he created a king for each of his islands. But then he thought again: there must be a king of kings, one who would be greater than the others. He chose the son of Day (*Ao*) and Night (*Po*) to be this ruler. But when the boy was about to be born, Tagaloa saw that the baby was attached too strongly to his mother's womb. The boy was stuck by his abdomen, inside his mother's body. When he was born, his belly ripped away, and the wound was great. The scattering of islands that would be his home was thus named Samoa—"Sacred Abdomen."

✦ INTRODUCTION AND HISTORY

Samoans are a western Polynesian people whose home is about 2300 miles south of the Hawaiian Islands. The islands of Samoa all resemble one another, topographically. They are of volcanic origin, with sandy beaches along a coral reef coast. Inland, there are ridges that rise to as much as six thousand feet. Tropical climate and abundant rainfall yield lush vegetation, with dense green ferns and bushes covering the slopes. The temperature rarely drops below 70 degrees, and does not peak much above 88 degrees. Tradewinds blow year-round, cooling the stickiest days. Although the nearly two hundred inches of rain that falls annually might seem to result in a marsh underfoot, the volcanic soil quickly absorbs the water, which falls in short torrential bursts, and not a slow, steady rain.

The Samoan Islands cover about twelve hundred miles and have a population of about 193,000. The island chain is divided into two political units. The eastern islands have been a territory of the United States since 1925, and these seven islands—American Samoa—have a total area of seventy-six square miles and a population of about thirty-seven thousand. Six of the islands form the Samoan chain; the seventh lies two hundred miles north of the others. The islands of Western Samoa have been an independent nation since 1962.

The Dutch West India Company sent ships to the Samoan Islands in the early 1700s, but there is some evidence that Europeans had visited the islands even earlier (Holmes 1974). Toward the middle of the eighteenth century, French sailors traded cloth for yams, coconuts, and small implements. Most impressive to these visitors was the Samoans' prowess as boat builders, and it was this French expedition that called the chain "Navigator's Islands," in recognition of this talent. These visits all took place at sea, trading between ship and outrigger canoe. It was not until the late eighteenth century that Europeans disembarked on any of the islands.

In the early nineteenth century, missionaries arrived in Samoa, and their influence has been profound. Nearly one hundred percent of Samoans have embraced Christianity.

Samoan woman making traditional siapo cloth (bark or tapa cloth) in the village of Saláilva.

America, Germany, and Britain all had commercial interests in Samoa during the mid-nineteenth century. Coconut oil was the main commodity, but the United States was far more interested in Samoa as a location for a naval base. The first formal agreements to secure rights to build and maintain such a base in Pago Pago were secured by treaty in the late nineteenth century. The U.S. Navy originally administered the territory, but in the early 1970s, this responsibility was transferred to the Department of the Interior. American Samoa has elected its own governor since 1977. In addition, the territory has a legislature with an eighteen-member Senate, and a twenty-member House of Representatives. American Samoans send a delegate to the United States House of Representatives.

✦ SOCIOPOLITICAL ORGANIZATION

The *Aiga*

Samoan villages are organized around the household and the extended family unit. Each household is headed by a man, the *matai*, who is responsible for those who live under his roof. The household is generally made up of a husband, wife, and their children, as well as elderly parents and other kin. One feature of Samoan household structure is mobility, with individuals having the ability to live with a wide variety of people, and often changing residence to do so. Within the village, each household owns a plot of land with separate houses for sleeping, cooking, guests, and an outhouse.

The household head is given a title by his extended family, the *aiga*. The *aiga* "owns" the title it confers—which will be either Chief or Talking Chief—although it is a title that is bestowed for life upon the *matai*. Each *aiga* has a home village where it owns land, and where its elected *matai* resides. The portion of the *aiga* that resides with the *matai* must answer to the larger group for its maintenance of their property in the village.

Aiga are large because membership may be claimed not only through blood ties, but also those of marriage and adoption. Individuals can therefore trace ties to as many as a dozen *aiga*, and it is a rare Samoan who cannot claim kinship ties to a king or "paramount chief" (Holmes 1974).

The *aiga* is an active group only on certain occasions. Chief among these are upon the death of a *matai*, when they must convene to elect his replacement, or those occasions when *aiga* members must supply the *matai* with goods for exchange purposes. More salient divisions are branches of the family, which are referred to as *faletama*, or "houses of the children." Each son and daughter of the *aiga*'s original *matai* would initiate a branch. The sons would each constitute a male branch, and the daughters a female branch. Thus, the number of sons and daughters of the original *matai* would fix forever the number of branches and their "gender." The relationship between the male and female branches has been described as an oath of sorts, on the part of the male branches, to "pay respect, to render services, and to observe certain obligations towards those descendants" who are members of the female branches of the family (Milner in Holmes 1974:20). There appears to be a special deference paid to the female branches, despite the fact that it is the male branches from which future *matais* will be elected. To ignore the preferences of female branch members is believed to result in misfortune at best, and sickness and death in the worst of cases. This special attention to the male and female branches of a family is reflected in a specific pattern of behavior between men and women. It is expected that those who stand in the classification of brother and sister to one another (which would include cousins as well as siblings) will not use sexual language in each other's presence, dance together, spend time alone together, or express affection openly.

The *Matai*

Electing a *matai* is a process of deliberation that may span weeks, and is often hotly contested. Different branches of the family each have a candidate they wish to put forth, and they offer a variety of arguments to support him. These are generally based on the man's intelligence, wealth, ceremonial knowledge, previous service to family interests, and, in recent years, both his years of formal education and his ability to negotiate with Europeans in issues of politics and economics. Generally, if a son of the former *matai* meets all these criteria, he will have an advantage over other candidates. However, proven service to the greater good of the family may often take precedence over purely genealogical qualifications. It is also advantageous to have resided in the household of a *matai,* which affords the ability to begin participating in family service events at an early age. Men are rarely considered for election as *matai* before they are forty, and those young men who aspire to the position one day may begin to plan their strategy long in advance. A man may choose to live in a household where he will be the only male of his age, thereby being the likely candidate put forth by the household when the time comes. Or he may move to his wife's household, if there are no male competitors, should he currently be residing in a household where he is one of several young men.

The process of electing a new *matai* is under the guidance of a *matai* who is related to the deliberating family. He will listen to all the arguments put forth in support of each candidate, and preside over the vote. Once a new *matai* has been chosen, there is a feast for the family only, followed at a later date by an inauguration ceremony and feast that involves the entire village. It is at this time that the village council, with all the other *matais* in the village present, will observe the newly elected *matai*'s skill in delivering a traditional inauguration address. He is expected to display not only his wisdom, but also his skill as an orator and recounter of Samoan myth.

Once he has pleased the other *matais* in this display, it is incumbent upon him to turn his attention to the community at large, providing food for a villagewide feast, at which occasion he will present the other *matais* with gifts. When this protocol has been accomplished, he is officially ensconced as the *matai* to his household, a position he will hold for the rest of his life. On rare occasions, a man who has been found to be either ineffective or cruel has been stripped of this title, but such events are rare. A more common occurrence is the election of a new *matai* before the death of the current man at the latter's request, when he is elderly and infirm and wants the family to have more active leadership than he can continue to provide.

The responsibilities of a *matai* are many. He is expected to provide leadership in all facets of family life. If there is a dispute, he is the arbiter. He encourages warm family relations, offers advice, directs religious participation. He oversees all family lands, and represents the family in village affairs. His demeanor must be different from his former posture as a man of lesser import. One *matai*, elected at a younger age than is the norm, observed:

> "I have been a chief only four years and look, my hair is grey, although in Samoa grey hair comes very slowly. . . . But always I must act as if I were old. I must walk gravely and with a measured step. I may not dance except upon most solemn occasions, neither may I play games with the young men. Old men of sixty are my companions and watch my every word, lest I make a mistake. Thirty-one people live in my household. For them I must plan, I must find them food and clothing, settle their disputes, arrange their marriages. There is no one in my whole family who dares to scold me or even to address me familiarly by my first name. It is hard to be so young and yet be a chief" (Mead in Holmes 1974:22).

Traditionally, families tend to the land communally, under the direction of the *matai*. The village as a whole may pool their labor for projects that have the entire community as a focus, but work is generally family-bound. The yield is also equally shared by family members, and it falls to the *matai* to see to it that every individual has received a fair share. It is also incumbent upon him to make certain that there is a reserve of wealth accumulated to offset times of economic need or social obligation. This is changing somewhat in modern times, as individuals wish to add to their personal fortunes. However, such changes are occurring within the framework of the traditional system, as an addition more than a replacement of older values. Lowell Holmes, in his ethnography of the village Fitiuta, on the island of Ta'u, observes that despite increased financial opportunities for young people, their family and *matai* obligations remain unaltered. He writes:

> In spite of the greater emphasis now being placed on the individual in the economic and social interactions of the household, the average Samoan is still committed to the traditional system. Even among teachers and government office workers in Tutuila (the most acculturated of Samoans), it was found that better than three-fourths believed that the *matai* system is adequate for shaping the future of Samoan society (1974:23).

Historically, there has been some misunderstanding of the *matai* system, in that his leadership has been reported to be dictatorial and oppressive. However, Holmes finds the Samoan household to be structured "very democratically." In fact, the freedom of movement between Samoan households works to effectively counter any excessive authoritarianism in *matais*. They must strike a balance between effective leadership, which assures that tasks are efficiently accomplished, and a harsh and unreasonable style. If he is overly demanding, household members may simply move elsewhere. (One informant confided to Holmes that his strategy was to move to another household just before he knew he was to have a particularly dreaded set of tasks assigned to him.)

Chiefs and Talking Chiefs

The title *matai* is a chiefly one, but within this designation we can speak of Chief or Talking Chief. The former category has three ranked levels within it: High Chief, Chief, and Between the Posts Chief. Talking Chiefs also have three levels of status: Orator Chief, Legs of the Talking Chief, and Common Chief.

The roles of Chiefs vary, to some extent, according to village structure. In some villages there is but one High Chief, and his singularity affords him more power. In larger villages there may be several "brother chiefs" who all hold this uppermost rank. In all cases, it is the role of the High Chief to oversee the village council, serve as host to visitors to the village, and mediate disputes. He receives the first servings (and most desirable portions) of food and drink at feasts. Chiefs of the secondary and tertiary rank participate less in village council decisions, and are clothed in less grand costume.

High Talking Chiefs are the village orators, and are famed for their exquisite ceremonial speech. In public ceremonies, the High Talking Chief bears the responsibility for all oratory portions of meetings, sports competitions, property and marriage exchanges, and other ceremonies. When exchange parties set out to another village, the High Talking Chief is always in attendance, and upon arriving in the host village, he must recite, from memory, a highly stylized recitation of salutations. In turn, the High Talking Chief of the host village must deliver an oratory to welcome the guests, entertain them for their stay, and bid them an elaborate ceremonial farewell. The art of oration is highly prized, and while there is ample opportunity for a High Talking Chief to improvise in spinning his speeches, peppering them with tales from mythology or phrases from the Bible, there is also protocol to be followed. Certain speeches are to be structured in a particular way, and committed to memory. Talking Chiefs often employ poetics in their performances, usually in the form of *solo,* rhyming couplets with a prescribed meter, often concerned with mythological themes.

Holmes (1974) describes the oratory of Talking Chiefs in the ceremonial context as "[functioning] less as communication than as art" (p. 29). Talking Chiefs are superb performers, who are experts at commanding their audiences' riveted attention. Holmes describes a typical performance:

> Generally the voice volume rises from a whisper to nearly a shout as the speech proceeds. Now and again a special point will be emphasized with a gesture of the fly whisk or a sudden clipped phrase. A momentary pause or sudden reduction of voice volume highlights a thought of which the orator wants his audience to make special note. When interest appears to lag, a bit of sarcasm or humor or a proverbial cliché may be used to renew flagging attention spans (p. 30).

In Samoa, as elsewhere in the Pacific, debates about the position and power of the traditional chief figure prominently in the modern national political agenda. Lindstrom and White (1997) call attention to this "renewed visibility of chiefs" (p. 2) in a number of modern nation-states, pointing out that chiefs occupy a strategic position today as they did in the colonial past.

Occupying a powerfully strategic position between local groups and national authority, chiefs find themselves "mediating local realities and larger spheres of national and transnational interaction" (p. 3).

The *Aumaga* and the *Aualuma*

Chiefs, Talking Chiefs, and *matais* are the titled men of the village. Those who are untitled belong to a work cooperative called the *aumaga*. This group is sometimes called "the strength of the village" (Holmes 1974:31) because these men are truly the labor core of the entire community. The *aumaga* builds houses, repairs roads, plants and harvests the gardens, fishes from the coral reef, and cuts copra (coconut meat) for sale. There are ceremonial responsibilities that fall to the *aumaga* as well, largely concerning assisting the Chief in ritual and cooking and serving food at ceremonies. They serve as informal keepers of the peace, and interact with one another as a large group of friends might, playing cards and cricket, or gathering for dances and parties. The *aumaga* is under the leadership of a relative of the Chief, called the *manaia,* who convenes the group to plan their activities. Although the *manaia* need not be a true son of the Chief, he is in a fictive kinship relationship, such that he is referred to as "son" by the Chief, whatever his actual kinship tie may be.

Unmarried women have a parallel group, called the *aualuma.* This association, like the *aumaga,* serves the needs of the village by undertaking all of the social, economic, and ceremonial tasks that older Chief's wives can no longer accomplish. In the past, there was a woman who was in some ways analogous to the *manaia,* in that she was the "fictive daughter" of the Chief, much in the way the *manaia* was a "fictive son." However, hers was not a leadership position. The *taupou,* as she was known, was a ceremonial figure whose function was to publicly represent virginity. At the occasion of her marriage to a High Chief or *manaia* from another village, she was publicly "tested" by the village High Talking Chief, who wrapped his finger in white bark cloth, and broke her hymen, displaying the blood as proof of her virginity. Although there is still an *aualuma* in every Samoan village, the position of *taupou* has changed. *Taupous* are women appointed by the Chief—often married women with children—who function as official hosts to entertain visitors from other villages, or assist with ceremonial duties. The ranks of the modern *aualuma* are made up of unmarried women and widows who are a subset of the Women's Committee. All these women work together on community projects such as fund-raising events for the church, staging dances for village celebrations, shellfish gathering at the water's edge, and helping out at the local clinic.

The *Fono*

The *fono,* or village council, is the central decision-making forum of the village. Informal gatherings of Talking Chiefs, which set the agenda for the council meetings, are important precursors of the formal *fono,* allowing all the *matai* to know what issues are to be debated and resolved. They can then prepare their thoughts about the matters and seek council and opinions from other family members. Such preliminary meetings also make evident the general sentiment about issues, so that all concerned will know which proposals are likely to have support, and which are potentially more hotly contested.

The *fono* begins with a formal welcome provided by the Talking Chief. The *aumaga* sits outside the council house, and the Chiefs and Talking Chiefs convene within. In all Samoan villages, *fono* begin with the *kava* ceremony. *Kava* is a root which is cut and pounded into a pulp, and then strained in water to make a drink. The preparation of the *kava* is a highly ritualized act, performed by the Talking Chief, who selects the root, and various members of the *aumaga.* One man cuts the root, another pounds it into a pulp, and it is then the job of the *manaia* to strain it over and over, until it is the proper consistency. The *manaia* carefully observes the color of the *kava,* to judge its strength; as it splashes into the bowl from the strainer, he listens to the sound of the liquid falling, and can determine when he has achieved the perfect concentration of pulp and water. At this, he pours the *kava* from a great height, so the assembled Chiefs can see it. It is the Talking Chief who sings out that it is ready, and the Chiefs applaud to signal their acceptance.

Serving the *kava* has a formal protocol as well. The order in which Chiefs are served denotes their rank. Beginning at the top of the hierarchy, High Chief and then High Talking Chief are served; then the next level of these two categories of Chief, and so on. Prestige is accorded both the man who drinks first, and the man who drinks last. The High Talking Chief serves the *kava,* sometimes calling out the names of the men; in the case of Chiefs of very high rank, he calls out not their names, but the names of their cups. Only the most elite of Chiefs have cup titles, which are usually phrases that allude to sacred myths, events, or places. Talking Chiefs are given their *kava* while being told "your *kava;*" Chiefs without cup titles are given theirs with the directive, "drink."

Now the meeting can begin in earnest. Each item of the agenda is addressed in turn, with time allowed for discussion, differences of opinion, and evidence to support both sides of an argument should there be one. Each *matai* has the opportunity to speak, and it is the speech that is the official casting of a vote. No count is taken of raised hands, or ballots cast, or verbal "ayes" and "nays." Compromise and consensus are sought, but majority rules. This is not calculated in numbers of votes, because those of higher status hold greater sway in decision making. The vote of a High Chief counts more than that of a secondary one. Whatever the outcome of a decision, it is always assumed to be an issue that may be reopened at a future *fono.* Solidarity in the community is promoted by reaching solutions that satisfy all council members. If a decision leads to hard feelings, this will be counterproductive for the village as a whole, and thus no decision is seen as irrevocable.

Marriage and the Family

Gift giving holds an important place in Samoan social relations, and weddings are a primary venue for this sort of exchange. Because it is so central a feature, the planning of a marriage ceremony involves extensive preparation for the transfer of property: *toga* (female property) will be exchanged for *oloa* (male property).

The households of the bride and groom are equally involved in the planning and expense of the wedding. They provide the bulk of the enormous feast, with guests bringing smaller dishes to contribute. There are generally two ceremonies performed, one following the other. The bride and groom march through the village, wedding party attending them, to the district judge, who conducts a civil ceremony. From there, the newly married couple and their attendants walk to the church, where all the guests are gathered. A religious ceremony is performed, after which the feasting and gift giving begin.

Newly married couples do not establish their own new household. However, they are free to choose which side of the family they will join. This is owing to the fact that Samoans have an ambilineal kinship system; individuals may choose to affiliate with any of a number of groups, through either their fathers or their mothers. There is a tendency to become most closely involved with the group where one resides, but membership in several groups is recognized.

Wherever a husband and wife reside, they are expected to work cooperatively with the rest of the household. Large families are economically advantageous, and older children are expected to care for their younger siblings when they themselves are hardly more than toddlers. For the first few years, children sleep with their mothers and their days are largely playful. By the time they are three or four, they begin to shoulder some responsibilities. Girls are directed toward childcare and housework; boys help with animals and water gathering, though their days are more leisurely than are those of their sisters. By the time children are seven or eight, they have been fully indoctrinated into the usual tasks of Samoan life, having participated to some degree in agriculture, fishing, cooking, and childcare. It is at this age that formal schooling begins, and the bulk of a child's day is spent at the village schoolhouse.

As Samoans age, status increases as responsibilities lighten. The elderly are valued by their fellow villagers, and are shown special deference at public gatherings. Restrictions regarding food and social interaction become lax, and older people feel they are at the best time of life, visiting with family and friends, doing as much as they care to and no more.

When death occurs, funeral preparations begin immediately. The church choir is dispatched to the mourner's home, where the body has been bathed, dressed in white, and placed on a cushions of woven mats. During the twenty-four hours between death and burial, the family of the deceased stays with the body while the burial site is selected. The burial itself is a religious ceremony, followed by a meal for all those who assisted in the care and burial.

✦ ECONOMIC ORGANIZATION

Property

It is the *matai* who controls the land, in that he holds sway over allocation of plots and the ways in which those plots are used. He does not, however, have the authority to sell the land or will it to his own children upon his death. Family land essentially belongs to the corporate group. They vote on its disposition, and work it cooperatively.

Land in a Samoan village is divided into four categories. The first contains village house lots, not agricultural sites. There may be trees on the land from which fruits may be picked, or an occasional taro patch may be encouraged to grow. By and large, however, this land is where houses are built in clusters—main sleeping houses, a guest house, and latrines.

True plantation plots are situated outside the village, either on the hills overlooking the houses, or along the coast. The former are best for breadfruit and bananas; the latter support coconut groves. Holmes (1974) describes these plots as deceptively overgrown; plants and trees grow in a seemingly haphazard placement, not an cultivated rows. Underbrush covers the land, and the uninitiated eye could easily survey a plantation plot and not recognize it as land under cultivation. Despite this appearance, however, these plots are owned by families, and their boundaries—rocks, streams, certain trees—are easily recognizable to all villagers.

A third category of land is the family reserve section, the plots where taro and yams are cultivated. These plots may be lent to other villagers, who may use them to grow crops for their own consumption. They are then regarded as owning the crops, but not the land. Because the foodstuffs planted in these sections are those that mature and are harvested quickly, these sites are cultivated less intensively than the plantation plots.

The fourth type of land is village land, and it is both farther removed from the village sites and less often cultivated. Permission to plant here is granted by the village council because the land is community property and not family owned. An individual who is willing to expend the enormous effort required to clear the overgrown land may petition to do so. If he is given leave to undertake the project, he may continue to use it as long as he cares for it. Village land also provides a site for hunting wild pigs and birds. In addition to this land high up in the mountains, some coastal land is also village property. There, any individual who wishes to fish is free to do so.

Cultivation

Clearing the land for planting is hard work. Large trees and bushes are cut down with axes; knives slice down tall grass, ferns, and smaller scrubby bushes. Felled vegetation is left to dry, and then is cut up further for burning. Small, well-controlled fires clear the land.

Digging sticks are then employed to dislodge rocks and loosen the soil for planting. Some crops—banana trees, chief among them—never need to be reestablished in a formal way. Although new taro and yam patches are started from old plants, banana groves can be cut back, encouraging new suckers to grow from the base of trees and develop into another plant. Papaya trees are easier still: workers in the field eat papaya and toss the pits to the ground. Trees spring up regularly from discarded seeds. Oranges and mangoes grow wild, but are sometimes planted from seed if additional trees are desired.

In this tropical climate, irrigation is unnecessary. Leaves from trees planted in the fields fall and decay into fertilizer, enriching the soil.

Coconut is the most important crop, and the one with the widest variety of uses. Copra is produced for cash income, but the coconut meat is a dietary staple as well. The meat is eaten raw; it can be grated and pressed into "coconut cream"; and the nut of the mature plant is eaten as a snack. The wood of the tree is used for building a host of items, from houses to cricket bats. Leaves are woven into fans, hats, floor mats, baskets, toys, and shoes. The fibers in the outer husk provide rope for outrigger canoes. The shell of the coconut serve as bowls, water bottles, and utensils. Oil from the coconut kernel has cosmetic and medicinal uses.

Despite the value of coconut, it is taro that is preferred as a food. Boiled or baked, it is eaten cold at nearly every meal. Breadfruit is eaten more often, but probably because it is so abundant.

There are many specialists in Samoan society, each with a distinctive talent. One may be an expert boat builder, or tattooer, or surgeon. There are, however, no agricultural specialists. Cultivation is the major part of everyone's day, whether it is organized by family, or a project of an *aualuma* or *aumaga*, or Women's Committee. Although everyone is expected to work, harvests are shared without regard to individual effort. Holmes (1974) observes, "[t]he industrious and lazy alike enjoy adequate food, clothing, and shelter" (p. 40).

Village councils generally set up a work schedule to organize the agricultural life of the community, day by day. These are hardly arbitrary lists of tasks; the schedule is planned with particular ends in mind. One of the most important of these is to regulate thievery. If copra is only to be cut on Tuesday, an individual sneaking into the bush to do so on a Thursday can be easily detected. Situating families in their banana groves on Mondays and Wednesdays assures that no one else can be there, picking their bananas; for a thief to do so on another day would not go unnoticed: one is not to be carrying harvested bananas on any other days.

Fishing

Unlike cultivation, fishing does have its specialists. These are the *tautai*, who captain the thirty-foot-long outrigger canoes, and sit in the stern of the boat, fishing for bonito, a breed of mackerel. Paddlers locate a school of bonito and keep the canoe in position. A fourteen-foot-long bamboo pole is secured on a shelf of blocks, which hold it steady at a 45-degree angle to the water. Line from the rod dangles a lure just at the surface of the water. The *tautai* keeps close watch on the bait, so he can jerk the catch out of the water quickly, sending it flying into the back of the canoe. The most skilled *tautai* have perfected the motion such that the fish is freed from the hook, eliminating the time it would take to manually remove the hook from the fish's mouth. The line can then be placed back into the school of bonito as quickly as possible. The paramount sign of a highly skilled *tautai* is the necessity of many of his crew to swim alongside the boat, on the return trip, owing to the quantity of bonito now occupying their place.

Much ritual is associated with bonito fishing, most of it after the catch has been brought back, and is centered around the division of the fruits of the day's labor. At the end of the day, all boats head to the outside of the reef to report the number of their catch to the fleet's chief. He offers a prayer of thanks for that day's yield, and requires each *tautai* to state how many bonito are in his hold. Every boat must arrive home with an equal number of fish. Before heading for home, there is a ceremonial meal where the crews of each boat eat raw bonito, given to them by the Chief as part of his allocation of the catch. *Tautai* eat first, the crew next, and then the boats return to shore. Families meet their canoes, pay the crew in more fish, and return home with the remainder of the catch. While the boats have been out, villagers have been at home, cultivating at a standstill, encouraging successful fishing with their prayers. Each time a fish slips off the hook is an occasion for the *tautai* to remark that the family at home is not offering adequate prayer.

Bonito fishing from large outrigger canoes is only one form of angling. Gathering along the coastline yields reef worm and turtle. Nets ensnare fish swimming close to the shore, and wooden traps capture lobsters, eels, and crabs. Pole and spear fishing for bass and snapper is popular. Entire schools of fish can be poisoned or dynamited inside the reefs, and men shoot spear guns armed with heavy wire, attacking from within the water and wearing the captured fish around their waists.

Those who enjoy the risk take to the water in row boats in search of sharks. They entice them to the boat's edge by throwing meat into the water, and when the shark comes alongside to devour the bait, men slip heavy nooses of rope around the shark's head. Women are expert in reef gathering, and their efforts are sometimes rewarded with the discovery of an octopus, which they kill by biting it, or by thrashing it against a rock.

Fishing took up more subsistence time in the past than it does in modern times. The Samoans' love for fish can be more easily satisfied by purchasing cans of sardines, tuna, and salmon at the local bush store.

Domestic Work

The traditionally strict division of labor between men and women is less pronounced in modern times. Traditionally, however, cooking was the exclusive domain of men. In Samoa today, men are still primarily responsible for food preparation, but they are especially involved in cooking traditional foods. When women prepare parts of the meal, their domain is "foreign" food—new items that are prepackaged, such as cake mixes or canned goods—which they often cook in modern vessels, among them pressure cookers and deep fryers. In the past, most dishes were prepared in an earth oven, and men still cook in them today. On the floor of a cooking house, stones are arranged to form the base, and kindling is lit on top to heat the stones. Another layer of stones is added once the blaze is at its peak, and in less than an hour the embers are removed, leaving hot rocks that can be spread out to accommodate the amount of food to be cooked. The food is placed on top of the rocks in the center and covered with leaves, and rocks from the edges are placed on top of the food. Layer upon layer is built, with the leaves acting to prevent the food from burning. The topmost layer is a canopy of broad leaves, which serve as a lid, trapping the heat. This method is most commonly employed for cooking fish and vegetables. When pigs are roasted, their preparation is more complex. Pork is the focus of ceremonial meals, and both preparation and division of the meat once cooked are of the utmost importance. Holmes (1974) describes this process:

> Pigs are strangled by laying them on their back and standing on a stick placed across their throat. The carcass is then dragged across the heated stones of the earth oven in order to singe off the hair and bristles. The abdomen is then cut open, the internal organs removed and wrapped in leaves to be cooked separately, and the hollow abdominal cavity is filled with papaya leaves, which supposedly flavor the meat and act as a tenderizer. The whole pig is then placed on the circle of heated cooking stones with the feet tucked under the carcass. After receiving a cover of leaves, and sometimes a layer of damp burlap bags, the pig is allowed to cook for approximately one hour (pp. 49–50).

Although the pork is not cooked thoroughly enough to eat in this amount of time, it is much easier to distribute in a partially raw state, when it can be cut accurately without falling apart. Meat is given based on rank, with certain parts designated for particular groups of individuals.

Barkcloth is an important commodity in Samoa, and its production is exclusively the domain of women. Cloth is made from mulberry bush bark. Branches are stripped, and the inner bark soaked to soften. Sharpened clam shells scrape it smooth, and several strips are bundled together and beaten into strips of cloth about a foot long. They are then dried and decorated. Finished barkcloths have a variety of functions. They are worn as ceremonial garb, wrapped around as skirts; are used by women as shawls; serve as bedspreads; and are hung as room dividers. Women also weave pandanus leaf floormats and sleeping mats.

While young girls are introduced into the art of clothmaking and weaving by older women, young men are directed toward carpentry. Boat and house building are done without blueprints; young apprentices watch more skilled artisans, and participate in more stages of the process as they become more skilled.

House building is often a ceremonial affair, with feasts arranged to mark the beginning and end of construction.

✦ RELIGIOUS LIFE

The Supernatural Ones: *Atua* and *Aitu*

Samoan myth tells of the Tagaloa gods, the *atua*, who live as a family on the ten mountain tops that form heaven. These gods appear not to have been attended to in the ways in which many peoples worship their deities. There were no priests who attended them, although *matai* and Talking Chiefs might invoke their names at feasts and other ceremonies. At mealtime, spoken prayers of thanks might be offered. The *atua* were the higher level of deities. Beneath them were the *aitu*, the spirits of ancestors. Several *aitu* are known throughout Samoa, and are something of 'national figures,' associated with particular activities (such as fishing) or sacred places. *Aitu* are a part of modern Samoan belief, often thought to be capable of wreaking havoc if displeased. They sometimes take human form again, dressing in white and appearing in the night. Certain spots are known to attract these ghosts, and it is the rare Samoan who does not have an experience to relate regarding a brush with an *aitu*.

If their families are behaving improperly, *aitu* send an illness, which is characterized by chills, fever, and bouts of delirious behavior. Cures may be effected by herbal remedies administered by local specialists. Families examine the recent past to see if any activities or decisions made could have incited an *aitu*'s wrath. Recovery can be hastened by remedying such mistakes.

Some *aitu* are significant only to a particular family or village. Taking the form of birds, fish, or game animals, these often become taboo food items for the group that recognizes them as spiritually important.

Christianity

Holmes (1974) reports that Samoans were long regarded, by other Polynesian peoples, as having no religion. Although the Tagaloa gods are mentioned in mythology, there was an absence of ritual life surrounding the supernatural. Whereas Chiefs functioned in a way that might be deemed "priestly," their power derived from the social and political spheres, and not the divine. Thus, when Christian missionaries came to Samoa in the early nineteenth century, they were met with very little resistance. In fact, some Chiefs argued that this new religion ought to be quickly accepted, as it brought with it the promise of acquiring valuable material goods such as those owned by the missionaries, and others agreed that wars might be prevented by embracing Christianity. For their part, missionaries recognized the power of the Chiefs, and realized that chiefly acceptance of Christianity was the means to successfully convert entire villages. The political influence of the Chief meant that their acceptance of Christianity was, in essence, on behalf of their whole family, and thus the conversion of a village *matai* "[won] the souls of entire villages for the Lord" (MacPherson 1997: 276). Samoan appreciation for verbal skills, institutionalized in the Talking Chief, resulted in their delight in "listening to the almost interminable sermons delivered by the mission pastors" (Holmes 1974:60).

Although there were some villages that were slower in their acceptance, Christianity took hold in Samoa quite easily. Communion was accepted as being much like the *kava* ceremony, which it now accompanied; sermons were greeted with the same rapt attention Talking Chiefs inspired. The church became the focal point of community life, and while Samoa is now almost entirely Christian, there remains great affection for, and knowledge about, their own local spiritual traditions and mythology.

✦ MARGARET MEAD IN SAMOA

One of the greatest debates in modern anthropology concerns the questions raised by Derek Freeman in 1983 about Margaret Mead's work in Samoa.

Mead, one of the discipline's most well-known and respected members, conducted ethnographic research among Samoan adolescents in the 1920s. At this time in the United States, the rebellion and turmoil that characterized the teenage years was regarded as a "natural" and universally human consequence of growing into adulthood. It was Mead's hypothesis that this turbulent time of life for American youth was not necessarily a biological dictate shared by adolescents everywhere. Rather, it was also greatly influenced by the culture in which children were raised. Mead found very little evidence among Samoan youth of the anguish and emotional upheaval so common to American teenagers. Her ethnographic studies were at the forefront of establishing the view that individuals are very much a product of the environments in which they live and are nurtured. Freeman, a sociobiologist, took issue with Mead's position, claiming that she painted a false picture of Samoa in order to promote her belief in the primacy of "nurture" over "nature." Mead's depiction was of a culture that had less repressive sexual mores than contemporary American society of the time, and one in which there were fewer conflicts and tensions. Freeman asserted that Samoa was, in fact, a culture replete with tension and aggression. Moreover, he believed Mead was misled by her informants, who provided her with false report. Serena Nanda (1994:147) writes:

> Freeman uses his criticisms of Mead's ethnographic work to put forth his own sociobiological view in which a large component of human behavior, particularly aggression, is seen as biologically determined. Many of Mead's former colleagues and students have defended her work, pointing out that her ethnography was done in 1925, when anthropology was still in its infancy as a science, and that she worked well within the tradition of ethnographic methodology as it was known at that time. They point out that although she may have been wrong about some of her facts and emphases, reinterpretation of ethnography is a standard practice in anthropology and is part of the growth and development of the field. Freeman's critics aptly point

out that the attention given to his book in the media represents a current sympathy with politically conservative implications of his sociobiological stance. Both Mead's and Freeman's work must be seen in the context of the "nature/nurture" controversy. It was due in great part to Mead's work that the theory that we are products of our environment and that we can reshape that environment if we are willing took hold in American scientific and popular thinking in the decades between 1930 and 1960. Beginning with the publication of Edward Wilson's *Sociobiology: The New Synthesis* (1975), the stage was set for criticism of the kind of cultural emphases that Mead's work embodies.

In 1990, a lengthy volume was published, bringing together dozens of anthropologists commenting on the "Mead-Freeman debate." Many different viewpoints were represented. Some took issue with the manner in which Freeman's challenges were presented; some agreed that Mead's original fieldwork was flawed. Most offered insightful commentary on the fact that it was more than two peoples' contradictory interpretations that were at issue; the nature of truth, the meaning of science, the power of myth, and the politics of academics were all in play. As the editor of the collection, Hiram Caton (1990), observed, the controversy led to an entire discipline's taking stock of itself, past and present.

✦ "The Great Migration" and Beyond

In 1950, the Navy turned its governance of American Samoa over to the Department of the Interior. Nearly six thousand Samoans had been employed by the Navy, some acting as local police, called *Fitafita* guardsman, and their livelihoods were in jeopardy. In 1952, Samoan naval employees and their families were given the opportunity to move to Hawaii, in search of employment. This began the so-called Great Migration of the 1950s; between 1952 and 1956, an estimated seventy-five hundred Samoans resettled in Hawaii (Pouesi 1994). For those who remained, change came again in the 1960s, when the United States government escalated its interest in the islands. With budget appropriations for Samoa tripled, programs regarding industry, education, and tourism were vigorously mounted. Holmes (1974:97) observes that prosperity brought changes to Samoa:

> Because of employment in the new construction program and in a tuna cannery, Samoans had more money. Beer and soft drink consumption had soared. Bush stores sold a wide variety of European tinned food. Taxi-cabs and private cars were numerous and traffic was becoming a problem. Girls ... had begun to wear makeup and European hairstyles ... stereo[s] were not uncommon household products.

In the 1970s, Samoan emigration to Hawaii and the United States mainland increased dramatically. California is home to over ninety thousand Samoans, and Los Angeles alone has a Samoan community of more than twelve thousand, many of whom maintain ties with traditional Samoan values. Southern California has a number of Samoan community organizations, designed to provide assistance to newly arrived individuals, as well as social and financial aid to those already established. Chief among these are *Samoa Mo Samoa* ("Samoans for Samoans"), a nonprofit organization in San Francisco, and the National Office of Samoan Affairs (NOSA), based in Los Angeles.

Village *fonos* continue to wield considerable local power, with recent legislation securing the rights of local leaders to exercise authority in accordance with established village custom (MacPherson 1997). The traditional *matai* system also exerts a powerful influence on Samoan life in the United States. *Matai* leaders are local community leaders, called upon to settle disputes and organize activities. *Matai* leaders who emigrate retain their ties to their *aiga,* and as part of the obligation they incur to maintain their position, send money home to their family and villages. Some return to Samoa to vote in elections, as another way to nurture their ties. Meleisea (1992) reports that it is not uncommon for representatives of political factions in Samoa to visit California and Hawaii to collect campaign donations. Janes (1990) refers to the ways in which Samoan migrants have responded to the urban, capitalist life they found stateside as "a creative kind of cultural consolidation" (p. 163). Within churches and local organizations, familiar forms of association and obligation have been altered to suit new demands. He points especially to the *fa'alavelave* (literally "problem" or "difficulty"), events that constitute a life-crisis and demand communal effort. Funerals, weddings, and nonritual events that require economic assistance are the primary examples. In Samoa, *fa'alavelave* are characterized by the exchange of food and handmade goods. In the United States, these reciprocal exchanges are primarily made in cash. Local members pay dues and donations to help with the cost of weddings and funerals, housing and education, knowing that they will be guaranteed similar assistance if they should need it (Pouesi 1994). By tailoring traditional redistribution practices to local needs, Samoan migrant communities maintain solidarity (and prestige) and provide support. Janes, a medical anthropologist, has investigated the health effects of the social stressors involved in migration and adaptation of Samoans in California. He finds that the "monetization" of traditional Samoan institutions such as *fa'alavelave* can take its toll. The economic burdens involved, stress resulting from status shifts, and the exigencies of daily life in a new community have all resulted in ill health. However, those Samoans who are closely connected to church groups, who have kin groups that buoy them in times of economic crisis, and who are able to maintain traditional ties and values within their communities seem buffered from the health effects of stress.

Pouesi (1994) notes that in the late 1960s and early 1970s, Samoan-born adolescents were eager to define themselves as "Hawaiians" and "Californians," and not Samoans. However, young Samoans born in California and Hawaii, while perhaps less reliant on kin-based mutual support organizations, seem nonetheless to be part of a "revival of pride in Samoan heritage" (p. 86). Local Samoan organizations are experiencing a resurgence, with an infusion of young people attempting to maintain a "collective personality in the face of increasing individualism" (Pouesi 1994:86).

✦ FOR FURTHER DISCUSSION

One of the greatest debates in modern anthropology surrounded the questions raised by Derek Freeman about Margaret Mead's work in Samoa. It was Mead's hypothesis that the rebellion and turmoil that characterized American teenage years was not the "natural" and universally human consequence of growing into adulthood it was believed to be. In Samoa, she found that adolescents experienced less repression, conflict, and tension, and displayed none of the emotional turbulence of "typical" Western teenagers. This supported the view that individuals are very much a product of the environments in which they live and are nurtured. Freeman, a sociobiologist, took issue with Mead's position, claiming that she painted a false picture of Samoa in order to promote her belief in the primacy of "nurture" over "nature." He asserted that Samoa was, in fact, a culture replete with tension and aggression.

Using what you have learned about anthropology's holistic and comparative perspective, how might you address the Mead-Freeman debate? What might be the consequences, positive and negative, of such controversy to the discipline of anthropology? How might the potential for such challenges influence future fieldwork?

CHAPTER 13

THE TIWI

Tradition in Australia

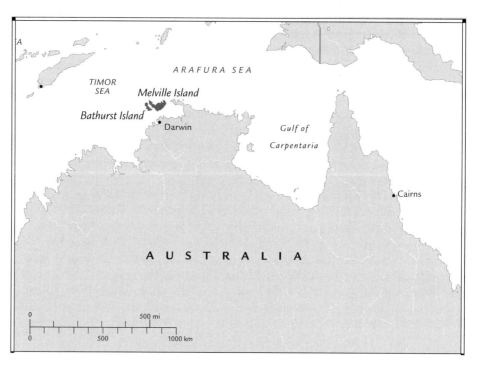

Location of the Tiwi on Melville and Bathurst Islands.

✦ THE BEGINNING

In the beginning the earth was flat, and dark, and silent. No hills or valleys, no trees or rivers. No birds called; no sun shone.

Out of the ground rose an old, old woman. She was blind, and in her arms she carried three babies: two girls and one boy. Across the land she crawled, clutching her children, and in the furrows left by her knees fresh water bubbled up. She turned westward and formed the shores. She crawled further and created the ports.

After a time she thought perhaps she was making the island too large, so she journeyed northward to create the straits that separate the islands where we are. On her last journey, she did the final thing; she separated the land of the Tiwi from all others. Before she crawled away—we do not know where—she turned back to create green on the bare land, and animals. Because here she was leaving her children; and her children must have food.

✦ INTRODUCTION AND HISTORY

The Tiwi occupy Melville and Bathurst Islands, which form a cultural as well as geographical unit. Taken together, they span about three thousand square miles. Located off the north coast of Australia, they lie about thirty miles north of Darwin.

The land is generally flat, with a low central ridge on Melville Island rising to about three hundred feet, and running west to east. Along this ridge running south to north are nine rivers that flow north to the sea. Along the headwaters of the larger rivers are open marshlands; on the northern and especially the southern coasts are areas of sandy beach and rocky cliffs. On Bathurst, which boasts less elevation, rivers are small and largely tidal.

Both islands are heavily forested, characterized largely by mangrove forests, mixed eucalyptus and cypress, woolly-butt, ironwood, and string-bark. As is found on the mainland, marsupials—wallaby, opossum, bandicoot—are present in large numbers. Snakes and lizards abound, and fruit bats populate the mangrove swamps. Crocodiles pose great danger both in rivers and on the coast. Monsoons occur between November and March, while little or no rain falls from June to September.

Northern people most likely came into contact with outsiders before those living to the south. It has been suggested, for example, that the coastal region of Arnhem Land probably hosted Indonesian fishing expeditions hundreds of years before British contact. Aided by northwest monsoon winds, these fishing parties most likely depended upon native Australian labor in their exploitation of the rich beche-de-mer fishing grounds. These individuals did not settle in the islands; when, after several months, the monsoonal winds blew homeward, they returned. In Queensland, native populations probably had contact with the peoples of New Guinea.

The Tiwi, too, most probably had contact with outsiders long ago, although definitive records are not available. Perhaps sailors blown off course landed accidentally (Goodale 1971). The Dutch, during the seventeenth century, sighted and named the islands that are home to the Tiwi. In the eighteenth century the Portuguese seized native Australians from the northern coast as slaves. The nineteenth century brought Malay fishing parties and Japanese pearl shell collectors.

It was during the early part of the nineteenth century that French exploration and British occupation brought intensive Western contact. The first foreign settlement was a British establishment (Fort Dundas) that was abandoned after five years of hardship. It was not for another seventy-five years that further European settlement was attempted. In the early twentieth century, Catholic missions were established on the southeastern coast of Bathurst Island and, in the years following, there was growing contact with white Australians.

In 1986 the Tiwi population totaled roughly 2000, with Bathurst Island home to about thirteen hundred, and two Melville Island townships totaling seven hundred.

✦ SUBSISTENCE

Native Australians are traditionally hunters and gatherers. Although there are overall similarities among native groups—to a much larger extent, for example, than among the very different tribal people of Africa—there are also differences.

The Tiwi live in a varied environment that provides them with dietary abundance today as it did in the past. This generous supply of fish, game, and vegetable foods is connected very firmly to what may be the most familiar characteristic of Tiwi culture—their system of marriage. Nanda (1994) points out that polygyny among the Tiwi appears to be adaptive to these foragers much in the same way it is in horticultural societies.

Men hunt turtles, geese, lizards, fish, and wallabies, all of which are in ready supply. However, as is typical of foraging subsistence, it is the edible plants, fruits, and vegetables gathered by women that make up the bulk of the daily food supply. In addition to providing the gathered items that are the staple of daily meals, women also hunt small game, using tools they manufacture. There is no problem securing food in the Tiwi environment; however, the collection of the abundantly available supplies does pose a challenge as it demands many hands.

The traditional day began with women and children fanning out to begin the day's subsistence activities. Typically, only younger men hunted and fished. Young boys and older men participated least in daily foraging activities.

Increasingly after European settlement, Tiwi became employed in a variety of jobs related to settlement life, including education, health, community service, and government. Although each community has a shop where food and other material goods may be purchased, the majority of Tiwi are concerned with the maintenance of hunting and foraging skills among the young. With a preference for "bush" food over "store-bought" goods, Tiwi still make up much of their weekly diet with native foods.

Tiwi man in ceremonial dress.

Settlement

Modern-day Tiwi live in two- to four-bedroom houses built by outside contractors during the past fifteen to twenty years, complete with kitchen and bathrooms, electricity, and plumbing. Some families, settling on the land owned by their own local group, have built housing for themselves.

Traditionally, however, Tiwi set up camp in a cleared area around a fire, with the kind of shelter constructed dependent largely on the season. During the rainy season, which lasts from early November through late April, sheets of bark were stripped from trees and supported on wooden poles. During the dry season, shelters were needed only to provide shade, and were constructed by merely leaning leafy branches together.

Every Tiwi woman and man owns land, and thus has a landowning name. Although the boundaries (and number) of these "countries" have changed many times over the past hundred years since their demarcation was first recorded, whichever group claims hold over an area has distinct responsibilities. In 1976 the islands were deeded back to the Tiwi under the Land Rights Bill, which created a Tiwi Land Council. The council recognizes seven countries, each represented by delegates. One is considered to own the land owned by one's father (although in the past, ownership of the land was conferred by one's father's burial in the land). All the individuals recognized as owners of a country are collectively held responsible for its maintenance, which includes not only natural but also spiritual resources. It is further expected that both knowledge of the land and responsibility for that country will be passed on to the next generation.

✦ Social Organization

The word "*tiwi*," in their own distinctive tongue, distantly related to other native Australian languages, means "people." As is the case with many indigenous names, it refers not to the human species but rather means "real" people, or primary beings. Traditionally, Tiwi referred to themselves by names indicating their membership in one of several landowning groups, which they call countries.

A key feature in the history of the Tiwi was their isolation. Reports of first contact between Tiwi and all other outsiders are characteristically quite hostile, and even fatal to the unfortunate visitors. Hart et al. (1988:10) point out that this feeling of being "distinct from any other alleged human beings who might show up from time to time on the beaches" and the accompanying feeling that these others were, in fact, "[excluded] from real 'human-ness'" (p. 10) may account for their bellicose reception.

Because they were so isolated and rarely disturbed, Tiwi thought less of protecting or identifying their group as a whole; the unit within which they functioned on a daily basis was the band. Bands were large (typically one hundred individuals) and tended to move in a dispersed fashion, so fellow members might not see one another for weeks. As is typically the case, Tiwi bands were characterized by flexible and often-shifting membership.

Hunting and gathering activities were organized as a band, but the focus of the daily routine was the household, which were fairly autonomous units of production and consumption. Often it was one household that decided where to set up camp and when to break camp and move on. This autonomy was especially likely in larger domestic units, such as those belonging to a "big man." Hart et al. (1988:37) write of one such household as constituting "a complete community in itself, with the old man as executive director. He laid down the daily, weekly, and monthly work and travel schedules for the women, the young men, and the children. Most of the time the work went automatically because all the adults and the older children knew their jobs."

A distinction is drawn between a residential group—that is, the people who live in a particular locale together for a time—and a landholding group—meaning those to whom a "country" belongs. Residential members of a group have rights of access to the resources around them, come to the aid of members of other households in their residential group (for example, during times of conflict), and carry out certain ceremonial responsibilities (as, for example, when there is a death in the group). Rights of landholding, acquired through one's father, may extend beyond the residential unit, if ones' father lived or died and was buried in a "country" of which he was not also an owner.

Kinship

Tiwi belong to their mother's matrilineal descent group, which they call their "skin." This matrilineal clan is a group whose members reckon their common descent from a group of unborn spirit beings living in or near a body of water. The traditional belief system explains pregnancy as occurring when a man discovers one of these unborn spirits and sends it to his wife, whose clan origin must be the same as the spirit's. Members of each of these named clans, further grouped into four larger exogamous units, provide one another with both moral and practical support. For every individual, it is important to recognize two clans: one's own clan (that of one's mother), and one's father's clan, from whom one chooses an individual to marry.

In the social system of the Tiwi, everyone is, at base, kin to everyone else. Kinship terms can be extended to every member of the population. The most basic division of kin is between those who are "close" (geographically) and those who are "far away" (called long-way kin).

Marriage

Customs surrounding Tiwi marriage have undergone enormous change in modern times, largely due to the influence of Catholic missionaries settling on the islands after World War II. However, traditional marital patterns are of crucial importance in understanding the larger Tiwi social, political, and economic system.

Traditional Tiwi culture mandated that all women *must* be married. This belief is a more extreme version of the belief held by Australian mainland tribes, in which marriage is expected, but not required—and certainly not contracted for before birth. Thus, in the past, every female was at all times married. From birth—in fact, before birth—to death, there was no concept of an unmarried female. (In fact, there was no word in Tiwi language to convey this state, even about a newborn girl.)

To begin to understand this mandate, one must first understand the indigenous beliefs about conception. Again, the Tiwi shared with mainlanders the belief that a woman becomes pregnant because a spirit enters her body. A man has no physical role in the creation of a child. But the Tiwi took another step in order to handle the potentially dangerous lack of predictability demonstrated by these impregnating spirits. Because a spirit could impregnate any female at any time, if every female were always married, every child could be assured a father. Thus, as soon as a baby girl was born, she was betrothed, if she had not been already; in most cases, when girls reached puberty their "future" daughters were betrothed. A woman who was widowed did not leave the graveside of her husband without a new spouse.

The consequences of such a system are many, not the least of which is that at any given time, the entire female population—but only part of the male population—was married. As is found in most human groups, roughly equal numbers of males and females are born to the Tiwi. Consequently, this situation mandated a high degree of plural marriage.

It fell to a baby girl's father to betroth his infant daughter, and he did this with an eye to his own future economic, political, and social advantage. Baby girls were not promised to baby boys. Hart et al. (1988:19) comment, "Put bluntly, in Tiwi culture daughters were an asset to their father, and he invested these assets in his own welfare." Therefore, he chose either someone who was an important friend or ally or whom he wished to engage as a friend or ally. This might very likely be a man of his own age, perhaps one who had already promised a daughter to him. If this were the case, such an individual would be at least thirty or forty years older than his bride. A father also used this process to grant him security in his old age. Rather than selecting a man as old as himself, he might choose a man in his twenties who showed great promise of one day becoming an influential and wealthy man. The father could then be assured that by the time his daughter was old enough to comply with the bargain, he would have a wealthy son-in-law obligated to care for him in his waning years.

The intricacies of daughter bestowal go far beyond this description. Suffice it to say that, ordinarily, a Tiwi girl was old enough to take up residence and act as a wife at about age fourteen. Her husband would generally be about forty. The arrival in his household of his first resident wife was usually followed quickly by two or three others. This was because after one father of a newborn girl had surveyed the prospects and set his stock in one young man, other fathers were likely to decide to do the same, based on their trust in the original bestower's "research." This was the first step to any man becoming a big man; once his wives were in residence he was assured future babies that he could bestow upon others.

A man's list of wives was, of course, always longer than the actual wives in residence. He continued to receive bestowals of baby girls well into his seventies, and it was not unusual for a man to die while the last of his promised wives were still infants. What becomes of the wives he has left behind, both those he has been living with, and those too young to have joined him? No female must ever be without a husband. And what of men upon whom babies were not bestowed? Widow remarriage solved both of these problems.

Bestowal was the primary method of acquiring *young* wives. But because widows had to be immediately remarried, those Tiwi men who were not regarded as the most promising hunters or most likely to succeed in acquiring big man status could depend on marrying widows, who in some cases would still be quite a bit younger than themselves.

Catholic missionaries were successful in putting an end to the majority of polygynous marriages, unions between people of vastly different ages, and all childhood (and prenatal) betrothals. By the middle 1950s, a young woman (sometimes with the guidance of her father) would identify an individual whom she would like to marry, and negotiations would begin. Widows are no longer encouraged to remarry. In fact, widows whose fathers are alive are encouraged *not* to remarry, but to join their father's households instead, and help care for them.

Tiwi Wives

Bestowal of infant daughters and immediate remarriage of all widows resulted in households in which successful old men had as many as twenty wives, while men younger than thirty had none. Men who were between thirty and forty had wives who were elderly widows. This is an unusual household structure but one that linked together all the aspects of Tiwi culture—kinship, subsistence, politics, economics, and law.

The Tiwi explicitly made the connection between their polygynous system and their subsistence. When a missionary opposed to polygyny confronted the head of a large, multiple-wife household, the husband responded, "If I had only one or two wives I would starve; but with my present ten or twelve wives I can send them out in all directions in the morning and at least two or three of them are likely to bring something back with them at the end of the day, and then we can all eat" (Hart et al. 1988:38).

The crucial importance of food gathering was a driving force behind the necessity for men who were starting their own households to begin by securing older widows as wives. It was older women who were experts in the environment and knew where to find food. Younger women acted as their apprentices, performing manual labor and learning all they could. Although younger wives were important in that they could be counted on to provide infants to bestow, it was older women who were responsible for the household's standard of living. It was unusual for a household to begin in any other way than with a younger man and an older wife.

It is not surprising that older men were reported to be unendingly hostile toward the younger men in the camp. This was one consequence of a household structure in which elderly men had multiple wives, many of them young, while men in their twenties were unmarried, and those slightly older were married to elderly women. Although this was economically quite efficient, it presented a social and "moral" problem. Older men had no difficulty in maintaining the food gathering and prestige enhancing facets of their households. It was a considerably greater challenge to keep young women who were out gathering every day away from young men who were at the same time out hunting. These purported daytime trysts gave rise to accusations hurled by older men to younger ones across the encampment fires nearly every night.

From all the foregoing, it would certainly seem that men and their interests are of sole importance in this system, with women being reduced to little more than pieces to be moved around a chessboard. Early ethnographic data collected among the Tiwi (and, for that matter, among most other groups) certainly reflected the perspectives of male ethnographers at this time. Regardless of the impressions given to an outsider, however, the Tiwi system functioned to the advantage of both men *and* women. Despite the early interpretations that made it appear favorable only to men, more recent ethnography among the Tiwi has allowed for reevaluation.

Anthropologist Jane Goodale (1971) presented a different picture of marriage and kinship among the Tiwi, one gathered from the perspective of Tiwi women. Although male ethnographers have typically described Tiwi women primarily as wives, Tiwi men might be viewed as part of the "fluctuating inventory" of woman's husbands (Nanda 1994:236). Under the traditional system, a Tiwi girl became a mother-in-law as soon as she met the man who would marry any daughters she might bear. Her relationship to her prospective son-in-law was a very important one. He must provide both food and favors to his mother-in-law, and may join her camp at that time.

Regardless of the verbal jousting between older and younger men, Goodale (1971) reports that until a woman had her first pregnancy, she maintained both her sexual and social freedom, traditionally engaging in several extramarital unions with men her own age. This practice might not have been "officially" approved of, but was certainly acknowledged and tolerated. Once a woman gave birth to a girl, her son-in-law was thereafter expected to remain in his mother-in-law's service.

Power and Prestige

As a woman progressed through her inevitable series of marriages, both her status and influence increased. In her role as manager of the household, an older woman was the linchpin of the Tiwi economy. As senior wife she was at the center of the powerful, cohesive social and economic unit that included her daughters and co-wives. In addition, she retained great influence over her sons. Goodale (1971) cautions us against the assumption that women in a polygynous society are by definition repressed by male authority. Tiwi woman had, in their solidarity with other women and their economic importance, both great power and great prestige.

Amassing the authority and eminence necessary to gain big man status among the Tiwi was a lifelong process. Influence was gained over decades of making alliances and currying favor. Because material goods were few (Hart et al. 1988), prestige derived more from intangibles such as respect, control, friendship, and influence. One of the most important markers of success was a larder of food, which could be given as gifts to individuals or distributed at feasts. (Surplus food also afforded a man the leisure time to pursue social connections.)

Women were crucial in the acquisition of status for men in that their labor was the vehicle for his amassing food surplus. As Hart et al. (1988:58) summarize, "in the final analysis it was the control of women that was the most tangible index of power and influence. Women were the main currency of the influence struggle. . . ."

As noted above, women, even in traditional Tiwi society, wielded considerable power, in part due to their centrality in men's pursuit of big man status. Power, for both men and women, came with age. Young Tiwi men had few assets and knew that they would have to wait many years for any return on an investment. Young Tiwi women were treated as property, "given away" as pawns in the strategy to gain influence. But older men had patiently amassed capital; older women had more control of their fate, and could not be coerced into joining a household unwillingly. Widows' decisions about which group to join in her subsequent marriages were effective instruments of power.

The complex systems of daughter bestowal and widow remarriage allowed young men to build the social alliances and food-surplus capital that would result in their elevation to big man status once they were elders.

✦ RELIGION AND EXPRESSIVE CULTURE

Religious Beliefs

The Tiwi emphasize relationships between people far more than those between people and the supernatural. There are three worlds of existence: the world of the unborn, the world of the living, and the world of the dead. Each individual passes through these three but once; each has a "life" in all three.

The world of the unborn—of the spirit children—is not one that is of much significance to Tiwi women. It figures greatly into the lives of Tiwi men, however, because it is men who "see" these children.

Earliest accounts reported that Tiwi recognize no biological contribution of a man to the conception of a child. Goodale (1971), in her pursuit of this line of questioning, was told in no uncertain terms that sexual intercourse with either a husband or a lover can result in pregnancy. However, this is a necessary but not sufficient contribution. In order for any Tiwi child to be conceived, it must be dreamed by its mother's husband.

Spirit children wait in their own world to be found by their parents. (When she asked what happens to those spirit children who were never found, Goodale [1971] was told that they married other unfound children, had children, grew old and died. That is, they lived out a complete life in the world of the unborn.)

The spirit children inhabit the country owned by their potential father, and all the locations where these children are to be found are well known. Men see these children in their dreams, and they look human. They are playing in the sand, pretending to hunt, always wishing to be found. The ultimate goal of every spirit child is to be located and brought into the next world, that of the living.

The time spent in life is focused on personal achievement and economic independence. Children know that when they are very young or very old, they may be certain someone will see to their needs, care for them, provide them with food. They must learn enough about their environment to be able to be successful in operating within it for the majority of their time in this middle sphere of existence.

In the world of the dead, important relationships formed while alive are continued. Mothers live with their children, wives live with their husbands. All that one knows stays with one; all of ones talents are retained too. The world of the dead is the one static world. No one will move on to anyplace else, nor will they change in any way.

Tiwi religion revolves primarily around the taboos established for daily life, rituals involving death, and male initiation ceremonies. There is, conspicuous in its absence, none of the repertoire of "magical" means so commonly found elsewhere as a mechanism to deal with the unpredictability of the universe and the hostility of outsiders. Hart et al. (1988) suggest there was no need to develop these beliefs in the benign Tiwi environment. Food and water were abundant; with the exception of snakes and crocodiles, the threat of wild animals was absent; there were few tropical diseases; natural disasters (such as earthquakes or hurricanes) were rare. Perhaps of singular importance was the absence of threatening neighbors. The isolation of the Tiwi resulted in their protection.

Taboo

The word *pukamani* is given both to a wide range of things seen as taboo as well as to the important funeral ceremony. In a generic sense, anything forbidden was *pukamani*, as were any people who, while not themselves "untouchable," were, nonetheless, in a ritually special state—such as in mourning, or having just given birth, or undergoing initiation rites. The overwhelming majority of circumstances surrounding *pukamani* have to do with death.

People who were in a *pukamani* state had elaborate sets of restrictions to follow, most often regarding food and sex. These requirements were not taken lightly, since the price generally exacted for their violation was failure in some desired enterprise. One's prestige surely suffered when the explanation given for perpetual misfortune was breaking *pukamani* restrictions.

Religion had little to do with everyday Tiwi life, except as it related to *pukamani* observances, which were viewed not as active ways to petition spirits or effect change, but rather as obligations one undertook at certain times, quite out of one's own volition.

Kulama Initiation Ceremony

The annual *kulama* ceremony is one of the rare occasions (the other being funerals) necessitating that ordinarily dispersed households come together in joint activity. Because of the rarity of Tiwi gathering in large groups, the *kulama* is charged with excitement.

The *kulama* is a yam ceremony, part of the initiation into Tiwi adulthood. It is held each year at the end of the rainy season (March or April), and residents of a particular locale take part in the ceremony each year, passing through a series of named statuses. In addition to initiates, fully adult (that is, initiated) individuals must participate in order to assure one's own good health, and that of one's children.

The ritual spans several days, beginning with the digging up of the *kulama* yam, a type not ordinarily consumed. Yams, which symbolize reproduction and health, are cooked and eventually eaten by the participants, who will attain the next *kulama* status at the completion of their participation.

Sickness and Healing

It is the expectation of all Tiwi that they will live a long life, grow old, and die of old age. Although they do recognize that illness or accident may strike, they still feel it is likely that they will one day be among the elderly.

Most unfortunate occurrences are thought to be brought upon people by their own behavior, either in the form of breaking taboos, improper performance of ritual, or breach of social custom. The consequences of these infractions are varied. A hunter may have an accidental fall, or his eyesight grow dim. He may find not game, but a poisonous snake in his path. In most cases, Tiwi look no further than the individual for the source of the trouble. (Children's accidents are not subject to the same blame; they are the fault of the child's parents, whose laxity in teaching proper observation of rules is held to be the cause of a child's misfortune. It is not until children clearly know right from wrong that they can be held accountable.)

There are some occasions when bad luck, sickness, accidents, or even death are blamed on a spirit, but these are most certainly the exception. Sometimes the spirit of an individual will yearn so for a loved one that it will send illness and death out of sheer loneliness and desire for a former companion.

In general, though, the responsibility for sickness is placed squarely at the feet of the person who is ill. This being the case, it is the patient who is the focus of the treatment, because he or she is, in effect, the causative agent. (This focus on the person as agent of illness or injury extends beyond self-blame; it is also imperative that individuals take responsibility for injury they have caused others. If one Tiwi injures another accidentally, the expected course of action is that the perpetrator will inflict the same injury on himself. When one dancer's spear accidentally cut another dancer's hand, the owner of the spear simply cut his own hand as an indication of its unintentional nature, and the dance continued uninterrupted, with nothing more said.) (Goodale 1971.)

The Tiwi have no ritual medical specialists. Healing is either first aid or it is preventive medicine, and both categories are common knowledge.

Bloodletting and application of heat are considered effective in any illness, and frequently both are used in tandem. Burning sticks cauterize wounds very effectively, and the practice of bleeding the area around a snake bite is quite successful. The only "medicine" taken internally besides a potion of boiled grass is the drinking of the patient's own urine.

The prevention of illness is attended to much more assiduously than is treatment, since prevention is largely bound up with observance of taboo. Thus, the bulk of learning about illness prevention is actually contained in lessons about proper behavior.

Death and *Pukamani*

When a person dies, the spirit rises up out of the body but does not travel far. After burial, the spirit hovers near the gravesite, making occasional visits to the camp to see loved ones still alive. In an attempt to convince the spirit to stay in the area of the grave, food, water, and tobacco are left at the burial site, and the area around the grave is designated as hunting ground accessible only to that spirit. Although at first the spirit is very lonely for the people left behind, it gradually seeks companionship instead in the other spirits also residing at the burial grounds. Once fully accepting of the world of the dead, these spirits go on to have a "life" that is structured identically to the one left behind.

Spirits of the dead are generally believed to be invisible, but many individuals report having seen them. The sick are visited by spirits who tell them how long it will be until they will join the world of the dead. However, healthy people, too, have had occasion to happen upon these spirits.

Despite the close and loving relationships one might have had with persons before their death, once they are gone and only their spirit remains, the spirits are not to be trusted. This necessitates participation in certain rituals aimed at showing the spirits that they are not forgotten and, at the same time, beseeching them to be content with the new company they have found in the world of the dead and kindly let them continue living. On the first night after death, fires are built around the grave and kept burning all night. It is on this first night that the spirit will be loneliest and most sorely tempted to come back for those left behind. The fires act as insurance that the spirits will be contained. (Accordingly, such elaborate precautions are not taken after the burial of an infant; this tiny spirit would not have had a chance to know even its mother, and is not likely to want to come and claim any relative.)

The *pukamani* funeral ceremony is deemed the most important of a person's life. It is the individual who has died, not the mourners, who is the focus of the ceremony. One's time in this middle world, the world of the living, cannot be finished until the completion of the funeral ceremony. Thus, although already dead, an individual's *pukamani* is still part of that individual's life.

The *pukamani,* like the *kulama* initiation ceremony, brings Tiwi together in a gathering of unusual size. Unlike the *kulama,* however, which is organized to include only those who live within a circumscribed territory, the *pukamani* is intended to cast a much wider net. All those who have any sort of social tie with the deceased are expected to participate, making it the only event in Tiwi life (with the possible exception of full-scale warfare) that is organized around such a varied group. This event demands an unusual degree of organization to prevent utter chaos, especially because the entire process will last several days. Participants are divided into groups based on their kin ties. Individuals from among a group of leaders, also determined by kinship, are each assigned responsibility for a segment of the assemblage. Ritual behaviors are also prescribed based on one's affiliation with the deceased, adding an additional element of structure. The actual degree of contact the participants have had with the deceased on a daily basis is not at issue; ritual tasks are assigned by membership in certain social categories (for example, "close kin" versus "long-way kin").

Ordinarily, a person's close family will be in attendance at the time of death, and it is these individuals who must observe the most stringent taboos; they become *pukamani*. Although the very young and very old are exempt from these requirements (because some are considered too strenuous), all others who are close consanguineal or affinal kin living in the camp must conform.

Immediately following the death, those who are *pukamani* smear white clay over the entire surface of their bodies, including their faces and hair. The surviving spouse will have his or her hair cut close to the scalp; men shave their beards. This will be done again at the conclusion of the mourning period. These outward signs display one's entry into the *pukamani* state, and often the clay is not washed off for the entire duration of the ceremonies. They may, in fact, be repainted each day, with elaborate designs added.

Once burial has taken place, all women who are *pukamani* tear pandanus leaves into strips and weave armbands to be worn along the entire length of both arms by men and women who are also *pukamani*. The number of armbands worn varies by the degree of closeness to the deceased. These are painted over as the daily clay is added, incorporating them into the design as if they were bare skin. The painting and armbands serve to at once hide and identify: living Tiwi will see they are *pukamani*; spirits of the dead will not recognize them. (A murderer will paint himself after the crime—as if he were a mourner and not the assailant—to escape the vengeance of his victim's spirit.)

Once painted, those who are *pukamani* begin a period of severely circumscribed behavior that may last several months. They may not be close to any source of water (which may explain why they do not wash one body painting off before applying the next), and cannot touch their own food. Their meals must be fed to them; even water must be lifted to their lips, as they cannot touch even the containers in which their food and drink are served. Sexual intercourse is forbidden.

The taboos established by death go well beyond the actions immediately restricted for close kin. Everything owned by the deceased becomes taboo. Many items are brought to the gravesite and placed atop the burial mound. Once so situated, they are not to be touched, lest they cause illness. The purpose in removing these belongings is to remove the sadness that would be engendered for the mourners were they to see these things again. Large and valuable items (such as canoes or tools) can be inherited by women and men close to the deceased, after they have been ritually cleansed by "smoking" (a process much like curing meat), which repels the spirit of the dead.

Items that have been touched by the deceased are also taboo, and anyone who handled them would swell up and die. Special care is taken not to place food in any container previously belonging to the deceased.

The name of the deceased, along with the names he bestowed on others, and any words that sound like the name of the deceased, become taboo. (This led to a crisis when a man named Tibuki died, preventing Tiwi in the area from requesting tobacco at the local mission; the similarity in sounds made the word *pukamani* [Hart et al. 1988].) The name of the surviving spouse is similarly *pukamani*, thus he or she must instead be referred to by the terms for widow or widower, rather than either a proper name or nickname.

The preparation for the elaborate *pukamani* ceremony begins with messengers sent out to announce the death in all the regions where there are kin who must attend. These messengers paint themselves bright red, and carry special message sticks. Thus attired, they are noticeable at quite a distance, and a crowd gathers to hear whose death has occurred. When the death is announced, relatives of the deceased fall into each other's arms and weep.

Singing and dancing figure prominently into the *pukamani* ceremony, and Tiwi can gain great prestige for their prowess as composer and performer. Songs usually center around mythological or historical themes, with items of current events woven through. (Much to Goodale's horror, as she listened to a "modern" *pukamani* song during a return trip to the Islands and asked for an explanation of the text—which sounded suspiciously like it had been inspired by a movie depicting the old Wild West—she was told, "Why, it's [about the cowboy] Hopalong [Cassidy] and the Indians, you should know that!" [1971:294])

Dance is central to funeral ritual because it is through dance that the three usually separate spiritual worlds—the dead, the living, and the unborn spirit children—can interact (Grau 1998). Transcending reality, performers move through the parallel worlds, embodying a grieving mother, an unborn child, a grandfather, experiencing in dance social roles they never played (Grau 1998).

Dancing sometimes becomes frenzied with grief, resulting in performers beating and cutting themselves. This is most often done as a display by people who are not close relatives of the deceased, in order to "join" in the grief of those who are *pukamani*. Goodale (1971) suggests that this is reminiscent of the "guilty" self-inflicted cuts which serve as displays of remorse after accidentally injuring another.

Dances performed by close family members demonstrate kinship relationships. There are specific matrilineal, patrilineal, and affinal dances, with specific body parts associated with particular relatives. A dancing man uses his shoulder to represent his mother-in-law, a woman indicates her husband with her big toes. Legs indicate one type of sibling, cheeks another, dancers holding the representative body part with their hands, while moving their feet (Grau 1998). Anthropologist Andree Grau (1998) found that Tiwi dancers' "embodiment" of their kinship ties extended beyond performance: when individuals felt pain, they interpreted it as a sign of illness or impending death of the relatives represented by that bodily site. He describes several instances of the unnerving experience of being in the bush gathering food when a Tiwi companion, experiencing pain, expressed worry about a certain relative, only to return home at the end of the day and learn of the relative's illness or death.

Perhaps the best known feature of the *pukamani* ceremony are the carved and brightly painted poles that are set up around the gravesite. Both the shaping and painting of the poles are done with elaborate intricacy, with no two alike. Since the poles represent the status and prestige of the deceased, great pains are taken to ensure the creation of the most beautiful and complicated poles possible.

At the conclusion of the mourning period, those about to leave the *pukamani* state wash off their clay body painting, rip off the pandanus armbands, and throw them on top of the grave.

✦ MODERN TIWI LIFE

In the eighty years since the first anthropologists visited Melville and Bathurst Islands, much has changed. In the 1920s Japanese pearlers were active; by the 1940s Catholic missions were exerting great influence. The islands, victims of bombing and strafing by Japanese war planes, did not escape involvement in World War II.

By the conclusion of the war, Tiwi had become largely dependent upon the products supplied to them by military bases, and most had settled near a

Catholic mission on Bathurst Island. Polygamous marriages, traditionally the cornerstone of so much of Tiwi social and economic structure, were outlawed. This policy was put into effect by missionaries who "purchased" young women, and then "allowed" them to select a single mate from among their own age group (Hart et al. 1988). By the 1950s many young Tiwi women had been converted to Christianity and did not wish to share their households with co-wives.

Residence patterns were altered dramatically as nearly all Tiwi lived in one of four European sites with centralized village patterns. By the early 1950s, polygamous households had all but disappeared. Rather than adopting the nuclear family of the Europeans, Tiwi maintained large households of extended families. Although there was only one wife, older widowed women were taken into the home to care for the children while younger women went out to gather food.

Perhaps the most significant change concerning native Australian peoples was the return of ownership of their land under the Land Rights Act of 1976. The Tiwi thus became owners once again of Melville and Bathurst Islands, establishing the Tiwi Land Council with elected representatives from each of the traditional "countries."

Contemporary Tiwi society is very much a part of the modern world system. Tourism and industry organized around the selling of indigenous Tiwi art has become an important part of the Tiwi's economic base. (Venbrux [1995] reports that after the traditional *pukamani* ceremony, the elaborate mortuary poles can be sold to art galleries in Japan and the United States.) However, they remain active hunters and gatherers, and the traditional *kulama* and *pukamani* ceremonies endure. These may be less elaborate in form, but retain all the most fundamental elements.

After many years of "development" by outsiders, the Tiwi are now faced with the determination of their own future, as they were in the past. Venbrux (1995, 1998) notes that community and land councils work to lessen dependency on the state, while still resisting "a mainstream Australian lifestyle" (1995:43). Returning to the islands in the late 1980s, anthropologist Goodale observed that, in the development of their tourist trade, Tiwi retained their non-commercial perspective. They embrace the challenge of balancing their desire to keep traditional culture alive for their children, while aspiring to participate in the global economy. Venbrux (2000) reports that the Tiwi are now widely recognized as pioneers in tourism controlled by indigenous peoples.

✦ For Further Discussion

Although this practice no longer survives in modern times, Tiwi tradition dictated that all women must be married, resulting in both the betrothal of baby girls and the mandatory remarriage of every widow. This practice served several important social ends. How do the bonds forged by such a practice resemble or differ from some of the other social functions of marriage with which you are familiar in other cultures? How do they compare to the rules and functions of marriage in our own society? Have those changed over time? If so, why might that be the case?

CHAPTER 14

THE TROBRIAND ISLANDERS
The Power of Exchange

Location of the Trobriand Islands.

✣ THE BEGINNING

The world started underground. There, below, all the people were, and they were as they would be above. Underground, there were villages. Underground, there were clans. Underground, there were magic and land, gardens and canoes, there was art and there was craft.

The people wanted to start the world. They gathered their belongings, and they chose their earth. A brother and a sister came together, up through to the hole to their land, up through the hole to start their lineage above the ground. Through each hole came only one clan: one brother and sister, one garden, one magic, one village. Except for the hole of Obukula.

All of humanity makes four clans. Which of these is yours can never be changed. It is for more than one life, it is carried to the next world, it is brought back unchanged when the spirit returns. These have their names, and they are named Malasi, Lukuba, Lukwasisiga, and Lukulabuta. There is a hole called Obukula. First from the hole came Iguana, totem of the Lukulabuta, and up he came, scratching and scratching to reach the earth. Up to the surface he came, and he ran to a tree, and he waited, and he watched. Soon came Dog, and Dog is the animal of Lukuba. Below the earth, they were the highest. Next through the hole Iguana had scratched came Pig. Pig is Malasi. Last to appear was the animal of Lukwasisiga. Some say it was Crocodile, some say Snake, some say Opossum. He is of least importance.

Dog and Pig played together on the earth. As Dog ran through the bush, he saw the fruit of the *noku* plant. This is not good food, this is foul. Only when famine is near should it be eaten. But Dog smelled it, and Dog ate it, and Pig proclaimed "You eat *noku*? You are a commoner! I am the real chief." This is how it came to be, and this is how it is. To eat unclean food, this causes your downfall. The Malasi rose to the top.

✣ INTRODUCTION, HISTORY, AND GEOGRAPHY

The Trobriand Islands are flat coral atolls off the coast of Eastern New Guinea. Four main islands form the group referred to as the Trobriands, but they are surrounded by over one hundred smaller uninhabited islands. The island of Kiriwina is the most populous; it runs a length of twenty-five miles and is eight miles wide at its widest point. The twelve hundred individuals who live on Kiriwina are settled in sixty villages. The other three islands are home to only a few hundred, with none of them organized into more than eight villages.

The Trobriands are hot and humid year-round, with beaches of sand giving way to coral reefs that reach ten feet high off some shores. These extend some six miles out into the water, and provide a vantage point for fine fishing.

The Trobriands were sighted by European sailors more than two hundred years ago. American whalers visited in the mid-nineteenth century. In the late nineteenth century, Germans who had settled in parts of Melanesia traveled to the Trobriands to buy yams. For the better part of the twentieth century, the

Trobriands were under Australian administration. Papua New Guinea gained independence in 1975.

✦ SETTLEMENTS AND SUBSISTENCE

Trobrianders live in thatched huts, some of which have metal roof coverings. Yam houses cluster in a central clearing, towering over the other buildings. Huts have a veranda in the front, where time can be spent carving, chewing betel, and visiting with neighbors.

Yams and pork are the most important foods, but lush Trobriand gardens also yield taro, squash, corn, bananas, tapioca, breadfruit, beans, and cassava. Pigs are only slaughtered on ritual occasions; it is fish that provide the major source of protein in the Trobriand diet. Open-sea fishing is not a year-round occupation, because two seasons of tradewinds churn up the waters and limit access. The lagoons, however, protected from the violent winds, provide good fishing year round. Those who live in the coastal villages that line the lagoon sell fish to the inlanders. Thirty canoes set out to fish, and when they return to shore, their customers are waiting. Within a few minutes they have sold their entire catch. Found among many of the coral outcroppings are sheltered coves where fresh drinking water is abundant, and which are favored places for swimming.

The production of yams is a central focus of daily life. Annette Weiner, the ethnographer who is most associated with Trobrianders in modern times, reports her informants as saying, "If a man has yams, he can find anything else he needs" (1976:137).

Yams are used both raw and cooked. Because raw yams can be stored for nearly half-a-year, they have a long potential exchange life. Once they have been cooked, they cannot function as investments. Thus, yams are both food and wealth, and there are different gardens for each. Food gardens are harvested as the yams are needed to eat. The yams are kept inside after harvesting, and great care is taken in planting to assure there will be enough yams for food as well as exchange. Exchange gardens have a different character entirely. It is yams from these gardens that are displayed in the yam houses, and which remain raw as long as possible.

Growing yams is primarily the domain of men. Some women have their own yam gardens, but these yams never enter into the formal cycle of exchange. A boy's first yam exchange garden is of great importance, and he cannot establish it independently. Boys prepare to enter the exchange system with their move out of their parents' houses in their early teenage years. Some boys will move into bachelor houses with their older brothers; others will live with other boys their age.

In order to make his first garden, a boy must work for an older male who has already established a garden. The younger will receive seed yams from the older, plant and reap the garden, and present the older man with the yield. Often a boy will plant a second garden, and these yams he will give to his father. This will enable him to claim rights to his father's land.

The planting of yam gardens is strenuous labor. Plots are cleared, and the soil is prepared. After planting, as the yams grow, their vines must be staked. Fences must be built around the garden plots to prevent pigs from destroying the new vines.

Taro gardens are planted by all Trobriand men and women, and food gardens, grown by women, yield all the rest of the Trobriand diet.

A Day in the Village

A village on Kiriwina today looks remarkably like it did when famed ethnographer Bronislaw Malinowski first conducted fieldwork there more than three-quarters of a century ago. Huts ring the yam houses, which circle a clearing in the village center. Though villagers at times wear Western clothes, they are most often dressed in fiber skirts and colorful cotton cloth.

The village rises early and, after breakfast, women gather water as men sit on the front porch, chewing betel, a nut which has roughly the same stimulant activity as coffee. Children play in the central clearing and, while it is still early, most of the adults leave the village to begin their day's gardening. Those who have a special task before them—men who are carving, or women who are preparing for a mortuary ceremony—may stay behind, but, except for the few months in the summer when gardening is not a daily pursuit, it is the garden that sets the rhythm of a Trobriand day.

Trobriand man in ceremonial dress.

By mid-afternoon the village fills again, as preparation for the evening meal begins. As dusk arrives, teenagers begin their rituals of self-beautification, preparing to set off into the outskirts of the village, where they will dance and sing and court. Evening is a time to visit and gossip, work at crafts, chew betel, and relax. Nighttime is dangerous, as the threat of sorcery in the dark looms large. The village is quiet by midnight, with adults and young children sleeping until dawn takes them back to the gardens.

✦ SOCIAL AND POLITICAL ORGANIZATION

Life's Beginnings

The island of Tuma, near the Trobriands, is a special place. It is there a spirit goes after death, and it is there that a new spirit child is created, returns to Kiriwina to enter a woman's body, and grows to be her child. This spirit seeks a woman who belongs to the same matrilineage to which the spirit belonged when housed in a previous body. A baby is formed from the mixture of this spirit and the woman's own blood, and when the baby is born, its mother gives it a name that had belonged to a now-deceased member of her matrilineage. It is in this way that the matriline's identity continues through time. However, as the pregnancy progresses, a woman's husband contributes to the development of the baby through frequent intercourse. Additionally, though the child's "true" ancestral name is given by its mother, the baby's father asks his sister for a name from their own matriline. It is generally by this name that the child will be called. As Weiner (1988) points out, a child's father thus "supplies the fetus with something more than its own inherited matrilineal substance, but his contribution does not in any way alter the basic physiological connection between a woman's blood and a spirit child" (p. 57).

Women nurse their children for the first eighteen months of life, and Trobriand babies are the center of attention for all the villagers. Babies are cuddled and carried, affection bestowed upon them by all their neighbors. Villagers are often seen carrying babies who are not theirs, and elderly men who stay behind when others are off gardening delight in caring for their grandchildren.

In a practical sense, however, the responsibility to see to it that children are fed and clothed and have all they need rests squarely on the shoulders of their fathers. To fall short in these caretaking responsibilities has grave social and political consequences. Fathers are deeply involved in their childrens' care from the time they are quite small. While babies are still being nursed by their mothers, their fathers feed them bits of mashed food. Weaning is accomplished when babies are left with others for several days. As soon as this occurs, babies sleep with their fathers.

Fathers are charged with their childrens' beauty, which is part of every youngster's social persona. Weiner (1988) distinguishes between a child's "physical" beauty and "social" beauty. It is the latter for which a father is responsible. Infants are adorned with shell decorations, which demonstrate a father's wealth, power, and political connections to those with whom he has had to trade to secure highly prized shells. The adornments displayed on a child announce that there is wealth and power in the family.

Life's Endings

Death is never met with equanimity in the Trobriands. Its immediate effects are dramatic, but there are repercussions that last for the better part of a year.

When a person falls ill, a sense of danger is aroused in all the kin. A child who falls sick and dies is clearly the vehicle for someone's desire to strike at the power of the matrilineage. When a powerful adult is stricken, this threat is intensely magnified. All illness is seen as an enemy declaring the intent to do harm. As word of an illness spreads throughout and between villages, questions arise. Who wishes this person harm? And what of the victim's close kin? The sick individual may be asked "Who gave you betel to chew?" "With whom did you go fishing?" The culprit could be anyone. People do not simply die; people are killed. And once illness has resulted in death, the question becomes. "Who has killed my kin?" (Weiner 1976)

As life ebbs, people surrounding the dying individual begin to perform tasks that differentiate them into two distinct categories. Some kin—members of the matrilineage—are "owners," and along with members of the village who are clan members, it is they who are responsible for organizing both the burial and the exchange rituals that follow. Owners are not permitted contact with the body, and must not participate in the public display of grief. They do not shave their heads or wear the clothes of mourners. Theirs is a heavy burden nonetheless; it is incumbent upon them to perform crucial economic duties, distributing the deceased's valuables, and repaying all those who were important during their relative's lifetime.

Other kin are designated as "workers." They are not members of the individual's matriline, but are clan members from other villages, or those related patrilineally or by marriage. The first task for some of the women workers, as death draws nearer, is to bathe, dress, and decorate the sufferer. They paint the face of the victim, rub oils into the body, carefully position shell body ornaments. The body is being prepared for its journey back to Tuma, where it will join the other spirits of Trobrianders who died before. On Tuma, the spirit will be renewed, and have a different life. As they do this, they cry. Once death occurs, the process of mourning begins with dramatic wailing. Shrill cries fill the air, and the house where death has occurred is soon filled with sobbing relatives who embrace the corpse and give vent to their grief. The matriline is diminished with every death. This is felt especially keenly at the death of young women, who hold within their bodies the power to renew the lineage.

From the time of death to the beginning of the mortuary ceremonies, crying becomes formalized. Four times a day, family members engage in ritualized crying. Male workers begin the process of binding the arms and legs of the deceased, and closing off all bodily orifices with coconut husks, so the body will remain straight and there will be no odor. Once the body is prepared, it is placed across the legs of those who have decorated it, with the spouse of the deceased cradling the head.

Men sing mourning songs, telling of the ancestors of the matriline. This unites the group in their grief, and helps to channel some of their fear, engendered by the sorcery which has caused the death. No workers sleep through the first night, so as not to show disrespect to the owners. There is another function served by appropriate mourning; its lack casts suspicion of involvement in causing the death.

The death of an important man brings a multitude of mourners. When a chief fell ill and died during her fieldwork in Kiriwina, Weiner (1988) writes "[b]y early evening, several hundred men had congregated in the central plaza close to Uwelasi's resting place. The workers sat together in village groups, [and] in the dim light of the small fires I could see little except a sea of bodies" (p. 37).

Burial does not signal the end of these mourning obligations; in fact, it sets a whole chain of observances in motion. The spouse in particular must bear the brunt of these traditions, beginning with months of strict seclusion. The fear of sorcery in the Trobriands is great. Despite obvious care and affection displayed in their lives together, suspicion may nonetheless fall on the spouse, and lengthy seclusion is one demonstration of innocence regarding the cause of death.

For several days after the burial, widow or widower is prohibited from speaking to anyone. It is taboo to touch food, and so the spouse must be hand-fed by another. Work of any sort is forbidden, and for many months it is permissible to leave the house only for toileting purposes, which consist of running into the bush, wrapped from head to toe in a woven mat, and returning to the hut as quickly as possible.

As the months pass, members of the spouse's matriline bring offerings of valuables to the owners, and one by one the bans are lifted. Such taboos extend to some other close relatives of the deceased. These prohibitions are of great seriousness, and one signifier of the way in which mourners are transformed, during this period is that their names become taboo and are replaced, for a time, with terms that signify their mourning status. Weiner (1988) recalls, "When Dabweyowa's father died, I forgot that his name had become Tomilabova (the son of a dead man). One day, shortly after his father was buried and while we were working together, I called him Dabweyowa. Immediately, without saying a word, he got up and left my house. I did not see Tomilabova for two days, and when he did reappear we never discussed the incident. I never made that mistake again" (p. 43).

During the time the spouse and certain members of the deceased's matriline are in mourning, their ritualized weeping sets divisions of the day in the village. Four times a day, their wails can be heard, and this pattern is altered only when someone who has missed the funeral returns to the village. It is their obligation to go first to the mourning house and cry with the family.

For other workers, a host of mourning taboos are observed. Many pertain to foods, and some to clothing and personal adornment. Many who are only distantly related wear black clothing or a black cloth armband; almost all shave their heads. These are undertaken once workers receive payment from owners for their part in the burial.

Such payments involve only small amounts of money; the bulk of the payments is made in yams. The size of the yams bestowed, as well as their number, is dependent upon the closeness of the relationship to the deceased. Making these payments is done publicly, and often takes all day. Owners call up workers, one by one, and distribute the yams. The process is usually slowed by constant interruptions, as the amount of payment is challenged and negotiated, before the next name can be called. For an important individual, who may have had hundreds of workers participating in the burial, the number of yams necessary to make adequate payments is staggering. Because this is so, the owners must depend on others to help with the payments. It is here that we can begin to see the importance of a strong matriline, and the power of exchange in Trobriand life.

The Politics of Yams: "Fathers and Brothers Give Yams; Husbands Receive Yams"

It is almost impossible to overstate the importance of Yams in Trobriand culture. They are social signifiers of the highest order.

Men expend tremendous effort in their making of yam gardens. It is hard work, and nearly constant work. Yet this work is not for themselves; it is all directed toward others. Men grow yams to give to women.

Once yams are harvested, they are displayed in the gardens for all to see, and then the gardener delivers them to their rightful owner, the woman for whom he has grown them. Young relatives of the gardener paint and adorn themselves and prepare to participate in the distribution. The yams are unstacked from their display, apportioned into baskets, and the youngsters set off to the home of the woman owner. Singing and shouting, they announce their arrival and pile the yams up again in front of the yam house of the owner's husband. It is the grower himself who will come, after they have been displayed for a few days, and stack them into the yam house. Once this has been accomplished, the owner's husband must repay the gardener and his young helpers. Yams and taro and pork are roasted and distributed. This entire exchange is a public presentation of the relationship between the two men, gardener and owner's husband. They are linked by the woman who owns the yams.

Yams and marriage are significantly linked. A couple declares that they are married by eating yams together, and after the first year of the marriage has passed, a woman's father begins a garden for her, which he will plant yearly. Her brother will eventually take over this obligation. This garden is small, but it is the hope of every man that his wife's brother will deem him worthy and grow more yams for his sister; enough so that in addition to growing yams for his sister, he will have to build a yam house to store them in. A yam house is a symbol of great accomplishment. It proclaims, "this is a man whose power has been recognized by his wife's brother." No man—not even a chief—can build a yam house for himself.

Not all men ever reach the position, and those who do will not achieve this status until a daughter is of marriageable age. At that time he will begin a garden for her, as well as continuing the garden he makes for his sister. While he is doing this, his wife's father and brothers are making gardens for him. Thus, all men are linked together around women. It is only through his wife's family that a man can garner political strength and social power. (Later in life, men can develop other relationships through which they can amass yams.) In this way, marriage begins the yam exchanges that will cement relations throughout a person's life. When a man's life ends, his yam house is taken down. Although the yams may be distributed in mortuary payments, the structure itself cannot be passed on; it is an edifice that has grown directly out of a singular and unique relationship between the dead man, his wife, and her brother.

✦ HIERARCHY AND POWER

Chiefly Competitions: Yams and Dances

For two months of the year, the daily focus on the work of yam gardening is shifted. Although the growth of yams is so central that the months of the year are named for the growing cycle of the yams, the time from July to September is a time when yam work is finished, and something on the order of a "vacation" ensues. Yams are harvested, the yam houses are filled, and the holiday begins. In years when harvests are large enough, this period is highlighted by yam competitions.

These events are meticulously planned festivals, designed to allow a chief or hamlet leader to enhance his status and become known in other villages. When new gardens are being prepared in September, the chief declares his intention to hold a *kayasa*, a yam competition, after harvest. This is an endeavor that demands the work of other men in the village, who must agree to grow additional gardens solely for the purpose of contribution to the competition. Members of his matriline are the first to join him in this, and his success will reflect directly upon them. But other community members will help too, because the chief will reward those who produce abundantly. Thus it is made a village-wide event, with gardeners competing to earn the valuables—money, ax blades, and other goods—with which the chief will compensate them. (And therefore even before declaring his intent to sponsor such a yam competition, the chief must amass the goods he will bestow upon the village gardeners.)

The year progresses, gardens are tended, and the harvest produces an abundance of yams. The chief rewards his gardeners and they, in turn, carry yams, pigs, and betel nut to another chief or hamlet leader, who, in future years, will reciprocate in kind. It is in this way that yam competitions solidify alliances across clans.

During these holiday months, a chief also may choose, instead of a yam competition, to host dance competitions. Throughout these months, nightly dances are hosted by the chief. Unmarried Trobrianders from villages across the island are invited to come, dance, and find sexual partners in what the tourist trade now advertises as "the high point" of the summer months in the Trobriands. After two months of this "bacchanal of sorts" (Weiner 1988), the competition culminates in the display of traditional dances, taught by the founding ancestors, hundreds of years ago. For this night, Trobrianders come from far and wide to watch the brightly costumed and painted dancers perform. Weiner (1988) describes one such night:

> To mark the end of the dancing and the competition, yam house are metaphorically "overturned" and emptied of their harvest. Pigs are chased, tied up, and hung on poles; and wooden crates 10 or 15 feet tall, fastened against coconut palms, are filled with yams; one crate and one pig are divided among the residents of each hamlet who participated as guests and dancers. By the end of this event, by hosting nights of dancing and giving food to hundreds of people, a chief or hamlet leader demonstrates that he and his matrilineage are "best" (p. 113).

Trobriand Cricket

Missionaries were especially disturbed by the overt sexual activities associated with the yam competitions and dances, and introduced the British game of cricket expressly for the purpose of attempting to substitute it for these indigenous activities, as well as to supplant the fighting that always accompanied harvest time. In this replacement, they met no success. The cricket matches were accepted as a fine sport, but the Trobrianders made the game their own, and used cricket competitions much in the same way yam competitions and dances had previously been employed. The element of sexuality is displayed in dress, chants, and dances. As Weiner tells us, "The words are sexual metaphors, used as one team taunts the other and exhibits their physical and sexual prowess to the appraising eyes of the young women on the sidelines" (1988:114). The cricket matches continue over the months, and the host village holds a feast when they are through. Pigs and yams and betel are distributed as they always were, and the chief's fame and wealth are known across the island.

Such fame and largesse are not without a dark side. Jealousy leading to sorcery and enmity is often an unwelcome outcome of these events. There is an unspoken assumption that the hosts of these lavish cricket matches must win. The guests, who must lose even if they have in "reality" won the game, return to their home village proclaiming that they had been treated unjustly by the umpire, and talking of revenge. In the 1980s, one such cricket match resulted in arson, with men on the losing team burning down houses in the host village.

Harvest-time fighting often springs from men asserting their gardens' superiority, which is generally done in abusive language, belittling the gardening abilities of others. Losers in these informal competitions are thought to be so humiliated by the process that they plot to destroy, through sorcery, the entire matrilineage of their taunters. Fear over sorcery invoked in this way can be passed down through several generations.

❖ TROBRIAND EXCHANGE

Kula

The Trobriand *kula* ring is perhaps one of the best-known systems of exchange in the anthropological literature. In his classic ethnography, *Argonauts of the Western Pacific,* Malinowski described in exquisite detail the Trobriand practice of exchanging shell goods. His writing was a turning point in the understanding of non-Western economics; previous to his description, economies of other peoples were regarded as haphazard and "primitive." Malinowski's work influenced the theoretical perspectives of many of the most important anthropologists of the twentieth century.

Malinowski recognized the centrality of *kula,* referring to it as "vast, complex, and deeply rooted" for which Trobrianders have "a passion in their hearts" (1922:86). While *Argonauts of the Western Pacific* spanned more than five hundred pages, Malinowski still referred to *kula* as "a very simple affair [which] only consists of an exchange, interminably repeated, of two articles intended for ornamentation, but not even used for that. . . ." (1922:86). In the years since, much more has been learned about *kula* exchanges throughout New Guinea, and its importance has been underscored as its meaning has been illuminated.

Kula shells move through a series of islands, on a particular path. There are two types of shells used in the exchange, white armshells (*mwali*) and red shell necklaces (*bagi*). The *mwali* move in a counterclockwise path through the villages in which *kula* partners reside; the *bagi* pass through the same hands, but circulate in the opposite, clockwise, direction. Men who do *kula* have partners on other islands. If we were to begin with any one man, draw a line tracing the path of the shells, as in a picture made by connecting the dots, we would have described a circle leading back to the origin point. A shell makes this circuit in anywhere from two to five years. Men generally know their *kula* partners whose islands are closest to them, because they sail to these islands to trade, and they host *kula* sailors who arrive. Those who are more distant are not known personally, but are known by name.

A village chief will act as the leader in organizing a *kula* expedition. Generally, men from several local villages set off to the neighboring island to do *kula.* They set off ready to *receive* shells, not to bring them. When they return home, they will have the shells that other *kula* partners will come to receive. Six months to a year may pass between individual *kula* voyages. There are women who do *kula,* especially nowadays, but they are still in the minority. And those who do participate will often do so without leaving home to sail to other islands; men are designated to carry out the shell transactions on their behalf.

The *mwali* and *bagi* are assessed in value based on their size, color, and the beauty of their polish. In addition, shells increase in value with age, and both men and shells gain prestige in their association with one another. A man may gain fame and notoriety for having possessed a particularly fine armband; similarly, a necklace may be highly regarded for having been owned by a great man.

Such great men help younger ones enter into their *kula* career. A boy may be invited by his father or his mother's brother to come along on a *kula* expedition. There the young man will be able to observe the transactions, meet the *kula* partners, and begin to learn the ways of the *kula* ring. It is important to be well trained, because inexperience can cost dearly. A man's *kula* path and the partners therein are passed along to his heirs at death. But when the living *kula* partners are unsure about the younger man's expertise, they will not necessarily honor his "rightful position." Weiner (1988) reports:

> . . . although Peter's father was a chief and he left him three *kula* paths
> when he died, he lost two of them and his *kula* shells; his closest partner did
> not believe that Peter was "strong" enough, so he diverted Peter's shells onto
> a different path (p. 148).

Malinowski presented the *kula* exchanges as anchored in tradition in such a way that the shells appeared to move between men effortlessly, as if they were propelled by nothing more than the force of custom. Subsequent investigations into the workings of the system have uncovered aspects of the exchange that eluded Malinowski and that expand the foundation of *kula* beyond simple reciprocity. There are profits to be made. Weiner (1988) sums up the ultimate meaning of *kula* this way:

> The histories of shells written through *kula* participation are of individuals'
> talents and exploits, of partners long dead whose faces were never seen.
> Through the shells, a villager transcends the history of his or her own
> ancestral lineage and becomes a part of *kula* history. What is of consequence
> is that *kula* history legitimizes a person's right to win while others lose. In
> Kiriwina, *kula* participation enables players, if they are "strong," to create
> long-standing debts, to hold on to valuables for years, and to keep these
> shells free from kin-related obligations like marriages or deaths. In this way,
> *kula* allows individuals to protect their wealth from the exigencies of
> everyday social and political life. . . . [T]he ability to hold on to a *kula* shell
> allows a person to store wealth, even if only momentarily, in the face of
> continual kinship or affinal obligations (p. 156).

Women's Wealth

The momentous position of yams and the fame of *kula* are two weighty aspects of Trobriand life. Another is the special wealth that is produced and controlled by Trobriand women.

Women manufacture skirts and "bundles" from banana leaves. These are crucial to the Trobriand economy, and are intricately tied to other forces—chief among them yams and the matrilineages—in Trobriand culture.

As we have seen, the death of a villager sets in motion a huge amount of work. The loss of any group member disturbs the many social ties in which that individual was bound up. In a sense, exchanges at mortuary ceremonies are one step in the process of "mending the hole" left in social networks by that death.

One women's mortuary ceremony may consist of the distribution of as many as five thousand banana leaf bundles, and thirty intricately woven red fiber skirts. Women deal in skirts and bundles, as currency, throughout the year. But they are of central importance when kin die.

Women make skirts and bundles from the leaves of banana trees, which they own. They inherit trees from their mothers and sisters, and often men plant banana trees for their wives, expressly for the purpose of creating her wealth. Men are dependent upon such wealth.

Women work for months, producing the skirts and bundles which they will distribute to those who participate in mourning. "Workers," both male and female, will receive bundles and skirts commensurate with their work. Men do not receive these directly; their mothers or sisters will collect these for them. Every individual who has had any association with the deceased will receive bundles. The chief distributor is the wealthiest woman, and she is distinguished by the long skirt of singular design she wears. She makes the first payment in every distribution.

Women's wealth is connected to yam production in several ways. When a death occurs in a woman's matrilineage, it will be her responsibility, as an "owner," to distribute bundles. Because her brothers have made her a garden every year and put those yams in her husband's yam house, it is incumbent upon a husband to secure bundles for her to distribute, in addition to those she will make herself. In order to participate fully in mortuary distributions, a woman needs far more bundles than she can manufacture herself. One way in which a husband provides his wife with bundles is through his sisters, those women for whom he makes gardens. These women will present their "sister-in-law" with bundles in appreciation for the yams provided by their brother, her husband. It is not only for his "true" sisters, but also for other women who stand to him "like a sister." Thus, there may be a great number of these "sisters" who will contribute bundles. A man is also expected to exchange pigs, money, and other valuables for bundles to provision his wife. In fact, the debt which is set in motion by the giving of yams from a man to his sister and her husband can *only* be repaid in women's wealth. If a husband does not use his own wealth to buy the needed extra bundles for his wife's mortuary obligations, her brother will not produce as big a garden the following season. The husband will suffer, in yams. When a man's wife's brothers build him a yam house, they are contracting with him to provide her with bundles. In fact, the eventual accumulation of skirts and bundles is what underpins much of the work to produce large yam gardens. There are intricate layers of rights and obligations between matrilineages, all of which coalesce around women's wealth. Their economy spurs men's productivity.

Women's wealth, in bundles, is an economic force in modern Trobriand life. Weiner tells of meeting Joshua, a young single man from Kiriwina who had been away from the village for some time, attending medical school. They talked as they rode to the village together, and when they passed a village where a women's mortuary distribution was visible, Joshua remarked that he thought it was imperative that women put an end to this tradition. Weiner (1988) writes:

> [Joshua said] "If women stopped needing so many bundles, then men would have plenty of money for other things." In his shrewd comment, Joshua put his finger on the vulnerability of using such bundles as currency. From a capitalist perspective, he was right. Men take money, which can be used to purchase all sorts of things, and turn it into bundles. Yet despite the demanding need for money to pay school fees, government taxes, trade store goods, and even airfare to the capital, men continue to spend their money on bundles. Why women's wealth has not diminished in importance over the past one hundred years is a serious question, which Joshua, in his own way, was asking. But Joshua was not married and so his interest in the cost of bundles was limited. Had Joshua lived in a village where his wife's brother produced yams for him each year, he would not have framed his comments in Western economic terms (p. 120).

✦ Malinowski in the Trobriands

Bronislaw Malinowski stands at the earliest edges of the science of anthropology. His first trip to New Guinea, in 1914, marked the beginning of a prodigious career. Few people before him had undertaken such intensive observation of a group of people over several years. Upon his return, he was tireless in his insistence that ethnography depended on rapport built up over time with local informants, and had to be conducted in the local language, squarely situated in the center of a culture's own context. The detail with which he presented his own work set a standard in the early science.

Malinowski's theoretical views have given way in popularity to other perspectives, but his influence is undisputed. It was this legacy that Annette Weiner carried into the Trobriands with her, some sixty years after Malinowski's tenure there. Her work is a prime example of the ways in which the dynamic science of anthropology continues to grow, both relying on past studies and illuminating them.

The most serious points of divergence between Malinowski's work and Wiener's, so many decades later, grow out of her recognition of the importance of women's economic role in the Trobriands. Malinowski took note of women's importance, but his interpretation was one that rested on women's reproductive role. In a matrilineal society, where descent will be reckoned through women, they are surely of genealogical significance. In addition, Malinowski's explanation of Trobriand kinship centered around this same feature, that of matrilineality. In such a system, children are members of their mothers' matrilines, and thus belong to the same group as their mothers' brothers, but not their fathers. Malinowski felt Trobriand fathers were both biologically and economically unimportant in their children's lives, and pointed to the making of yam gardens by men for their sisters as evidence to support the tie between a mother's brother and his sister's son over that of a father. It is true that men make yam gardens for their sisters, but as Weiner has described, the motivation for this is not to assure that a man's sister's children are adequately fed, as Malinowski assumed. Because he was unaware of the economic ties which grow out of women's wealth, he could not fully understand the complex exchange relationships that grew out of the production of skirts and bundles. Weiner (1988) summarizes:

> That Malinowski never gave equal time to the women's side of things, given the deep significance of their role in social and political life, is not surprising. Only recently have anthropologists begun to understand the importance of taking women's work seriously. In some cultures, such as the Middle East or among Australian aborigines, it is extremely difficult for ethnographers to cross the culturally bounded ritual worlds that separate women from men. In the past, however, both women and men ethnographers generally analyzed the societies they studied from a male perspective. The "women's point of view" was largely ignored in the study of gender roles, since anthropologists generally perceived women as living in the shadows of men—occupying the private rather than the public sectors of society, rearing children rather than engaging in economic or political pursuits (p. 7).

✣ MODERN TIMES

Since 1975, the Trobriand Islands have been counted as part of Papua New Guinea, a nation-state that is one of the largest developing counties in the South Pacific. Trobrianders are not eager to give up their traditional culture, and have consistently taken new ideas and made them their own, made them "Trobriand."

In the early 1970s, tourists were a constant presence on the islands, with charter flights arriving weekly. Villagers greeted visitors at the airstrip and at the local hotel, waiting to sell their carvings for cash. Traders and missionaries also bought indigenous arts and crafts to sell. As the tourist trade grew, some Trobrianders were unhappy; they were offended at their islands' portrayal, in travel brochures, as "The Isles of Love." Some believed the impetus to produce carvings to sell took its toll on gardening because some men were more eager to produce salable items than yams. However, most felt that the end result would be a positive one—economic security.

One Trobriander, John Kasaipwalova, studying nationalist movements as part of his university studies, left school to return to Kiriwina and urge fellow islanders to take control of their island's economic fate. It was his intention to build local industry—a hotel, stores, a shipping company—so that Trobrianders could truly be in charge of their economic future.

When a fire destroyed the island's hotel, the tourist industry came to an abrupt halt. This led to more villagers throwing their support to John Kasaipwalova, in opposition to local chiefs. Great debates ensued, and in the end Kasaipwalova was unsuccessful. Tourism never regained its foothold, and although there are still some carvings to sell to the occasional visitor, ebony forests have been ravaged and selling local arts and crafts can support no one.

Weiner (1988) points out that there is a long Trobriand tradition to resisting change: "tradition wins out despite people's willingness to try something new" (p. 25). The islands in the South Pacific were extensively involved in World War II, and despite the Trobrianders' contact with missionaries, soldiers, tourists, and a colonial government, they exhibit a fierce tenacity to traditional culture. Weiner sees the fundamental importance of women's wealth as playing a central role in this resolve. She explains:

> Throughout all the years of public disputes, fighting, competition between chiefs, and changes brought about by colonial law and traders' enterprises, women have gone about their business undisturbed by government officers and missionaries, who, like Malinowski, never thought they played any economic role. Men are the carvers, the gardeners, the fishing experts, the orators, and the chiefs. No one recognized the activity that is central to women's position and power in Trobriand society. Yet it is an activity that deeply interpenetrates the economics and the politics of men (p. 27).

Jutta Malnic (1998) undertook three expeditions, over four years, traveling the *kula* circuit. She notes that the Trobrianders are undergoing great change, with both tourism and a cash economy diverting the time and energy previously devoted to traditional social pursuits. Modern modes of transportation and communication hold the potential to alter the *kula* ring, but those with whom Malnic sailed are resolute that the essence of *kula* will endure. As one trader explained:

> Kula has lasted over time and will last into time. It will take on different dimensions and expressions; it may extend into new areas and change characteristics. But underneath it will always be an act of Giving and Receiving, which allows the receiver to grow and extend, materially and spiritually (p. 31).

In the course of his fieldwork on Kiriwina Island, anthropologist Gunter Senft (1999) has analyzed interactions between tourists who have been promised a chance to "'meet the friendly people' and 'observe their unique culture, dances, and art'" (p. 21) and the Trobriand Islanders who dance and sing for the European audiences. He describes the Islanders as creating, for these "customers," the performance they expect to see, retaining the upper hand through their control of the situation. Because it is staged, Trobrianders know that "neither they nor the core aspects of their culture will suffer any damage within a tourist encounter that is defined [by them]" (p. 21). Analyzing the texts of the songs, Senft describes humorous instances of the Trobrianders ridiculing their listeners, which he sees as evidence of indigenous pride and self-confidence, through which they protect their cultural identity while using it as a tourist commodity.

→ FOR FURTHER DISCUSSION

Bronislaw Malinowski's first trip to New Guinea in 1914 marked the beginning of a long tradition of ethnography that depended on rapport built up over time with local informants, conducted in the local language, and squarely situated in the center of a culture's own context. Some sixty years later, anthropologist Annette Weiner undertook her own fieldwork in the Trobriands. Her findings both added to Malinowski's earlier work and challenged some of its assumptions.

How did Malinowski's and Weiner's approaches differ? What are some of the factors that might account for each of their perspectives? What are some of the challenges faced by ethnographers in the twenty-first century? How might modern technology change the way anthropologists conduct their fieldwork?

CHAPTER 15

THE YANOMAMO

Challenges in the Rainforest

Location of the Yanomamo in South America.

✦ THE BEGINNING

One of the ancestors shot Moon in the belly. Moon's blood fell on the earth, and the drops of blood became men. These men were alone, and went out collecting vines one day. There they saw the *wabu* fruit, and the fruit had eyes. The *wabu* began to fall to the ground, and where it fell, up sprang women. And the Moonblood men and the *wabu* women together made the Yanomamo (Chagnon 1992b).

✦ INTRODUCTION: THE YANOMAMO ENVIRONMENT

The Yanomamo are a tribe of 22,500 who live in about 250 widely dispersed villages in Brazil and Venezuela. Although they are well-known to students of anthropology, owing largely to the lifelong study of Napoleon Chagnon, they have remained remarkably isolated and undisturbed until very recently. While some sources (Chagnon 1992a) claim theirs is a history of very little contact and retention of indigenous patterns, others (Ferguson in Salamone 1997) report that the Yanomamo have been influenced by European contact since the early seventeenth century, when Spanish, Portuguese, and Dutch slave traders entered their territory. Moreover, contact continued after slave trading times, with missionaries being chief among those with whom the Yanomami have dealt closely. In any case, the most recent contact—with gold miners—has been dramatic, and cause for international outcry.

The tropical forest in which the Yanomamo live is dense and green, with varied growth. Its thick floor of vines and scrub makes it difficult to traverse; on cloudy days its impenetrable canopy keeps out most light.

Villages are at varying distances from one another, and have differing degrees of social closeness as well. Those that harbor good relations host frequent visitors, and it is not unusual for individuals to travel several days to pay a visit (Smole 1976).

✦ SUBSISTENCE AND MANUFACTURE

Gardening and Foraging

The earliest reports about the Yanomamo erroneously described them as solely hunters and gatherers, with no portion of their diet grown in gardens. Chagnon (1992a) postulates that this was based on the assumption that a tribe as isolated as the Yanomamo could not possibly possess the sophistication to be cultivators. Currently, the vast majority of Yanomamo (more than 95 percent) live within the Amazon forest and rely on both foraging and horticulture. The remainder have settled along the rivers, where fishing has replaced hunting (Salamone 1997). For those Yanomamo who are forest-dwellers, the abundant jungle supplements their diet. Ordinarily a tribal society settled in villages, the Yanomamo exploit the wild foods found in their environment by trekking, mostly during the dry season. They break into small family groups to go off on collecting expeditions, traveling for several weeks when the jungle fruits and vegetables are ripe. Honey is the ultimate wild prize, and honeycombs are often consumed with the larvae still inside. Good (1991) estimates that roughly 40 percent of their time is spent on a *wayumi* (trek).

Game is plentiful, and during these expeditions they commonly hunt wild pigs, large and small birds, monkeys, deer, rodents, and anteaters. Armadillos, which live in underground burrows, cannot be hunted with bow and arrow. They are ingeniously smoked out. Once an entry to a burrow is located, a slow smoky fire is lit. Smoke escaping from other burrows indicate exits to be dammed up. Once all escape routes are blocked, hunters listen with an ear to the ground for the scurrying of the animal, and dig straight down to retrieve it. Insects and shellfish round out the protein portion of their diet.

Fish do not provide an extensive portion of the inland Yanomamo diet, but when the rainy season is over and pools formed by overflowing rivers dry out, stranded fish can be opportunistically gathered by women. This practice includes the use of mild poisons, introduced into the water upstream. The drugged fish float to the surface where they are easily grabbed and tossed into baskets. Larger fish, which are less stunned by the poison, are bitten behind the head by the women and killed.

The bulk of Yanomamo food (more than 80 percent) is grown in their village gardens. Garden sites are cleared by cutting down trees and brush and burning them, although not with the systematic precision of other slash-and-burn practitioners. Large tree trunks that have been felled but are too wet to burn are simply left where they fall, and either used as firewood once dry, or allowed to serve as boundary markers between the gardens of different families.

The size of a garden plot is usually dictated by the size of the family it must feed. Since village headmen will have the responsibility of entertaining visitors and sponsoring feasts, they plant and care for larger plots.

Plantain is the most important domesticated crop. Manioc, taro, and sweet potato are also cultivated. Cane used in arrow manufacture is grown in village gardens, as is tobacco, a crop of central importance. All women, men, and children chew it daily and guard it jealously. Adults will often have wads of the soft leaves rolled into their lower lips all day long (Smole 1976). Chagnon (1992a) reports that it is the only crop that is fenced off to warn potential thieves. The value of tobacco (to which every Yanomamo above the age of 10 is reportedly addicted) is evidenced by the fact that the local word for being "poor" is literally "without tobacco" (Chagnon 1992a).

Cotton grown in village gardens is used predominantly for the construction of hammocks, which are owned by everyone. It is also used to make what little clothing is worn. Men typically wear little more than a string around the waist, while more ornate belts are generally worn by the women. Single strands of cotton string are also tied around wrists and ankles.

Manufacture

The technology found among the Yanomamo is not complex. Any necessary tool can be manufactured from materials readily available in any village. The knowledge of how to do so is widely held. The level of manufacture has been compared to that of typical foraging societies, despite the fact that they are horticulturalists (Chagnon 1992a).

Palm wood is used to make numerous items, among them bows and arrow points. A type of palm wood arrow point that is highly prized is the one used in hunting with curare, a poison extracted from a local vine. The point is dipped in curare and shaved to insure that it will break off underneath the skin, preventing the victim from removing it. The curare, which induces muscle relaxation, is then sent into the bloodstream. Poison arrow tips are among the most popular items of trade between villages. Quivers that hold them are made from bamboo, and are worn hanging on the back. Arrows themselves are fashioned from cane, and are quite long, resembling spears.

Other manufactured items include large shallow baskets used to collect fish, and a rudimentary "razor," used to create the Yanomamo's unique haircut, bowl-shaped with a circle shaved bald at the top center of the head, a style worn by both men and women. The exception is during a severe bout with head lice, when it is simply easier to completely shave the heads of affected men, women, and children.

Village Construction

Houses are constructed from readily available local materials, predominantly saplings for support posts, vines and leaves for thatching. These are not very durable, despite the substantial labor that goes into their construction. In addition to being little protection against rains, after only a year or two the leafy roofs become so infested with insects that there is no other option but to burn them and start again. (Chagnon comments that roaches often grow to the size of small birds [1992a]).

Living space, called the *shabono,* is a series of individual homes, sheltered underneath a common roof. Men sink the four main posts into the ground, and women and children gather the vines and leaves used for thatching. Thousands of leaves are needed to cover the structure. Each family builds the section of the roof that covers their own compartment. When the structure is complete, there are numerous individual sections with a few feet between them, all underneath a long stretch of connected thatching, surrounding an open central plaza. The building site is chosen with an eye to the suitability of the surrounding land for gardening, access to potable water, and proximity of both allies and enemies.

If there is continual threat of enemy attack, a tall wooden fence is constructed behind the *shabono.* The fence is covered with dry brush at night, so that intruders will be heard by village dogs, who will in turn wake the residents.

Village size will, of course, reflect the size of the population, which may be as small as forty or as large as three hundred. But another factor determining size is the number of neighboring villages with whom friendly relations are maintained. It is important to be able to accommodate any allies who will be visiting regularly. Thus, a village size may reflect not the number of permanent residents, but the number of people it will have to house when visitors are expected.

To house visitors or to provide shelter on extended food gathering forays, less elaborate temporary shelters are constructed. These are usually made by lashing three poles together and covering them with broad banana leaves.

✦ Religion and Expressive Culture

The relatively simple technology and material culture of the Yanomamo is not replicated in their systems of belief and expression. Although they have no tradition of writing, their use of language is elegant and verbal skills are highly prized.

The Yanomamo envision the universe as being constructed of four layers hovering atop one another with a thin layer of space between them. The topmost stratum is empty, and has least to do with current Yanomamo life. Long ago, things may have come from here, but now it lies fallow. The layer below it is the sky. People can only see its underside, onto which stars are stuck, but the surface of the sky is believed to look much as the earth does, with trees and plants and animals. The most important residents of this layer are the souls of the dead, who carry on an existence there much like the one they had as living Yanomamo. This layer—the sky—is believed to float quite close to the earth, as Chagnon (1992a) deduced from the repeated questioning about bumping into it when he flew in airplanes.

The third layer down, on which the Yanomamo live, was created when a section of the "sky" layer cracked off and toppled down. The bottommost layer, which exists under the earth, was formed when sky fell to earth on top of a particular settlement, and pushed it down through the earth to the underside. There it has settled as the last layer, along with the people, their homes and garden. Unfortunately, their hunting grounds were left behind. Loss of the jungle in which to find game led them inevitably to cannibalism, and the unfortunate souls of Yanomamo children are their usual prey. The belief that souls are regularly carried off to be eaten down below reflects the Yanomamo's fear that natives of the earth can indeed fall into the practice of cannibalism. This possibility apparently both terrifies and disgusts them. Chagnon (1992a) elaborates:

> Whenever I hunted with them and we shot a tapir, I would always cut off a thick juicy slice of tenderloin and fry it lightly on both sides—a rare steak that dripped juicy delicious blood as I cut it and ate it. This so disgusted and alarmed them that they could not bear to watch me eat it, and invariably accused me of wanting to become a cannibal . . . a disgusting eater of raw flesh. For their part, they cook their meat so much that you could almost drive nails with it (pp. 101–102).

These dwellers of the bottom layer of the universe were in existence when the first people originated. Those original human beings were different from people today in that they were part human, part animal, and part spirit. When they died, they became all spirit—the *hekura* who figure prominently into Yanomamo shamanism.

Myths

Many Yanomamo myths are built around these original humans, called "those who are now dead." Although tales of their origin are spotty, they themselves are responsible for the creation of many plants and animals, and are in fact the spirits of those living things that bear their names.

Men are generally the storytellers in Yanomamo society, and they "perform" the recounting of a myth more than simply reciting it. Their histrionic style, often enhanced by drugs, leads to dramatic embellishments and provides enjoyable diversion for the audience.

Some stories incorporate a moral, designed to teach the ways of Yanomamo. Others are told to explain why the world is as it is. Many are sheer entertainment.

The relationship of humankind to the jaguar is a theme that predominates in many stories. Chagnon (1992a) suggests that the jaguar may have been chosen because it effectively exemplifies a fundamental theme in Yanomamo culture (and many others)—the distinction between "nature" and "culture." Jaguar is in some ways a figure in which nature and culture overlap. The Yanomamo are proud that humans have culture and animals do not, yet the jaguar is a hunter as skilled as a Yanomamo. Jaguar is an animal (a creature of nature) who shares traits with people (bearers of culture) and is both feared and respected. In many of their jaguar stones, the fierce and powerful jaguar is reduced to a clumsy, inefficient beast. In the creation of these stories, culture triumphs over nature.

The Yanomamo Soul

The soul plays a central part in the "spiritual" world of the Yanomamo. It is the soul that is consumed by the cannibals in the netherworld, and it is a rather sophisticated "organ."

The soul consists of several different portions, each of which has a function in both life and death. The part of the soul that is the "will" is the part that makes the journey to the afterlife. At death, it shimmies up the ropes of the deceased's hammock, entering the layer of the universe above the earth, and begins a journey down a road that divides into two separate paths. This fork is guarded by a spirit charged with assessing the generosity shown by the soul's mortal owner during life, and then sending it down the appropriate path. Generous souls are directed down the path to the comfortable earth-like place; stingy ones are shepherded down the fork to a fiery place. (This latter fate is not one that causes them great worry; they are unimpressed by the intelligence of the guard, and plan simply to lie and be sent down the preferred route.)

There is another part of the soul that is freed upon cremation of the body and lives, thereafter, in the jungle. This portion has the potential for evil, clubbing people who visit the jungle at night. Great caution is exercised to avoid them.

The most crucial portion of the Yanomamo soul resides within the chest or flank (interestingly, that portion of the body attacked in stylized chest- and side-pounding duels), and is most vulnerable to attack. This component can be stolen, and then subject to supernatural attack. If this happens, the individual sickens and will likely die unless this portion of the soul is restored.

The last aspect of the soul lives both inside and outside the individual. Inside, it is a part of the individual spirit (the part captured by the camera when a person is photographed); outside it is a person's animal counterpart, which leads a parallel life. When the person eats, his or her animal self is doing the same. When the person is asleep, so too is the animal. Ordinarily one will never meet this animal alter ego, but if by some twist of fate one were to hunt and kill it, ones own death would follow (as it does when another hunter kills "your animal").

✦ ILLNESS, HEALING, AND DEATH

Illness is caused by the *hekura* spirits, which harm a person by consuming a portion of his or her soul, usually at the behest of someone from an enemy village. It is the charge of a shaman to call upon his own powerful *hekura* to counterattack, thus curing the sick villager.

Shamanism is a practice open only to Yanomamo men, however, it is not a role restricted by birth or special characteristics or suitabilities. Anyone who wishes may undertake the training, if they are willing to undergo the rigors entailed. These include a fast, which may last up to a year, during which the initiate becomes emaciated. Instructors, who are older shamans, guide the novices in the ways to call their own *hekura* spirits to them. They must learn the likes and dislikes of the *hekura*, in order to lure them into one's chest. This is not an easy task—they are difficult to seduce, and apt to be fickle and leave abruptly. An aspiring shaman must endeavor to make the interior of his body into attractive terrain in which the *hekura* may dwell in comfort. If they find verdant mountains and cool streams in the shaman's chest, they may stay. Older, more proficient shamans may have succeeded in attracting many *hekura* spirits to live within them, yet are always striving to keep them happy. Because *hekura* are repelled by sexual activities, younger novices have no hope of attracting and keeping the *hekura* unless they are celibate. This requirement alone often deters men from the pursuit of this status. Once a shaman has established a stable relationship with the *hekura*, he may engage in sex without fear of abandonment by his spiritual powers.

Hekura, which dwell among the Yanomamo in the thousands, are both male and female, but all are exceedingly beautiful. Different sorts have different temperaments. The most fearsome are the "hot and meat hungry" *hekura,* for these are the ones who devour the souls of enemies.

Shamans have access to the *hekura* only while they are under the influence of hallucinogens. These drugs are used on a daily basis, and their preparation

Yanomamo youth in ceremonial dress.

is ongoing. They are ingested in powder form, blown into the nose through a long hollow pipe placed in the mouth of another man. The initial effects are quite painful, leading to coughing, choking, watery eyes, and retching. Their power takes effect almost immediately. As the shamans begin to feel intoxicated, they begin their chanting, which calls their *hekura* to them. Since the *hekura* are themselves so beautiful, they require great attractiveness on the part of the shaman, who wear feathers and paint themselves elaborately. Once the *hekura* have danced down their trails and into the chests of their hosts, they can aid a shaman in curing They can also be manipulated to go to enemy villages and avenge the sickness sent on local villagers.

When a Yanomamo dies, the body is cremated. This is done by carrying the body to a prepared pile of firewood, where it is burned. One person is designated to watch the fire, making sure that the entire corpse is consumed, and nothing but ash and bone remains. A log is hollowed out to hold the teeth and bones, which are ground by a close kinsman and apportioned into several small gourds. Any ashes remaining in the log's hollow are consumed in soup, and then the log is burned. The gourds full of ashes are kept for a larger more elaborate ceremony during which they will be added to more soup and consumed by visiting kin from other villages.

If there are multiple deaths occurring at one time, all the bodies are taken into the jungle. Rather than being burned, they are wrapped with bark and positioned in trees until they decompose. Later the remaining bones are burned, and the same ash-drinking ceremony takes place.

→ SOCIAL ORGANIZATION

Leadership

The Yanomamo are generally egalitarian in that there is no ranked hierarchy. While women hold less status than men, among adult males prestige is achieved, and not ascribed, and "there are as many prestigious positions as there are people to fill them" (Salamone 1997:47). However, Yanomamo villages generally have a headman, an individual who usually belongs to the largest kin group represented in the village. He serves more as a representative of his own village in dealings with other villages than as a authoritarian figure within his own. Chagnon (1992a), who in his visits to more than sixty Yanomamo villages has seen the leadership styles of many headmen, reports that there is no one personality that typifies this status. Some headmen are quiet, introspective leaders; others are bombastic and dictatorial. What they have in common are the limitations inherent in the status afforded them. They act as hosts and negotiators. Their opinions carry somewhat more weight. They lead by example and not by decree. If there is trouble within the village, it is the headman's responsibility to attempt to restore order. Since he must model the behavior he wishes others to exhibit, his life is often fraught with risks. He demonstrates the bravery, self-control, or industriousness that he expects others to display.

Male and Female

The realities of daily life differ greatly for Yanomamo men and women. Chagnon (1992a) calls it "decidedly masculine," and this certainly seems borne out by other ethnographers as well (Good 1991, Lizot 1985, Salamone 1997).

Girls are aware at an early age that they have far less social room in which to maneuver than do their brothers. They begin to assume a productive role in their household very early on, and assume childcare responsibilities while they are themselves small children.

Most girls are betrothed while they are still quite young, and they have no opportunity to voice any preference (or register any dissent) in this regard. The men to whom they are promised are usually much older. In some cases, a man identifies a girl and asks his relatives to make marriage inquiries. She may then be "raised" to some extent by the man who is to become her husband. Regardless of the age at which she is promised, a girl does not generally take up residence with her husband until reaching puberty.

Even when their marriage "officially" begins, life changes little for a Yanomamo girl. She continues to spend her days as she has previously done: collecting firewood, cooking, and devoting herself to the needs of others around her. One aspect of her marital relationship, which does appear to be unique to the husband-wife dyad, is the physical cruelty to which Yanomamo women are subjected by their husbands. According to Chagnon this is commonplace and expected behavior. Others, while agreeing that domestic violence occurs, refer to it as "occasional" (Good 1991:73). Women are physically disciplined by their husbands for a host of "infractions," ranging from being too slow to prepare a meal to suspected infidelity. Punishment runs the gamut from blows with firewood or axes, burns, and arrow wounds to murder. Women often depend on their brothers to protect them from an "unusually" cruel husband, and despair of being promised to a man in another village where they will separated from this potential source of protection.

Although women appear to gain no status from the transition from single girls to married women, they are afforded more respect and fear less for their safety as they age. Elderly women can travel even between warring villages without fearing harm, which, according to Chagnon (1992a), is more than they can be assured in their own homes when they are young wives.

Boys are socialized early into this behavior through the encouragement they receive to strike others, especially little girls, when they are angry. Boys as young as four or five are well aware of their license to "[inflict] blows . . . on the hapless girls in the village" (Chagnon 1992a:126), and are cheered on by their parents and others who often goad them into this behavior during play. (However, once he is grown, a woman's brother assumes the aforementioned expected responsibility to protect her from the mistreatment of others [Salamone 1997]).

"Play" lasts nearly twice as long for boys as it does for girls. While a girl of ten spends the bulk of her day as a worker, boys in their late teens may still be enjoying childhood. This often causes difficulties, because boys of this age expend much effort attempting to seduce girls of their own age—who are generally married women, often with several children.

Children—both boys and girls—are particularly susceptible to malevolent spirits, often sent from enemy villages to attack their souls. They are vulnerable in this fashion because their souls are not yet moored securely within their bodies. Young souls, given to wandering, escape from the mouth when a child cries.

✦ Political and Economic Organization

Forging Alliances

The focus of "political" life among the Yanomamo centers on forging and maintaining ties between villages. There are several ways in which alliances may be formed.

Inherent in these ties is the obligation to offer asylum to residents of an allied village who are fleeing an enemy. Since leaving one's village means leaving one's garden—hence, one's economic base—it is sometimes necessary for this "visit" to be quite lengthy. Guests will stay in a village while they are establishing a new garden in a safer site. Chagnon (1992a) observed more than one occasion when an enemy's capture of a village led to the reliance of the displaced Yanomamo on the hospitality of an allied village for a year or more. Such an imposition exacts a commensurate cost, and payment is usually demanded in women. The other options open to an invaded group are either standing ground and attempting to withstand the hostile onslaught, or dispersing into small family units and joining other villages permanently. Neither of these is preferable to the pattern of "visiting" for only as long as it takes to establish a new garden elsewhere, and then moving on.

With the threat of attack always looming, no village can afford to be without the alliances that insure they will have somewhere to go after invasion. Chagnon (1992a) points out an inherent conflict in the need to forge alliances as protection against attack—warfare among the Yanomamo is predicated on the belief that stronger villages should overpower weaker ones. This encourages villages to present as strong a face to outsiders as they possibly can. This posture is difficult to maintain while engaging in the development of dependent friendships. He summarizes, "Allies *need* but cannot really *trust* each other" (p. 160).

Trade relations and feasting are the usual channels for creating ties between villages, but the most secure alliances are formed by marriage. Cross-cousin marriage is the preferred form. Villages can cement relations with one another through betrothals between families living some distance apart (Salamone 1997). Chagnon (1992a) reports that not all relations between villages proceed to this final step because the mistrust always beneath the surface in intervillage relations leads Yanomamo to suspect the promise of reciprocity. In fact, he observes that it is only the minority of villages that progress past the arguments and accusations about women that are produced in the course of trading and feasting, prerequisites for marital exchange. Salamone (1997), however, reports that Ramos found that 70 percent of the Yanomamo villages she studied in Brazil forged marital alliances with one another, thus preventing conflict.

Trading

Trade between Yanomamo villages follows a pattern that is self-propelling; that is, rules are established such that trade leads to more trade.

All items traded must be reciprocated with items that are different. Usually these are representative of the "specialty" of the village. The return gift must be presented in the proper time frame. It cannot be immediately exchanged. The former feature serves as an "excuse" to continue trading with a particular village.

One village doesn't usually possess a resource or skill which is unique. However, claiming that ties are being maintained with another village solely because it guarantees access to a needed item functions as a face-saving mechanism. It allows interdependence—in the form of repeated visiting to trade for the specialty item—without demonstrating weakness. The element of elapsed time results in an ongoing relationship of indebtedness; one village always owes payment to the other.

Chagnon (1992a) points out that these explanations for the "ulterior motives" of trading and feasting are not ones which the Yanomamo themselves readily volunteer. Outwardly, they never say "we must maintain these ties so that we can call upon them during times of war." Feasts and trading expeditions are ends in and of themselves. Likewise, the hosts of such events seize the opportunity to demonstrate their power and wealth, without overtly expressing the fact that it places them in a position of strength.

Feasting

Feasts among the Yanomamo are usually much anticipated occasions for both hosts and guests. They provide opportunities to eat, drink, and flirt; to display oneself proudly; and to affirm and deepen ties of mutuality. Given the constant undercurrent of defensiveness and opportunism, however, there is always the potential for something going awry and culminating in violence.

Men take the primary responsibility for preparing food for feasts. Because one hundred or more guests may be expected, hunting, gathering, and cooking is a large-scale task. Although a messenger is sent to the guest village with an invitation only on the day of the feast, preparation at the host village starts long before.

Game meat and plantain are the main foodstuffs that are served, and large quantities of plantain are harvested and hung to ripen in anticipation. Many of these will be used to make soup, cooked in large strips of bark that are cut and fashioned into troughs of sufficient size to hold up to one hundred gallons of soup.

A hunting party is organized to secure meat, and as the hunters set off, the excitement surrounding a feast begins to build. When they return, the meat is presented to the headman, smoked at his fire, and wrapped for later presentation.

Both village and villagers are groomed for the festivities. The central village clearing is weeded and swept to prepare it for dancing. Houses are neatened and scraps from the preparation of food and gifts are disposed of. Both men and women paint their faces and bodies and decorate themselves with bright feathers. Men further prepare by ingesting hallucinogenic drugs. Guests adorn themselves similarly, in anticipation of their formal parade into the center of the host village.

As the guest delegated to begin the processional enters the village, appreciative cheers erupt from the hosts. There is a formality in this presentation; he is elaborately painted and festooned with parrot feathers and monkey tails. Reaching the center of the clearing, he stops and strikes a predictable posture, standing still, haughty, weapons in the "visitor's pose" by his face. He maintains this stance for several minutes. He is there to be admired, but he is also there to express his peaceful intent. With his weapons held motionless and fully exposed, he declares himself to be without hostility and invites an easy shot if malice is contemplated.

This accomplished, he approaches the designated host (the village headman or his representative) and the two begin a chant that signifies the acceptance of the invitation by the guests, and officially initiates the feast. Spirited and at the top of their voices, the two dance and chant for five or ten minutes, and then the guest departs to arrange the formal entry of his village.

Guests assemble at the entryway, with the men in front and women and children holding gifts behind the front ranks. At their headman's signal, visiting dancers spring into the village in pairs, whirling and chanting along the edge of the central plaza, and then returning to the rest of the group, still outside the village walls. Each man enters the village in this manner, displaying his own unique body painting, chant, and aggressive facial expression. When everyone has a chance to do this, attended all the while by the enthusiastic cheers and whoops of their hosts, the assembled group enters, one by one, dancing along the rim of the clearing, coming to a halt in the center of the plaza where they stand for silent inspection.

One by one, hosts approach the throng of guests and lead each family unit off to his own house. As the guests eat their first serving of plantain soup, the host men gather their village to make a formal entrance and display of their own decoration.

From dusk to dawn, all are engaged in chanting and trading. Visitors tell their headmen which items they want; these requests are relayed to the host headman, who entreats his villagers to provide them. Once presented, they are inspected by the recipient and his friends, who praise them even as the donors apologize for their obvious inadequacies. (Unless it is, in fact, truly inadequate, in which case the presenter calls attention to all its finer attributes, while the recipient points out each flaw.) In any case, the hosts always claim to have given more than they should; guests always assert they have been undercompensated. Bickering accompanies every trade.

Should arguing escalate for any of a number of reasons, such as impoliteness, intimidation, or the exchange of insults, a chest-pounding duel may ensue. The entry into the host village to signify the acceptance of such a challenge bears little resemblance to that which begins a feast. Guests arrive waving their axes, clubs, bows and arrows. They are received with the noises made by hosts clattering their arrows together and thumping clubs and arrows on the ground as they surround the guests, each host selecting the guest he will fight.

A chest-pounding duel is not a spontaneous brawl. The blows delivered are carefully calculated and stylized. One partner presents himself, daring the other to hit him. The recipient of the challenge assesses the position struck, realigns his victim's arms or chest so they can be most effectively pounded. He measures and remeasures the distance he wants his arm to be from the victim's chest, feinting several trial punches. Finally, "he . . . [winds] up like a baseball pitcher . . . and [delivers] a tremendous wallop with his fist to the man's [chest], putting all of his weight into the blow" (Chagnon 1992a:179). The victim, reeling from the punch, is urged on by his fellows not to back down, but to present himself for another blow. A maximum of four blows may be struck before victim and aggressor change places. Each aggressor is required to return the same number of poundings he receives. Only if severely injured in his receipt of the retaliatory blows may a victim withdraw from the fight after receiving fewer hits than he has inflicted. Fighting may continue in this vein for several hours, often with many agitating for its escalation to the use of axes. Although headmen often oppose this, knowing it will lead to bloodshed, there is a variation on the chest-slapping duel, "side" slapping, to which it sometimes escalates. This open-handed smacking of the opponent's side between rib cage and pelvis often incurs greater injury, especially when a fistful of stones replaces an open hand. While chest-pounding blows are directed to the muscular portion of the chest, there is no such protection of the organs beneath blows to the flank. In one fight witnessed by Chagnon (1992a), two young men died after a side-slapping fight, most likely because of ruptured kidneys. (Death occurs after chest-pounding, too, and it is not uncommon that participants cough up blood for several days after these confrontations.) As is evidenced by the outright choreography of the chest-pounding duel, many forms of fighting among the Yanomamo are strictly regulated. The aggression so assiduously cultivated in males is released in these formalized duels, as an attempt to avoid warfare.

→ Yanomamo Violence and Warfare

Within the anthropological community, there have been few more public disagreements in recent years than that which has arisen regarding the portrayal of the Yanomamo as "the fierce people," as named by Napoleon Chagnon in his popular ethnography, first published in 1968. In it, Chagnon described the centrality of violence to the everyday life of the Yanomamo. In addition to chest-pounding duels, Chagnon (1992a) describes attacks with clubs, often the result of arguments over women and food. These are not restricted to outsiders; co-villagers can and do attack each other with clubs. He tells of an incident in which a father clubbed his son for eating some of the older man's bananas without permission. The son retaliated with his own club, and soon most of the men in the village had taken up the cause of one side or the other.

The clubs are actually heavy ten foot long poles. One end is sharpened to a point, allowing it to be turned and used as a spear should it be necessary. The most common scenario for the instigation of club fights is the accusation made by a husband that another man has been carrying on an affair with his wife. The jealous husband grabs his pole, and after accusing the other man, presents his own head to be hit. Once the accused succumbs to the challenge and strikes him, the husband may retaliate. As the first blood is drawn, much of this orchestration falls away. Most observers will yank a pole out of the framework of the house and join in the fight, soon to have blood streaming down their heads and necks.

It is not surprising that the tops of most male Yanomami heads boast a network of deep scars. Some of the men who keep the top central portion of their heads shaved do so to proudly display the impressive thick knots they have received in club fights.

Because larger villages afford more opportunity for adultery, they also are plagued with more club fighting. As sides are taken, often along kinship lines, large villages sometimes split in two over these confrontations.

An escalation to the next level leads to raids, which are considered true warfare. The objective is usually to kill as many of the enemy as possible and escape undetected. However, if any of the attacking group are killed, the raid is considered a failure, regardless of the number of enemies dispatched before one of the invaders was killed.

During the course of a raid on an enemy village, women are often abducted. This, however, is not usually the objective around which the raid is organized, but rather a "side benefit" of a successful endeavor. In villages with acute shortages of women, wars have been initiated for the sole intent of capturing them. One such war is an example of *nomohori* ("dastardly trick"), the ultimate form of treachery and violence. Raiders arrive at a distant village, saying they acquired machetes and cooking pots through prayer to a previously unknown spirit. The raiders offer to teach the unsuspecting villagers this prayer, so that they too might receive the goods. As the men kneel down and bow their heads, preparing to be instructed in prayer, the raiders kill them, capture the women of the village and flee (Chagnon 1992a).

Once villages are already at war with one another, stealing women is a common occurrence in ongoing raids. New conflicts are more likely to arise out of an accusation of sorcery or food theft.

Others have taken issue with Chagnon's presentation. Jacques Lizot, a French anthropologist whose work among the Yanomamo began in the 1960s, wrote an ethnography in 1985, which he explicitly aimed at helping to "revise the exaggerated representation" of Yanomamo violence (Lizot 1985:xiv). He maintains that while the Yanomamo are indeed warriors and can be both brutal and cruel, such "violence is only sporadic; it never dominates social life for any length of time" (Lizot 1985:xiv). This assertion that Yanomamo violence has been overemphasized is echoed by Kenneth Good, a former student of Chagnon's. While acknowledging, as Lizot did, that violence existed, he agreed with Lizot's position that this one aspect of Yanomamo behavior had been sensationalized out of proportion. Raiding, killing, and domestic violence did occur, but it was not the defining feature of Yanomamo life. Good offered an analogy: Chagnon's citing violence as the central cultural theme of Yanomamo life, he maintained, was as misleading as asserting that all New Yorkers are muggers and knife-wielding criminals, and as such, anyone on a New York street may expect to be robbed at knifepoint.

> Of course these things do take place. But that doesn't mean it's an accurate or reasonable generalization to make about New Yorkers. It doesn't mean that someone would be justified in writing a book entitled *New Yorkers: The Mugging and Murdering People* (Good 1991:73).

Brazilian anthropologist Alcida Ramos concurs, having found the Yanomamo to be an essentially peaceful group, despite acknowledged feuding. She characterizes Chagnon's ethnography as "sensationalistic," adding that the portrait of the Yanomamo as "a bloodthirsty 'fierce' people who regularly kill each other is not supported by other anthropologists or anyone who has lived with the Yanomamo for years" (in Rocha 1999:34).

Perhaps most significantly, the Yanomamo themselves appear to have taken issue with their portrayal as "fierce people." Salamone (1996:10) reports that the Yanomamo "argue that although there is violence in their society, they are not violent people." One Brazilian Yanomamo man explained "I have killed but I am not a killer" (Salamone 1996:10).

Some have suggested (Ferguson in Salamone 1997) that when Chagnon first visited the Yanomamo in the 1960s, violence had reached an unusual height because this particular group had been subject to epidemics, disruption in trading, and had experienced the loss of many aspects of their traditional way of life. The result was "violence [reaching] a level where it appears to be 'normal'" (Salamone 1997:49).

Brian Ferguson (1995), writing what he calls a "political history" of Yanomamo warfare, presents an argument tying Yanomamo violence specifically to unequal access to scarce and much-desired Western manufactured goods, especially steel and iron tools. He traces patterns of peace and violence through the presence and absence of Westerners (including anthropologists), and concludes that complex changes in Yanomamo exchange relationships, often leading to intervillage violence, is largely the result of Western presence.

Darkness in El Dorado

The controversy surrounding the veracity of claims regarding Yanomamo violence escalated in 2000, when an investigative journalist, Patrick Tierney, published a book with accusations that generated heated debate within the anthropological community and beyond. In his book, *Darkness in El Dorado,* Tierney made allegations in two realms of Yanomamo research. First, he claimed that Napoleon Chagnon and James Neel, a physician and geneticist, knowingly endangered the lives and health of the Yanomamo communities they studied. Second, he asserted that Chagnon not only misrepresented the Yanomamo as "fierce people," but in fact instigated and promoted violence and warfare.

Neel and Chagnon were among the Yanomamo during a measles epidemic in 1968. As a population with little immunity against such a disease, there was potential for disaster. Tierney claims that Neel caused thousands of deaths by deliberately using an outdated vaccine, and by withholding medical treatment from sick individuals, in order to test theories of eugenics. The scientific community (including the developer of the vaccine Neel used) and colleagues rallied to his support, vigorously refuting all such claims (Baur 2001, Cantor 2001). They provided evidence that Neel had carefully chosen the proper vaccine, had administered it in a timely manner, and likely saved many lives by doing so. In addition, evidence points to the fact that Neel responsibly cared for sick Yanomamo, and in fact had none of the extreme eugenic beliefs attributed to him.

The second set of allegations assert that Chagnon breached ethnographic ethics in a number of ways, including inappropriate gift-giving that incited jealousy and enmity among villagers, using coercive methods to elicit information, instigating and staging the violence he wished to portray as central to Yanomamo culture, and exploiting the Yanomamo and their territory. Reactions to these charges were far more varied than to those against Neel, which were overwhelmingly refuted. Anthropologists were divided in their judgments: some came to Chagnon's defense against what they saw as Tierney's sensationalistic claims supported by flimsy and misrepresented sources; others pointing out the long history of controversy surrounding Chagnon's fieldwork practices and data. Numerous investigative bodies were assembled to investigate the charges, with the American Anthropological Association task force publishing their several hundred page report in 2002. The task force found that Tierney's book was, in fact, riddled with errors and unfounded accusations, but also concluded that Chagnon did not, in fact, put the best interests of the Yanomamo ahead of his own research agenda, a practice required by anthropology's ethical standards. They represent their charge as having been "not to find fault with or to defend the past actions of specific anthropologists, but to provide opportunities for all anthropologists to consider the ethics of several dimensions of the anthropological enterprise" (Preface, El Dorado Task Force Papers).

✤ YANOMAMO: CHANGING CULTURE AND MODERN TRAGEDIES

Life for the Yanomamo is changing. Contact with missionaries began many years ago in some villages. In others, direct contact has yet to occur. Groups of Yanomamo whose lives remain relatively unchanged from their traditional patterns are few, and becoming fewer.

The introduction of disease to indigenous populations who have no immunity can have devastating effects. As we have seen, this was the case among the Yanomamo, who were exposed to measles during an epidemic in 1968 that is believed to have started at several mission posts and then spread to surrounding villages (McElroy and Townsend 1989). Physician James Neel's team immunized as many unexposed individuals as they could in an attempt to curb the decimation such as that wrought by previous measles epidemics among other indigenous peoples in Brazil. Their efforts, which included providing medical care to those already infected, greatly reduced the death rate as compared to that of the earlier epidemics (McElroy and Townsend 1989).

Encroachment on Yanomamo land began in the 1970s, as roads began to be built inside their territory (Ramos 1979, Rocha 1999). However, the most dramatic—and horrific—changes to Yanomamo life are the consequence of the 1987 gold rush in Brazil, which brought not only miners with guns and heavy machinery and a usurpation of land, but previously unencountered diseases, which indigenous peoples could not withstand.

In the late 1970s, as the price of gold began to climb steadily, the Brazilian government opened up the Amazon to miners. Wildcat miners—*garimpeiros*—began to flood into the area over the next decade, with some estimating the invasion at anywhere between 250,000 and one million *garimpeiros*. In 1995, 300,000 were camped out throughout the Amazon (MacMillan 1995). Brazilian authorities were asked to expel the illegal miners, firmly entrenched in Yanomamo territory, with little success. In fact, in response to this threat, *garimpeiros* claimed that if their presence was illegal, so was that of others working with the indigenous populations. The government acquiesced, expelling anthropologists, missionaries, and health workers. This brought an onslaught of *garimpeiros,* who, in a short time, had cleared more than one hundred airstrips in Yanomamo territory (Chagnon 1992b). Brazilian president José Sarney's government refused to help, and, in fact, contributed to the devastation by reducing a proposed Yanomamo reserve from eight million to 2.4 million hectares, partitioned into nineteen little "islands" of communities (MacMillan 1995).

The Yanomamo were devastated by the introduction of diseases such as malaria and tuberculosis, among others, to which they had little resistance. Hundreds died. It is estimated that in two short years, between 1988 and 1990, 15 percent of the Yanomami population was lost (MacMillan 1995). The destruction of the environment also took its toll. Hunting was compromised as game was either shot or scared off by miners. Vegetation was stripped from along streams, altering water courses. Drinking water was polluted, and the churning up of riverbottom sediments disrupted the life cycle of fish, endangering an important protein source (MacMillan 1995). More toxicity resulted from the use of mercury in the gold mining process, which enters the waterways and contaminates fish and reptiles, poisoning those who consume them. Hair-sample analysis from Yanomamo living near mining centers revealed toxic levels of mercury (MacMillan 1995).

Further devastation has been wrought on both social organization and cosmology. Ramos (in Rocha 1999:31) describes the trails that connect Yanomamo villages as "conveyer belts carrying the social impulses that keep alive the great chain of relationships between communities." It is these trails and streams that link the three hundred Yanomamo communities in Brazil and Venezuela, and it is these trails and streams that are being destroyed. The loss of territory also means that they are unable to resolve disputes in the traditional way, which involved feuding groups leaving a village to set up a new homestead elsewhere. Not only were new groups established in this way, but it also alleviated competition for resources in too concentrated an area.

In 1990 José Sarney was replaced by Fernando Collor de Melo, who revoked the privileges given to the *garimpeiros* and who, in 1991, made a dramatic and public trip to Yanomamo territory in response to a growing international outcry for their protection. He ordered the illegal airstrips destroyed, and the numbers of *garimpeiros* began to wane. However, this didn't last long; only a dozen airstrips were closed down, and these soon reopened (Chagnon 1992b). By 1992 Collor resigned under the specter of impeachment for corruption, and was succeeded by his vice-president, Itamar Franco, who held office until 1995, when he was replaced by Fernando Henrique Cardoso.

In 1993 the world was stunned by reports of a massacre among the Yanomamo, perpetrated by *garimpeiros* in their territory. Eighteen Yanomamo, including many children, were murdered in their village, their bodies desecrated. To a people for whom proper funerary preparations—cremation and the preservation of the ashes for the family—are so important, the state in which the bodies were left was particularly horrifying.

The destruction of the natural world has dire consequences for the spiritual world (MacMillan 1995). Davi Kopenawa, a Brazilian Yanomamo who has emerged as a spokesman for the tribe, explains that during mining a vaporous spirit is released from the soil and causes sickness. Moreover, this spirit has the power to destroy the *hekura* spirits, who hold up the sky, preserve the forests, and cure through the actions of shamans. Thus, continued mining will result in the eradication of the *hekura*, which, for the Yanomamo, "heralds the end of the world" (MacMillan 1995:51).

In 1995, after eight years of requesting permission from the Brazilian government to be allowed to investigate human rights violations in Yanomamo territory, an international Human Rights commission was allowed entry. Their report was scathing, and the following year, nearly three hundred Yanomamo leaders representing thirty villages came together to address their dire situation and make a formal plea to national leaders and international agencies, to no avail. In December 1997 President Cardoso instituted a human rights program, promising that indigenous peoples and their organizations would have a voice. In March of 1998 disaster struck again in the form of raging fires resulting from a drought. With the Yanomamo rainforest threatened, international attention was once more focused on the area (Rocha 1999).

In 1969 Survival International was founded in direct response to the endangerment of indigenous peoples in the Amazon (Rocha 1999). For the past twenty years, various nongovernmental organizations (NGOs) have worked with the Yanomamo to defend their land and culture. The Pro Yanomami Commission (CCPY) administers health and education projects. Anthropologist Napoleon Chagnon, after a career invested so heavily in the Yanomamo people, has devoted extensive efforts to their protection and the task of safeguarding the rights and cultures of other indigenous groups. The Yanomamo, in many ways, have come to represent indigenous peoples worldwide, though their role as such has been played "unwittingly and often reluctantly" (Rocha 1999). The structure of traditional Yanomamo society is such that no one "leader" may speak for the group as a whole. Thus, there are those who are skeptical about any spokesman who may claim to do so (Sanford 1997). However, Davi Kopenawa has eloquently expressed views that appear to be representative of the wishes and beliefs of other Yanamamo (Salamone 1997). His 1992 plea to the General Assembly of the U.N. was to:

> stop the destruction, stop taking minerals from under the ground and stop building roads through forests. Our word is to protect nature, the wind, the mountains, the forest, the animals, and this is what we want to teach you (Rocha 1999:40).

The Yanomamo are engaged in efforts to help themselves, but Chagnon has urged the international community to join forces with them. He writes, "The Yanomamo are now a symbol for all tribesman everywhere, perhaps the ultimate test case of whether ordinary concerned, educated and determined people can stay a destructive process that will [otherwise] be inevitable" (1992a:246).

In January 2003, Worker's Party candidate Luis Inacio Lula da Silva took office as the president elected by the largest popular margin in Brazil's history. Leaders in Brazil's Indigenous Movement are hopeful that as a representative of the political party identified with social justice, change, and the struggle of the oppressed, President Lula will work to overcome the threats to their land, health, and culture. In a document following a national indigenous congress in April 2004, after a year of escalating violence, they petitioned President Lula, with a simple declaration: "Fear should not overcome hope." (Indigenous Leaders' Document to President Lula Brasilia-DC, May 10, 2004.)

✦ FOR FURTHER DISCUSSION

Recently there has been great controversy surrounding ethnographic work among the Yanomamo, including questions about the introduction of disease, the accuracy of reported violence, and the role of social scientists who witness political and economic victimization of indigenous peoples. These issues bring to the fore many important questions about ethnographic fieldwork and the role of the anthropologist. Napoleon Chagnon has said that the Yanomamo stand as a symbol for tribal peoples everywhere. What are some of the ethical issues involved in fieldwork among peoples who have had very little previous contact with outsiders? Does this differ from ethnographic work carried out in an industrialized setting? What is the role of the anthropologist in conflict between indigenous peoples and the governments of the countries in which they reside? Should an anthropologist be an objective observer, an advocate, or neither of these? What are some of the difficulties involved in choosing a position?

REFERENCES

Abdullah, T. Modernization in the Minangkabau World: West Sumatra in the Early Decades of the Twentieth Century in *Culture and Politics in Indonesia*. C. Holt, ed. Ithaca, NY: Cornell University Press, 1972.

Abdullah, T. *Schools and Politics: The Kaum Muda Movement in West Sumatra*. Ithaca, NY: Cornell University Press, 1971.

Anders, Gary C. "Indian Gaming: Financial and Regulatory Issues." In *Contemporary Native American Political Issues*. T. R. Johnson, ed. Altamira Press, 1999.

Anthony, S. *Haiti*. New York: Chelsea House, 1989.

Barrett, R. A. *Culture and Conduct*. Belmont, NY: Wadsworth, 1991.

Barth, F. *Nomads of South Persia*. Oslo: Universitetsforlaget, 1964.

Baur, M., P. Majumder, C. Amos, J. Feingold, T. King, N. Morton, M. Province, M. Spence, and D. Thomas. IGES-ELSI Committee. *Genet. Epidemiol.* 21(2):81–104, 2001.

Berdan, F. *The Aztecs of Central Mexico: An Imperial Society*. New York: Holt, Rinehart & Winston, 1982.

Berland, J., and A. Rao. "Unveiling the Stranger: A New Look at Peripatetic Peoples." In *Customary Strangers: New Perspectives on Peripatetic Peoples in the Middle East, Africa, and Asia*. J. Berland and A. Rao, eds. Westport CT: Praeger, 2004.

Biesele, M. "Aspects of !Kung Folklore." In *Kalahari Hunter-Gatherers*. R. B. Lee and I. DeVore, eds. Cambridge, MA: Harvard University Press, 1976.

Biesele, M. *Shaken Roots: The Bushman of Namibia*. Marshalltown: EDA Press, 1990.

Biesele, M. *Women Like Meat: Folklore and Foraging Ideology of the Kalahari Ju/'hoan*. Bloomington: Indiana University Press, 1993.

Blackwood, E. "Breaking the Mirror: The Construction of Lesbianism and the Anthropological Discourse on Homosexuality." In *Culture and Human Sexuality*. D. N. Suggs and A. W. Miracle, eds. Pacific Grove, CA: Brooks/Cole, 1993.

Blackwood, E. *Webs of Power: Women, Kin, and Community in a Sumatran Village*. Lanham: Rowman and Littlefield Publishers, 2000.

Bonfil Batalla, G. *Mexico Profundo: Reclaiming a Civilization*. Austin: University of Texas Press, 1996.

Bourgignon, E. *Possession*. San Francisco: Chandler & Sharp, 1976.

Bradburd, D. "Producing Their Fates: Why Poor Basseri Settled but Poor Kamachi and Yomut Did Not." *American Ethnologist* 16(3): 502–517, 1989.

Brand, W. *Impressions of Haiti*. London: Mouton & Co., 1965.

Brown, J. S. H., and R. Brightman. *The Orders of the Dreamed*. St Paul: Minnesota Historical Society Press, 1988.

Cantor, N. A Special Message from University of Michigan Provost Nancy Cantor Regarding the Research of

James V. Neel. *Medicine and Michigan* 3(1), 2001.

Carrasco, D., and E. Matos Moctezuma *Moctezuma's Mexico: Visions of the Aztec World.* Boulder: University Press of Colorado, 2003.

Catanese, A. *Haitians: Migration and Diaspora.* Boulder, CO: Westview Press, 1999.

Caton, H. *The Samoa Reader: Anthropologists Take Stock.* Latham: University Press of America, 1990.

Chagnon, N. *Yanomamo.* Fort Worth: Harcourt Brace Jovanovich, 1992(a).

Chagnon, N. *Yanomamo: The Last Days of Eden.* San Diego: Harcourt, Brace & Company, 1992(b).

Chan, S. *Hmong Means Free: Life in Laos and America.* Philadelphia: Temple University Press, 1994.

Conquergood, D. *I Am a Shaman: A Hmong Life Story with Ethnographic Commentary.* Minneapolis: Center for Urban and Regional Affairs, University of Minnesota, 1989.

Courlander, H. *The Drum and the Hoe: Life and Lore of the Haitian People.* Berkeley: University of California Press, 1960.

Davis, C. *Women's Conversations in a Minangkabau Market: Toward an Understanding of the Social Context of Economic Transactions.* Hull: Centre for South-East Asian Studies, 1997.

Davis, W. *The Serpent and the Rainbow.* New York: Simon & Schuster, 1985.

Dejean, P. *The Haitians in Quebec.* Ottawa:Tecumseh Press, 1980.

Doggett, S., and L. Gordon. *Dominican Republic and Haiti.* Hawthorn: Victoria Press, 1999.

Douglas, M. *Purity and Danger.* London: Routledge & Kegan Paul, 1980.

Douglas, M. *Purity and Danger.* London: Routledge & Kegan Paul, 1966.

Dyer C. "Nomads and Education for All: Education for Development or Domestication?" *Comparative Education* 37(3): 315–327, 2001.

El Dorado Task Force Papers, Preface. http://www.aaanet.org/edtf/final/preface.htm.

Erikson, K. *A New Species of Trouble: Explorations in Disaster, Trauma, and Community.* New York: Norton, 1994.

Evans-Pritchard E. E. *Nuer Religion.* New York: Oxford University Press, 1956.

Evans-Pritchard E. E. *The Nuer.* New York: Oxford University Press, 1940.

Evans-Pritchard, E. E. *The Azande: History and Political Institutions.* Oxford: The Clarendon Press, 1971.

Evans-Pritchard, E. E. "Witchcraft amongst the Azande." In *Witchcraft and Sorcery.* M. Marwick, ed. Baltimore: Penguin Books, 1970 (original 1929).

Evans-Pritchard, E. E. Witchcraft in *Oracles and Magic among the Azande.* Oxford: The Clarendon Press, 1937.

Fadiman, A. *The Spirit Catches You and You Fall Down.* New York: Farrar Straus and Giroux, 1997.

Farmer, P. *The Uses of Haiti.* Monroe: Common Courage Press, 1994.

Feld, S. *Sound and Sentiment.* Philadelphia: University of Pennsylvania Press, 1990.

Feld, S. "Waterfalls of Song: An Acoustemology of Place Resounding in Bosavi, Papua New Guinea." In *Senses of Place.* S. Feld and K. Basso, eds. Santa Fe, NM: School of American Research, 1996.

Ferguson, B. *Yanomami Warfare: A Political History.* Santa Fe, NM: School of American Research Press, 1995.

Freeman, D. *Margaret Mead and Samoa: The Making and Unmaking of an Anthropological Myth.* Cambridge, MA: Harvard University Press, 1983.

Frey, K. S. *Journey to the Land of the Earth Goddess.* Jakarta: Gramedia Publishing Division, 1986.

Geddes, W. *Migrants of the Mountains.* Oxford: Clarendon Press, 1976.

Gedicks, A., and Z. Grossman. "Native Resistance to Multinational Mining Corporations in Wisconsin." *Cultural Survival Quarterly* 25:1, Spring 2001.

Gedicks, A. *The New Resource Wars: Native and Environmental Struggles against Multinational Companies.* Boston: South End Press, 1993.

Good, K. *Into the Heart: One Man's Pursuit of Love and Knowledge among the Yanomama.* New York: Simon & Schuster, 1991.

Goodale, J. C. *Tiwi Wives.* Seattle: University of Washington Press, 1971.

Grau, A. "On the Acquisition of Knowledge: Teaching Kinship through the Body among the Tiwi of Northern Australia." In *Common Worlds and Single Lives: Constituting Knowledge in Pacific Societies.* V. Keck, ed. Oxford: Berg, 1998.

Gross, D. *Discovering Anthropology.* Mountain View, CA: Mayfield, 1992.

Grossman, Z. and D. McNutt. *From Enemies to Allies in Multiracial Formations: New Instruments for Social Change.* G. Delgado, ed. Oakland: Applied Research Center, 2003.

Grossman, Z. "Linking the Native Movement for Sovereignty and the Environmental Movement." *Z Magazine* 8(11): 42–50, November 1995.

Gujadhur, T. *Alcohol Abuse Intervention Strategies for Rural (Bushmen) Settlements Embarking on CBNRM.* Gabarone: IUCN/SNV Support Programme, 2000.

Gutiérrez, N. *Nationalist Myths and Ethnic Identities: Indigenous Intellectuals and the Mexican State.* Lincoln: University of Nebraska Press, 1999.

Hall, D. G. E. *A History of South-East Asia.* London: Macmillan, 1964.

Hallowell, A. I., and J. S. H. Brown. *The Ojibwa of Berens River, Manitoba.* Fort Worth: Harcourt Brace Jovanovich, 1992.

Harner, M. "The Ecological Basis for Aztec Sacrifice." *American Ethnologist* 4:117–135, 1977.

Harris, M. *Culture, People, Nature.* New York: Harper & Row, 1988.

Hart, C. W. M., A. R. Pilling, and J. C. Goodale. *The Tiwi of North Australia.* New York: Holt, Rinehart & Winston, 1988.

Heinl, R. D., and N. Gordon Heinl. *Written in Blood: The Story of the Haitian People 1492–1971.* Boston: Houghton Mifflin, 1978.

Hickerson, H. *The Chippewa and their Neighbors.* Prospect Heights: Waveland Press, 1988.

Hitchcock, M., and V. T. King, eds. *Images of Malay-Indonesian Identity.* Oxford: Oxford University Press, 1997.

Hitchcock, R., and M. Biesele. Controlling Their Destiny: Ju'hoansi of Nyae Nyae. *Cultural Survival Quarterly* 26(2): 13, 2002.

Hitchcock, R., M. Biesele, and R. Lee. *The San of Southern Africa: A Status Report, 2003.* http://www.aaanet.org/committees/cfhr/san.htm.

Holmes, L. *Samoan Village.* New York: Holt, Rinehart and Winston, 1974.

Holtzman, J. *Nuer Journeys, Nuer Lives.* Boston: Allyn & Bacon, 2000.

Hones, D. F. *Educating New Americans: Immigrant Lives and Learning.* Mahwah: L. Erlbaum Associates, 1999.

Houseman, M. "Painful Places: Ritual Encounters with One's Homelands." *Journal of the Royal Anthropological Institute* 4(3), September 1998.

Hutchinson, S. *Nuer Dilemmas: Coping with Money, War, and the State.* Berkeley: University of California Press, 1996.

Indigenous Leaders' Document to President Lula Brasilia-DC, May 10, 2004. http://www.amazonia.org.br/english/guia/detalhes.cfm?id=113522&tipo=6&cat_id=82&subcat_id=395.

Iwanska, A. *The Truths of Others: An Essay on the Nativistic Intellectuals in Mexico.* Cambridge, MA: Schenkman Publishing Company, 1977.

Jackson, D. D. *"Our Elders Lived It": American Indian Identity in the City.*

DeKalb: Northern Illinois University Press, 2002.

Jackson, D. D. "This Hole in Our Heart": Urban Indian Identity and the Power of Silence. *American Indian Culture and Research Journal* 22(4): 227–254, 1998.

Janes, C. *Migration, Social Change, and Health: A Samoan Community in Urban California.* Stanford: Stanford University Press, 1990.

Jean-Pierre, J. *The 10th Department in Haiti: Dangerous Crossroads.* Deidre McFadyen and Pierre LaRamé, eds. Boston: South End Press, 1995.

Josselin de Jong, P. E. de. *Minangkabau and Negri Sembilan: Sociopolitical Structure in Indonesia.* New York: AMS Press, 1980 (1952).

Kahn, J. S. *Constituting the Minangkabau: Peasants, Culture and Modernity in Colonial Indonesia.* Oxford: Berg Publishers, 1993.

Kahn, J. S. *Minangkabau Social Formations: Indonesia Peasants and the World-Economy.* Cambridge: Cambridge University Press, 1980.

Katz, R. "Education for Transcendence: !Kia-Healing with the Kalahari !Kung." In *Kalahari Hunter-Gatherers.* R. B. Lee and I. DeVore, eds. Cambridge, MA: Harvard University Press, 1976.

Kebbede, G. "South Sudan: A War-Torn and Divided Region." In *Sudan's Predicament: Civil War, Displacement, and Ecological Degradation.* G. Kebbede, ed. Hampshire: Ashgate publishing, 1999.

Kirsch, S. "Acting Globally: Eco-politics in Papua New Guinea." *Journal of the International Institute* 3(3): 1–15, 1996.

Kling, Z. *Adat: Collective Self-Image,* in *Images of Malay-Indonesian Identity.* M. Hitchcock and V. T. King, eds. Oxford: Oxford University Press, 1997.

Knab, T. J. *A War of Witches: A Journey into the Underworld of the Contemporary Aztecs.* San Francisco: HarperCollins, 1995.

Koentjaraningrat, R. M. *Introduction to the Peoples and Cultures of Indonesia and Malaysia.* Menlo Park, CA: Cummings Publishing Co., 1975.

Koltyk, J. A. *New Pioneers in the Heartland: Hmong Life in Wisconsin.* Boston: Simon & Schuster, 1998.

Konner, M. *Becoming a Doctor.* New York: Viking, 1987.

Kottak, C. *Anthropology: The Exploration of Human Diversity.* 7th ed. New York: McGraw-Hill, 1997.

Krätli, S. Education Provision to Nomadic Pastoralists, IDS Working Paper 126. Brighton: Institute of Development Studies, 2001.

Laguerre, M. *American Odyssey: Haitians in New York.* Ithaca, NY: Cornell University Press, 1984.

Lee, K. C. *A Fragile Nation: The Indonesia Crisis.* Singapore: World Scientific Publishing Co., 1999.

Lee, R., and I. Susser. AIDS and the San: How Badly Are They Affected? Appendix to The San of Southern Africa: A Status Report, 2003. http://www.aaanet.org/committees/cfhr/san.htm.

Lee, R. B. *The Dobe !Kung.* New York: Holt, Rinehart and Winston, 1984.

Lee, R. B. *The Dobe Ju/'hoansi.* New York: Holt, Rinehart and Winston, 1993.

Lee, R. B. *The Ju/'hoansi.* Cambridge: Cambridge University Press, 1979.

León-Portilla, M. *The Aztec Image of Self and Society.* Salt Lake City: University of Utah Press, 1992.

Lindstrom, L., and G. White. Introduction in *Chiefs Today: Traditional Pacific Leadership and the Postcolonial State.* Stanford, CA: Stanford University Press, 1997.

Lizot, J. *Tales of the Yanomami: Daily Life in the Venezuelan Forest.* Cambridge: Cambridge University Press, 1985.

Lockhart, J. "Three Experiences of Culture Contact: Nahua, Maya, and Quechua." In *Native Traditions in the Postconquest*

World. E. Boone and T. Cummins, eds. Washington, DC: Dumbarton Oaks Research Library and Collection, 1998.

Loeb, E. M. *Sumatra: Its History and People*. Oxford: Oxford University Press, 1989 (1935).

Lomnitz-Adler, C. *Exits from the Labyrinth: Culture and Ideology in the Mexican National Space*. Berkeley: University of California Press, 1992.

MacMillan, G. *At the End of the Rainbow? Gold, Land and People in the Brazilian Amazon*. London: Earthscan, 1995.

MacPherson, C. "Chiefly Authority in Western Samoa." In *Chiefs Today: Traditional Pacific Leadership and the Postcolonial State*. G. White and L. Lindstrom, eds. Stanford: Stanford University Press, 1997.

Mair, L. *African Societies*. Cambridge: Cambridge University Press, 1974.

Malinowski, B. *Argonauts of the Western Pacific*. New York: E. P. Dutton, 1922.

Malinowski, B. *Coral Gardens and Their Magic*. New York: Dover, 1935.

Malnic, J. *Kula: Myth and Magic in the Trobriand Islands*. Wahroonga: Cowrie Book, 1998.

Marshall, J., and C. Ritchie. *Where Are the Ju/wasi of Nyae Nyae? Changes in a Bushman Society: 1958–1981*. Cape Town: University of Cape Town Press, 1984.

Marshall, L. "Sharing, Talking and Giving: Relief of Social Tensions among the !Kung." In *Kalahari Hunter-Gatherers*. R. B. Lee and I. DeVore, eds. Cambridge, MA: Harvard University Press, 1976.

McCall, G. "Ju/'hoansi Adaptations to a Cash Economy." *African Sociological Review* 4(1): 138–155 2000.

McElroy, A. and P. Townsend. *Medical Anthropology in Ecological Perspective*. Boulder, CO: Westview Press, 1989.

McLeod, M. D. "Oracles and Accusations among the Azande." In *Zande Themes*. A. Singer and B. V. Street, eds. Oxford: Basil Blackwell, 1972.

Mead, M. *Coming of Age in Samoa*. New York: William Morrow, 1928.

Meleisea, M. *Change and Adaptations in Western Samoa*. Christchurch: University of Canterbury Press, 1992.

Miller, J. *The Plight of Haitian Refugees*. New York: Prager Publishers, 1984.

Muller, K. *Spice Islands: Exotic Eastern Indonesia*. Lincolnwood: Passport Books, 1990.

Murad, A. *Merantau: Outmigration in a Matrilineal Society of West Sumatra*. Canberra: Australian National University Press, 1980.

Nanda, S. *Cultural Anthropology*. 5th ed. Belmont, CA: Wadsworth Publishing, 1994.

Nanda, S. *Cultural Anthropology*. Belmont, CA: Wadsworth, 1991.

Neill, W. T. *Twentieth-Century Indonesia*. New York: Columbia University Press, 1973.

Nicholls, D. *From Dessalines to Duvalier: Race, Colour and National Independence in Haiti*. New Brunswick, NJ: Rutgers University Press, 1996.

Nicholls, D. *Haiti in Caribbean Context: Ethnicity, Economy and Revolt*. New York: Macmillan, 1985.

Northrup, J. *The Rez Road Follies: Canoes, Casinos, Computers, and Birch Bark Baskets*. New York: Kodansha International, 1997.

Nusit, C. *The Religion of the Hmong Njua*. Bangkok: Siam Society Press, 1976.

Overholt, T. W. and J. B. Callicott. *Clothed-in-Fur and Other Tales*. Lanham: University Press of America, 1982.

Ovesen, J. *A Minority Enters the Nation State*. Uppsala: Uppsala University, 1995.

Pacquin, R., and R. Doherty. *Not First in Nobody's Heart: The Life Story of a Contemporary Chippewa*. Ames: Iowa State University Press, 1992.

Parkes, C. *Southeast Asia Handbook*. Chico: Moon Publications, 1998.

Parsons, A. *Belief, Magic, and Anomie.* New York: The Free Press, 1969.

Peacock, J. L. *Indonesia: An Anthropological Perspective.* Pacific Palisades: Goodyear Publishing Company, Inc., 1973.

Peletz, M. *Social History and Evolution in the Interrelationship of Adat and Islam in Rembau, Negeri Sembilan.* Singapore: Institute of Southeast Asian Studies, 1981.

Peters, C. *Progressive Activism in the United States* in *Haiti: Dangerous Crossroads.* Deidre McFadyen and Pierre LaRamé, eds. Boston: South End Press, 1995.

Pommer, M. *Madison Capital Times,* Madison, Wisconsin, October 28, 2003.

Posposil, L. *The Kapauku Papuans of West New Guinea.* New York: Holt, Rinehart and Winston, 1963.

Pouesi, D. *An Illustrated History of Samoans in California.* Los Angeles: KIN Publications, 1994.

Ramos, A., and K. Taylor. *The Yanoama in Brazil 1979.* Copenhagen: IWGIA, 1979.

Reavis, D. *Conversations with Moctezuma: Ancient Shadows over Modern Life in Mexico.* New York: William Morrow and Company, 1990.

Reining, C. C. *The Zande Scheme: An Anthropological Case Study of Economic Development in Africa.* Evanston, IL: Northwestern University Press, 1966.

Robbins, J. "God Is Nothing but Talk: Modernity, Language, and Prayer in a Papua New Guinea Society." *American Anthropologist* 103(4): 901–912D, 2001.

Rocha, J. *Murder in the Rainforest: The Yanomami, the Gold Miners and the Amazon.* London: Latin America Bureau Ltd., 1999.

Rodman, S. *Haiti: The Black Republic.* New York: Devin-Adair, 1954.

Rotberg, R. I. *Haiti: The Politics of Squalor.* Boston: Houghton Mifflin, 1971.

Sahlins, M. "The Segmentary Lineage: And Organization of Predatory Expansion." *American Anthropologist* 63 (1961):322–343.

Salamone, F. "Theoretical Reflections of the Chagnon-Salesian Controversy" in Salamone, F., editor, *Who Speaks for the Yanomami?* Williamsburg: Studies in Third World Societies, 1996.

Salamone, F. *The Yanomami and their Interpreters: Fierce People or Fierce Interpreters?* Lanham: University Press of America, Inc., 1997.

Salzman, P. C. Political Organization among Nomadic People in *Man in Adaptation.* Y. A. Cohen, ed. Chicago: Aldine, 1974.

Sanford, G. Who Speaks for the Yanomami? in *Who Speaks for the Yanomami?* F. Salamone, ed. Williamsburg: Studies in Third World Societies, 1997.

Schieffelin, B. B. *The Give and Take of Everyday Life.* Cambridge: Cambridge University Press, 1990.

Schieffelin, B. "Introducing Kaluli Literacy: A Chronology of Influences." In *Regimes of Language: Ideologies, Polities, and Identities.* P. Kros krity, ed. Santa Fe, NM: School of American Research Press, 2000.

Schieffelin, B. "Marking Time: The Dichotomizing Discourse of Multiple Temporalities." *Current Anthropology* 43(54), August–October 2002.

Schieffelin, E. L. *The Sorrow of the Lonely and the Burning of the Dancers.* New York: St. Martin's Press, 1976.

Schoolcraft, Henry Rowe. *The American Indians: Their History, Conditions and Prospects.* Buffalo: Derby, 1851.

Schwartz, S. *Victors and Vanquished: Spanish and Nahua Views of the Conquest of Mexico.* Boston: Bedford/St. Martin's, 2000.

Senft, G. "The Presentation of Self in Touristic Encounters: A Case Study from the Trobriand Islands." *Anthropos* 94: 21–33, 1999.

Smith, M. *The Aztecs*. Cambridge: Oxford: Blackwell Publishers, 1996.

Smole, W. *The Yanoama Indians: A Cultural Geography*. Austin: University of Texas Press, 1976.

Stepick, A. *Pride Against Prejudice: Haitians in the United States*. Boston: Allyn & Bacon, 1998.

Street, B. V. The Trickster Theme in *Zande Themes*. A. Singer and B. V. Street, eds. Oxford: Basil Blackwell, 1972.

Tanner, H. H. *The Ojibwa*. New York: Chelsea House, 1992.

Tan-Wong, N. and V. Patel, *Adat Perpatih: A Matrilineal System in Negeri Sembilan, Malaysia*. Kuala Lampur: Wintrac Malaysia, 1992.

Townsend, R. F. *The Aztecs*. London: Thames and Hudson, 1992.

Trouillot, M. R. *Haiti: State against Nation*. New York: Monthly Review Press, 1990.

Trueba, H. T. *Cultural Conflict and Adaptation: The Case of Hmong Children in American Society*. New York: Falmer Press, 1990.

Unny, G. *Kinship Systems in South and Southeast Asia*. New Delhi: Vikas Publishing House, 1994.

van Reenan, J. *Central Pillars of the House: Sisters, Wives, and Mothers in a Rural Community in Minangkabau, West Sumatra*. Leiden: CNWS Publications, 1996.

Vang, L. *Grandmother's Path, Grandfather's Way*. San Francisco: Heritage Preservation Project, 1984.

Venbrux, E. "Tales of Tiwiness: Tourism and Self-Determination in an Australian Aboriginal Society." *Pacific Tourism Review* 4: 137–147, 2000.

Venbrux, E. "Why Do the Tiwi Want a New Township?" In *Common Worlds and Single Lives: Constituting Knowledge in Pacific Societies*. V. Keck, ed. Oxford: Berg, 1998.

Venbrux, Eric. *A Death in the Tiwi Islands: Conflict, Ritual and Social Life in an Australian Aboriginal Community*. Cambridge: Cambridge University Press, 1995.

Vizenor, G. *Crossbloods: Bone Courts, Bingo, and Other Reports*. Minneapolis: University of Minnesota Press, 1990.

Vreeland, N., G. B. Dana, G. B. Hurwitz, P. Just, P. W. Moeller, and R.S. Shinn. *Area Handbook for Malaysia*. Washington, DC: American University Press, 1977.

Weil, T. E. *Haiti: A Country Study*. Washington, DC: American University Press, 1985.

Weiner, A. B. *The Trobrianders of Papua New Guinea*. New York: Holt, Rinehart and Winston, 1988.

Weiner, A. B. *Women of Value, Men of Renown*. Austin: University of Texas Press, 1976.

Westermyer, J. *The Use of Alcohol and Opium among Two Ethnic Groups in Laos*. Master's Thesis, University of Minnesota, 1968.

Willcox, D. *Hmong Folklife*. Marion: Copple House Books, 1986.

Woldemikael, T. *Becoming Black American: Haitians and American Institutions in Evanston, Illinois*. New York: AMS Press, 1989.

Wood, S. *Transcending Conquest: Nahua Views of Spanish Colonial Mexico*. Norman: University of Oklahoma Press, 2003.

Yang, D. *Hmong at the Turning Point*. Minneapolis, MN: World Bridge Publishers, 1993.

Young, K. R. Minangkabau Authority Patterns and the Effects of Dutch Rule in *The Malay-Islamic World of Sumatra: Studies in Politics and Culture*. J. Maxwell, ed. Barus: Monash University, 1982.

Zéphir, F. *Haitian Immigrants in Black America: A Sociological and Sociolinguistic Portrait*. Westport: Bergin & Garvey, 1996.

INDEX

N